BRITISH GEOLOGICAL SURVEY

T P YOUNG
W GIBBONS
D McCARROLL

Geology of the country around Pwllheli

CONTRIBUTORS

Biostratigraphy
W T Dean
F Martin

Geochemistry
R E Bevins
J M Horák

Pleistocene stratigraphy
C Harris

Seismic interpretation
P J Brabham
R McDonald

Memoir for 1:50 000 Geological Sheet 134
(England and Wales)

This memoir and the 1:50 000 Series geological map that it
describes are the products of a mapping contract between the
Natural Environment Research Council and Cardiff University.
The interpretations presented are those of the authors.

London: The Stationery Office   2002

The grid used on the figures is the National Grid taken
from the Ordnance Survey map. Figure 2 is based on
material from Ordnance Survey 1: 50 000 scale maps,
numbers 123 and 124.
© Crown copyright reserved.
Ordnance Survey Licence No. GD272191/2002

ISBN 0 11 884561 6

Bibliographical reference

YOUNG, T P, GIBBONS, W, and McCARROLL, D. 2002.
Geology of the country around Pwllheli.   *Memoir of the
British Geological Survey*, Sheet 134 (England and Wales).

Authors

T P Young, MA, PhD
GeoArch, Cardiff

W Gibbons, BSc, PhD, CGeol
Cardiff University

D McCarroll, BA, PhD
University of Wales, Swansea

CONTRIBUTORS

R E Bevins, PhD, CGeol
J M Horák, BSc, PhD
W T Dean, BSc, PhD, DSc
National Museum of Wales, Cardiff

P J Brabham, BSc, PhD
C Harris, BSc, PhD
Cardiff University

R McDonald, BSc
Terradat, Cardiff

F Martin, Licenciée en Biologie, Docteur ès Sciences
*formerly Institut royal des
Sciences naturelles de Belgique, Brussels*

Geology of the country around Pwllheli

The district described in this memoir covers the central area of the Llŷn Peninsula in north-west Wales. It lies on the north coast of Tremadog Bay with the Harlech Dome to the east and the mountains of Snowdonia to the north-east. The rocks include Precambrian in the west, Cambrian on St Tudwal's Peninsula and Ordovician underlying most of the area.

This work contains a wealth of new stratigraphical, palaeontological, petrographical, geochemical and geomorphological data. The solid rock types described vary from deformed mélange and Precambrian granites, through an array of Cambrian and Ordovician clastic sedimentary rocks, to an extraordinarily wide range of tholeiitic to alkaline and ultrabasic to acid igneous rocks. A new centre of late Ordovician volcanicity is identified, the Llanbedrog centre. Detail presented for the igneous rocks in this area provides the first opportunity for comparisons and correlations to be made between Pwllheli and the classic eruptive sequences of Snowdonia. The structure of the area is integrated for the first time and a number of new faults and folds are identified. The economic geology chapter includes a description of the once important mining industry that extracted manganese, lead, zinc, copper and silver on St Tudwal's Peninsula, and the major resources of sand and gravel that were deposited during the retreat of the last glaciers over 14 500 years ago. Finally, the detailed Quaternary chapter reconstructs the evolution of the present landscape, emphasising the close link between geology and scenery that is so much a characteristic of the Pwllheli district.

The memoir includes several classic sequences and sites such as the famous Cambrian rocks of the St Tudwal's Peninsula, with its superb sub-Ordovician angular unconformity exposed on the cliffs at Trwyn Llech-y-doll. Equally well known, but at the other end of the Phanerozoic timescale, are the glacial Quaternary deposits around Glanllynnau which have been described as one of the most intensively studied glacial sites in the world.

Cover photograph

View looking east to the Arenig unconformity at Trwyn Llech-y-doll, St Tudwal's Peninsula.

The cliffs in the background are of Arenig sandstones (St Tudwal's Formation) which dip gently east and rest on more steeply dipping Middle Cambrian sediments of the Ceiriad Formation. Foreground cliffs expose Middle Cambrian Cilan Formation sediments. (GS 658).

a

b

c

d

Frontispiece   Mineral specimens from Carreg-yr-Imbill (Gimlet Rock) [3885 3435]. All from National Museum of Wales mineral collection (GS 673).

a   Euhedral prismatic quartz, coated by white albite.
    Specimen size 10 cm. NMW 27.111.GR352.
b   Translucent and white analcime coating euhedral quartz.
    Field of view 9 cm. NMW 27.111.GR376.
c   Close-up of pectolite on quartz. Field of view 7 cm.
    NMW 27.111.GR29 8 357.
d   Radiating pectolite crystals in quartz. Field of view 10.5 cm.
    NMW 27.111.GR29.

CONTENTS

FIGURES

TABLES

PLATES

Acknowledgements

This memoir has been compiled and written mostly by T P Young and W Gibbons (solid) and D McCarroll (drift). It represents the completion of NERC mapping contract F60\G2\28 to map sheets 133 Bardsey and 134 Pwllheli that was awarded to W Gibbons at Cardiff University (Gibbons and McCarroll, 1993). The mapping of the Pwllheli district was carried out on a 1:10 000 scale by the three authors over the period 1988–1991. In addition, R Bevins (National Museum of Wales — NMW) contributed to the interpretation of the geochemical data, especially the REE analyses, and to the study of the low-grade metamorphism. P J Brabham (Cardiff University) and R McDonald (Terradat) undertook a seismic reflection and refraction survey of the thick Quaternary drift deposits around Porth Neigwl. The late F Martin (Institut royal des Sciences naturelles de Belgique, Brussels) provided a report on the micropalaeontology of the Cambrian succession and W T Dean (NMW) studied Cambrian and Ordovician trilobites. J M Horák (NMW) provided petrographical and geochemical details on the Sarn Complex and of mineral specimens in the Museum collections. C Harris (Cardiff University) helped in the interpretation of the complex drift sequences exposed on the coast. A report on the Caradoc graptolites, principally those held in the collections of the British Geological Survey, was made by A W A Rushton and J Zalasiewicz (formerly BGS; Biostratigraphy Research Group Report PD 91/221). Material from this survey, notably the thin section collection, has been archived in the National Museum of Wales.

Rushton and Zalasiewicz also reported on graptolites held in the National Museum of Wales, and those collected by T P Young.

Material from this survey, notably the thin section collection, has been archived in the National Museum of Wales.

The authors acknowledge the supervision and encouragement provided by R A B Bazley (BGS), the excellent editing support provided by T Charsley, and valuable discussions in the field with D Bate (BGS), M J Branney (University of Leicester), T Druitt (University of Clermont Ferrand) and M F Howells (formerly BGS). Professor M Brooks (Cardiff Univeristy) provided help with the seismic surveying and as Head of Department was highly supportive of this mapping contract. P T Leat and R Thorpe (Open University) kindly lent thin sections of rocks with published analyses. G Tegerdine (Production Geoscience Ltd.) and A Beckly (British Petroleum) loaned their maps of Arenig outcrops. H Ivimey-Cook facilitated examination of the Matley fossil collection in the BGS. The authors also acknowledge discussions with A W A Rushton and J Zalasiewicz (BGS) on aspects of Ordovician biostratigraphy, and with D J Hughes (Portsmouth) on igneous geochemistry. W Gibbons would particularly like to thank G M Power (Portsmouth) and A J Reedman (BGS) who together initiated and supported both his early work on Llŷn and the subsequent preparation of BGS Memoirs 133 and 134. The memoir was edited by A A Jackson. Figures were produced by R J Demaine, P Laggage and G Tuggey, BGS Cartography, Keyworth.

Notes

Throughout this memoir the word 'district' refers to the area covered by the 1:50 000 Series Sheet 134 Pwllheli.

National grid references are shown in square brackets; all fall within the 100 km grid square SH.

Authorship of fossil species are shown in the Fossil Inventory (page 00).

Llŷn is used throughout in preference to the Lleyn Peninsula, which appears on the published OS 1:50 000 scale map.

Numbers preceded by GS refer to BGS photograph collection.

PREFACE

This memoir and the new 1:50 000 Series geological map Sheet 134 Pwllheli that it describes are the products of a mapping contract awarded to Cardiff University by the Natural Environment Research Council. The funding provided allowed for the continuation of fieldwork from the adjacent Aberdaron sheet. The contract stems from a NERC policy of encouraging academic researchers to transfer their data and information into the public domain. In addition to the map and memoir, the detailed field maps and other material will be lodged in the National Geosciences Record Centre at BGS Keyworth.

The primary survey of this part of the Llŷn Peninsula was carried out at a scale of one inch to one mile, and sheets 76S, 75SW, 75NW were published by the Geological Survey in 1850–51. An accompanying memoir was not published at that time, but details of the area were incorporated into a memoir on the whole of North Wales (Ramsay, 1866, 2nd edition 1881). Thus despite early interest, this is the first comprehensive account of the district.

The Llŷn Peninsula with its rocky coastline along the north coast of Cardigan Bay and views towards Snowdonia and the mountains of central Wales, the Rhinogs and Cadair Idris, is one of the most beautiful parts of Wales. The geology described here includes Precambrian mélange, Cambrian sedimentary rocks, Ordovician volcanic centres and the well-exposed Quaternary sediments that record past ice movement from both the north and the east; it provides interest for both academic and amateur geologists.

David A Falvey PhD
Director

British Geological Survey
Kingsley Dunham Centre
Keyworth
Nottingham
NG12 5GG

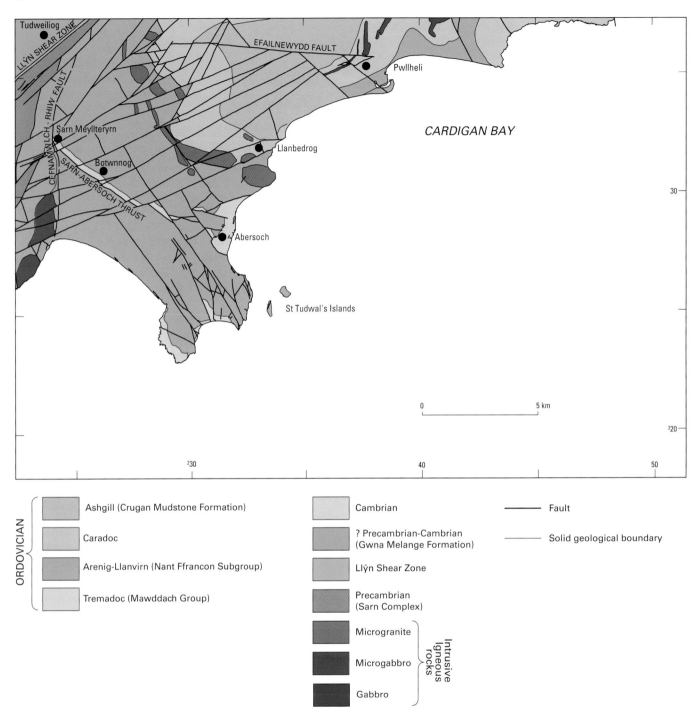

Figure 1 Geology of the Pwllheli district.

ONE

Introduction

The Pwllheli district lies on the Llŷn Peninsula in north-west Wales (Figures 1, 2). The coastline includes both wide, sand and gravel beaches backed by Quaternary glacial deposits, and low rocky shores and high cliffs that expose the Lower Palaeozoic succession. Inland, exposure is poor, low hills and drift plains are mainly cultivated, and only the higher hills remain as rough pasture. The main towns, Pwllheli and Abersoch, are heavily dependent on the tourist industry for employment.

The district is bounded to the west by a line of hills extending northwards from Mynydd Penarfynydd near the south coast to Mynydd Rhiw (304 m) and Mynydd Cefnamwlch (182 m). The high ground curves eastwards to Garn Fadryn (371 m), and thence southwards to Mynytho Common (194 m) (Figure 2). This line of hills encircles a broad depression centred on Botwnnog, which slopes southwards into a large drift plain behind Porth Neigwl (Hell's Mouth); it is incised by the steep-sided north-south valleys of Nant Llaniestyn and Nanhoron. To the north of Garn Fadryn, the ground falls away into the north-western coastal plain of the Llŷn.

The most spectacular scenery in the district is along the southern coast (Plate 1) where the thick drift deposits of Porth Neigwl have been excavated by the sea between the two headlands of Mynydd Penarfynydd (north-west) and Mynydd Cilan (south-east). The latter hill forms the highest point on the rocky headland of the St Tudwal's Peninsula which is severed from the hills to the north by the deeply incised Soch valley (Figure 1). Farther to the east, around Pwllheli, the coast is generally flat and relatively featureless, with long sweeping stretches of Quaternary deposits at Traeth Crugan and Morfa Abererch punctuated by the low rocky headlands of Carreg-yr-Imbill and Pen-ychain. Inland in this north-eastern corner of the district rise low hills running north-east from Y Garn (71 m) and curving eastwards to the Broom Hall area (30 m) to contain the low ground of Morfa Abererch, drained by the Afon Erch. Finally, one of the more notable inland areas of Quaternary deposits lies between Pwllheli and Garn Fadryn, where the bogs of Cors Geirch and the gravel terraces of Penrhos and Efailnewydd decline into the coastal plain of Morfa Abererch (Figure 1).

The Mynydd Tîr-y-cwmwd to Garn Fadryn range divides the district into two catchment areas. West of the hills drainage is via the incised valleys of Nanhoron, Nant Llaniestyn and Sarn Meyllteyrn into the Soch as it swings eastwards across the plain behind Porth Neigwl. Despite being only 800 m from the coast near Llanengan, the Soch flows north and then eastwards to eventually reach the sea at Abersoch (Figure 2). East of the Fadryn range

Plate 1 View south-west across the low, drift-filled plain behind Porth Neigwl (Hell's Mouth) (GS640).

The plain is bordered to the west by the steep slopes of Mynydd Rhiw, underlain by the Mynydd Penarfynydd layered intrusion. The north-eastern slopes of Bardsey Island are visible in the distance (left). The slopes in the foreground are underlain by Arenig rocks that form the northern margin of the St Tudwal's block.

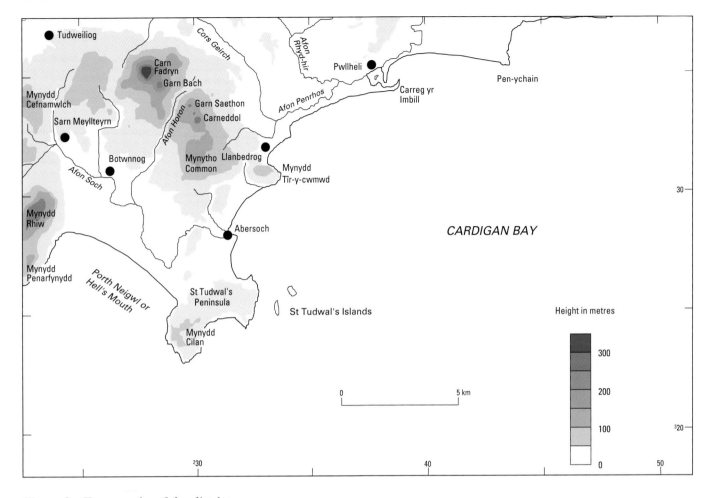

Figure 2 Topography of the district.

of hills, drainage is mainly via Afon Penrhos, Afon Rhyd-hir and Afon Erch into Pwllheli harbour, although the Cors Geirch drains north-westwards towards the north coast of Llŷn.

At the present time farming and tourism are the main economic activities of the district although in the past mining was significant. The earliest records of mining in the St Tudwal's Peninsula for lead, zinc and copper are in the mid 17th century. Mining took place for at least two and a half centuries, before finally ceasing in 1892. In the northern part of the St Tudwal's Peninsula ironstones near Llanengan were worked intermittently from about 1820 to 1885. The Mynydd Tîr-y-cwmwd 'granophyre' intrusion has been extensively quarried for aggregate, and numerous similar small quarries existed throughout the district, but now the only working quarry is at Nanhoron.

PREVIOUS RESEARCH

The first geological accounts of the district were by Sedgwick (1843, 1844, 1847), who recognised in particular the volcanic origin of many the rocks. Sharpe (1846) considered that all the igneous rocks were intrusive. The

Geological Survey subsequently mapped the region (sheets 76S, 75SW, 75NW, published in 1850–1), and the memoir (First edition, Ramsay, 1866) designated the rocks of St Tudwal's Peninsula as 'Cambrian sandstones' or Harlech Grits, largely following observations by Selwyn. However, Sir Henry De la Beche favoured a correlation with the Silurian grits of Denbighshire, whereas Ramsay considered that the Lower Llandovery grits of Cardiganshire were a more likely correlative. By the time the second edition (Ramsay, 1881) was published, Middle Cambrian (St David's) fossils ('Upper Lingula Flags') had been distinguished near Nant-y-big, which clarified the age of at least some of the strata of the St Tudwal's Peninsula. The unconformity between the Ordovician and the Cambrian sequences at Trwyn Llech-y-doll was illustrated in both editions of the memoir and interpreted as 'merely a case of false bedding'. The lower Ordovician sequences received little attention from the early workers, but Ramsay (1881) recognised the probable Arenig age of grits, slates and a pisolitic iron ore at Llanengan, and, apart from some tuffs near Pwllheli, considered (like Sharpe) that most of the igneous rocks were intrusive. Hicks (1878) claimed that many of the igneous rocks of the district were Precambrian, but favoured Sedgwick's extrusive interpretation for many of them. Harker (1889) incorporated descriptions of the igneous rocks of the district in his classic essay on the Bala volcanic rocks of North Wales, and Raisin (1889) described the 'felsites' in the coastal exposures of Carreg y Defaid and Pen-ychain.

Fearnsides (1910b) described the 'Lingula Flags' as being unconformable on the Harlech Grits in the St Tudwal's Peninsula, and Nicholas (1915) determined these rocks to be of Ordovician age, which together with his description of the Arenig succession of the St Tudwal's Peninsula made a significant advance. His terminology for the Cambrian and lower Ordovician succession on St Tudwal's Peninsula is the basis for the current scheme. Further studies were made by Matley (1928) on the Precambrian of western Llŷn, Matley and Heard (1930) on the sequence in the northern limb of the Llŷn syncline, Matley (1932) on the igneous complexes of Mynydd Rhiw and Sarn, Matley and Smith (1936) on the age of the Sarn Granite, and Matley (1938) on the Llanbedrog, Mynytho and Pwllheli areas. The Sarn Granite and associated rocks of the Sarn Complex were later remapped and described by Shackleton (1956), Gibbons (1980, 1983) and Horák (1993).

Bassett and Walton (1960) described the turbidites of the Hell's Mouth Formation and the occurrence of Lower (Comley Series) Cambrian fossils which Bassett et al. (1976) formally described. Crimes (1966, 1969a, 1969b, 1970a), Crimes and Oldershaw (1967), and Crimes and Sly (1964) described aspects of the ichnology and sedimentology of the Upper Cambrian (Merioneth Series) strata. Apart from studies on the St Tudwal's area by Crimes (1969a, 1969b, 1970b), there was little revision of the Lower Ordovician strata until the work of Beckly (1987, 1988) who remapped the area between Rhiw and Sarn and detailed the biostratigraphy.

More recent research on the upper Ordovician rocks has mainly been on the Caradoc volcanic succession with some map interpretation (Fitch, 1967; Tremlett, 1965, 1969, 1972). Geochemical studies (Croudace, 1982; Leat and Thorpe, 1986) distinguished several suites of intrusive rocks which have been incorporated into various petrogenetic models. Studies of the biostratigraphy have been mainly to support these various studies. However, the fauna of the Caradoc, Dwyfach Formation (Buttler, 1991) and the Ashgill, Crugan Mudstone Formation (Price, 1981; Cocks and Rong, 1988) have also been described. This resurvey has allowed revision of the Lower Palaeozoic stratigraphy. The lithostratigraphy of the Cambrian rocks of the St Tudwal's Peninsula has been described by Young et al. (1994).

The first detailed descriptions of drift deposits in the district were made by Jehu (1909), who described evidence for two southerly directed ice movements. In the St Tudwal's area, Nicholas (1915) recognised evidence of ice moving from the east from Snowdonia. Synge (1964) described coastal sections throughout Llŷn, suggesting evidence for three glaciations but with the last terminating on the north coast, leaving the Pwllheli district ice-free. Matley (1936) and Saunders (1968b) described the landforms of the centre of the district, interpreting them as evidence of an ice-dammed lake.

The Pleistocene history of the area was summarised by Whittow and Ball (1970), and has recently been reinterpreted in terms of a glaciomarine model (Eyles and McCabe, 1989a,b, 1991). Late glacial and Holocene organic sediments at Glanllynnau, one of the most important Quaternary sites in Wales, have been described by Simpkins (1968, 1974) and Coope and Brophy (1972).

This memoir extends and develops several of the observations and interpretations on both solid and drift geology instigated during the remapping of the adjoining Aberdaron area by Gibbons and McCarroll (1993).

GEOLOGICAL HISTORY

The oldest rocks are exposed in the north-west of the district (Figure 1) as the Sarn Complex, which is separated from the Gwna Mélange by the Llŷn Shear Zone, which is not exposed here. The Sarn Complex comprises late Precambrian calc-alkaline plutonic rocks intruded within an 'Avalonian' magmatic arc setting (Horák et al., 1996). The Gwna Mélange is a pre-Arenig chaotic unit of uncertain age, and appears to represent the termination of sedimentation within a 'Monian' arc-related basin. The steeply dipping mylonitic rocks of the Llŷn Shear Zone form a south-westward continuation of the north-east-trending Menai Strait Fault System, a prominent tectonic boundary initiated as a transcurrent fault system slicing through the Avalonian arc (Gibbons and Horák, 1996). Continued movements along the Menai Straits Fault System influenced sedimentation, volcanism and deformation in the Pwllheli district throughout Early Palaeozoic time.

The Cambrian sequences exposed on St Tudwal's Peninsula (Figure 3) are some 1100 m thick (a minimum figure as the base is not exposed). They belong to the Dyfed Supergroup of Woodcock (1990). The succession bears a strong resemblance to that in the Harlech district, about 30 km to the east (Young et al., 1994, Young and Dean, 1995).

The lower and middle Cambrian (Comley and St David's Series) succession on St Tudwal's Peninsula is dominated by coarse-grained turbidites in the Harlech Grits Group (Hell's Mouth, Trwyn y Fulfran and Cilan formations), with mud- and silt-grade turbidites interbedded with shelf mudstones and siltstones being more typical of the overlying Ceiriad and Nant-y-big formations. The late Comley Series age of the Hell's Mouth Formation, and the St David's age of the Trwyn-y-Fulfran, Cilan, Ceiriad and Nant-y-big formations reflect a period of at least 12 Ma, according to the timescale of Harland et al. (1990). Bentonites, commonly manganiferous, record repeated distant volcanic activity and are especially prevalent within the Ceiriad and Nant-y-big formations.

A complex erosional unconformity occurs between the St David's Nant-y-big Formation and the Merioneth Maentwrog Formation, and represents an interval that could be as much as 10 Ma. The Cambrian and lowest Ordovician (Tremadoc) succession, the Mawddach

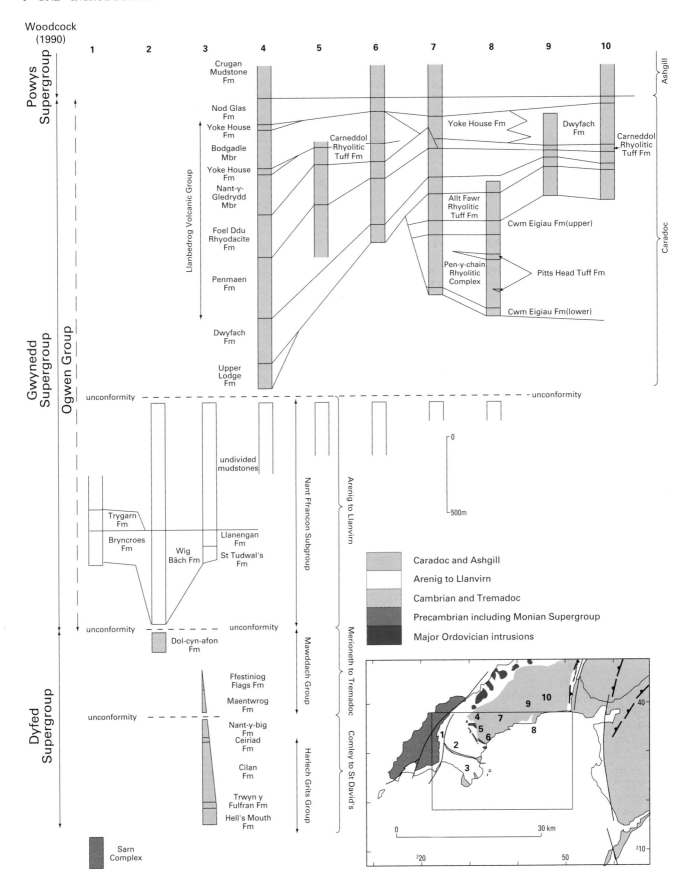

Group, above this unconformity (Maentwrog, Ffestiniog Flags, and Dol-cyn-afon formations) corresponds to more open-shelf environments.

During early Ordovician times (later Tremadoc?) the Cambrian and earliest Ordovician strata of the Harlech Dome and of the St Tudwal's Peninsula were tilted and uplifted. These areas of early Cambrian basinal sedimentation became structural highs during the remainder of Ordovician times.

Lying unconformably above the Mawddach Group is the Nant Ffrancon Subgroup (part of the Gwynedd Supergroup of Woodcock, 1990) which records sustained (Arenig to Llanvirn) basin development in the Pwllheli area. In early to middle Arenig times (Moridunian to Whitlandian Stage) a narrow basin, initiated parallel to the Menai Strait Fault System, extended north-eastwards across the central part of the Pwllheli district (Wig Bâch Formation). By late Arenig (Fennian Stage) times, marine conditions had extended across both the northwestern (Bryncroes Formation) and south-eastern (St Tudwal's Formation) margins of this Wig Bâch Formation basin. To the north-west the Bryncroes Formation lies unconformably on the Sarn Complex, and to the south-east the St Tudwal's and Llanengan Formations are unconformable on the previously tilted and uplifted St Tudwal's area. The east to west overstep of the St Tudwal's Formation over the entire exposed Cambrian to Tremadoc succession on St Tudwal's Peninsula is particularly striking.

The Arenig shallow marine sedimentary rocks consist mostly of storm-reworked sandstones interbedded with 'fair-weather' mudstones. They have been lithostratigraphically subdivided on the basis of differing bed thicknesses, differing mud:sand ratios and degrees of bioturbation. The Bryncroes and St Tudwal's formations are interpreted as having been deposited on relative 'highs'. During late Arenig times the district was affected by falling sea level, followed by a rapid rise in early Llanvirn times (Fortey et al., 1990; Young, 1992). The sediment starvation produced by the sea-level rise caused the generation of the Hen-dy-Capel Ironstone on the St Tudwal's high, the abundant ooidal ironstones of the Trygarn Formation in the north-east of the district and minor, similar ironstones in other areas. Uplift on the Wig Bâch basin-bounding faults in earliest Llanvirn times is interpreted as causing a fresh influx of coarse-grained clastic material interbedded with volcaniclastic sediments (Trygarn Formation), emplacement of a welded ash flow tuff, and the injection of a complex of basic sills in the west of the district. The upper part of the Nant Ffrancon Subgroup comprises 600 m of mudstones deposited in an outer shelf environment.

Within the district there is no evidence of strata of the Llandeilo Series, or of the lowermost part of the Caradoc

Figure 3 Summary of the stratigraphy of the Lower Palaeozoic rocks of the district. The Ogwen Group includes the sedimentary formations of the Gwynedd Supergroup of the district (Nant Ffrancon Subgroup, Cwm Eigiau, Dwyfach and Nod Glas formations).

Series. The district at this time formed part of a relatively uplifted block to the west of a 'Pitts Head Graben' (Kokelaar, 1988), so that an unconformity separates the Llanvirn Nant Ffrancon Subgroup from rocks of mid-Caradoc age (Figure 3).

During late Ordovician times, major volcanism developed across much of North Wales, with magmatic activity being recorded in Llŷn as three successive magmatic centres through late Soudleyan to Woolstonian times, and each of these has left some record in the Pwllheli district. These centres are referred to, in order of decreasing age, as Llywd Mawr (in the north-east), Upper Lodge (in the north), and Llanbedrog (centred on the Pwllheli district). The lowermost Caradoc strata in the district are conglomeratic sandstones (Cwm Eigiau Formation) and ashflow tuffs (Pitts Head Tuff Formation), both associated with the development of the Llwyd Mawr centre. Above the Pitts Head Tuff Formation, the upper part of the Cwm Eigiau Formation comprises early Longvillian marine siltstones with subordinate basic tuffs and sandstones (Figure 3).

In the north-west of the district, the lowermost Caradoc strata rest unconformably upon the Nant Ffrancon Subgroup and comprise basaltic trachyandesites (Upper Lodge Formation) erupted from a transitionally alkaline volcanic centre, thought to have been located near Nefyn. These volcanic rocks are interpreted as coeval with a prominent ashflow tuff (Allt Fawr Rhyolitic Tuff Formation) which extends farther east across the Pwllheli district. Both of these volcanic units are overlain by shallow marine siltstones and sandstones (Dwyfach Formation), of Longvillian age (Figure 3).

A further phase of intermediate volcanism (Penmaen Formation), was the forerunner of a second major igneous centre of mildly alkaline nature, this time centred on Llanbedrog. This centre is of Woolstonian age, developed in the area south of the Efailnewydd Fault, and produced thick volcanic deposits which dominate the upper Ordovician geology of the district. In the western and south-western parts of the district, the basaltic trachyandesitic and dacitic lavas and tuffs of this formation are up to 300 m thick, and are overlain by the more acidic tuffs and lavas of the Foel Ddu Rhyodacite Formation, which has a maximum thickness exceeding 250 m. This trend of increasingly evolved volcanic products was continued by the eruption of two major rhyolitic tuffs, the Nant-y-Gledrydd and Bodgadle members of the Carneddol Rhyolitic Tuff Formation. These tuffs together are up to 500 m thick between Llanbedrog and Madryn, an area interpreted as lying within a Llanbedrog caldera, but are represented by only up to 45 m of rhyolitic tuff at Pwllheli, outside the caldera. The volcaniclastic sedimentary apron to the Llanbedrog volcanic centre, the Yoke House Formation, passes progressively to the north-east into the fine-grained clastic sediments of the upper part of the Dwyfach Formation (Figure 3).

Following the Carneddol Tuff eruption there was regional subsidence, and graptolitic mudstones were deposited across the district (Nod Glas Formation). These mudstones have intercalated basaltic volcanic rocks associated with the east-west Efailnewydd Fault, running approximately along the northern margin of the former Llanbedrog volcanic centre. In contrast to the earlier more alkaline volcanicity, these basic rocks are markedly tholeiitic. Evidence for the age of the youngest parts of the Nod Glas Formation is poor, and no definite *linearis* Biozone faunas have been recorded. The district appears to have been starved of sediment, and rocks of latest Caradoc and early Ashgill age are probably not represented.

The youngest Ordovician rocks in the district are the calcareous siltstones and mudstones of the Crugan Formation, which were deposited in a relatively deep-water outer-shelf environment. This formation defines the base of the Powys Supergroup of Woodcock (1990). There was probably a considerable lapse of time between the deposition of these sediments (the base of which is of Rawtheyan age) and the underlying Nod Glas Formation. The renewal of sedimentation may have been associated with a major reactivation of the fault systems of the Welsh Borderlands, and probably elsewhere in the Welsh Basin, recorded in mid-Ashgill times.

The Caradoc volcanic rocks were contemporaneous with a wide variety of intrusive igneous rocks. The basic rocks are represented by numerous dolerites, particularly around the town of Pwllheli itself, and by the layered igneous complex at Rhiw, which is probably also of this age. Acid intrusive rocks include the Mynydd Tîr-y-cwmwd Granophyric Microgranite, the Wyddgrug Porphyritic Microgranite, a peralkaline suite (Nanhoron Suite) including the Mynytho Common, Foel Gron and Nanhoron granophyric microgranites, and an alkaline suite (Carn Fadryn Suite) including the Garn Bach Dacite, the Glynllifon Trachydacite and the Carn Fadryn Quartz-microdiorite.

The Acadian (late Caledonian) deformation which affects all Lower Palaeozoic rocks of the district is probably of mid-Devonian age. The earliest structures include the Sarn–Abersoch Fault and the reactivation of the north-western Wig Bâch basin bounding faults as reverse faults. The Sarn–Abersoch Fault was itself folded by the deformation phase associated with a main regional cleavage. The folding was followed by the development of important south-south-east-trending reverse faults, particularly in the southern part of the area. Some of the latest deformation in the area was associated with the development of a north-east-trending fault set, which cross-cuts earlier structures. There is much evidence for reworking of structures and many of the faults active during the deformation were those active during basin extension and subsidence.

Pb–Zn–Cu–Ag mineralisation in the St Tudwal's orefield post-dates the main Acadian deformation. Dating of mineralisation in similar contexts in the Harlech Dome suggests there that the mineralisation followed immediately after the main deformation. The mineralisation is concentrated in an east-west belt across the northern part of the St Tudwal's Peninsula, interpreted as the position of a major basement fault.

The large-scale features of the Pwllheli district landscape, particularly the steep-sided hills, probably predate the Pleistocene glaciations, but their origin and the timescale involved in their development is the subject of debate. The classical interpretation involves marine erosion of a Cainozoic (Tertiary) peneplain, but a more recent interpretation suggests a much longer history of Mesozoic and Cainozoic differential weathering under tropical conditions following emergence as early as the Triassic.

The region is presumed to have been glaciated at least three times during the Pleistocene. It is probable that the spectacular meltwater channels of the district were initiated at an early stage and re-excavated during successive glacial events. All of the glacigenic deposits of the district are, however, assigned to the last (Late Devensian) glaciation when the district was inundated by ice from two sources. Ice from the mountains of Snowdonia moved west into Cardigan Bay and over eastern Llŷn as far as St Tudwal's Peninsula. Ice carrying Scottish erratics moved down the basin of the Irish Sea. The uncoupling of the two ice streams, and the stalling of active ice fronts at topographical highs, with stagnation of debris-rich ice elsewhere, produced a complex proglacial environment. The thickest accumulations of drift, exposed in the larger bays, represent redistribution as flow tills of debris released from stagnant ice on the surrounding hills. Stepped terraces of sand and gravel in the centre of the district record the pulsed release of meltwater ponded by active and stagnant ice. The Cors Geirch wetland represents the site of a stagnating lobe of active ice which extended through a gap in the northern hills. Environmental changes during the Late glacial and Holocene are recorded by cryoturbation structures and by organic sediments developed in kettle holes.

TWO

Precambrian to ?Cambrian

The oldest rocks of the Pwllheli district crop out in the north-west, from around Tudweiliog [237 368], past Mynydd Cefnamwlch [230 340], to north-west of Mynydd Rhiw [225 296] (Figures 1, 2). These exposures form a small part of a broader outcrop of similar rocks that runs for 23 km south-westwards from Nefyn to Bardsey Island on Llŷn, and continues over a much larger area on Anglesey (the Mona Complex of Greenly, 1919). On Llŷn these rocks are better exposed in the adjacent Bardsey district (Gibbons and McCarroll, 1993) where they comprise the Gwna Mélange and the Sarn Complex, these being separated by the near-vertical Llŷn Shear Zone which is interpreted as a transcurrent mylonitic terrane boundary (Gibbons, 1983, 1987). In the Pwllheli district, only Gwna Mélange and Sarn Complex rocks are exposed, but the Llŷn Shear Zone is assumed to occur beneath the drift cover.

A minimum age for the Sarn Complex is provided by a contact with overlying Ordovician rocks, which, although probably a fault in most places, is exposed as an unconformity at Mountain Cottage Quarry [230 347] (Matley and Smith, 1936), where the Bryncroes Formation of late Arenig age lies on the Sarn granite, one of several plutonic lithologies that comprise the Sarn Complex. U–Pb isotope data on plutonic rocks in the Sarn Complex indicate a crystallisation age of 615 ± 2 Ma (Horák et al., 1996). Pebbles similar in lithology to the Sarn Complex and possibly the Llŷn Shear Zone occur within the Middle Cambrian Cilan Formation (see Chapter 3) on St Tudwal's Peninsula, suggesting these two units formed an exposed basement by that time. The age of the Gwna Mélange is less well constrained and could be latest Precambrian or Cambrian (Gibbons et al., 1994). Given the uncertainties, both over the absolute age of the mélange and Llŷn shear zone mylonites and of the Precambrian–Cambrian boundary itself, the Gwna Mélange is placed within this chapter to avoid confusion with the apparently younger, and certainly much less deformed, Cambrian sedimentary sequence of St Tudwal's.

SARN COMPLEX

The Sarn Complex crops out only along the western edge of the district. In its main outcrop on Llŷn, the Sarn Complex includes plutonic rocks with compositions ranging from gabbro to leucogranite, and rare metamorphic lithologies of ultrabasic and quartzo-feldspathic gneiss (Gibbons and McCarroll, 1993, Horák et al., 1996). However, within the Pwllheli district only the leucogranite is exposed, this being part of the Sarn Granite which is the largest exposed unit within the complex.

The main exposure of leucogranite crops out over 6 km² on Mynydd Cefnamwlch to the north-west of Sarn Meyllteyrn. Ramsey (1866) referred to the rock as an 'intrusive feldspathic porphyry' of probable Cambrian age. Later, Hicks (1879) named it the Rhos Hirwaun Syenite of Precambrian age. Tawney (1883) examined the contact between the 'syenite' and Palaeozoic shales at Mountain Cottage Quarry [230 347] and with some uncertainty, decided it was a fault. Harker (1889) designated it to be a granite intruded into the Arenig sedimentary rocks of Mountain Cottage Quarry just outside the Pwllheli district, and Matley (1932) agreed with this interpretation until the recognition of a basal conglomerate overlying the granite (Matley and Smith, 1936).

The contact between the country rock and the granite is not exposed within the Pwllheli district, and the western boundary of the intrusion is the Llŷn Shear Zone (Gibbons, 1983). Exposure of the granite is limited by the overlying Ordovician sedimentary rocks and by a veneer of drift. Furthermore much of the main outcrop on the south-west and north-east slopes of Mynydd Cefnamwlch [2265 3390] is forested. The main exposures are afforded by a series of small quarries on the road which skirts the northern side of the hill, as well as southwards from Mynydd Cefnamwlch for 1.5 km along the ridge of Foel Meyllteyrn [231 331]. The most southerly exposures are seen in the track at Muriau [2306 3109, 2307 3115] 1.5 km south of Sarn. North-east of Mynydd Cefnamwlch a small inlier is exposed on a hilltop at Pen-yr-Orsedd farm [2425 3525]. This exposure lies 1.5 km south-east of Tudweiliog and is pitted by small quarries, the largest of which reveals Palaeozoic olivine dolerite dykes cutting the granite (see Pen-yr-Orsedd dykes, Chapter 5).

PETROGRAPHICAL DETAILS

The Sarn Granite is typically a medium- to coarse-grained, pale weathering leucogranite. Chloritized biotite is the only visible ferromagnesian phase and most samples show some evidence of cataclasis and chlorite-filled fractures and quartz veins. Small (100 to 200 mm) rounded, unfoliated, granitoid enclaves and white felsite dykes are seen in some exposures, such as along the south part of Foel Meyllteyrn [e.g. 2319 3288].

In thin section, the leucogranite shows considerably greater textural heterogeneity than is noticeable in hand specimen, and this is expressed both in grain-size variation and by micro-granitoid enclaves or glomeroporphyritic clots. All samples fall within the monzogranite field on the Q–A–P modal plot (Streckheisen, 1976). The subsolvus granite is medium grained but demonstrates the full range of grain size within this category (1 to 5 mm).

The most homogeneous facies is highly leucocratic with an equigranular, allotriomorphic texture composed of anhedral plagioclase, biotite, microcline and quartz. Microcline forms the largest crystals, up to 7 mm in size but more commonly 1.5 to 3 mm. The larger microclines commonly contain inclusions of plagioclase, quartz and biotite, which less commonly ghost the former crystal outline of K-feldspar, although subsequent K-feldspar growth has resulted in an anhedral form. Plagioclase inclusions within microcline display a clear albitic rim. Such rims are common in plagioclase-perthite bearing rocks and represent the growth of albite during the formation of perthite. Small microcline crystals show the best developed cross-hatched twinning whereas larger crystals display a range of exsolution textures from fine to coarsely perthitic. Plagioclase crystals are typically 1.75 to 3 mm, as are anhedral quartz grains. Low temperature plastic deformation and cataclastic textures are common with most quartz showing undulose extinction and some feldspar displaying microfracturing. The least homogeneous granite texture displays glomeroporphyritic clots dominated by fine-grained plagioclase (0.5 mm), quartz and biotite.

Although only two enclaves have been identified at a macroscopic scale, they are relatively common under the microscope. Of 20 thin sections of the Sarn granite, 8 contained evidence of enclaves or glomeroporphyritic textures. The modal mineralogy of these is dominated by plagioclase and plots as tonalite on the Q–A–P plot (Streckheisen, 1976). Typical of many similar enclaves (e.g. Vernon, 1983, Castro et al., 1990) they are fine grained with a hypidiomorphic-allotriomorphic texture consisting of plagioclase, biotite and quartz, with accessory apatite and zircon. Euhedral to subhedral plagioclase crystals are up to 0.9 by 0.6 mm in size, but are most commonly 0.3 by 0.1 mm. A faint zoning is discernable in the larger crystals as the cores are more intensely sericitised, presumably indicating an originally more calcic composition. Biotite, with some remnants of its original foxy-red pleochroism, commonly encloses zircon crystals. It is generally pervasively chloritized and occurs as anhedral flakes interstitial to plagioclase or as smaller tabular inclusions (120 x 90 mm) within plagioclase. Quartz occurs interstitial to plagioclase. Acicular apatite crystals up to 0.1 mm are abundant within the enclaves. The contact between the enclaves and host granite is sharp, but apophyses of granite may invade the enclaves. The fine grain size and similar mineralogy of the enclaves to the host granite suggests that they represent early fractionates. The glomeroporphyritic clots are interpreted as having a similar origin, although their smaller size may be a result of fragmentation of the enclaves or be a primary feature.

GEOCHEMICAL DETAILS

The Sarn Granite shows a highly evolved composition with samples from Cefnamwlch and Foel Meyllteyrn having an average SiO_2 content of 80% and plotting within the leucomonzogranite field. It contains up to 4.25% K_2O and its high molar $Al_2O_3/(CaO + Na_2O + K_2O)$ ratios of up to 1.9 are interpreted as resulting from alkali (dominantly Na_2O) loss rather than a primary peraluminous signature (Table 2). In the adjacent Bardsey district, Rb–Sr, Ba–Sr and Rb–Ba data for Sarn Complex granitoid compositions other than leucomonzogranite indicate that plagioclase fractionation is the main control on the distribution of these elements (Gibbons and McCarroll, 1993). This is consistent with both the occurrence of plagioclase-rich enclaves and the presence of a Eu anomaly of up to 0.64 on chondrite normalised REE profiles (Horák et al., 1996). Average SREE contents of 333 ppm have a Ce_N/Yb_N of 6.1. High Nb and Y values are related to incompatible behaviour within such a highly fractionated, plagioclase-rich magma.

Table 2   Analyses of rocks from the Sarn Complex.

%	1	2	3
SiO_2	71.60	79.64	80.41
TiO_2	0.54	0.13	0.29
Al_2O_3	15.29	12.84	12.90
Fe_2O_3	3.26	0.69	1.56
MnO	0.03	0.01	0.04
MgO	0.93	0.10	0.22
CaO	0.30	0.07	0.11
Na_2O	3.80	1.91	3.39
K_2O	3.84	4.29	0.79
P_2O_5	0.09	0.01	0.02
ppm			
Ba	1434	895	408
Ga	20	21	22
Nb 16	29	31	
Rb	167	170	45
Sr	172	62	92
Y	42	87	84
Zr	65	364	408

Key to analyses

1   Average analysis of Sarn felsite (N = 2)
2   Sarn Granite (high K), Pen-yr-Orsedd
3   Sarn Granite (low K)

NOTE   Total iron expressed as Fe_2O_3

Samples containing less than 1% K_2O are predictably poor in K-feldspar and also show low contents of Rb but similar Nb, Y, Zr and REE contents to 'normal' leucomonzogranite. The low content of K_2O may result from albitisation of K-feldspar. Alternatively, it may represent a primary plagioclase -rich composition rather than K_2O loss directly from alteration of K-feldspar which is precluded because plagioclase shows more extensive alteration than microcline. The felsitic rocks exposed on the Foel Meyllteyrn ridge [2319 3279] have an average SiO_2 content of 71.6%, an alkali saturation index of 1.3, and are less evolved than the typical Sarn leucomonzogranite.

Ocean ridge granite (ORG) -normalised profiles for the Sarn Granite show the strongest correlation with calc-alkaline granite (I-type), although the tectonic discrimination diagrams of Pearce et al. (1984) reveal a within-plate affinity (A-type). This A-type component is attributed to the high degree of fractionation and the incompatible behaviour of Nb and Y. Such compositions correspond to the A2 category of Eby (1992) who interprets A-type granites as derived from fractionation of I-type magma. This explanation is supported by the less evolved Foel Meyllteyrn felsite which, with average values of Nb 15 ppm, Y 40 ppm, Rb 167 ppm, plots within the volcanic arc field.

U–Pb isotopic analysis of zircons from metagabbro from the adjacent Bardsey district date the plutonic rocks of the complex as 615 ± 2 Ma (Horák et al., 1996). Sm-Nd isotopic data recalculated to this age reveal the isotopically heterogeneous nature of the plutonic rocks (ϵNd_{615} −7.6 to −1.2) and indicate that the Rb–Sr age of 549 ± 19 Ma (Beckinsale et al., 1984) is not a magmatic cooling age but may represent a resetting of previously heterogeneous isotopic Sr. A TDH model age of 1.2 Ga for the Sarn Granite (Horák, 1993) supports the interpretation of Davies et al. (1985) that ancient crustal basement has not played a significant role its generation.

MONIAN SUPERGROUP

Gwna Mélange

The Gwna Mélange lies at the top of the Monian Supergroup, the lower parts of which are exposed on Anglesey (Gibbons and Ball, 1991). Within the district, the mélange is well exposed along the coast south-west of Porth Towyn [229 375], but also occurs in isolated exposures along the stream flowing north-westwards to the coast west of Porth Towyn [232 3750] (Plate 2). The most south-easterly exposures occur in streams and trenches across thinly drift-covered ground south of Tudweiliog [2348 3601]. The typical lithology is a grey-green, low grade, semi-pelitic metasediment with a well-developed slaty foliation. Neither top nor base of the mélange is exposed in the Pwllheli district. Although bedding is preserved in several coastal exposures west of Porth Towyn [e.g. 2285 3752], the mélange is more typically pervasively disrupted subparallel to original bedding so that any original lithostratigraphical sequence has been destroyed. The dominant foliation dips moderately to steeply north-west and is commonly contorted by minor folds (Plate 3). The mélange is estimated to be about 1200 m thick in the district; this probably representing only a small part of the total thickness for the Gwna Mélange outcrop in north-west Wales.

Within the disrupted grey-green sandstones and siltstones that comprise most of the mélange are isolated lenticular clasts of basic lava, limestone and quartzite, which are best exposed on the coast 300 m west of Porth Towyn. The largest of these clasts, of purple basaltic pillow lava, measures 145×25 m [2265 3744] and overlies (to the north-east) a mixed mélange facies of limestone, quartzite, basic lava and small jasper fragments within a slaty matrix [2275 3750]. Farther south-east, the mélange is dominated by disrupted fine-grained sandstones and siltstones with relatively few 'exotic' clasts. The siliciclastic rocks within the mélange include litharenites crowded with intraformational siltstone and fine sandstone fragments, porphyritic, feldspathic volcanic rocks, quartzites, micaceous tourmaline-bearing psammites, and monocrystalline quartz, alkali feldspar and plagioclase. The more pelitic beds are overprinted by low-grade metamorphic slaty chlorite-muscovite fabrics. West of Towyn beach [2287 3752] the north-westerly dipping mélange contains large overturned slabs of south-easterly younging bedded grey turbiditic siltstones, fine-grained sandstones and minor conglomerates, previously referred to by Gibbons (1980) as part of a disrupted 'Towyn Member'. For a discussion of Gwna Mélange structure see Chapter 8.

Plate 2   Coastal exposures of Gwna Mélange overlain by Quaternary sediments south-west of Porth Towyn [2260 3745] on the north-west coast of Llŷn (GS641).

The mélange in the foreground contains glacially smoothed white quartzite clasts, whereas across the bay the mélange is dominated by large dark metabasaltic clasts. View towards the south-east.

Plate 3   Gwna metasediments on south side of Porth Towyn [2280 3754] showing abrupt transition from relatively undisrupted clast (left) into mélange. The strong fabric is a composite S_1/S_2 foliation. The pen is aligned parallel to a more gently north-west-dipping poorly developed S_3 crenulation cleavage (GS642).

THREE

Cambrian

Within the district, rocks proved to be of Cambrian age crop out only on St Tudwal's Peninsula (Figure 4). The base of the Cambrian succession is not seen, but the turbiditic sequences of the Hell's Mouth, Trwyn-y-Fulfran and Cilan formations of the Harlech Grits Group form imposing sea cliffs around Mynydd Gilan. The coarser sandstone turbidites contain clasts of igneous and metamorphic rocks similar to some of the Precambrian rocks of western Llŷn and Anglesey, and it is likely that the Cambrian succession rests unconformably on a basement similar to the Sarn Complex. The overlying Ceiriad and Nant-y-big formations, well exposed in Porth Ceiriad, represent a waning in the supply of coarse detritus to the basin, as mudstones and siltstones become dominant over sandstones. There are numerous intercalations of fine-grained volcaniclastic debris, within both the Ceiriad and the Nant-y-big formations. Sedimentation rates were significantly reduced in the upper part of the Nant-y-big Formation, and the overlying erosion surface indicates

that there was a complete hiatus spanning the later part of the St David's Series (Middle Cambrian) and the early Merioneth Series (Late Cambrian). This unconformable erosional surface is overlain by thin coarse conglomeratic, locally bioclastic, sandstones at the base of the Merioneth Series (Maentwrog Formation) which record deposition in shallow marine, storm-influenced conditions. The upper part of the Cambrian succession is poorly exposed, with parts of the generally finer grained Ffestiniog Flags Formation being seen only on St Tudwal's Island East.

Macrofossils are scarce in the Cambrian succession; apart from Comley Series (Lower Cambrian) trilobites in the highest Hell's Mouth Formation recorded by Bassett and Walton (1960) and described by Bassett et al. (1976) nothing significant has been added to the collection made by the late T C Nicholas over the course of many years (reviewed by Rushton, 1974). Most of the macrofossils are St David's Series trilobites, particularly agnostids

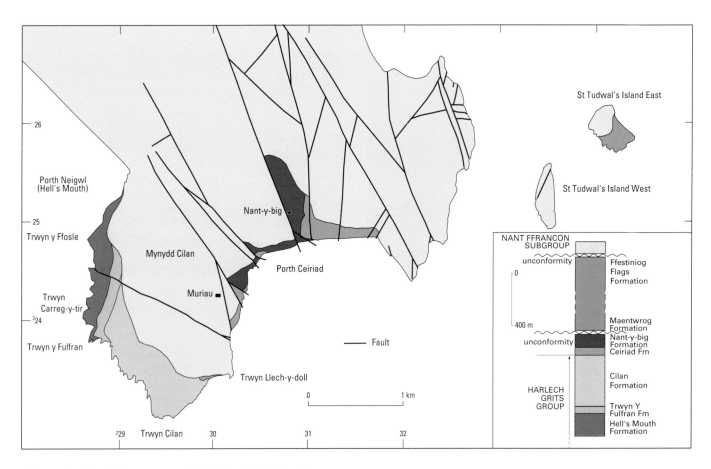

Figure 4 Cambrian strata of St Tudwal's Peninsula.

or eodiscids; the former provide zonal indices for many of the classic 'reference' successions in Sweden (Westergård, 1946) and were widely distributed with a preference for deeper marine environments. An investigation of acritarchs in the St Tudwal's Cambrian succession (Martin in Young et al., 1994) has improved correlation with eastern Newfoundland (Martin and Dean, 1981, 1983, 1988), where macrofossils, which have many species in common with those of the Welsh Basin, are more numerous.

The Cambrian to Tremadoc succession in the district is considered to form part of the Dyfed Supergroup of Woodcock (1990). The base is not exposed due to the unconformable overstep of the Nant Ffrancon Subgroup (Arenig, Ordovician); the latter rests on the Dol-cyn-afon Formation (possibly lower Tremadoc) near Abersoch, and progressively older parts of the Cambrian from Ffestiniog Flags Formation in the east, to Hell's Mouth Formation in the west of St Tudwal's Peninsula (Rushton and Howells, 1999). In the north-west of the district the Dyfed Supergroup is overstepped completely by the Arenig sequence which rests directly on the late Precambrian Sarn Complex.

The lithostratigraphy (Figure 5) of the Dyfed Supergroup on Llŷn (Young et al., 1994) differs from that previously proposed in the adjacent Harlech district (Allen et al., 1981; Allen and Jackson 1985; discussion by Pratt, 1995 and by Young and Dean, 1995). The cessation of coarse-grained turbidite deposition (top of the Harlech Grits Group) occurred later in the Harlech district than in the Pwllheli district. Furthermore, overlying strata in the Harlech district (Mawddach Group) appear uniform and contain no recorded unconformities (Allen et al., 1981) whereas equivalent strata on Llŷn are more variable and contain a mid- to late Cambrian unconformity which separates silt-grade turbidites (Ceiriad and Nant-y-big formations) from coarser sandstones (Maentwrog and Ffestiniog Flags formations). Exposures of the highest levels in the succession on St Tudwal's Peninsula are not stratigraphically complete and have been correlated directly with the Maentwrog and Ffestiniog Flags formations, previously defined in the adjacent Harlech district (Allen et al., 1981)

The lower part of the Cambrian succession on St Tudwal's Peninsula includes two thick sandstone turbidite-dominated units (Hell's Mouth and Cilan formations) separated by finer grained manganiferous siltstones (Trwyn y Fulfran Formation). The observed succession is over 630 m thick but the base of the group is not exposed. In the Harlech district (Allen et al., 1981) the lower part of the Cambrian succession (Harlech Grits Group) has been subdivided into Dolwen, Llanbedr, Rhinog, Hafotty, Barmouth and Gamlan formations. There is a broad lithological similarity between the Rhinog, Hafotty and Barmouth formations and the Hell's Mouth, Trwyn-y-Fulfran and Cilan formations. This lithostratigraphical correlation suggests that on Llŷn equivalents of the lower part of the Rhinog, the Llanbedr and the Dolwen formations (1500 m thick at Harlech) are concealed beneath drift in the Hell's Mouth area. The top of the Harlech Grits Group is placed at the base

of the overlying Ceiriad Formation (Young et al., 1994) which is marked by a significant and abrupt decrease in sediment grain-size from sand to silt, and a corresponding absence of coarse-grained turbidites.

HARLECH GRITS GROUP

Hell's Mouth Formation

This unit, equivalent to the 'Hell's Mouth Grits' of Nicholas (1915), is over 190 m thick and comprises laterally persistent coarse- to medium-grained, graded, green sandstone beds, interbedded with thinner green and grey siltstones. Its base is not exposed and the lowest visible beds crop out near sea level on the west side of Trwyn Cilan.

The type section (Young et al., 1994) (Figure 6) is at Trwyn y Ffosle from sea level [2868 2482] to the base of the overlying Trwyn y Fulfran Formation [2894 2464], which is marked by a line of old trial pits for manganese. Here the upper part of the section is not well exposed, so the base of the overlying Trwyn y Fulfran Formation was defined at Trwyn Carreg-y-tîr [2876 2402] (Figure 6).

Bassett and Walton (1960) demonstrated that sole structures to the turbidites indicated derivation from the north-east, with the mean direction on individual beds varying between 042° and 053°. The bases of some sandstone beds are loaded up to 0.6 m into underlying siltstone and mudstone. Individual sandstone beds may be up to 4 m thick and are typically medium- to coarse-grained, massive, crudely graded and locally pebbly lithic arkoses; the basal layers consist of coarse granule to sand grade fining up to silt with parallel laminations and, in places, ripple cross-beds at the very top. Intercalated siliceous mudstones with beds of micaceous siltstone, together with thin beds and lenses of coarse sand to granule grade sediment, suggest some reworking or winnowing of the sediments between the major turbiditic incursions. The sandstone clasts, which range up to 1.4 mm in size, are mostly monocrystalline quartz, although single crystals of plagioclase, perthite, biotite, and muscovite are all conspicuous and indicate a dominantly granitic source. Trachytic clasts form a minor constituent (less than 5%) but are present in all thin sections. Siltstone intraclasts also occur, and are locally abundant.

The trilobites *Hamatolenus (Myopsolenus) douglasi* (Plate 4i) and *Kerberodiscus succinctus* (Plate 4, ii, xiv) were described (together with a fragment of *Serrodiscus*) by Bassett et al. (1976) from a level 16.5 m below the top of the formation at Trwyn Carreg-y-tîr [2875 2404]. The former species, a protolenid, belongs to a genus known from the highest Comley and lowest St David's Series of the Anti-Atlas Mountains, Morocco; the latter is one of a number of eodiscids widespread in only the highest Comley Series of what is now Europe and eastern North America, regions that formed part of the Gondwana 'supercontinent' during the early Palaeozoic. A 'Protolenid-Strenuellid' Biozone was introduced by Cowie et al., (1972) to designate the topmost zone of the Comley

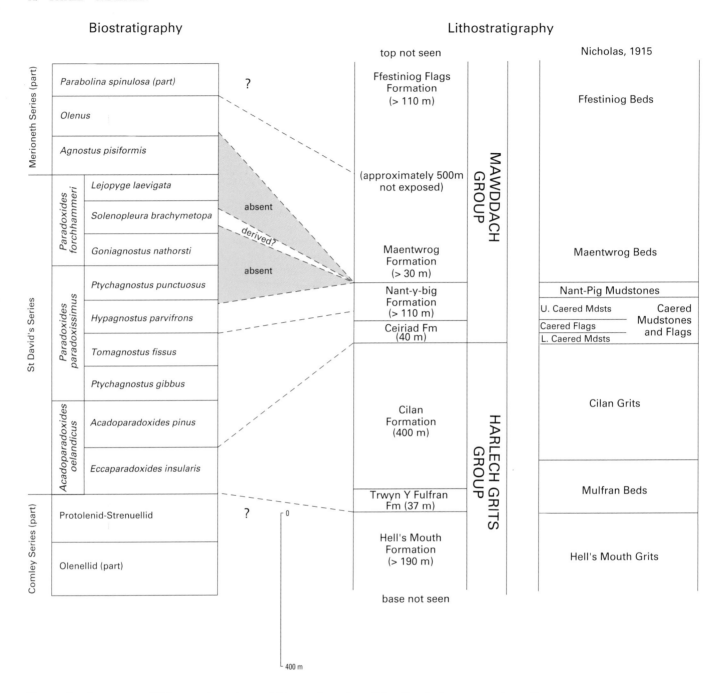

Biostratigraphy   Lithostratigraphy

Figure 5 Summary of lithostratigraphy and biostratigraphy of the Cambrian succession of St Tudwal's Peninsula.

Series, and the Hell's Mouth Formation assemblage is of this age; the position of the Comley–St David's Series boundary has not been determined in the St Tudwal's Peninsula.

In some parts of the type section of the Hell's Mouth Formation, east of Trwyn-y-Ffosle, acritarchs are numerous, but only moderately well preserved and mostly not restricted in range to the Comley Series. They include *Annulum squamaceum*, *Comasphaeridium* sp., *Eliasum llaniscum*, *Retisphaeridium dichamerum* and *R. howellii*,

recovered from between 99.5 and 5 m below the top of the formation; all range upwards to the Nant-y-big Formation (St David's Series, *Tomagnostus fissus* Biozone), and were found up to at least 30 m above the base of that unit below Pared Mawr. Only *Skiagia scottica*, (commonly abundant in the upper part of the Hell's Mouth Formation) and *Peramorpha manuelsensis*, (occurring rarely at a level 66 m below the top) are limited to the Comley Series. *Skiagia scottica* is known from the middle of the Comley Series in the Holmia Shales of Norway, the Bastion Formation in

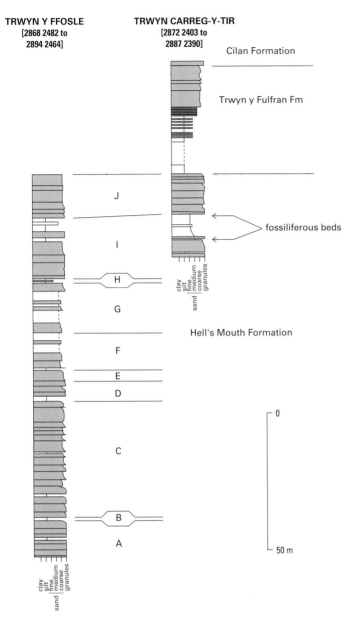

TRWYN Y FFOSLE
[2868 2482 to
2894 2464]

TRWYN CARREG-Y-TIR
[2872 2403 to
2887 2390]

Cilan Formation

Trwyn y Fulfran Fm

J

fossiliferous beds

I

H

G

Hell's Mouth Formation

F

E

D

C

B

A

clay
silt
fine
medium
coarse
granules
sand

clay
silt
fine
medium
coarse
granules
sand

0

50 m

Figure 6   Graphic logs of sections through the lower part of the Harlech Grits Group.

A–J   Pecked lines indicate gaps in exposure lithofacies divisions of Bassett and Walton (1960); their fossil localities are indicated

Greenland and the Fucoid Formation in north-west Scotland (Downie, 1982; Cowie, 1974, p. 145, 148). Both Bastion and Fucoid formations contain the *Olenellus* Biozone of North America, correlated with the '*Protolenus* Biozone' of Europe, itself equivalent to the '*Protolenid-Strenuellid* Biozone' of Cowie et al. (1972). All the type specimens of *S. scottica* illustrated by Downie (1982) were from the Fucoid Formation and their age is late Comley Series. *Peramorpha manuelsensis* was described from the late Comley Brigus Formation of eastern Newfoundland (Martin and Dean, 1983) from a level dated as '*Catadoxides*

Biozone', correlated by Hutchinson (1962) with the '*Protolenus* Biozone'.

Trwyn-y-Fulfran Formation

This formation (37 m thick) is equivalent to the lower part of the 'Mulfran Beds' of Nicholas (1915), and is dominated by dark manganiferous siltstones which, in the upper part of the unit, are interbedded with fine- to medium-grained sandstones. The type section lies above Trwyn Carreg-y-tîr, from the old manganese trials [2877 2402] onto the hillside above [2885 2394] (Young et al., 1994). The base of the formation coincides with that of the first thick manganiferous siltstone and the disappearance of the typically thick sandstone beds of the Hell's Mouth Formation. The lower part of the formation can be easily traced along strike through almost continuous manganese trial pits, and comprises approximately 20 m of manganiferous siltstone with a few (around 15% by thickness) medium-grained sandstone beds, generally less than 10 cm thick.

The upper part of the formation is approximately 17 m thick, but is poorly exposed, apart from the inaccessible cliff section south-east of Trwyn-y-Fulfran; it shows a gradual increase in both thickness and grain size of the sandstone component (up to around 80%). Nicholas (1915) assigned the base of the succeeding 'Cilan Grits' to a level marked by the disappearance of the manganiferous siltstones. A difficulty with his interpretation is the fact that manganiferous siltstones occur throughout the Harlech Grits Group, and in the present study the top of the Trwyn-y-Fulfran Formation is placed at the first appearance of very coarse-grained sandstones that characterise the overlying Cilan Formation. The total thickness of 37 m is significantly less than the 140 m of Nicholas's 'Mulfran Beds'.

No macrofossils have been recorded from the formation, and acritarchs are only sporadically present, and poorly preserved; there is thus no faunal evidence whether the age is late Comley or St David's Series.

Cilan Formation

This succession comprises 400 m of coarse-grained, thickly bedded turbidites and, because of poor inland exposure, its type section (Young et al., 1994) is in the mostly inaccessible cliffs around Trwyn Cilan. No macrofossils have been recorded from the Cilan Formation, and acritarchs, recorded up to a level about 64 m above the base, are badly preserved. The base of the formation is well exposed in the sea cliffs, but as these are accessible only by boat it has been defined on the poorly exposed slopes above the cliffs [2885 2394], at the base of the lowest very coarse-grained sandstones. The top contact with the overlying finer grained lithologies is sharply defined at Trwyn Llech-y-doll [2995 2340]. The formation is broadly equivalent to the 'Cilan Grits' of Nicholas (1915), but its base is approximately 100 m lower.

The turbiditic sandstones are typically coarser grained than those of the Hell's Mouth Formation. The bases of

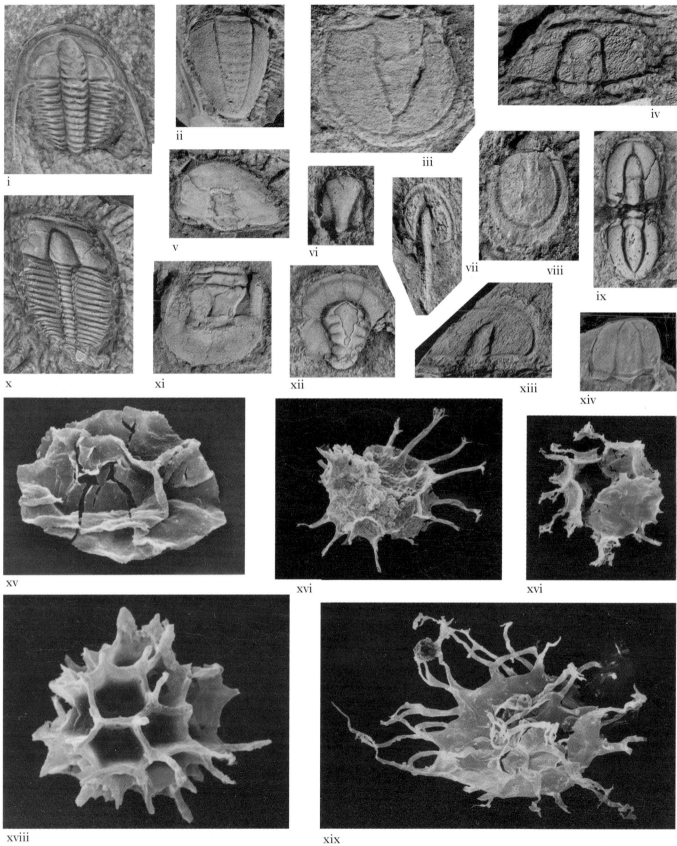

i

ii

iii

iv

v

vi

vii

viii

ix

x

xi

xii

xiii

xiv

xv

xvi

xvi

xviii

xix

individual beds are generally of granule and pebble grade, and some beds (up to 1 m thick) are very coarse sand grade throughout. The coarse sandstone beds contain rip-up clasts of mudstone and siltstone, commonly up to 0.8 m long; clasts up to 3 m in length have also been recorded. Sole structures are less common than in the finer grained sandstones of the Hell's Mouth Formation. Rippled bedding planes with trough cross-lamination indicate palaeocurrents from 060 to 085°.

The sandstones are typically medium- to coarse-grained lithic wackes. Coarser beds contain lithic fragments up to 3 cm in length, including granitic rocks similar to those exposed in the Sarn Complex, quartzitic rocks showing various degrees of dynamic recrystallisation from mildly strained quartzites to quartz mylonites, together with fine quartz-mica schists, and siltstone intraclasts. Most of the other clasts are monocrystalline quartz (50%), unfoliated polycrystalline quartz (10–15%),

feldspar (about 21% K-feldspar, commonly perthitic; 7% oligoclase), muscovite, biotite, ore, epidote, and tourmaline; rare volcanic clasts are mostly basic in composition. The sandstones are interpreted as derived from the reworking of lithologies similar to the Sarn Complex, together with possible Gwna Mélange, and Llŷn Shear Zone rocks.

MAWDDACH GROUP

Ceiriad Formation

This formation comprises at least 40 m of red, brown and green siltstones with subordinate similarly coloured sandstones, and corresponds to the 'Lower Caered Mudstones' and 'Caered Flags' of Nicholas (1915). Since no complete section exists, the base and lower part of the unit was defined at Trwyn Llech-y-doll [299 233] and the upper part in the north-west corner of Porth Ceiriad [3033 2425 to 3056 2469]. The relationship between these two sections is not known but it is likely that, at most, only a small thickness of intervening strata is missing.

The base of the formation is marked by a cherty, intraclast-bearing sandstone with diffuse cross-laminae of sandstone and a strongly sulphide-mineralised top. Some 40 m of the lower part of the formation crop out at Trwyn Llech-y-doll [299 233] and a little farther to the north [3018 2387]. This lower part of the formation comprises 5 to 20 cm beds of red and brown siltstones with fine-grained sandstones, probably turbidites, and abundant thin pale bentonite horizons some of which show grading, suggesting that they represent ashfalls reworked by turbidity currents. In contrast, the upper part of the formation exposed at Porth Ceiriad is sandstone — rather than siltstone — dominated and was assigned to the 'Caered Flags' by Nicholas (1915). These rocks comprise some 12 m of red, green and purple very fine-grained, moderately to well sorted, lithic arkose sandstones with siltstone interbeds. The finer grained interbeds of this upper part are similar to the dominant lithology of the lower part of the formation at Trwyn Llech-y-doll, whereas the sandstones contain clast assemblages like those of the Hell's Mouth Formation, with quartz (dominant), plagioclase, alkali feldspar, biotite (minor, but prominent), muscovite, trachyte, and rare green tourmaline. The uppermost beds of the formation, in the north-western corner of Porth Ceiriad, are green siliceous mudstones with pyrite mineralisation which closely resembles that within the basal bed of the unit (Figure 7). The top of this formation has been placed where a gradational change from these green mudstones to grey siltstones more typical of the Nant-y-big Formation is interrupted by a distinctive, coarse-grained sandstone layer.

Matley et al. (1939, p.85) reported a complete agnostid trilobite about 30 m above the base of the formation, but no further specimens have been found (Bassett et al., 1976, p.639). Acritarchs are of variable abundance and preservation between 3.1 and 23 m

Plate 4 Microflora and macrofauna of the Cambrian rocks of St Tudwal's Peninsula.

i   *Hamatolenus* (*Myopsolenus*) *douglasi* Bassett, Owens and Rushton. Hell's Mouth Formation, Trwyn Carreg-y-tîr. Latex cast of holotype, NMW 75.4G.1, ×2.

ii, xiv   *Kerberodiscus succinctus* Bassett, Owens and Rushton. Horizon and locality as for i.

ii   Paratype pygidium, NMW 75.5G.8, ×4; xiv, paratype cephalon, NMW 75.5G.14a, ×4.

iii   *Peronopsis*? cf. *scutalis* (Hicks). Highest part of Nant-y-big Formation, locality α16 of Nicholas (1915), Porth Ceiriad. Pygidium, SM A.52679, ×7.

iv   *Parasolenopleura* cf. *applanata* (Salter). Nant-y-big Formation, loose block 9.2 m (est.) below top. SM A.54665, ×4.

v   *Agraulos longicephalus* Hicks. Nant-y-big Formation, locality as for iii. Cranidium, SM A.264a, ×2.

vi   *Corynexochus cambrensis* Nicholas. Nant-y-big Formation, locality as for iii. Syntype cranidium, SM A.276b, ×6.

vii   *Eodiscus punctatus* (Salter). Nant-y-big Formation, locality as for iii. Cephalon, SM A.54233, ×6.

viii   *Phalagnostus* sp. Nant-y-big Formation, locality α14 of Nicholas (1915). Pygidium, SM A.257, ×6.

ix   *Ptychagnostus longifrons* (Nicholas). Nant-y-big Formation, locality α8 of Nicholas (1915). Pared-mawr. Internal mould of holotype, SM A.248, ×6.

x   *Parasolenopleura applanata* (Salter). Nant-y-big Formation, locality α9 of Nicholas (1915). SM A.272a, ×2.

xi, xii   Plutonides hicksii (Salter), Nant-y-big Formation, locality α10 of Nicholas (1915).

xi   pygidium, SM A.54661, ×4. xii, immature cranidium with long preglabellar field, SM A.54637, ×7.

xiii   *Meneviella venulosa* (Salter), Nant-y-big Formation, locality as for iii. Incomplete cranidium, SM A.265, ×3.

xv   *Cristallinium cambriense* (Slaviková) Vanguestaine, 1978. Ceiriad Formation, IRScNB b 2465, ×2000.

xvi, xvii   *Cymatiogalea* sp. Maentwrog Formation, highest part of 'calcareous grit' of Nicholas (1915, locality a15).

xvi   IRScNB b 2466, x1000; xvii, IRScNB b 2467, ×1000.

xvii   *Izhoria* sp. Horizon and locality as for xvi. IRScNB b 2468, ×2000.

xix   *Heliosphaeridium*? *llynense*. Martin in Young et al., 1994, Nant-y-big Formation, IRScNB b 2469, ×2000.

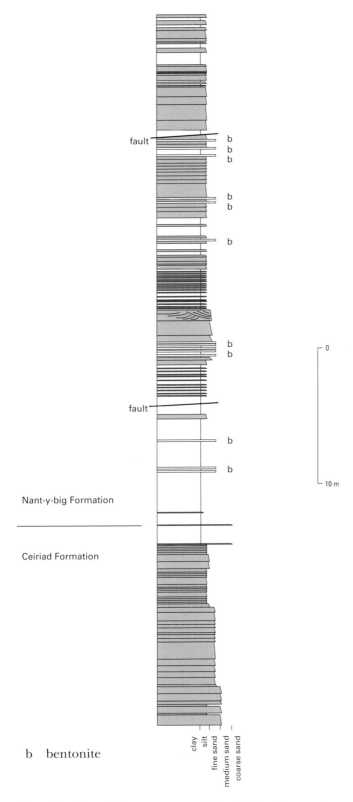

b   bentonite

above the base at Trwyn Llech-y-doll. *Cristallinium cambriense* (Plate 6, xv), found 6.5 m above the base, is here accepted as indicating St David's Series. The species has a long range within the Cambrian, and in eastern Newfoundland (Martin and Dean, 1988) it appears in the middle St David's Series *Ptychagnostus atavus–Tomagnostus fissus* Biozone. A level 3.8 m below the top of the formation in Porth Ceiriad has yielded rare badly preserved acritarchs, none of which indicates a more specific age than St David's Series.

Nant-y-big Formation

This formation comprises dark grey and blue-grey siltstones, with subordinate thin beds of pale sandstone/quartzose siltstone in the upper part. It is equivalent to the 'Upper Caered Mudstones' and the 'Nant Pig Mudstones' (Nicholas, 1915) which are juxtaposed in Porth Ceiriad by a poorly exposed fault zone at the eastern end of the prominent cliff of Pared-mawr. Nicholas (1915) claimed that there was a stratigraphical gap between the highest 'Upper Caered Mudstones' to the west and the lowest 'Nant Pig Mudstones' to the east, but it is not possible to verify this relationship on current coastal exposure. The similarity of the two mudstones led Young et al. (1994) to merge them into a single formation, the thickness of which is uncertain because of faulting. In the type section at Porth Ceriad, approximately 110 m are seen to the west of the major fault (of which the lowest 37 m are well exposed at beach level) and 50 m to the east.

The contact between the Nant-y-big Formation and the underlying Ceiriad Formation (Figure 7) is exposed in the north-western corner of Porth Ceiriad [3056 2469]. The lower part of the Nant-y-big Formation (Nicholas's Upper Caered Mudstones) is well exposed at beach level. It is lithologically similar to the lower part of the Ceiriad Formation, but slightly finer grained and darker. The basal 6 m are characterised by laminated siltstones and mudstones and these become increasingly interbedded with massive to crudely graded siltstones, interpreted as turbidites, that form the dominant lithology thoughout much of the formation. Bentonite beds occur in several places and are particularly common 13 m above the base (Bennett, 1989; Roberts and Merriman, 1990) (Plate 5).

The upper part of the succession, east of the fault in Porth Ceiriad (Nicholas's 'Nant Pig Mudstones'), again comprises 10 to 20 cm beds of graded, internally structureless, grey-brown turbiditic siltstones, interbedded with darker laminated siltstones. The turbiditic siltstone beds commonly have sand-grade bases, which may show development of diagenetic or metamorphic sulphides. These silty turbidites assume less importance upwards through the formation. They become subordinate to the laminated interbeds which are interpreted as evidence of sea floor reworking and sorting of the sediment into coarse and fine laminae. Towards the top of the formation, the coarse-grained laminae thicken and commonly form lenticular beds of starved ripples (Plate 6), with local concentration of sulphides. Thicker

Figure 7   Log of the upper part of the Ceiriad Formation and lower part of the Nant-y-big Formation, north-west part of Porth Ceiriad [305 247]. The upper part of the Ceiriad Formation comprises green and red cherty siltstones and sandstones. The Nant-y-big Formation includes numerous graded siltstone turbidite beds, within a background of fossiliferous laminated dark siltstones.

Plate 6 Dark siltstones with paler fine-grained sandstone laminae and lenticular sandstone beds formed by starved ripples, uppermost part of the Nant-y-big Formation, Porth Ceiriad [3103 2484]. Length of hammer: 40 cm (GS647).

Plate 5 Pale bentonites interbedded with siltstone turbidites from the lower part of the Nant-y-big Formation in Porth Ceiriad [3058 2471]. Length of hammer: 40 cm (GS646).

sandstone beds, containing large carbonate concretions, occur in the top 15 m of the formation and are interbedded with dark grey fossiliferous siltstones. The top metre of the formation is formed of siltstones with large wavelength, low-amplitude, cross-lamination, picked out by thin beds of darker (possibly phosphatic) material which also occurs as intraclasts. The uppermost 20 cm are highly indurated, rich in carbonate and phosphate concretions, and interpreted as a hardground beneath the overlying unconformity (Figure 8; Plate 7). As a whole, this upper part of the Nant-y-big Formation is interpreted as recording a waning influence of turbidity currents, increased reworking by wave and storm action, and decreasing sedimentation rate.

Nicholas (1915, 1916) recorded several species of trilobites, mostly agnostids, from the lower part of the Nant-y-big Formation (his 'Upper Caered Mudstones'); nearly all were found close to the base of the unit. His

faunal list, now revised, includes *Eodiscus punctatus* (Plate 4vii), *Peronopsis scutalis* (previously recorded as *Agnostus exaratus*), *Ptychagnostus longifrons* (Plate 4ix; for which this is the type locality and horizon), *Tomagnostus fissus* and *Plutonides hicksii*, which Rushton (1974) identified as indicating the *T. fissus* Biozone of the St David's Series, or Middle Cambrian. *Plutonides hicksii* (Plate 4 xi, xii), first described from the Mawddach valley, east of Barmouth, is a widespread species, known also from South Wales, the English Midlands, eastern Canada (especially in the Manuels River Formation of eastern Newfoundland), Siberia and Scandinavia.

Within the upper part of the Nant-y-big Formation, trilobites are most common in the higher levels. Only *Peronopsis scutalis*, *Plutonides hicksii*, *Eodiscus punctatus* and *Parasolenopleura applanata* (Plate 4x) are recorded from 50 to 20 m beneath the top of the formation. *P. scutalis* has a long range, from the *gibbus* Biozone to the *punctuosus* Biozone; *P. hicksii* occurs in the *gibbus* and *fissus* biozones; the remaining two are not recorded below the *fissus* Biozone, to which the assemblage is considered to belong.

The more diverse fauna in the upper part of the section at Porth Ceiriad (0 to 20 m below the top of the formation) includes agnostids such as *Peronopsis?* cf. *scutalis* (Plate 4iii), *Ptychagnostus punctuosus* and *Phalagnostus* sp. (Plate 4viii) together with *Eodiscus punctatus* (Plate 4vii), *Meneviella venulosa* (Plate 4xiii), *Centropleura pugnax* (figured Lake, 1934), *Agraulos longicephalus* (Plate 4v) and *Corynexochus cambrensis* (Plate 4vi), for which this is the type locality and horizon. The fauna indicates the *parvifrons* Biozone of the St David's Series, despite the record of *Pt. punctuosus* which ranges below its named zone. Nicholas's (1916) record of '*Solenopleura variolaris* (?)', a species now referred to *Solenopleuropsis* (a genus of zonal value in the Mediterranean region), from two levels in the highest 10 m of the Nant-y-big

Plate 7 Contact between the Nant-y-big and overlying Maentwrog formations in Porth Ceiriad [3104 2483]. The exact contact lies just below the top of the pale part of the hammer shaft. The hammer base lies at the base of the 'calcareous grit' of Nicholas (1915) and the top of the hammer shaft lies at the top of this unit. Nicholas's 'calcareous grit' therefore includes within it a significant intra-Middle Cambrian unconformity. Length of hammer: 40 cm (GS648).

Formation suggests a possibly younger horizon, the *punctuosus* Biozone. But his record has not been confirmed and the specimen could have been the superficially similar *Parasolenopleura* cf. *applanata* (Plate 4iv), a long-ranging species that occurs in the *parvifrons* Biozone. Nicholas's (1916) record of *Paradoxides hicksii* was also not confirmed. There is no evidence at St Tudwal's of *Paradoxides davidis*, the very large trilobite so conspicuous in the Menevian Beds of St David's, South Wales, and in the Clogau Formation of the Harlech Dome, units that belong to the *punctuosus* Biozone. As was appreciated by Nicholas, there is a considerable stratigraphical break between the top of the Nant-y-big Formation and the overlying Maentwrog Formation.

Acritarchs are of variable abundance and preservation. In western Porth Ceiriad [306 247], approximately 35 m above the base of the formation (*T. fissus* Biozone: locality α10 of Nicholas, 1915), *Heliosphaeridium? llynense* (Plate 4xix) is present and continues to occur through the succeeding 24 m of strata. *Adara alea* appears 53 to 59.5 m above the base of the formation (upwards from the upper part of locality α8, Nicholas, 1915, *T. fissus* Biozone) in the youngest assemblage containing *Annulum squamaceum*. In eastern Newfoundland, the *Adara alea* Biozone is correlated, with confidence, with the upper part of the *T. fissus–P. atavus* Biozone, and with the '*Paradoxides hicksii* Biozone'; it may extend to about the middle of the *P. punctuosus* Biozone and the '*Paradoxides davidis* Biozone'. All the acritarchs from the upper part of the Nant-y-big Formation were undeterminable.

Maentwrog Formation

The boundary between the Nant-y-big Formation and the Maentwrog Formation in the Porth Ceiriad section is an irregular erosion surface locally encrusted with stromatolites and overlain by coarse conglomeratic sandstones containing boulders greater than 30 cm in diameter. These conglomeratic sandstones are 25 to 120 cm thick , and are overlain by another irregular erosion surface which locally preserves upstanding remnants of bioclastic limestone. The previously described 'calcareous grit' of Nicholas (1915) (Figure 8; Plate 7) [3106 2482] included both the concretionary top of the Nant-y-big Formation and the coarse conglomeratic sandstones at the base of the Maentwrog Formation. The double unconformity now recognised at this stratigraphical level is interpreted as recording a significant time gap in mid- to late Cambrian times. The combination of low sedimentation rates and erosion surfaces means that the biostratigraphical data at this level must be treated with caution, especially where previously described specimens are not very accurately located within the sequence.

Above the second unconformity the Maentwrog Formation is characterised by grey, very fine-grained sandstone and coarse-grained siltstone, up to 40 cm thick, cemented by calcite and commonly showing soft-sediment deformation features such as convoluted beds and ball-and-pillow disruption. Thinner sandstone beds commonly comprise amalgamated ripple sets, whereas the thicker beds show sole structures, parallel lamination and wave rippled tops. The siltstone interbeds contain rippled sandstone laminae and discontinuous trains of starved ripples. The sequence is interpreted as having been deposited in a storm-influenced shallow marine environment.

These beds pass upwards into a succession of laminated siltstones with sandstone laminae but this upper part of the formation is poorly exposed and the relationship between the lower and upper levels is not clear. In the Pwllheli district these lithologies are seen at the east end of Porth Ceiriad, where they are unconformably overlain by the St Tudwal's Formation [3172 2490], but no proof exists as to whether the exposures

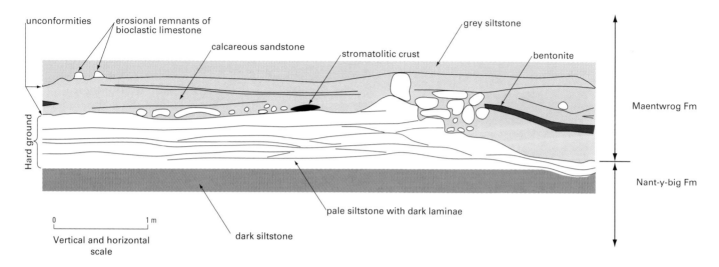

Figure 8 Section of the contact of the Nant-y-big and Maentwrog formations as exposed in Porth Ceiriad [3106 2482]. The complex of units included in Nicholas's 'calcareous grit' includes at least two major unconformities.

belong to the Maentwrog or to the lithologically similar Ffestiniog Flags formations. In contrast to the incomplete, poorly exposed sequence on Llŷn, the type section of the Maentwrog Formation, on the south side of the Harlech Dome, is 700 to 1200 m thick (Allen et al., 1981)

Limestone clasts from the base of the Maentwrog Formation at the shore section in Porth Ceiriad [3106 2482] (Figure 4) have yielded a small number of fragmentary trilobites (Nicholas, 1915,1916, locality α15) which were interpreted as belonging to the highest part of the St David's Series, equivalent to the *Paradoxides forchhammeri* 'Stage' of Sweden, and to the *punctuosus* Biozone (Lake, 1940). The precise level of the fossils obtained is unknown, but the collection includes (Young et al., 1994) *Dorypyge* sp., *Bailiaspis glabrata*, *Linguagnostus aristatus* and *Dolichometopus* cf. *suecicus*, the age of which approximates to that of the Andrarum Limestone (late St David's Series, *Paradoxides forchhammeri* 'Stage', *Solenopleura brachymetopa* Biozone) in Sweden. The trilobite specimens collected by Nicholas lie within a matrix of bioclastic limestone similar to the lithology locally preserved beneath the second unconformity (i.e. the top of his 'calcareous grit'). However, the presence of Merioneth Series acritarchs (*Cymatiogalea* sp. (Plate 4xvi, xvii) and *Izhoria* sp. (Plate 4xviii) immediately below these in situ bioclastic limestones suggests that the trilobites were derived from some lower stratigraphical level. Above the second unconformity the only macrofossils known are poorly preserved small agnostid and olenid trilobites from the highest beds of the incomplete section exposed at the beach at Porth Ceiriad [3112 2487]. The material was recorded and determined by Nicholas (1915) as *Agnostus pisiformis* var. *obesus* (later made type species of *Homagnostus*) and *Olenus* sp., an assemblage indicative of the *Olenus* Biozone, and this interpretation was supported by Young et al., (1994).

Acritarchs from the section at Porth Ceiriad beach are abundant and variably preserved (Young et al., 1994). Compared with the zonation based on acritarchs and trilobites on the Avalon Platform, eastern Newfoundland (Martin and Dean, 1981, 1988), *Timofeevia microretis*, recorded 10 cm above the top of the conglomeratic sandstone at the base of the section, could possibly represent the middle of the upper part of microflora A2, which ranges from the *Agnostus pisiformis* Biozone into strata without trilobites that underlie the *Olenus* Biozone. If this correlation is correct, and if the trilobite-bearing horizon from the upper part of the same section belongs to the *Olenus* Biozone, then the species of *Cymatiogalea* and *Stelliferidium*, amongst others, appear earlier in the Merioneth Series than was recognised by Martin and Dean (1988) in the Avalon platform and by Volkova (1990) in the East European Platform. *Timofeevia lancarae, T. pentagonalis, T. phosphoritica, Cymatiogalea aspergillum, Cymatiogalea* cf. *C. cristata, Stelliferidium pingiculum* and *Vulcanisphaera turbata* appear 10 cm above the top of the basal conglomerate. *Leiofusa stoumonensis* and badly preserved specimens attributed to *Cristallinium* cf. *C. randomense* appear 3.85 m above the top of the basal conglomeratic sandstone, and *Leiofusa* cf. *L. gravida* appears 27.20 m above. All these taxa have also been identified in the lower part of the Ffestiniog Flags Formation on St Tudwal's Island East. All except the last-named are known from the top of the upper part of microflora A2 and from microflora A3a, and do not permit a distinction to be made between the upper part of the *Olenus* Biozone and the lower part of the *Parabolina spinulosa* Biozone. It should be noted that *Veryhachium dumontii*, which appears at the base of microflora A3a in eastern Newfoundland and is abundant in the Ffestiniog Flags Formation at Llŷn Carreg-wen, west of Porthmadog, has been found neither in the Maentwrog

St Tudwal's Formation

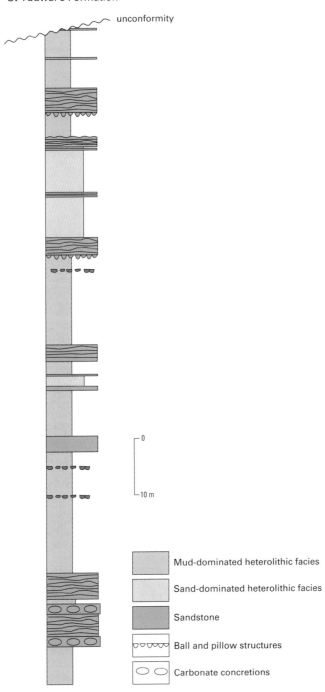

Figure 9   Section in the Ffestiniog Flags Formation as exposed on St Tudwal's Island East.

Formation at Porth Ceiriad Beach nor in the lower part of the Ffestiniog Flags Formation on St Tudwal's Island East.

Ffestiniog Flags Formation

In the Pwllheli district this unit is lithologically very similar to, but slightly finer grained than, the underlying Maentwrog Formation and is exposed only on St Tudwal's Island East where it is about 110 m thick (Figure 9). Exposures are characterised by groups of beds of fine-grained sandstone, commonly with soft-sediment deformation structures, interspersed in background sediments of bioturbated siltstones and mudstones.

Acritarchs are abundant in the lower part of the succession and are relatively well preserved. In addition to the taxa noted above from the Maentwrog Formation, several new species occur, together with the very rare *Poikilofusa* cf. *P. squama* and *P.* cf. *P. chalaza*. Such an association is as yet unknown elsewhere in deposits dated by means of trilobites, but may be compared broadly, with reservation, with microflora A3a of eastern Newfoundland, found in the *Parabolina spinulosa* Biozone below the appearance of diacrodians.

FOUR

Ordovician

Ordovician sedimentation in the Pwllheli district is recorded by marine siliciclastic rocks of Tremadoc to Ashgill age, and was interrupted by late Tremadoc uplift and several periods of volcanism. Representatives of all three Welsh Basin supergroups (Dyfed, Gwynedd, and Powys), as defined by Woodcock (1990) with each separated by basin-wide unconformities, are present within the Ordovician succession. The oldest Ordovician rocks, of Tremadoc age, are those of the Dol-cyn-afon Formation (Mawddach Group) and lie in the upper part of the Dyfed Supergroup. These are overlain by the Gwynedd Supergroup which comprises a thick sequence of Arenig to Caradoc marine sediments (Ogwen Group of Rushton and Howells, 1999) and intercalated deposits from several volcanic centres. The Powys Supergroup is represented by the Crugan Mudstone Formation, which is of Ashgill age and provides the youngest record of Ordovican sedimentation in the district.

Most Ordovician exposures within the Pwllheli district are of rocks belonging to the Gwynedd Supergroup, the stratigraphy of which is complex but may be overviewed as recording background sedimentation (Ogwen Group) locally interrupted by various volcanic events (Figure 3). The lower part of the Ogwen Group is represented by the Nant Ffrancon Subgroup, which is of Arenig to Llanvirn age and is divided into the Wig Bâch, Bryncroes, St Tudwal's, Llanengan and Trygarn formations (Figure 3). The deposition of these marine siliciclastic formations took place within, and on either side of, a marine basin initiated in early Arenig times. The youngest strata within the Nant Ffrancon Subgroup are of Llanvirn (probably early Llanvirn) age. Above this is an unconformity, with no evidence for strata of later Llanvirn, Llandeilo or early Caradoc age. Sedimentation was renewed in late Soudleyan to Longvillian times with a stepwise marine transgression across this previously uplifted area, with the onset of volcanism interpreted as controlling the onset of local subsidence.

The Caradoc marine sedimentary sequence forming the upper part of the Ogwen Group includes the Cwm Eigiau Formation (restricted to the east of the district), the Dwyfach Formation and the Nod Glas Formation (Figures 10, 16, 17). Intercalated into this succession of sedimentary rocks are the products of four distinct phases of volcanism. The earliest is the Pitts Head Tuff Formation, erupted from the Llwyd Mawr centre, intercalated within the Cwm Eigiau Formation and restricted to the east of the district (Figure 10). In the north, the second phase of volcanism is represented by the Upper Lodge and Allt Fawr formations, probably erupted from a centre in the adjacent Nefyn district, and at least in part younger than the Pitts Head Tuff Formation. The Upper Lodge and Allt Fawr formations are overlain by the

siltstones and sandstones of the Dwyfach Formation. The third volcanic phase was the Llanbedrog Volcanic Group, erupted from a centre within the Pwllheli district where over 1000 m of lavas and tuffs are preserved intercalated within the Dwyfach Formation (Figure 16). The Dwyfach Formation and Llanbedrog Volcanic Group are blanketed by dark mudstones of the Nod Glas Formation, which contains basalts that record a final, basaltic, phase of Ordovician igneous activity in the district (Figure 10).

The overlying Crugan Mudstone Formation comprises a thick succession (at least 600 m) of siltstones and mudstones belonging to the lower part of the Powys Supergroup. The oldest faunas in the Crugan Mudstone Formation are of Rawtheyan age, and there was therefore probably a major hiatus between the Nod Glas Formation and the Crugan Mudstone Formation above (Figure 10). This hiatus is the local expression of a widespread sub-Powys unconformity which has been interpreted as related to the onset of a phase of strike-slip faulting in the Welsh Borderlands (Woodcock and Gibbons, 1988; Woodcock, 1990). Elucidation of the local palaeo-geography during the deposition of the Crugan Mudstone Formation is hindered by the paucity of rocks as young as this in north-west Wales, but contrasting faunas between Llanbedrog and Llanystumdwy suggest a south-east-dipping palaeoslope on the north-west margin of the Welsh basin (Bevins et al., 1992). The top of the Crugan Formation is not exposed, although the equivalent Dwyfor Mudstones are overlain by Silurian strata in the Llanystumdwy syncline, just to the north of the Pwllheli district, and these Silurian rocks may be present beneath the drift of the north-east corner of the district.

The Upper Ordovician lithostratigraphy described in this chapter has been recently formalised and interpreted by Gibbons and Young (1999). This latter publication discusses the geochemistry of the Upper Ordovician magmatism and places it within the broader context of the Snowdon volcanic corridor of north-west Wales. A wider ranging lithostratigraphical correlation of Welsh Ordovician rocks, including those of the Pwllheli district has been published by Rushton and Howells (1999).

MAWDDACH GROUP

Dol-cyn-afon Formation

The Dol-cyn-afon Formation ('Tremadoc Slates' of earlier authors) was defined in the Harlech Dome where it forms part of the Mawddach Group (Allen and Jackson, 1985). In the Pwllheli district, it is exposed only in the hanging wall of the north-dipping Sarn–Abersoch Thrust to the north of Abersoch, near Sarn Meyllteyrn where siltstones are exposed in an old quarry north-west of the farm of

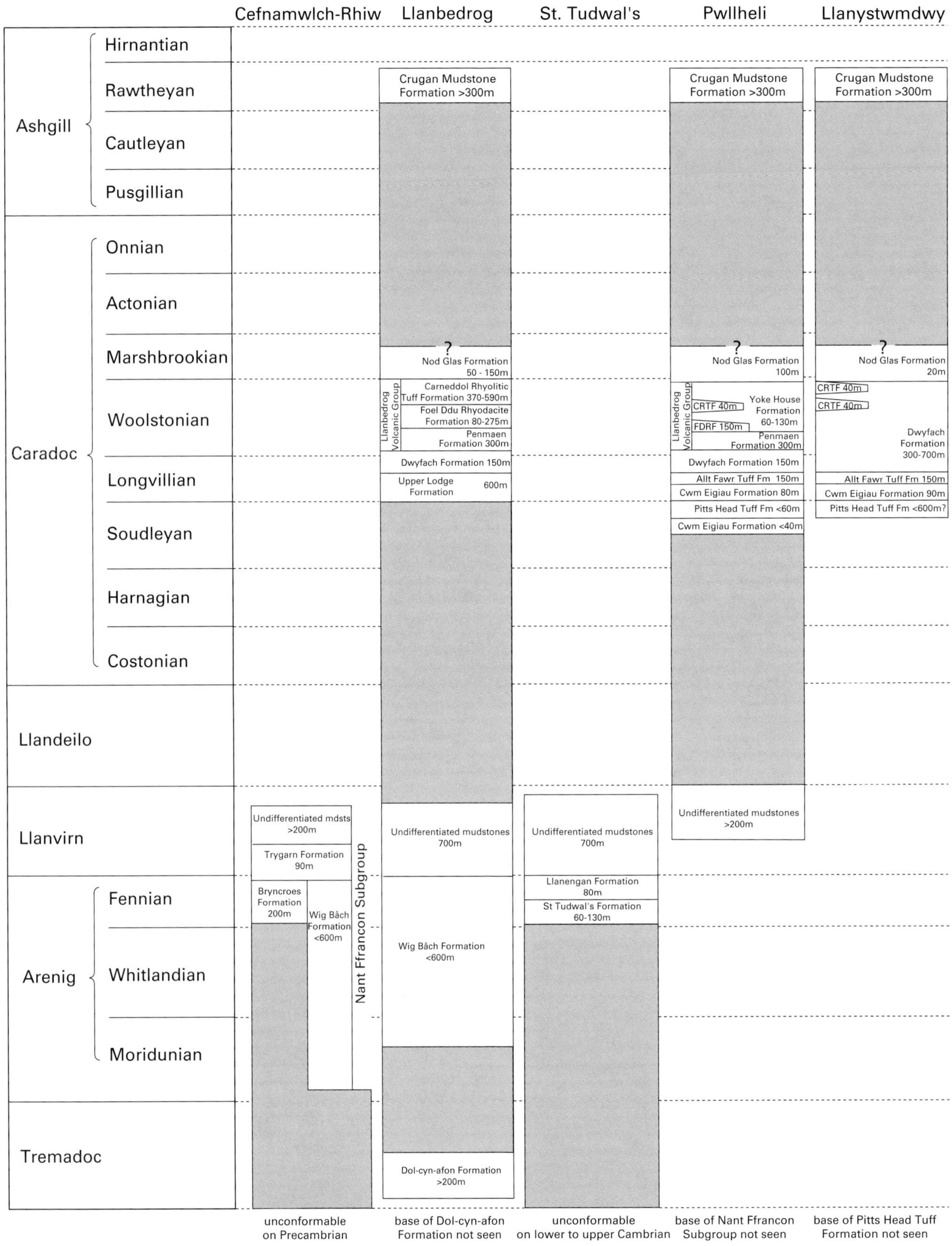
Cefnamwlch-Rhiw
Llanbedrog
St. Tudwal's
Pwllheli
Llanystwmdwy
Ashgill
Hirnantian
Rawtheyan
Cautleyan
Pusgillian
Caradoc
Onnian
Actonian
Marshbrookian
Woolstonian
Longvillian
Soudleyan
Harnagian
Costonian
Llandeilo
Llanvirn
Arenig
Fennian
Whitlandian
Moridunian
Tremadoc
Crugan Mudstone Formation >300m
?
Nod Glas Formation 50 - 150m
Llanbedrog Volcanic Group
Carneddol Rhyolitic Tuff Formation 370-590m
Foel Ddu Rhyodacite Formation 80-275m
Penmaen Formation 300m
Dwyfach Formation 150m
Upper Lodge Formation 600m
Undifferentiated mudstones 700m
Wig Bâch Formation <600m
Dol-cyn-afon Formation >200m
Undifferentiated mdsts >200m
Trygarn Formation 90m
Bryncroes Formation 200m
Wig Bâch Formation <600m
Nant Ffrancon Subgroup
Undifferentiated mudstones 700m
Llanengan Formation 80m
St Tudwal's Formation 60-130m
Crugan Mudstone Formation >300m
?
Nod Glas Formation 100m
Llanbedrog Volcanic Group
CRTF 40m
Yoke House Formation 60-130m
FDRF 150m
Penmaen Formation 300m
Dwyfach Formation 150m
Allt Fawr Tuff Fm 150m
Cwm Eigiau Formation 80m
Pitts Head Tuff Fm <60m
Cwm Eigiau Formation <40m
Undifferentiated mudstones >200m
Crugan Mudstone Formation >300m
?
Nod Glas Formation 20m
CRTF 40m
CRTF 40m
Dwyfach Formation 300-700m
Allt Fawr Tuff Fm 150m
Cwm Eigiau Formation 90m
Pitts Head Tuff Fm <600m?
unconformable on Precambrian
base of Dol-cyn-afon Formation not seen
unconformable on lower to upper Cambrian
base of Nant Ffrancon Subgroup not seen
base of Pitts Head Tuff Formation not seen

Crugeran [2422 3219], and in new excavations north of the farm [243 321]. In the main outcrop, north of Abersoch, the formation is at least 200 m thick; it usually shows tight folding and thrust imbrication, and only the coastal exposures around the headland of Penbennar [31 28] (Figure 11) are well preserved (Nicholas, 1915; Roberts, 1979; Cattermole and Romano, 1981). The occurrence of the Dol-cyn-afon Formation in the hanging wall of the Sarn–Abersoch Thrust suggests that the fault may have exploited the horizon of the carbonaceous mudstones of the Dolgellau Formation which underlie the Dol-cyn-afon Formation elsewhere in north-west Wales.

The sequence is formed dominantly of grey, well bedded, possibly turbiditic siltstones (e.g. near the old lime kiln, Abersoch [3145 2835]) with subordinate sandstones, commonly calcareous and locally phosphatic (e.g. east side of Penbennar), or volcaniclastic (e.g. near Bryn Cethin Bach [3060 2912]). Farther east from the lime kiln the sediments are generally finer grained, have yielded *Rhabdinopora* [*Dictyonema*] sp. (and also *Clonograptus*; Nicholas, 1915), and can be correlated with some confidence with the lower Tremadoc succession at Porthmadog (the 'Dictyonema Band' of Fearnsides, 1910a). The top of the formation is marked by a distinctive very hard, dark, red, brown or purplish ironstone bearing green or black grains, and has been recorded at Fach [3120 2939], the chapel in Lon Garmon [3091 2863], north of Llangian [2982 2916] [2963 2913], and at Penbennar [3160 2836, 3158 2831, 3183 2821] where it is approximately 1 to 1.5 m thick. The grains are pellets of uncertain mineralogy, possibly glauconitic, and are cemented by sphaerosiderite. It is this unit which apparently was described from near Fach Farm by Matley as an ash. It is interpreted as the product of alteration and early lithification of the sea bed during a period of nondeposition, and as such is the local expression of the late Tremadoc uplift seen elsewhere as defining the break between the Dyfed and Gwynedd Supergroups in the Welsh Basin (Woodcock, 1990).

OGWEN GROUP

NANT FFRANCON SUBGROUP

The lithostratigraphy of the Ordovician sequence from the base of the Arenig to the base of the Snowdon Volcanic Group in North Wales has long been problematic (Williams, 1927; Shackleton, 1959; Howells et al., 1973, 1981, 1983, 1991; Orton, 1992; Gibbons and McCarroll, 1993). The Nant Ffrancon Subgroup has been established to encompass this entire sequence and three major subdivisions can be distinguished.

Figure 10 Time-correlation diagram of Ordovician strata of the district and adjacent area to the north-east around Four Crosses and Llanystwmdwy.

CRTF   Carneddol Rhyolitic Tuff Formation
FDRF   Foel Ddu Rhyodacite Formation

i a varied succession of sandstones and siltstones of Arenig (Moridunian to Fennian) age (locally more than 600 m thick)
ii a dominantly argillaceous unit of siltstones and mudstones of Llanvirn age (up to 1200 m thick) with some restricted acid volcanic rocks
iii a succession (up to 2200 m thick) of siltstones and mudstones with intercalated acid volcanic rocks of early Caradoc age (Costonian to possibly Soudleyan)

The Nant Ffrancon Subgroup of the Pwllheli district includes the Wig Bâch, Bryncroes, St Tudwal's, Llanengan and Trygarn formations, together equivalent to subdivision (i) above, with a considerable thickness of overlying siltstones of subdivision (ii), which do not have a formal lithostratigraphical name. Subdivision (iii) of the Nant Ffrancon Subgroup is not present in Llŷn (Figure 10).

The stratigraphy of the Nant Ffrancon Subgroup of the district is complex, reflecting a varied palaeogeography in early Ordovician times. In the south-west part of the district, the Wig Bâch Formation crops out, representing the north-eastwards continuation of the sedimentary basin seen in the Aberdaron area, the deposits of which have been referred to the Aberdaron Bay Group by Gibbons and McCarroll (1993). The Wig Bâch Formation may also underlie much of the central part of the district, but is unexposed except for a belt in the hanging wall of the Sarn–Abersoch Thrust. The onset of sedimentation was in the Moridunian (early Arenig), with a marine transgression over a basement of Sarn Complex rocks in the west and over the Tremadoc Dol-cyn-afon Formation in the central part of the district. The basin accumulated a thick (locally up to 600 m) fill of Arenig sedimentary rocks and late Arenig rocks are found overstepping the basin margins to both north-west and south-east.

The north-west margin of the Arenig Wig Bâch Formation basin is now defined by a belt of north-north-east- to north-east-trending faults (including the faults near Bodgaeaf, the 'boundary thrust' to the west of Mynydd Rhiw and the faulting of the manganese mining belt). Across this fault system the Arenig succession thins extremely rapidly and the Wig Bâch Formation is replaced laterally north-westwards by the Bryncroes Formation (200 m in thickness). Continued subsidence across this margin into Llanvirn times was accompanied by igneous activity during the later deposition of the overlying Trygarn Formation.

To the south-east of the Wig Bâch Formation depocentre, the thin (up to 210 m) Arenig succession of the St Tudwal's Peninsula, south of the Sarn–Abersoch thrust, records transgression over a basement of tilted Cambrian rocks. The lower, arenaceous, part of this succession is referred to as the St Tudwal's Formation and comprises a storm- and tide-dominated inner shelf facies. The upper, argillaceous, part forms the Llanengan Formation, which represents a south-eastward spread of more offshore facies.

These thinner successions to the north-west (Bryncroes) and south-east (St Tudwal's and Llanengan)

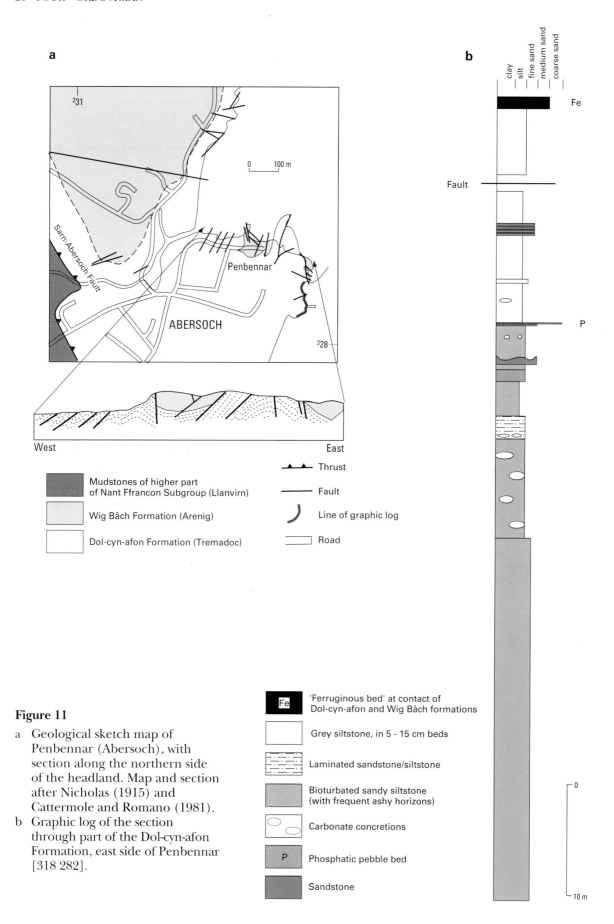

Figure 11

a Geological sketch map of Penbennar (Abersoch), with section along the northern side of the headland. Map and section after Nicholas (1915) and Cattermole and Romano (1981).

b Graphic log of the section through part of the Dol-cyn-afon Formation, east side of Penbennar [318 282].

of the Wig Bâch Formation basin are of Fennian age in their upper parts, but the time of the initial transgression is not well constrained. There is no evidence, however, that the transgression was as early as that seen in the Wig Bâch Formation basin itself.

Close to the Arenig/Llanvirn boundary throughout the Pwllheli district there are distinctive ooidal ironstones generated during a period of sediment starvation. In the north-west, a locally substantial ooidal ironstone unit marks the base of the Trygarn Formation, and reworked ferruginous allochems are common in the sandstones higher in the formation. On the south-east side of the basin, the ooidal ironstones have been referred to as the Hen-dy-capel Ironstone and are 6 m thick (Nicholas, 1915; Young, 1991). The same ironstone unit has also been recorded in the central part of the district, lying immediately above the Wig Bâch Formation.

The Trygarn Formation is dominated by sandstones and dark ferruginous siltstones and mudstones, but also contains high-level basic sills, a basalt lava and, in the west of the district, a rhyolitic ashflow tuff. During the later Llanvirn, the district received fine-grained sediment, forming the mudstones of the higher parts of the Nant Ffrancon Subgroup. The Llandeilo Series has not been recognised in the Pwllheli district; any sediments deposited in the time interval between the mid-Llanvirn and the Longvillian (mid-Caradoc) have been eroded.

Wig Bâch Formation

The Wig Bâch Formation crops out in the south-west of the district, where it is very poorly exposed, and more centrally, in the hanging wall of the Sarn–Abersoch Thrust. In its type area in the adjacent Bardsey district to the west, the lower part of the formation (of probable Moridunian age) comprises mudstones and sandstones, and the upper part is dominantly grey siltstones and bioturbated muddy sandstones of Whitlandian to Fennian age. The type locality was not stated by Gibbons and McCarroll (1993), but is here taken as the somewhat faulted, but largely complete section on the eastern side of Aberdaron Bay which omits only the very top of the formation. The base is seen in a fault-bounded outcrop at the eastern end of Aberdaron Beach [1863 2570], and a more continuous section runs from Wig Bâch [1860 2567] up through the Wig Member (repeated by faulting), then south of Ogof Ddeudrws [1868 2550] through the upper part of the formation, reaching as high as the Trwyn Cam Member on the islet of Ebolion [1888 2514]. Only the very top of the formation is not seen in this section, but that is extremely well exposed in Porth Meudwy [1642 2560].

Within the south-west of the Pwllheli district, the only exposure of this formation occurs in small quarries and a track near Hen Felin [237 279] where highly sheared unfossiliferous siltstones are in faulted contact with phosphatic and volcaniclastic sandstones of the Trygarn Formation. The relationships and lithologies of these exposures strongly resemble those of the manganese mining belt of Nant y Gadwen and Benallt, just to the west of Rhiw. The formation is interpreted to crop out in the unexposed ground on the west side of Mynydd Rhiw and in a small area to the south-east of Rhiw. Fine-grained grey unfossiliferous siltstones referred to the Wig Bâch Formation, lying below the Trygarn Formation, were determined by a BGS borehole on Mynydd Rhiw [229 295] (Brown and Evans 1989). Similar sedimentary successions to that of the Wig Bâch Formation are seen at Trefor, Caernarfon and Bangor, reflecting the likely original continuation of the basin along the Menai Strait Fault System.

In the central part of the district, north of the Sarn–Abersoch Thrust and east of the Cefnamlwch–Rhiw Fault, the Wig Bâch Formation rests on Tremadoc rocks of the Dol-cyn-afon Formation, and it is well exposed in the area around, and to the north-west of, Castellmarch [314 297] and Fach [312 293] Farms. The base of the formation in this area is well exposed on Penbennar [318 283], and the top of the formation is seen 700 m west-north-west of Castellmarch [3085 2993].

The base of the formation in this central part of the district is characterised by a distinctive and complex ferruginous horizon which is interpreted as a combination of a diagenetically altered substrate of the top of the Dol-cyn-afon Formation overlain by a coarse-grained ferruginous sandstone, up to 1.5 m thick, at the base of the Wig Bâch Formation. This basal section is exposed on Penbennar [3160 2836] (where it is difficult to divide in the field from the underlying sphaerosiderite-cemented pelletal unit) near Aberuchaf [3106 2833], and north of Llangian [2982 2916, 2963 2913]. The ferruginous sandstone base to the formation is overlain by ooidal ironstones which are exposed near Aberuchaf [3106 2833] where they appear to be only a few tens of centimetres thick. Finely interlaminated, bioturbated sandstones (less than 3 mm thick) and mudstones (less than 10 mm thick) overlie the basal sandstone and ironstone. These sediments are much finer grained and more thinly laminated than the sandier Bryncroes Formation (see below) which crops out west of the Cefnamlwch–Rhiw Fault. The basal part of the formation resembles, but has coarser laminae than, the Llanengan Formation farther south, but there is no evidence of lateral continuity between the two formations, the laminated facies of which are likely to be of very different ages. The upper part of the formation is generally finer grained than the lower, and closely resembles the upper part of the Wig Bâch Formation in its type area. The top of the formation is seen 700 m west-north-west of Castellmarch [3085 2993] where laminated mudstones contain large carbonate concretions capped by poorly exposed ironstones. This sequence of carbonate concretion-bearing marine sediments overlain by ironstone is similar to that in the adjacent district, south-west of Aberdaron, although here the succession is generally more arenaceous (Gibbons and McCarroll, 1993).

Fossils are uncommon in the Wig Bâch Formation of the district, but Nicholas (1915) recorded '*Azygograptus* sp?', phyllocarids and cyclopygid fragments just above the base at Penbennar [3183 2825] and '*Azygograptus lapworthi*' with phyllocarids from Castellmarch Farm

[3145 2980]. In this survey, *Azygograptus* sp. and phyllocarids were recorded from 250 m west of Rhandir Bach [2986 2917]. Beckly (1985, 1987; Beckly and Maletz, 1991) has recorded *Pseudophyllograptus angustifolius* from west of Castellmarch [3079 2976] and has confirmed the *Azygograptus lapworthi* from Castellmarch Farm. Farther west, Matley (1932, 1938) recorded '*Didymograptus* cf. *deflexus*' and '*Azygograptus* sp?' from Bottwnog, and '*Didymograptus hirundo*' with '*Azygograptus suecicus*' in the Cefn valley [249 321]. These records suggest the presence of the Fennian Stage, but the age of the base of the formation in the Pwllheli district remains unconstrained, although in the adjacent Aberdaron district both the Moridunian and Whitlandian stages are reported within the formation (Gibbons and McCarroll, 1993).

Bryncroes Formation

The Bryncroes Formation comprises a sequence, about 200 m thick, of late Arenig, thinly interbedded and interlaminated sandstones and mudstones, cropping out north of the north-east-trending fault zone at Bodgaeaf and west of the Cefnamwlch–Rhiw Fault (the area west and north-west of Sarn Meyllteyrn: area 2 on Figure 3). The Bryncroes Formation is either mostly or entirely Fennian in age, and therefore is partly at least the lateral equivalent of the Wig Bâch Formation which represents a succession from the Moridunian to Fennian (Gibbons and McCarroll, 1993). The Bryncroes Formation passes southwards into the Wig Bâch Formation to the south of the Bodgaeaf Fault. The sedimentary rocks of the Bryncroes Formation were previously placed by Beckly (1988) within a diachronous 'Sarn Formation' which in addition included part of what later became defined as the Wig Bâch Formation (Gibbons and McCarroll, 1993). However, given the lithological and age differences between the Arenig sequences around Bryncroes and Aberdaron Bay, and the potential confusion engendered by the use of 'Sarn Formation' and the Precambrian Sarn Complex, the use of 'Sarn Formation' has been discontinued (Gibbons and McCarroll, 1993)

The conglomeratic base of the Bryncroes Formation rests unconformably on the Sarn Complex at Mountain Cottage Quarry [2300 3470] (Matley and Smith, 1936) and grades up rapidly into sandstones with beds up to 0.20 m thick. Above this, the dominant lithologies comprise sandstones in laminae and beds 0.1 to 5 cm thick, interbedded with mudstones up to 1 cm thick. Bioturbation is locally intense but the two lithologies rarely become homogenised, unlike the upper part of the Wig Bâch Formation (e.g. in the Trwyn Cam Member of Gibbons and McCarroll, 1993). The top of the formation is marked by the basal ooidal ironstone of the succeeding Trygarn Formation.

Beckly (1985) recorded azygograptids and lingulids from three localities in the Bryncroes Formation. At only one of these [2317 3150] was the material specifically identifiable as *A. lapworthi* (Beckly and Maletz, 1991). This locality (south-west of Ty Fair) is within 50 m of the top of the formation. At the others, including one much lower in the formation [2285 3114], *Azygograptus* sp. and

lingulids were recorded. The upper part of the formation can accordingly be dated as Fennian, but the lower part remains undated.

St Tudwal's Formation

The St Tudwal's Formation (60 to 130 m thick), equivalent to the 'St Tudwal's sandstone' of Nicholas (1915), crops out on the St Tudwal's Peninsula and the St Tudwal's Islands, and oversteps the underlying Cambrian succession. It is divided into four members: the Pared-mawr, Trwyn yr Wylfa, Penrhyn Du and Machroes members (Figure 12). The base of the formation is exposed at Trwyn Llech-y-doll [300 234], south-east of Muriau [3018 2385], and on Pared-mawr [305 247], and the lower parts of the formation (Pared-mawr and Trwyn-yr-Wylfa members) are well exposed on the cliffs of the southern part of St Tudwal's Peninsula at Trwyn Llech-y-doll [300 234], Pared-mawr [307 248] and Trwyn yr Wylfa [321 244]. The upper parts of the formation (the Penrhyn Du and Machroes members) are better exposed in the north-east of the peninsula in Porth Bach [324 265] and near Machroes [319 265].

The formation is characterised by intensely bioturbated muddy sandstones (most of the Pared-mawr and the Penrhyn Du members), alternating with well-bedded tidally-influenced sandstone packets (base of the Pared-mawr, Trwyn-yr-Wylfa and the Machroes members) and is interpreted as having been deposited in shallow marine conditions on an intra-basinal high. The basal part of the Pared-mawr Member at Trwyn Llech-y-doll [300 234], east of Muriau [3018 2385], at the east end of Porth Ceiriad [3173 2489], and the east end of Hell's Mouth [2909 2541] contains straight-crested megaripples of probable tidal origin, indicating currents toward N055–080°. The Trwyn-yr-Wylfa Member similarly yields east-north-east directed megaripple palaeocurrent indicators at Muriau [3017 2378], at Trwyn Llech-y-doll [300 234], and at Pant Gwyn [3077 2650]. This is consistent with a general decrease in grain size, a decrease in tidal influence, and a thickening of the formation in the same

Figure 12 Graphic logs of sections through the St Tudwal's Formation of the St Tudwal's Peninsula and islands.

1 North-east corner of Porth Neigwl [291 255]
2 Trwyn Llech-y-doll [301 235]
3 South-east of Muriau [242 238]
4 Pared-mawr [306 278] (type section for Pared-mawr Member)
5 Lower part of section: east end of Porth Ceiriad beach [317 248] upper part of section: Trwyn-yr-Wylfa [321 244] (type section of Trwyn-yr-Wylfa Member)
6 Lower part of section: east side of Penrhyn Du [324 266] (type section of Penrhyn Du Member), upper part of section: Machroes [319 265] (type section of Machroes Member)
7 St Tudwal's Island West [335 255]
8 St Tudwal's Island East [340 260]

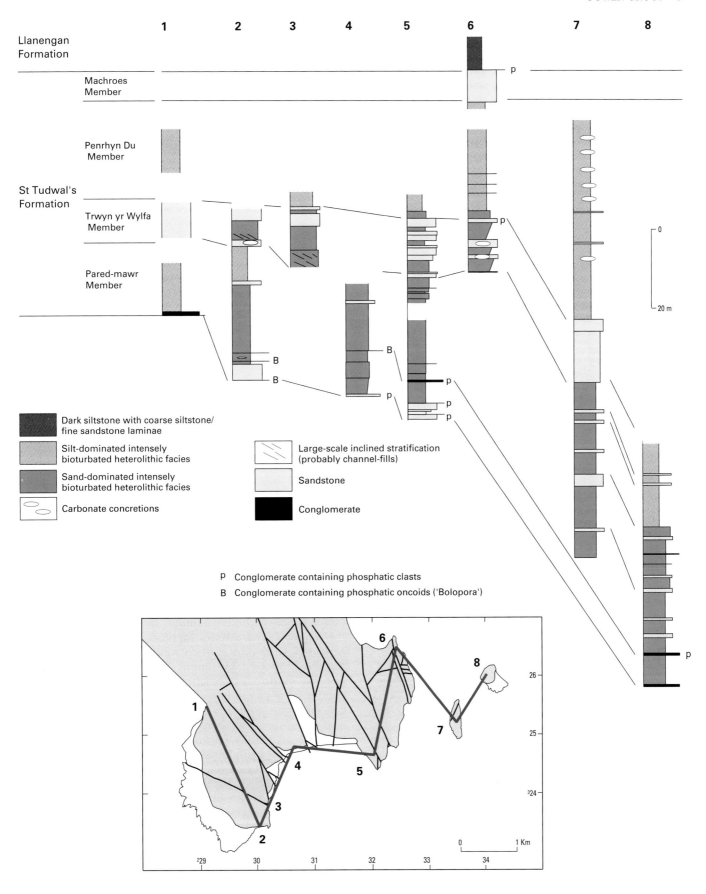

Llanengan
Formation

Machroes
Member

St Tudwal's
Formation

Penrhyn Du
Member

Trwyn yr Wylfa
Member

Pared-mawr
Member

Dark siltstone with coarse siltstone/
fine sandstone laminae

Silt-dominated intensely
bioturbated heterolithic facies

Sand-dominated intensely
bioturbated heterolithic facies

Carbonate concretions

Large-scale inclined stratification
(probably channel-fills)

Sandstone

Conglomerate

p   Conglomerate containing phosphatic clasts

B   Conglomerate containing phosphatic oncoids ('Bolopora')

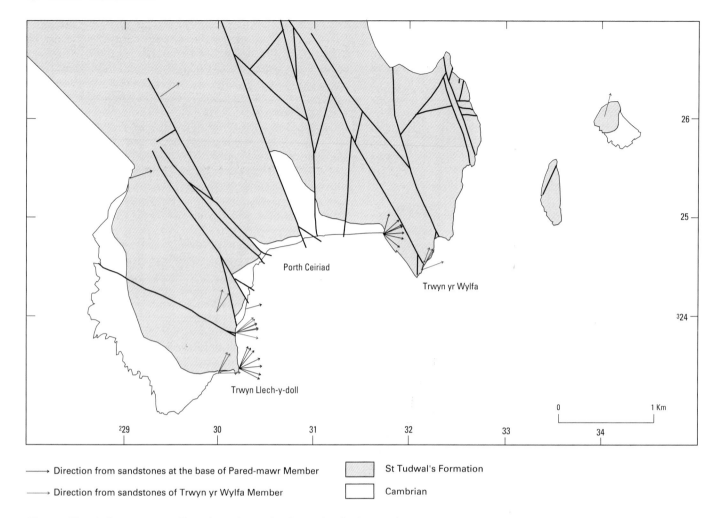

Figure 13 Palaeocurrent directions from the St Tudwal's Formation. Directions were derived from cross-bedding, bedding plane exposures of megaripples and reactivation surfaces. Flow directions were consistently to the north-east, interpreted as offshore flow down a palaeoslope controlled by north-west-trending extensional faults.

east-north-easterly direction away from the intra-basinal high (Figures 12, 13). This direction is perpendicular to the prominent set of reverse faults cutting the St Tudwal's Peninsula, which strike N135 to 175°. Nicholas (1915) noted that a member of this fault set cutting the Nant-y-big Formation in the cliffs of Porth Ceiriad [3089 2481] shows a pre-Arenig normal displacement, which was subsequently reversed. Extensional tectonics in the Arenig is likely to have produced an east-north-east- dipping palaeoslope during normal movements on this fault set.

The St Tudwal's Formation is interpreted as recording the fluctuation of minor transgressive and regressive events following the main Arenig marine transgression from the east-north-east. Initial tidal conditions deposited the basal sandstones of the Pared-mawr Member, and continued transgression led to sediment starvation and the development of oncoidal horizons. Later sedimentation of an upward- coarsening sequence is interpreted to have taken place during marine regression, and culminated in the re-

establishment of tidal conditions during the deposition of the sandy Trwyn-yr-Wylfa Member. This cycle was then repeated to produce firstly the muddier Penrhyn Du Member followed by renewed progradation of coarser grained sandstones (Machroes Member) although tidal conditions were not re-established this time. A third transgressive pulse produced a phosphatic lag marking the top of the Machroes Member.

The St Tudwal's Formation shows a similar development of facies to the Allt Lŵyd Formation (Allen and Jackson, 1985) of the Harlech Dome area, particularly to localities in the Cadair Idris district (Pratt et al., 1995). However, given the substantial variation in the development of the Allt Lŵyd Formation around the Harlech Dome and the inclusion within it of facies excluded from the St Tudwal's Formation, the maintenance of a distinct lithostratigraphical nomenclature for the St Tudwal's area is preferred. Furthermore, although biostratigraphical data for the St Tudwal's Formation are scarce, a Fennian age has been ascribed to the formation (Beckly, 1987), which would suggest it to be younger than the equivalent facies within the Allt Lŵyd Formation,' dated as Moridunian. The Pared-mawr Member has a variably developed coarse basal unit (see below) which is of a similar facies to the Garth Grit Member of the Allt Lŵyd Formation. However, since these tidally influenced facies recur at higher horizons in the St Tudwal's Formation, and because there is no evidence of lateral continuity with the Garth Grit Member in its type area, this term has not been employed in the Pwllheli district.

Pared-mawr Member

The Pared-mawr Member is 15 to 37 m thick, and forms the basal part of the St Tudwal's Formation. It comprises sandstones that are variously coarse-grained, locally conglomeratic, silt-dominated and bioturbated. The coarse sandstones above the base have prominent mud-draped reactivation surfaces (Plate 8), and at Trwyn Llech-y-doll they are interpreted as filling a tidal channel incised into the underlying Ceiriad Formation (Figure 14). The type section is the prominent cliff of Pared-mawr (Figure 12 column 4) where the basal unconformity on the Ceiriad Formation is exposed towards the western end of the section [3055 2472]. Here, the conglomeratic sandstones at the base of the formation are 0.5 m thick, and are overlain by approximately 8 m of bioturbated muddy sandstones, 2 m of finer grained muddy sandstones, and a thin conglomeratic horizon with the phosphatic oncoid Bolopora (Hofmann, 1975; Niedermeyer and Langbein, 1989). This distinctive conglomeratic lag horizon is overlain in most places by a thin horizon (up to 0.5 m thick) of fine-grained siltstones which locally yield inarticulate brachiopods and dendroid graptoloids. This horizon (obscured at the type section) passes rapidly up into bioturbated sandstones which in the type section are 15 m thick and, in the lower part, contain abundant carbonate concretions. These sandstones have a Cruziana ichnofacies trace fossil assemblage (Goldring, 1985) and contain several conglomeratic beds up to 0.3 m thick [3175 2484] dominated by rounded to sub-rounded quartzitic clasts (up to 7 mm diameter) that include quartz-mylonites probably derived from the Llŷn Shear Zone. Other clasts include granite (some with graphic intergrowth texture), perthite, basalt, siltstone intraclasts, and phosphatic brachiopod fragments.

The trilobite *Neseuretus* sp. occurs in the lower part of the Pared-mawr Member (Beckly, 1987). The siltstones immediately above the basal sandstones have yielded inarticulate brachiopods and dendroid graptoloids at the east end of Porth Ceiriad beach [3175 2484]. Dendroids were also reported by Nicholas (1915) from the Pared-mawr Member at Pistyll Cim [3235 2479], possibly from a similar horizon. None of these forms is diagnostic of age.

Trwyn-yr-Wylfa Member

The lithologically distinctive Trwyn yr Wylfa Member (10 to 15 m thick) is characterised by thickly bedded, pale weathering sandstones (0.1 to 0.6 m thick) which grade up from the underlying Pared-mawr Member; the type section is on the headland of Trwyn-yr-Wylfa [3206 2450] (Figure 12). This member defined one of the basic mapping units of Nicholas (1915), although it was not differentiated on the published map.

The lower part of the Trwyn-yr-Wylfa Member consists of storm-generated bioturbated sandstones, locally with large lateral accretion surfaces [e.g. at 3018 2375]. The upper part of the member consists of thicker, coarser grained, cross-stratified sandstones similar to those in the Pared-mawr Member at the base of the formation. Sedimentary structures include straight-crested dunes (in the thickest beds), and thickening- and coarsening-up parasequences [e.g. at Porth Bach 3245 2645], Figure 12, column 6), each approximately 3 to 4 m thick and commonly capped by phosphatic granule lags. The highest of these lags, marking

Plate 8 Coarse-grained, cross-bedded quartzose sandstones at the base of the Pared-mawr Member, St Tudwal's Formation, Trwyn Llech-y-doll [3009 2344] (GS678).

The upper sandstone bed shows low-angle mud-draped reactivation surfaces. These sandstones are interpreted as the fill of a tidal channel incised into the underlying Cambrian Ceiriad Formation (see Figure 14). Clipboard is 30 cm high.

West   East

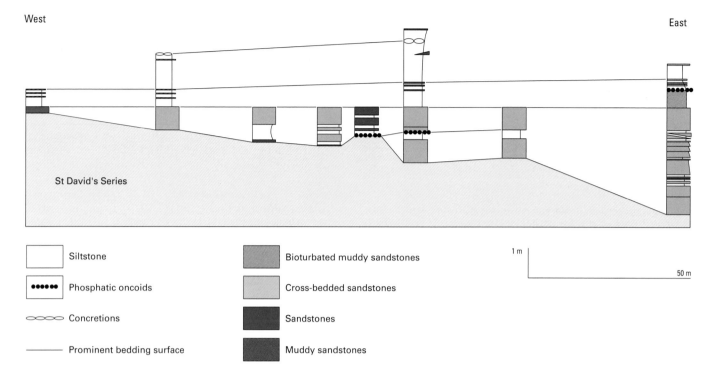

St David's Series

Siltstone

••••• Phosphatic oncoids

∞∞∞ Concretions

——— Prominent bedding surface

Bioturbated muddy sandstones

Cross-bedded sandstones

Sandstones

Muddy sandstones

1 m

50 m

Figure 14 Graphic logs of the base of the Pared-mawr Member at Trwyn Llech-y-doll.
The lowest part of the Pared-mawr Member here comprises sandstones with east- to
north-east-dipping cross-bedding and reactivation surfaces, lying on the irregularly eroded
surface of the underlying St David's Series. The sandstones are interpreted as having been
deposited by tidal currents and the irregular unconformity surface may represent a tidal channel.

the base of the Penrhyn Du Member, is particularly distinctive. The sedimentology of this member is well illustrated
by the exposures in Porth Bach where the lowest of four
parasequences grades up from the underlying Pared-mawr
Member and is overlain by a granule lag. Above this, a
second parasequence consists of 1 m of bioturbated sandstones (with beds 5 to 10 cm thick) that passes up into 2 m
of cross-bedded sandstones, locally with *Skolithos*; beds
increase in thickness upwards to 60 cm into a capping of
sandstone that contains large carbonate concretions. The
third parasequence (3.3 m) is similar to the first, but the
fourth (5 m) is dominated by much finer grained b
bioturbated sandstones, although it is capped by similar coarse-
grained cross-bedded sandstones with abundant phosphatised clasts.

The uppermost pale-weathering sandstones are well
exposed at several coastal localities (e.g. Trwyn Llech-y-
doll [300 234], east of Muriau [3018 2375], Pared-mawr
[305 247], Trwyn-yr-Wylfa [3206 2450], Porth Bach [3245
2645]), and contrast with the darker, pale green, bioturbated sandstones of the Pared-mawr and Penrhyn Du
members. The sandstones are also exposed at several
inland quarries worked for building stone (e.g. Pant
Gwyn [3077 2648], Sarn Bach [3038 2648], Tan-yr-allt
Farm [2940 2665] and Nant Farm [2945 2571]).

The coarse-grained sandstones are lithic subarkoses,
and are more mature than the coarse sandstones and
conglomerates of the Pared-mawr Member. The largest

grains are usually granitic, some with micrographic
textures. Polycrystalline quartz grains are rare; some have
the mylonitic textures typical of the coarser facies of the
Pared-mawr Member. Detrital tourmaline and zircon
occur locally. Feldspar clasts are not abundant, but
include both alkali feldspars and plagioclase.

Nicholas recorded graptolites from the Trwyn-yr-Wylfa
Member from several localities: Pant-gwyn quarry, γ1
[3078 2648]; the old quarry, Sarn Bach, γ2 [3038 2648];
Trwyn Llech-y-doll, γ3 [3008 2345]; quarry at Tan-yr-allt
Farm, λ1 [2940 2665]; Penrhyn Du, δ3 [3248 2648]. The
first two localities yielded '*Didymograptus* cf. *deflexus* Elles
and Wood' and '*Didymograptus extensus* Hall', the others
yielded '*D.* cf. *deflexus*' alone, although this material
cannot now be traced. Nicholas likened the '*Didymograptus* cf. *deflexus*' to material collected by Fearnsides (1905)
from the 'Llyfnant Flags' (now the Llyfnant Member of
the Allt Lwŷd Formation; Traynor, 1990) of the Arenig
area. The Llyfnant Member fauna has been revised
recently (Zalasiewicz, 1984; Beckly, 1987) and demonstrated to be of *D. extensus* Biozone age, Moridunian
Stage, but such graptolites are very long-ranging.

Penrhyn Du Member

The Penrhyn Du Member (approximately 35 to 40 m
thick) is lithologically similar to the Pared-mawr Member
except that the bioturbated sandstones are finer grained,

more muddy, and are commonly more strongly cleaved. Large carbonate concretions are common. The member is only well exposed on St Tudwal's Island West [33 25] and on Penrhyn Du [324 265] where the type section is exposed from Porth Bach [3244 2649] to the old Lifeboat Station [3240 2667]. The top of the formation is defined at Machroes [3185 2652] (Figure 12) where the contact with the overlying Machroes Member is exposed on the headland, east of the boatyard.

The base of the member, exposed in the low cliffs on the north side of Porth Bach, shows a basal 2 m of cross-bedded, bioturbated, muddy sandstones, with granule-grade clasts probably representing reworking of the underlying sandstones belonging to the Trwyn yr Wylfa Member. Above the basal 2 m, the member comprises some 31 m of fine-grained bioturbated muddy sandstone, with rare sandstone beds up to 30 cm thick. The lower part of the Penrhyn Du Member has yielded fragments of extensiform didymograptids from Penrhyn Du (Nicholas, 1915; δ2) [3245 2650].

Machroes Member

The Machroes Member ('Passage Beds' of Nicholas, 1915) passes up gradationally from the Penrhyn Du Member. The contact is exposed poorly, only in the type section at Machroes [3182 2652] where it shows less than 8 m of well-bedded storm-generated sandstones, up to 10 cm thick, interbedded with mudstones up to 5 cms thick, and capped by a 2 cm-thick phosphatic conglomerate. The member yields abundant specimens of *Azygograptus lapworthi* in the mudstone interbeds at Machroes [3195 2650] (Nicholas, 1915; Beckly, 1985, 1987). *Azygograptus lapworthi* has been demonstrated by Beckly (1985) and Beckly and Maletz (1991) to be a good indicator of the late Arenig, particularly the Fennian Stage. The upper part of the St Tudwal's Formation is therefore likely to be of Fennian age. The whole formation was placed in the Fennian by Beckly (1987), but the lower part of the formation may be older.

Llanengan Formation

The Llanengan Formation, 80 m thick, consists of dark grey mudstones with thin, pale grey siltstone or very fine-grained sandstone laminae, typically less than 1 mm in thickness. The type section lies on the south side of Borth Fawr where its base is well exposed [3198 2650] and shows the laminated mudstones that are typical of the formation lying abruptly on phosphatic conglomerate at the top of the Machroes Member. The upper part of the formation is relatively well exposed below Cornish Row [322 264], and the top is exposed in a faulted section beside the old tramway [3224 2646], where it is overlain by the Hen-dy-capel Ironstone. The uppermost 4 to 5 m of this formation show more bioturbation and slightly thicker sandstone beds (up to 10 mm) immediately below the ironstone. The generally undisturbed nature of the delicate, thin, coarse-grained laminae that characterise this formation contrasts with the more diffuse, bioturbated, and more thickly bedded nature of the Wig Bâch Formation.

The Llanengan Formation is interpreted as having been deposited during a third transgressive phase recorded by the Arenig rocks of the St Tudwal's Peninsula. The bioturbated sandstones at the top of the formation represent a third minor regressive phase, which was followed by a later transgressive interval which produced the Hen-dy-capel Ironstone of the Trygarn Formation.

The Llanengan Formation yields *Azygograptus lapworthi* at many localities. It was recorded by Nicholas (1915) from Llanengan, Nant and Borth Fawr, from horizons through the whole thickness of the formation, and in a small trial on the hillside south of the Hen-dy-capel quarry [2993 2706] '*Azygograptus lapworthi*' was found just below the base of the Hen-dy-capel Ironstone. Later, Elles (1922) erected *Azygograptus eivionicus* based partly on Nicholas's material from Nant, and indicated that this species was younger than *A. lapworthi*. In the current usage (Beckly, 1987; Beckly and Maletz 1991) *A. lapworthi* is a form indicative of the late Arenig (Fennian), whereas *A. eivionicus* occurs elsewhere in western Llŷn in the Moridunian to early Whitlandian. That part of the type material of *A. eivionicus* from the Llanengan Formation of Nant is poorly preserved and may belong to *A. lapworthi* Nicholson. The occurrence of *A. lapworthi* in the Llanengan Formation is indicative of its Fennian age. Nicholas (1915) also recorded '*Phyllograptus* sp.?' from near the base of the formation at locality β4 near Nant [294 254], '*Tetragraptus amii* (?) Elles and Wood' 20 m above the base of the formation at locality κ5, Llanengan [2948 2685] and '*Tetragraptus serra* Brongniart' some 20 m above the base of the formation in the Nant area [2955 2545].

Trygarn Formation

The Trygarn Formation, 90 m thick, comprises a distinctive succession of ironstones, ferruginous siltstones and sandstones, and crops out to the west of the Cefnamwlch–Rhiw Fault. It is well exposed around the farm of Trygarn [241 315], although here the sedimentary rocks are contact-altered adjacent to dolerite sills. The formation includes the beds referred to the Carw Formation of Beckly (1988) in its type area. In this study, the dominantly volcaniclastic nature of the type section of the Carw Formation has not been confirmed; many of Beckly's volcaniclastic sediments are interpreted here as hornfelsed siliciclastic rocks. Those volcaniclastic beds which have been recognised in the study did not prove to form a mappable unit. The Carw Formation has therefore been suppressed in favour of the broader scope of the Trygarn Formation. The type section for the formation is taken in Nant y Carw, where the base, seen in the bank of a small stream north-east of Ty Ruttan [2337 3234], is defined by an ooidal ironstone, which rests on the Bryncroes Formation, and lies immediately below the Sarn Hill basaltic sill (Trythall et al., 1987; Trythall, 1989a, b; Young, 1991a, b). The same ironstone, beneath the same sill, was seen in a borehole on Mynydd Rhiw in the south-west of the Pwllheli district, where it is 4 m thick (Brown and Evans, 1989). This ooidal ironstone is interpreted as being the same age as the Hen-dy-capel Ironstone which was deposited on the opposite (south-east) side of the Wig Bâch basin.

Above the sill in the type section are 3.2 m of ferruginous siltstones, bearing inarticulate brachiopods (seen in Sarn Hill Quarry [2343 3246]) and 2 m of ferruginous siltstones and conglomeratic sandstones containing granule-grade mylonitic detritus and ferruginous ooids (exposed in Sarn Hill quarry and in the hillside below [2341 3240]). In between the type section and Mynydd Rhiw, this part of the Trygarn Formation is exposed in the area around Hen Felin [237 279] as sandstones, locally volcaniclastic, with thin conglomeratic beds rich in phosphatic and ferruginous material. The overlying 20 to 30 m of the formation, seen in the type section ('Carw Formation' of Beckly, 1988), includes fine-grained volcaniclastic beds [2353 3233], commonly with soft sediment deformatid structures.

The sediments of the upper part of the Trygarn Formation are much less varied, comprising finely bedded (0.5 to 2 cm bed thickness) siltstones and sandstones, and are poorly exposed. The grain component of the sandstones is similar to the much coarser sandstones lower in the formation, and is commonly rich in Monian basement clasts. A major component of most sandstone beds, and in places the only component, are derived ferruginous (chlorite/goethite) ooids (Young, 1991a). Basalt fragments and detrital white mica also occur, and the rocks contain much chlorite, and locally have a siderite cement. Phosphatic concretions are locally abundant, particularly near the top of the formation, which grades up from thin-bedded ferruginous sandstones and siltstones into micaceous siltstones of the overlying undivided upper part of the Nant Ffrancon Subgroup.

The formation shows little change northwards from the type section, at least as far as Pen-yr-Orsedd, and again stays lithologically similar southwards to between Mynachdy and Ty Fair. Farther south however, on Mynydd Rhiw, the formation contains an increasing amount of volcaniclastic material, which, combined with extensive contact-alteration by abundant basic sills, has produced fine grained cherts. These cherts were used by Neolithic man as a source of material for tools, and have been quarried on Mynydd Rhiw [2341 2994]. The **Mynydd Rhiw Rhyolitic Tuff Member** (Fitch, 1967) occurs here, within the lower part of the formation on Mynydd Rhiw, but its outcrop can only be determined by displaced blocks. It is a fine-grained, purple-weathering, welded rhyolitic tuff with common flattened pumice (up to 10 mm across) discernable on weathered, bedding parallel surfaces. Its outcrop can be traced by loose blocks for 1 km across the northern hillside of Mynydd Rhiw [2353 2990] to near Ty'n-y-mynydd [2325 2900].

The Trygarn Formation contains a fauna of small inarticulate brachiopods and graptolites at most localities. Pendent didymograptid graptolites indicative of a Llanvirn age have been found at several localities in Nant-y-Carw (the lowest found approximately 30 to 40 m above the base of the formation [2359 3230]), near Mynachdy [2355 3180], north of Sarn [2356 3328], a locality approximately 5 m above the base of the formation, also yielding an indeterminate trinucleid trilobite), and near Rhiw [2277 2765], as well as occurring as clasts in float derived from the formation on the north side of Mynydd Rhiw. No identifiable graptolites have been recovered from the ooidal ironstone at the base of the formation, nor from the coarse clastic material immediately above the ironstone.

Nant Francon Subgroup undivided

The upper part of the Nant Ffrancon Subgroup comprises over 600 m of poorly exposed, lithologically uniform dark grey mudstones and siltstones which have not been assigned a formation. The terms 'Nevin Shales' (Matley and Heard, 1930, for the Garn Boduan area), 'Maesgwm Slates' (Shackleton, 1959, for the Cwm Pennant area; after Williams, 1927) and 'Tal-y-fan argillites' (Fitch, 1967, for the Llanbedrog area) have been previously utilised, and Matley (1938) described the unit as 'a monotonous series of obscurely folded and cleaved shales and mudstones'.

In the west of the district (west of the Cefnamwlch–Rhiw Fault) the Trygarn Formation grades up into mudstones via micaceous, locally fossiliferous siltstones [e.g. 2382 3332], with scattered laminae of reworked ferruginous ooids. Farther east, away from the sedimentary basin margin, the Trygarn Formation is absent, an ooidal ironstone is only locally present [3076 2998], and the undivided mudstones rest, in most places, directly upon the Wig Bâch Formation.

Higher stratigraphical levels of these undivided sediments are exposed south of the Sarn–Abersoch Thrust near Llangian [2975 2910], in the Soch Gorge [3095 2830], near Abersoch [3095 2805] and probably near Sarn [242 321]. At these localities ooidal ironstones and clastic debris flows, with large rounded sandstone clasts and phosphatic oncoids are interpreted as occurring approximately 600 to 700 m above the base of the formation. These may be the youngest exposed part of the Nant Ffrancon Subgroup in the Pwllheli district but are unfossiliferous, and so are of uncertain age. The lithologies, however, suggest a possible correlation with similar deposits of *gracilis* Biozone age at Tremadog.

In the Morfa Abererch area, the Nant Ffrancon Subgroup is overlain, probably unconformably, by conglomeratic sandstones at the base of the Cwm Eigiau Formation. The top of the group is faulted out by the Sarn–Abersoch Thrust in the south of the district, and faulted out against the base of the Upper Lodge Formation (e.g. Carreg Dinas [286 353]) or the Llanbedrog Volcanic Group (e.g. near Llanbedrog and Mynytho) farther north.

Hen-dy-capel Ironstone

In the St Tudwal's Peninsula, the bioturbated beds at the top of the Llanengan Formation are overlain abruptly by a 4 to 6 m thick, ooidal ironstone deposit, the Hen-dy-Capel Ironstone, which was commercially exploited in the last century (Trythall et al., 1987;

Trythall, 1989a, b; Young, 1991a, 1991b; Chapter 9). The ooidal ironstones are very variable in lithology, but most are reworked and mixed with clastic sediment. Locally, ferruginous debris flows have transported clasts of volcanic rocks of unknown provenance. The ooidal ironstones are interbedded in places with thin mudstone intercalations, up to 10 cm thick. They are correlated with the similar, but thinner, ironstones at this stratigraphical level in other areas of the district.

The Hen-dy-Capel Ironstone is overlain by approximately 5 m of laminated siltstone with abundant sponge spicules and graptolites, bioturbated siltstone and fine-grained sandstone with phosphatic concretions and oncoids, which suggest continuing low sediment accumulation rates after deposition of the ooidal ironstone.

Arenig to Llanvirn biostratigraphy

North of Sarn Meyllteyrn and west of the Cefnamwlch–Rhiw Fault [239 333], graptolite faunas of early Llanvirn age have been recorded from the lower part of the thick undivided mudstones (Matley 1932, 1938). In these assemblages the pendent didymograptids are subordinate to the abundant scandent biserials. Matley recorded only '*Cryptograptus* sp. (probably *tricornis*)' and '*Glyptograptus dentatus*', but pendent didymograptids (*Didymograptus* (*D.*) *spinulosus*) have been recovered from this locality during recent collecting, together with ?*Glyptograptus* sp., '*Amplexograptus*' *confertus* and *Cryptograptus* sp. (Figure 15). This fauna is very similar to that recorded by Gibbons and McCarroll (1993) from the lower part of the unit at Penarfynydd, just below the Mynydd Penarfynydd layered intrusion. The fauna occurs immediately above the Trygarn Formation which also yields poorly preserved pendent didymograptids of Llanvirn age.

Trythall et al. (1987) described an acritarch assemblage from a mudstone intercalation within the Hen-dy-capel Ironstone at Pen-y-gaer [2984 2829] (?*Arbusculidium filamentosum*, *Arbusculidium* aff. *gratiosum*, *Barakella fortunata*, *Dicrodiacrodium* spp., *Frankea* aff. *hamata*, *Frankea hamulata*, *Frankea longiusucula*, *Goniosphaeridium* spp, *Michrystridium acum brevispinosum?*, *Orthisphaeridium quadrinatum?*, *Pirea lagenaria?*, *Quadruilobus* sp, *Stellechinatum celestum*, *Stelliferidium* spp., *Striatotheca frequens*, *Striatotheca quieta*, *Veryachium trispinosum*, *Veryachium* sp. A, *Veryachium* sp. B). The assemblage was described as being very similar to assemblages from the Trefor, Betws Garmon and Llandegai ironstones in the lower part of the Nant Ffrancon Subgroup elsewhere in North Wales (their 'acritarch assemblage 2'). They ascribed an 'early Middle Llandeilo' age to the ironstone from the combination of the acritarch data and the *gracilis* Biozone age given by Nicholas (1916), but considerable reservation was placed on the reliability of the acritarch-derived age by those authors. Subsequently Molyneux (1988) reassessed the acritarch data presented by Trythall et al. (1987) together with unpublished data from near to the base of the Hen-dy-capel Ironstone in the small trial above Hen-dy-capel quarry [2994 2705]. Considerable doubt was

again expressed about the precise age of the acritarch assemblages, because of the long ranges of the taxa involved, but the pre-Caradoc *gracilis* Biozone age for Pen-y-gaer was supported, together with a similar, or slightly younger age for Hen-dy-capel. The Hen-dy-capel quarry sample also yielded the chitinozoans *Desmochitina minor* f. *typica* and *Belonechitina* sp.

Young (1991b) described pendent didymograptids (*Didymograptus* (*D.*) sp.) from mudstones immediately overlying the Hen-dy-capel Ironstone at Pen-y-gaer [2982 2827 and 2982 2823] and suggested that the previously supposed *gracilis* Biozone age for the ironstone (Nicholas, 1915; Trythall et al., 1987; Trythall, 1989a) is erroneous, and that it is actually of early Llanvirn age.

Other localities in the siltstones immediately above the Hen-dy-capel Ironstone near Llanengan also yielded graptolites to Nicholas (1915) compatible with the Llanvirn age proposed by Young (1991b, 1993) (∈2: debris from a trial adit, probably that at the rear of Gwel-y-Don [2972 2723], '*Glyptograptus* cf. *teretiusculus*', '*Climacograptus scharenbergi*'; ∈1: trial quarry, probably that near Ty Fry [2963 2716], '*Orthograptus calcaratus* var. *acutus*', '*Hallograptus bimucronatus*'). Most of the fauna occurs in grey siltstones containing pale weathering coarser laminae with graptolites and abundant sponge spicules, probably corresponding to the 'ashy mudstone' of Nicholas. The remaining material in the Sedgwick Museum includes scandent biserials with a straight septum from ∈2, and some *Orthograptus calcaratus*-like material from ∈1. Indeterminate scandent biserial graptolites have also been recovered in similar lithologies, both from the quarry face [3003 2715] and from the mine dump at Hen-dy-capel quarry.

The higher parts of the Nant Ffrancon Subgroup of the area south of the Sarn–Abersoch Thrust have yielded no fauna, apart possibly from a single specimen of '*Glyptograptus* sp.' recorded from the old mine dump at Pantgwyn Mine [about 308 267] by Nicholas (1915), derived from an uncertain horizon in the formation.

North of the Sarn–Abersoch Thrust, in the main outcrop of the mudstones of the upper part of the Nant Ffrancon Subgroup in the Pwllheli district, there are only sporadic records of fossils. Matley (1938) recorded isolated pendent didymograptids from the west side of Mynydd Tîr-y-cwmwd [322 311], from near Rhyd-galed smithy [284 316] and Nant-bach [263 346] and a diplograptid from Nant Bodlas [291 341]. He also recorded more abundant graptolite material from two localities near Carreg Dinas [285 352, 287 352] attributed to the *murchisoni* and *teretiusculus* Biozones respectively. The graptolite assemblages from this area have been more recently revised: Bate and Rushton (1991) recorded an assemblage of *Placoparia cambriensis*, '*Amplexograptus*' cf. *confertus*, *Didymograptus* (*D.*) cf. *spinulosus*, *Diplograptus* cf. *ellesi*, '*Glyptograptus*' sp.? and indeterminate ostracod? from a locality between Garn Bach and Carreg Dinas [2869 3502] close to that attributed by Matley to the *murchisoni* Biozone. They gave a revised age of rather lower in the Llanvirn, probably in the upper part of the *artus* Biozone. Rushton and Zalasiewicz (1991) revised the material collected by Matley, attributed to the *teretiusculus*

Figure 15 Graptolites from mudstones of the Nant Ffrancon Subgroup, north of Sarn Meyllteyrn [239 333].

i, ii   *Didymograptus* (*D.*) *spinulosus* Perner
iii   *Glyptograptus?* sp
iv   *Cryptograptus* sp
v, vi   '*Amplexograptus*' *confertus* (Lapworth)

Scale bar 1 mm

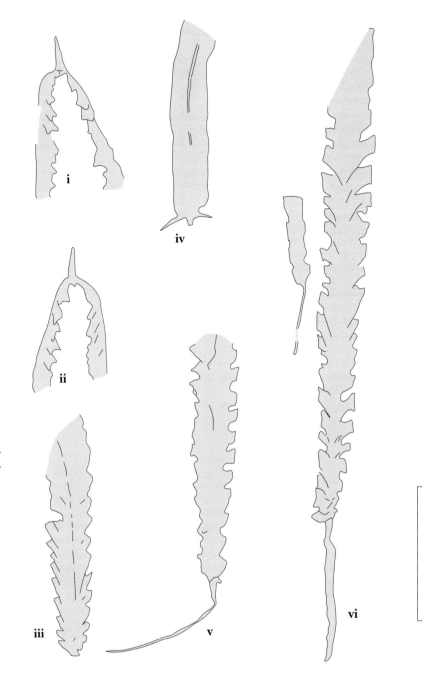

Biozone, from 'under Carreg Dinas, Madryn', and recorded an ostracod and diplograptid fragments all indeterminate, and *Pseudoclimacograptus scharenbergi*? This assemblage too is likely to be of Llanvirn age.

The cleaved mudstones below the Cwm Eigiau Formation in the Morfa Abererch area have yielded no biostratigraphical information. On the north limb of the Llŷn syncline a single locality close to the margin of the Wyddgrug intrusion has yielded an indeterminate pendent didymograptid (information from D Bate BGS, 1989).

The majority of the mudstones in the upper part of the Nant Ffrancon Subgroup are therefore likely to be of (probably early) Llanvirn age. The age of the youngest sedimentary rocks in the subgroup, exposed to the south and in the footwall of the Sarn–Abersoch Thrust, is unknown.

OGWEN GROUP: MIDDLE PART

Cwm Eigiau Formation

The oldest Upper Ordovician sedimentary rocks are represented by the Cwm Eigiau Formation (Howells et al., 1978) which, although up to 1300 m thick in central Snowdonia (within the Pitts Head/Llwyd Mawr caldera) is only some 120 m thick in the Pwllheli district (Figures 16, 17, 18). The relationship between the Pitts Head Tuff Formation and the Cwm Eigiau Formation in Snowdonia has been reviewed by Orton (1992), who has suggested the use of the terms lower and upper for those parts of the formation lying below and above the Pitts Head Tuff Formation. The lower Cwm Eigiau Formation in the Pwllheli district comprises about 40 m of sandstones, locally conglomeratic, which lie unconformably on Nant Ffrancon Subgroup mudstones and underlie the Pitts Head Tuff Formation. The upper Cwm Eigiau Formation comprises about 80 m of siltstones and subordinate sandstones of possible Soudleyan to Longvillian age, and lies between the Pitts Head Tuff Formation and the overlying Allt

Fawr Rhyolitic Tuff Formation. The Cwm Eigiau and Pitts Head Tuff formations are intruded by rhyolite sills of the Pen-y-chain Rhyolitic Complex, which obscure the original contacts with the Pitts Head Tuff Formation.

The base of the formation is marked by conglomeratic sandstones, with rhyolite cobbles (up to 70 mm across) in a coarse-grained sandstone matrix, exposed (Figure 19) west of Pen-ychain [4250 3630], and traceable as loose fragments east of Llwyngwyn Farm [4247 3688], and in exposures in the stream farther north [4358 3719]. Above the conglomerates are medium-grained brown sandstones, exposed west of Pen-y-chain [4251 3625] and just south of the railway [4247 3646]. The highest part of the lower Cwm Eigiau Formation (seen in the Broom Hill area in a small exposure north of Tan yr Allt [4126 3644])

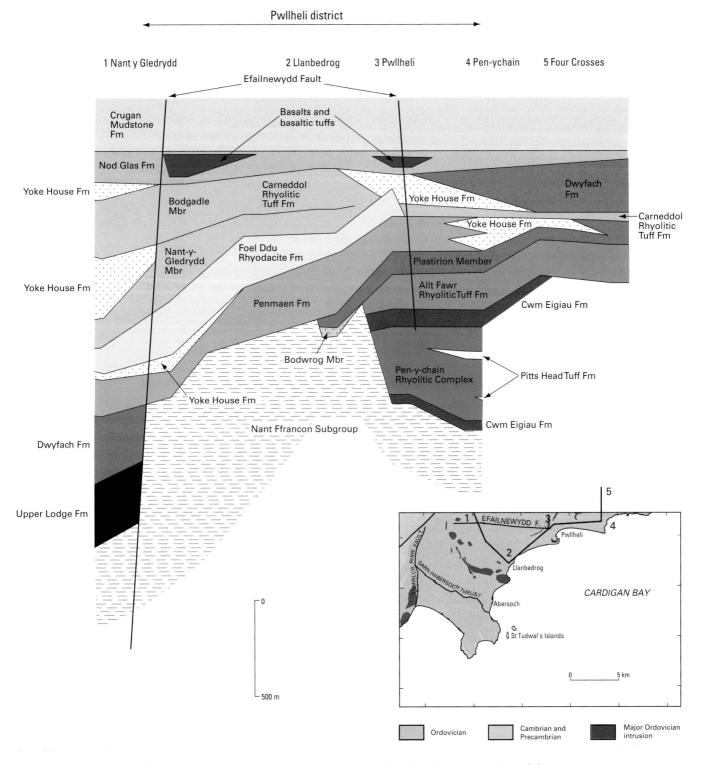

Figure 16 Schematic fence diagram showing lateral variation in the Caradoc succession of the Pwllheli district and immediately adjacent areas to the north. The fence runs westwards from the northern limb of the syncline east of Nant-y-Gledrydd, southwards along the outcrop of Caradoc strata around the syncline to Llanbedrog, and then north-eastwards to Pwllheli and Pen-ychain.

The Ogwen Group represents the background sedimentation to the intercalated volcanic rocks. It comprises the Cwm Eigiau, Dwyfach (Bodwrog and Plastirion Members) and Nod Glas formations. The volcanic units comprise the Pen-y-chain Rhyolitic Complex (Snowdon Volcanic Group), Allt Fawr and Upper Lodge formations (not assigned to a volcanic group), and the Penmaen, Foel Ddu Rhyodacite, Yoke House and Carneddol Rhyolite Tuff formations (Upper Volcanic Group). The Nod Glas Formation contains intercalated basalts and basaltic tuffs.

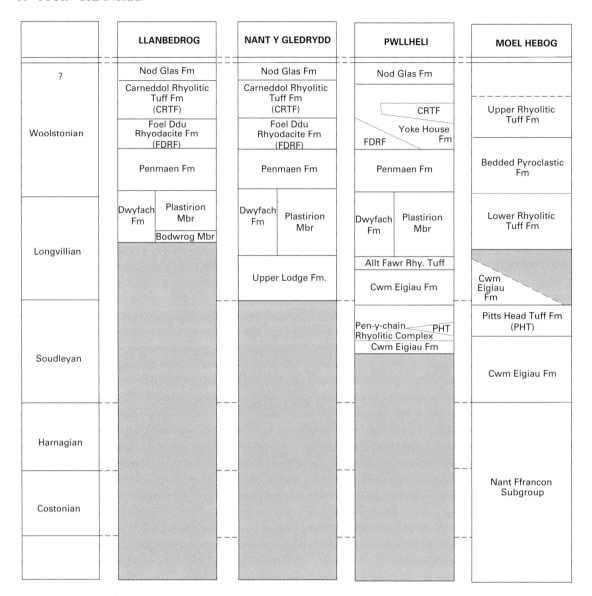

Figure 17 Time-correlation diagram for the Caradoc succession of the district, also showing correlation with the Moel Hebog area, 10 km to the east but situated to the east of the Cwm Pennant lineament. Progressive onlap of Caradoc strata to the west during mid-Caradoc times illustrates that subsidence and igneous activity encroached progressively on the margin of the Harlech Dome and on to the Anglesey high.

comprises dark grey mudstones and siltstones containing tuffaceous beds up to 2 cm thick. The top of the lower Cwm Eigiau Formation is intruded by a rhyolite sill which obscures the original contact with the Pitts Head Tuff Formation.

The upper Cwm Eigiau Formation comprises poorly exposed fossiliferous mudstones, siltstones, sandstones and tuffs, and is exposed only in the Pen-y-chain area. A basaltic lithic tuff, up to 15 m thick and exposed in the railway cutting [4304 3652] and north of Tal-y-bont [4272 3691], lies above the highest of the rhyolitic sills of the Pen-y-chain Rhyolitic Complex. The tuff is overlain by a tuffaceous sandstone, [4271 3694, 4279 3686], which fines up into dark grey siltstones with thin sandstone laminae. The silt-

stones have yielded brachiopods and trilobites from localities in the stream valley north of Tal-y-bont [4276 3702, 4281 3699, 4277 3710]. The top 10 m of the member are marked by an increase in the frequency and thickness of intercalated volcaniclastic sandstone beds. The sharp contact between the Cwm Eigiau Formation and the Allt Fawr Rhyolitic Tuff Formation is exposed in the bank above the stream north of Tal-y-bont [4279 3710]. The upper part of the member is also exposed at Llwyn-hudol [3880 3668] where poorly fossiliferous, fine-grained, brown sandstones and siltstones occur on the scarp below the Allt Fawr Rhyolitic Tuff Formation.

The only biostratigraphically important fossil obtained from the Cwm Eigiau Formation is *Broeggerolithus*

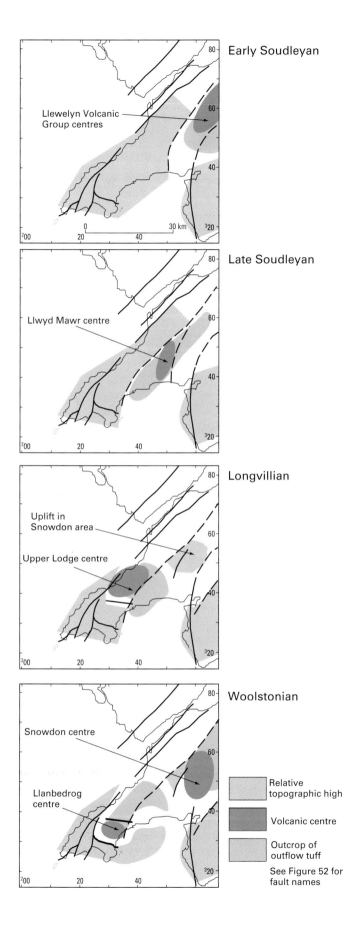

Early Soudleyan

Llewelyn Volcanic Group centres

Late Soudleyan

Llwyd Mawr centre

Longvillian

Uplift in Snowdon area

Upper Lodge centre

Woolstonian

Snowdon centre

Llanbedrog centre

Relative topographic high

Volcanic centre

Outcrop of outflow tuff

See Figure 52 for fault names

nicholsoni from a level less than 10 m below the top of the formation [4281 3701]. This trilobite indicates a horizon no older than the early Longvillian, in contrast to the claimed pre-Longvillian age (Harper, 1956; Roberts, 1967, 1979) for the fauna from Nant y Glyn [4580 3837] 3 km north-east, apparently from a similar, or slightly lower horizon, not far below the base of the Allt Fawr Rhyolitic Tuff Formation. Revision of the fauna from Nant-y-Glyn has identified *Brongniartella* cf. *minor, Broeggerolithus soudleyensis, Broeggerolithus* cf. *nicholsoni?, Remopleurides* sp., *Sericoidea* cf. *abdita complicata* and an indeterminate dalmanellid. This fauna indicates a Longvillian, probably early Longvillian, age. *Sericoidea* cf. *abdita complicata* also occurs in the siltstones of the upper Cwm Eigiau Formation [4281 3701]. The Upper Member yields a limited fauna (*Onniella?* sp., nuculoid bivalve indeterminate) at Llwyn-hudol [3880 3668] near Pwllheli, but this assemblage is not biostratigraphically significant.

In Snowdonia, the Cwm Eigiau Formation is dominated by shallow marine siltstones and sandstones which reflect a gradation from alluvial fan environments in the south-west of the Pitts Head graben to more offshore conditions in the north-east (Howells et al., 1991). In the east of the Pwllheli district, the much thinner succession (up to 120 m) lies close to the inferred source for the north-eastward prograding alluvial fans in Snowdonia, but the restricted exposure precludes detailed sedimentological analysis. The siltstone-dominated upper Cwm Eigiau Formation of the Pwllheli district contrasts strongly with the equivalent horizon above the Pitts Head Tuff Formation in southwest Snowdonia, where the Pitts Head Tuff Formation was apparently subaerially exposed and directly overlain by the Lower Rhyolitic Tuff Formation (Howells et al., 1991). The more siltstone-dominated offshore conditions occurring in the Pwllheli district may have been produced by subsidence associated with the generation of the new basin in north-western Llŷn in which the volcanic centre that produced the Upper Lodge Formation developed. This basin would have been beyond the influence of the Lower Rhyolitic Tuff Formation magma body, interpreted by Orton (1992) to be responsible for the lack of the upper Cwm Eigiau Formation in the central parts of the Pitts Head graben.

The Pitts Head Tuff Formation has been assigned to the Snowdon Volcanic Group (Howells et al., 1991), in a

Figure 18 Evolution of volcanic centres in north-west Wales during the Caradoc.

Early Soudleyan activity (Llewelyn Volcanic Group) was restricted to the 'Pitts Head Graben'. The Pitts Head Tuff Formation was subsequently erupted from the Llwyd Mawr centre immediately to the west of this graben. During the Longvillian, activity moved farther west, with the production of the Upper Lodge volcanic centre adjacent to the Menai Strait Fault System. Woolstonian activity centred both on the Llanbedrog area, where subsidence encroached on the northern margin of the Harlech Dome, and at the Snowdon Volcanic Group centre in the Snowdon graben.

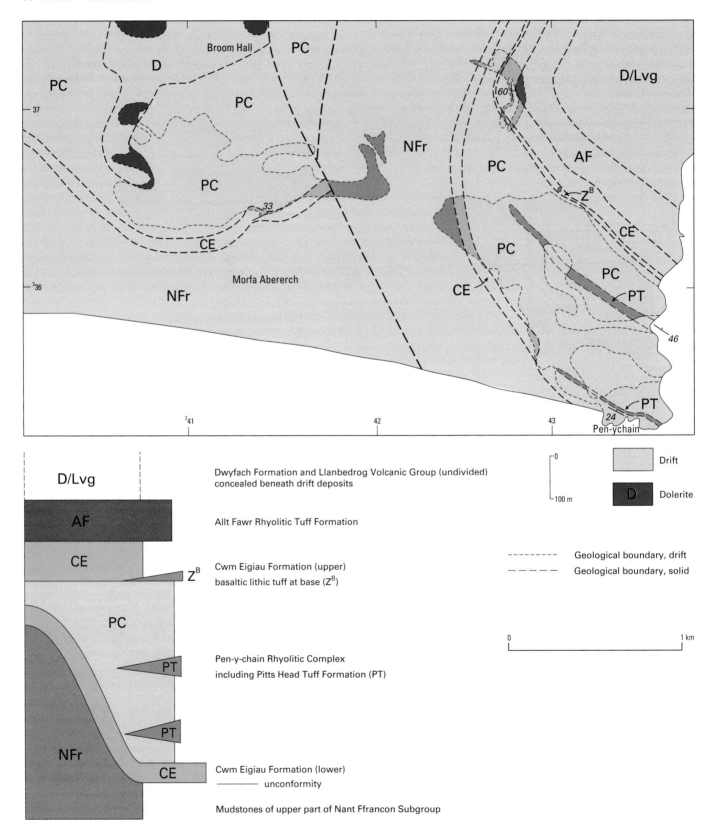

Figure 19 Geological map of the outcrop of the Pen-y-chain Rhyolitic Complex, with a generalised vertical section.

significant change from earlier usage in which the base of the Snowdon Volcanic Group had been placed at the base of the younger Lower Rhyolitic Tuff Formation (Howells et al., 1983; Reedman et al., 1987). Orton (1992) argued against such a change in stratigraphical nomenclature, on the grounds of the considerable length of time between the eruption of the two tuffs (up to a million years). The Pitts Head and Lower Rhyolitic tuffs were also erupted from geographically distinct centres (Llwyd Mawr and Snowdon respectively) some 15 km apart.

Pen-y-chain Rhyolitic Complex and Pitts Head Tuff Formation.

The Pen-y-chain Rhyolite Complex comprises sills, domes, an ashflow tuff (Pitts Head Tuff Formation), and possible lava flows: the distinction between rocks of an intrusive, extrusive or pyroclastic origin is commonly difficult to make, particularly in the poorly exposed Broom Hall area (Figure 19). Most exposures in the complex are pale weathered rhyolites, variously devitrified, silicified, porphyritic, flow-foliated, brecciated, and rich in siliceous nodules. The complex reaches a thickness of 835 m on the coast at Pen-y-chain [435 353], where it is mostly rhyolite (only 80 m of tuffs), but thins rapidly north-westwards along strike for 2 km where, just north of the A497, it is less than 100 m thick. A similar sequence, up to 400 m thick, is exposed in the Broom Hall area where the lowest rhyolites overlie siltstones with thin tuff horizons [4126 3644]. The uppermost rhyolites at the top of the complex are exposed in the railway cutting near the station [4304 3652] and north of Tal-y-bont [4272 3691] where they are overlain by the basic tuff at the base of the upper Cwm Eigiau Formation.

The rhyolite sills and rhyolitic tuffs of the complex have a distinctive geochemistry which is different from other acidic rocks in the Pwllheli district, but similar to that of the Pitts Head Tuff Formation in the Snowdon district (Howells et al., 1983; Campbell et al., 1987; Orton, 1992; Gibbons and Young, 1999) This tuff has been interpreted as having been erupted from a caldera that was subsequently filled by the Llwyd Mawr Tuff (Roberts, 1967; Kokelaar, 1988), which outcrops only 5 km east-north-east of Pen-ychain.

Most of the rhyolites are porphyritic, with phenocrysts, (rarely exceeding 3 mm) of quartz, perthitic alkali feldspar and oligoclase; the phenocrysts are commonly corroded and partially resorbed, and may be grouped into glomeroporphyritic clusters [4064 3639]. The alkali feldspar is commonly subhedral and partially envelopes euhedral oligoclase crystals. Quartz phenocrysts are fewer and smaller than the feldspars. The groundmass comprises a recrystallised, cryptocrystalline siliceous aggregate. Spherulitic textures are common and flow foliation is generally well developed.

The lowest rhyolite exposed on the coast west of Pen-ychain headland [4323 3536] illustrates the relationship between brecciated, siliceous nodular and flow-banded facies. The top 4 m of this rhyolite is flow-banded, with the banding folded into a series of asymmetric, south-easterly verging anticlines and complimentary synclines [4326 3533]. The axes of these folds plunge gently to moderately north-east, with axial surfaces dipping moderately north-west. The fold zone passes downwards into brecciated rhyolite [4329 3532]. Brecciated, massive rhyolite overlain by a strongly flow-banded zone (Plate 9) occurs also at other localities, for example in the highest rhyolite exposures on the coast [4363 3597]. The repetition of thin, strike-parallel, zones of similarly flow-folded rhyolite, parallel to topographical features, and the lobate nature of the outcrop pattern suggest that the rhyolites form a series of sills. A similar outcrop pattern is seen in the Broom Hall area where three topographical features are interpreted to relate to individual sills. The lowest of

Plate 9 Folded rhyolitic flow banding cut by rhyolitic breccias. Pen-y-chain Rhyolitic Complex, Pen-ychain [4329 3531]. Hammer is 30 cm in length (GS649).

these sills forms the prominent hill of Careg y Gath [4150 3655] and extends west-south-west to the A497 at Glan-y-Morfa [4080 3636]. The second rhyolite sill is exposed at Pen-y-Clogwyn [4107 3658], and the highest sill is exposed as flow-foliated, and locally highly porphyritic, rhyolite on the north side of the small gorge north of Ty'n-y-nant [4115 3677].

Two sequences of tuffs within the Pen-y-chain Rhyolitic Complex have been attributed to the Pitts Head Tuff Formation, and their distribution has been mapped in the Pen-ychain area. The lower of the two units are unwelded, bedded, lithic tuffs, and are exposed to the west of Pen-ychain [4345 3533], continuing south-eastwards along strike for 200 m, thinning from 14 m to 4 m. The tuffs show a coarse, block-rich base overlain by finer lithic tuffs with clasts of mostly pale rhyolite (including flow-banded varieties) locally mixed with black mudstones. The relationship between these tuffs and the underlying rhyolite is complex. At the base of the cliff, the pale, pink-weathering rhyolite exposed is thoroughly brecciated, with individual disoriented fragments in the breccia preserving flow banding. Just below the tuffs, the rhyolite contains of zones of breccia rich in black mudstone, suggesting interaction between hot rhyolite and unconsolidated wet sediment. The rhyolite is overlain by lithic tuffs, and individual tuff beds can be seen to thicken westwards away from the rhyolite, suggesting they were deposited upon an uneven surface of the rhyolite which had emerged through a mudstone carapace. The tuffs are overlain by porphyritic rhyolite with a flinty, fine-grained, brecciated base.

The higher of the two tuff units is exposed on the south side of the beach at Porth Fechan [4354 3579] where distinctively welded, fiamme-rich rhyolitic tuffs overlie brecciated, flow-banded pink rhyolite, and are overlain, on the north side of the beach, by rhyolites with flow banding, folding and siliceous nodules. The maximum thickness of these tuffs is approximately 60 m (of which only some 10 m are actually exposed) and they thin inland, to the west, to an estimated 40 m [4315 3605], beyond which no trace of this lithology is exposed. In the Broom Hall area, welded, pumiceous and shardic, rhyolitic ashflow tuffs were exposed only in a trench between Hendre and Ty'n-y-mynydd [4072 3682].

Upper Lodge Formation

The Upper Lodge Formation comprises a sequence of porphyritic basaltic trachyandesites and lithic tuffs (with porphyritic lava, glass, and siltstone fragments) that, in the Pwllheli district, occur only in small exposures at Ceidio Bach [290 374] on the northern limb of the Llŷn syncline. The formation is early Longvillian (possibly late Soudleyan) in age and is older than the Llanbedrog Volcanic Group, from which it is separated by the (Longvillian) Plastirion Member of the Dwyfach Formation. The unit is equivalent to the informal 'Upper Lodge Group' of Matley and Heard (1930) which was defined on exposures of intermediate to basic rocks near Boduan [323 388] in the adjacent Nefyn district where the formation is nearly 500 m thick. It is interpreted as broadly coeval with the Allt Fawr Rhyolitic Tuff Formation, emanating from an as yet undefined 'Upper Lodge' volcanic centre situated to the north of the Pwllheli district.

At Ceidio Bach [290 374] the lavas show plagioclase (andesine) phenocrysts up to 3.5 mm within a fine- to medium- grained groundmass of feldspar (0.02 to 0.05 mm), quartz, chlorite and ore. Some samples show a well-developed flow-foliated texture, and the groundmass is commonly recrystallised to a patchy mosaic of inter-locking quartz crystals. Other phenocrysts include altered clinopyroxene, ore (up to 0.5 mm across), and glomeroporphyritic feldspathic clots. Apatite is very common, with prismatic crystals up to 0.7 mm long. Plagioclase phenocrysts commonly display globular, hollow (resorption) textures and rounded crystal margins; some clinopyroxene phenocrysts show a faint rimming by alter-ation products (mostly ore), interpreted as having been produced by low pressure destabilisation during uprise from the magma chamber.

Allt Fawr Rhyolitic Tuff Formation

This formation is an alkali feldspar crystal-rich ash flow tuff, approximately 120 m thick in the Pwllheli area; it crops out on the southern limb of the Llŷn Syncline from Pwllheli to Llanystumdwy, and on the northern limb in the Llwyndyrys to Llanaelhaearn area. It is typically a pale weathering, variably welded and brecciated crystal tuff. Its base is only exposed north of Tal-y-Bont [4279 3708], where coarse-grained rhyolitic tuff overlies silt-stones and sandstones of the Cwm Eigiau Formation. The Allt Fawr Tuff Formation is well exposed in the Pwllheli district on a prominent ridge running north-east from Pont-y-Garreg-fechan [3633 3483] towards Four Crosses. It is interpreted to continue into the Nefyn district as thick ignimbrites exposed on Moel Bromiod [41 45] and Pen-y-gaer [42 45], east of Llanaelhaearn (Tremlett, 1964).

The main body of the Allt Fawr Rhyolitic Tuff Formation is crystal rich with abundant perthitic alkali feldspar, and lesser quartz and calcic oligoclase, crystals in a microcrystalline, variably welded matrix. Perthite crystals, up to 1.5 mm across, occur singly and in glomeroporphyritic aggregates and may partially or completely enclose plagioclase phenocrysts. Isolated quartz crystals lie scattered within the matrix, although quartz also occurs as aggregates with alkali feldspar. The matrix is a microcrystalline mosaic of quartz, sericitic mica, feldspar laths and chlorite, and is variously shardic, welded, devitrified, and pumiceous. The top few metres of this unit are noticeably poor in alkali feldspar phenocrysts.

In the area of Tan-y-graig [389 373] a more mafic unit, exposed at the base of the formation, is of broadly trachydacitic composition, and is interpreted as an initial eruptive phase. It is highly porphyritic, with a mixture of sodic andesine and prominent orthoclase phenocrysts (commonly perthitic and isolated or partially enclosing plagioclase phenocrysts, and with corroded possibly quench textures) which suggest that it is associated with the rhyolitic tuff above. Clasts of pale rhyolitic tuff suggest the unit is the product of a magma mixing event, with an initial phase of more mafic magma becoming overwhelmed by a main rhyolitic outburst.

Dwyfach Formation

The Dwyfach Formation forms the major part of the fill of a Longvillian and Woolstonian basin, lying approximately in the area now occupied by the Llŷn Syncline (Figure 16), and the outcrop spans the boundary between the Pwllheli and Nefyn districts. Only the lower 150 m of this formation crops out within the Pwllheli district, above which sedimentation was interrupted by the deposition of the Llanbedrog Volcanic Group. Farther north, in the Nefyn district, the Dwyfach Formation is much thicker (600 m) as background sedimentation of dark siltstones, with intercalations of tuffs and sandstones, continued away from the proximal influence of the Llanbedrog centre. Only the lower part of the Dwyfach Formation is exposed in the district and this can be divided into the Bodwrog Member and the Plastirion Member. However, the members have not been shown on Sheet 134 Pwllheli due to scale restriction. The stratotype for the Dwyfach Formation lies in the valley of the Dwyfach at Plas Talhenbont, north-west of Llanystumdwy. In this section the formation is seen lying on the top of the Allt Fawr Rhyolitic Tuff Formation [4618 3975] and is overlain by the Nod Glas Formation [468 397].

Bodwrog Member

The Bodwrog Member is equivalent to the 'Llanbedrog Grits' of Matley (1938) and only crops out with certainty within the Pwllheli district near Llanbedrog [321 314]. The type locality for the member is the hillside below Bodwrog farm in a quarry in the lower part of the member [3220 3137], and a small stream through the upper part [3205 3136]. The member is characterised by medium-bedded, medium- to coarse-grained sandstones (30 m thick) but its base is faulted out against the Nant Ffrancon Subgroup in the type area. In this Llanbedrog area the member crops out as a thin zone of sedimentary rock between the two sections of a trachydacite intrusion (Glynllifon Trachydacite, see Chapter 5).

The upper part of the Bodwrog Member grades upwards into the finer grained Plastirion Member, transitional sandstones being exposed in the stream below Bodwrog. From these sandstones and the immediately overlying mudstones Matley (1938) recorded a fauna including *Bicuspina* sp. This brachiopod is not a common element of the Dwyfach Formation assemblages, but also occurs in the sandstones in Penarwel Drive [3322 3226]. The sandstones in Penarwel Drive were interpreted to be above the Carneddol Rhyolitic Tuff Formation by Matley (1938); this interpretation was followed by Fitch (1967), who named them as the Penarwel Drive Beds. They have been referred to the Dwyfach Formation here. They have similar lithology and fauna to the Bodwrog Member, but their position within the formation is uncertain.

The member is interpreted as having been deposited during the earliest phase of subsidence of the region south of the Efailnewydd Fault. The area north of the fault had subsided in Soudleyan or earliest Longvillian times, during the eruption of the Upper Lodge Formation. The subsidence spread southwards during Longvillian times, allowing marine transgression over the area south of the fault, which subsequently, in the Woolstonian, became the site of the Llanbedrog volcanic centre (Figure 18).

Plastirion Member

The Plastirion Member comprises about 100 m of brown-weathering, grey calcareous mudstones and grey siltstones, commonly highly fossiliferous and locally with intercalated beds of brown fine- to medium-grained sandstone. In the mudstones, bedding is defined by concentrations of fossil debris. Coarser grained parts of the succession commonly show crudely graded beds of siltstone to medium-grained sandstone. Typically, the beds are up to 15 cm thick, and many show faint low-angle to parallel stratification which suggests the influence of periodic storm reworking. The type area for the member is north-east of Pwllheli [381 356], with one of the best sections being in a road section at Llanbedrog [32 31].

The base of the Plastirion Member, temporarily exposed in excavations in Pwllheli [3708 3515], comprises 8 m of siltstones and sandstones overlying the Allt Fawr Rhyolitic Tuff Formation; the contact is marked by a thin bed of cherty mudstone with dispersed large feldspar crystals. Near Pwllheli the member passes up rapidly into andesitic tuffs and breccias of the Penmaen Formation at the base of the Llanbedrog Volcanic Group. At Llanbedrog the uppermost parts of the member contain thin beds of fine-grained cherty tuffite [3220 3160] and are again overlain by andesitic tuffs.

The upper parts of the Plastirion Member are locally (e.g. near Llanbedrog) finer grained than the lower parts, although elsewhere (e.g. Pwllheli) there is a marked coarsening at the very top of the formation, representing renewed clastic input probably associated with the onset of the Penmaen Formation volcanicity. The Bodwrog and Plastirion members are together interpreted as a transgression of the Dwyfach Formation towards the south-west, over the margins of the basin in which the Upper Lodge Formation had been deposited, and overstepping on to the structural high (comprising denuded Nant Ffrancon Subgroup) south of the Efailnewydd Fault.

The finer grained parts of the Plastirion Member yield a fauna typically dominated by large examples of the trilobite *Brongniartella minor* (Plate 10ii, vi), usually accompanied by *Howellites* sp. (Plate 11i–v, viii) and *Kjaerina* sp. (Plate 11xx, xxi). This assemblage is typical of much of the Dwyfach Formation in the Nefyn district. In slightly coarser grained siltstones and fine-grained sandstones the fauna is more diverse, with, in addition, abundant *Broeggerolithus nicholsoni* (Plate 10ix, x) and *Sowerbyella* sp. (Plate 11x–xii, xiv, xv, xviii, xix), together

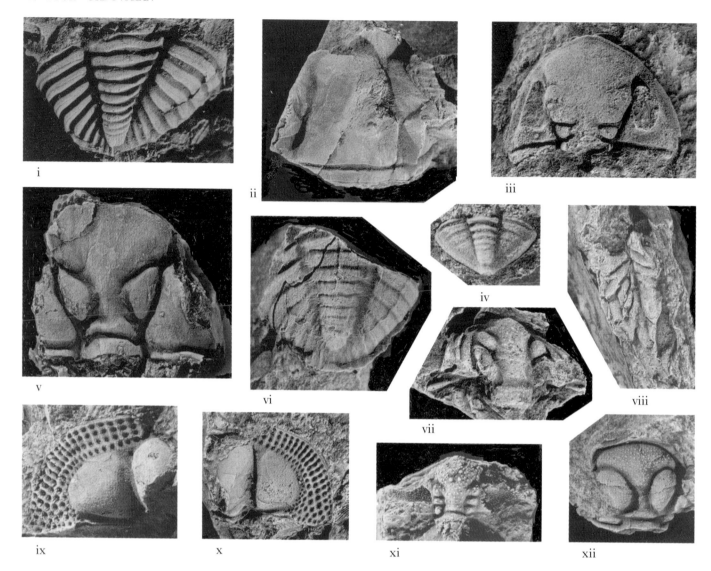

Plate 10   Trilobites of the Dwyfach Formation (GS675).

i, v   *Scopelochasmops cambrensis* (Whittington). Plastirion Member, Llanbedrog road cutting.
i   pygidium, NMW.83.19G.107b, ×4; v, cranidium, NMW.83.19G.76, ×4.
ii, vi   *Brongniartella minor* (Salter). Plastirion Member, Llanbedrog road cutting.
ii   cranidium, NMW.83.19G.113, ×3; vi, pygidium, NMW.83.19G.114, ×3.
iii, iv   *Kloucekia apiculata* (McCoy). Plastirion Member, 200 m east-south-east of Plastirion, Pwllheli.
iii   cranidium, NMW.83.19G.252, ×5; iv, pygidium, NMW.83.19G.253, ×5.
vii   *Primaspis semievoluta* (Reed). Nant-y-castell, Llanbedrog. Cranidium, NMW.27.110.G464, ×5.
viii, xii   *Platylichas* cf. *nodulosus* (McCoy). viii, pygidium, NMW.76.21G.200, ×2.5, Plastirion Member, 320 m E of
Creigiau Yoke House, Pwllheli; xii, cranidium, NMW.76.21G.239a, ×2.5, Plastirion Member, Llanbedrog road cutting.
ix, x   *Broeggerolithus nicholsoni* (Reed). Plastirion Member, Llanbedrog road cutting.
ix   cranidium, NMW.76.21G.230, ×4; x, cranidium, NMW.76.21G.235, ×2.5.
xi   *Deacybele pauca* Whittington, Plastirion Member, Llanbedrog road cutting. Cranidium, NMW.83.19G.163, ×3.

with *Conolichas* cf. *melmerbiensis*, *Dalmanella* sp., *Deacybele pauca* (Plate 10xi), *Decoroproetus calvus*, *Flexicalymene planimarginata*, *Illaenus* (s.l) sp., *Harpidella* sp., *Kloucekia apiculata* (Plate 10iii, iv), *Platylichas* cf. *nodulosus* (Plate 10viii, ix), *Primaspis semievoluta* (Plate 10vii), *Remopleurides* sp., *Scopelochasmops cambrensis* (Plate 10i, v) and *Stenopareia* sp. These siltstones also bear a diverse bryozoan fauna, described by Buttler (1991). The sandstone-dominated parts of the Plastirion Member bear a much sparser fauna, including *Dalmanella* sp. (Plate 11xiii, xvi) and *Broeggerolithus* sp. There is a particularly close resemblance to the trilobites of the Gelli-grin Formation in the Bala area, north Wales, but all are members of a widespread assemblage found elsewhere in north Wales and north-west England (Cross Fell inlier; Drygill area, northern Lake District), particularly in mudstone facies. Corresponding trilobites are less common in Longvillian sandstones in Shropshire, on the margin of the Welsh Basin, and have not been recorded in south Wales.

The abundant faunas from the Plastirion Member of the Dwyfach Formation indicate an early Longvillian age. Old reports of faunas of Soudleyan age from the lower part of the member at Llanbedrog (Matley, 1938) have not been substantiated in this study.

There are no fossiliferous localities recorded from the uppermost part of the Plastirion Member of the Pwllheli district. The highest horizons of the Dwyfach Formation at Glan-y-gors [3074 3782], just outside the district, yield a fauna with *Lonchodomas* sp., *Brongniartella* sp. and *Kjaerina* sp. This is probably of Woolstonian age, based on the presence of *Lonchodomas* which is not recorded below the Upper Longvillian in England and Wales, although occurring earlier elsewhere. Farther east, near Plas Boduan [3264 3810] and Pont Penprys [3504 3942], equivalent horizons at the top of the Dwyfach Formation yield *Estoniops alifrons* as well as *Lonchodomas* sp., allowing confident attribution to the Woolstonian. The age of the top of the Dwyfach Formation within the district is presumed to be of a similar Woolstonian age, but is not well constrained.

LLANBEDROG VOLCANIC GROUP

The Llanbedrog Volcanic Group is equivalent to the Mynytho Volcanic Group and the Llanbedrog Ignimbrites of Fitch (1967) and is well exposed around the village of Llanbedrog (Figure 20). The group shows a broad evolution from the dominantly basaltic trachyandesitic rocks of the Penmaen Formation, overlain in some areas by the lavas and tuffs of the Foel Ddu Rhyodacite Formation, to the rhyolitic tuffs of the Carneddol Rhyolitic Tuff Formation. The ashflow tuffs of the Carneddol Rhyolitic Tuff Formation thin rapidly northeastwards, and interdigitate with the volcaniclastic rocks of the Yoke House Formation and, in the Nefyn district, the Dwyfach Formation.

The Llanbedrog Volcanic Group was erupted across an area straddling the Efailnewydd Fault and west of an old lineament running along the southern limb of the

Llŷn Syncline (Figure 21). The group differs markedly from the broadly contemporaneous Snowdon Volcanic Group (Figure 18), not only in its mildly alkaline geochemistry, but in the major development of volcanic rocks of intermediate composition. Unlike the Snowdon Volcanic Group with its marked basalt/rhyolite bimodality, the Llanbedrog Volcanic Group includes significant volumes of basaltic trachyandesite, trachydacite and rhyodacite lavas and tuffs, together with rhyolitic tuffs.

Penmaen Formation

The Penmaen Formation comprises about 300 m of lava flows and tuffs of intermediate composition, and associated sedimentary rocks. The formation, the lowest division of the Llanbedrog Volcanic Group, is broadly equivalent to the 'Foel Fawr Dacites' of Fitch (1967). The type area for the formation is near Pwllheli where it comprises rocks of basaltic trachyandesitic composition, although in the Llanbedrog area the dominant lithology is trachydacite. Lavas are thickest to the west and north of Pwllheli, whereas farther north-east, beyond the Efailnewydd Fault, the formation grades into an apron of volcaniclastic sandstones belonging to the Yoke House Formation. The lithology at the base of the formation at Pwllheli varies, but is always characterised by the abrupt appearance of volcanic or volcaniclastic material. At Penmaen, for example, these lowest units are blocky andesitic lava breccias (7.5 m) above which are coarse-grained, cross-bedded sandstones and conglomerates (2 m), all well exposed in the cliff south of Penmaen [3620 3490]. A further 2 m of andesitic breccia lie beneath a topographically prominent porphyritic basaltic trachyandesite lava. The breccia can be traced for 300 m eastwards beyond which it thins and dies out, in passing into unwelded, andesitic crystal-lithic tuffs that are exposed both north [3636 3500] and east [3718 3530] of the lava.

The base of this formation is also exposed along strike farther east, on the north side of Pwllheli [3760 3551], where grey siltstones of the Plastiron Member are overlain by andesitic tuff; this, in turn, is overlain by a series of andesitic lavas capped by volcaniclastic andesitic tuffs, breccias and sandstones. The lavas are commonly highly vesicular [3736 3542]. The andesitic breccias lying above the lavas are best exposed near Denio chapel [3744 3566], but can also be seen in other localities such as along the north-east side of Allt Salem [3730 3556]. Andesitic tuffs were temporarily revealed at the track junction to Ffridd [3768 3578].

North of the Efailnewydd Fault at Pwllheli, the base of the formation is represented by coarse-grained, feldspathic, mud-rich sandstone, exposed 250 m east of Yoke House [3819 3667] where some 14.5 m of volcaniclastic sediments show sandstones rich in feldspar crystal fragments interbedded with grey cherty tuffites and ashy siltstones displaying intraformational cherty mud clasts and synsedimentary slump folds.

Between Llanbedrog and Mynytho, the Penmaen Formation comprises intermediate tuffs and trachydacite lavas. The lavas are exposed both in the valley

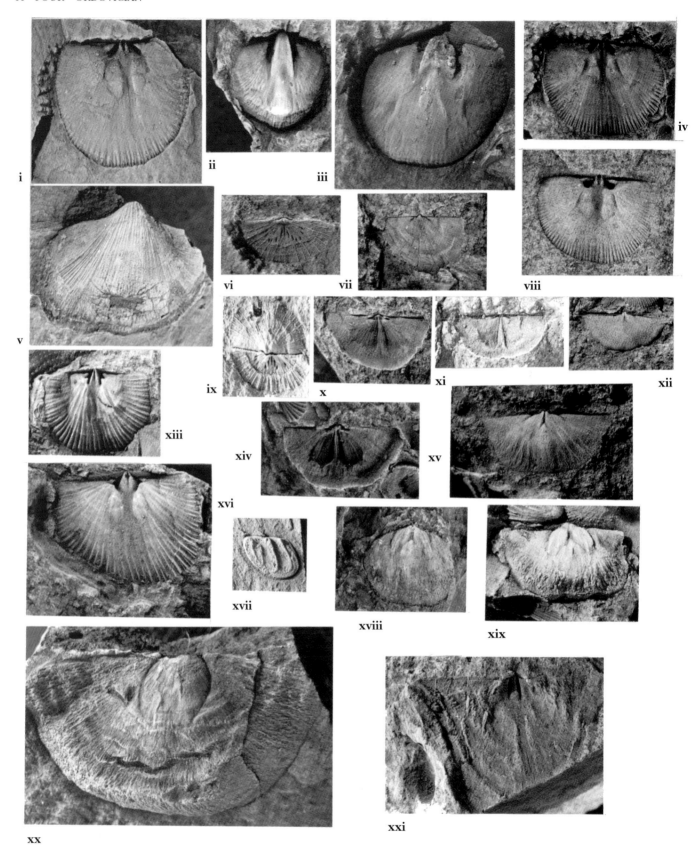

south of Llanbedrog near Nant-y-Castell and on the isolated hill of Foel Fawr, north of Mynytho. At Llanbedrog the base of the formation is not exposed, but the lowest exposures show andesitic tuffs [3208 3156] with intercalated fine-grained tuffite beds [3220 3161]. These andesitic tuffs are overlain by 180 m of trachydacite lavas with prominent columnar jointing (Matley, 1938, Figure 1) exposed beside the A499 [3236 3171, 3260 3181]. These pass up into andesitic breccias (probably autobreccias), overlain by westward-thickening trachydacitic tuffs which reach a maximum thickness of about 80 m. The same sequence of 180 m trachydacitic lavas is also exposed on Foel Fawr, locally with poor examples of columnar jointing. The low ground north of this hill probably conceals the andesite breccias and trachydacitic tuffs for the sequence passes northwards into tuffs belonging to the overlying Foel Ddu Rhyodacite Formation [306 323].

North of Foel Ddu the Penmaen Formation is absent, possibly due to faulting or post-eruptive erosion. However, it crops out east of Carn Fadryn at Carreg Dinas [2870 3530], where basaltic trachyandesites similar to those of the Penmaen Formation on the north limb of the Llŷn Syncline are overlain by tourmalinised sandstones [2875 3547] belonging to the Yoke House Formation (the clastic apron of sediment derived from the Llanbedrog Volcanic Group).

North of the Efailnewydd Fault, the basaltic trachyandesites seen to the south on Carreg Dinas again crop out for 1600 m along strike from their westernmost exposure north-east of Madryn Farm [2868 3644]. The cliff southeast of Wyddgrug exposes the upper part of this unit which is further seen on Mynydd Meilian and north of Glan-y-gors [307 378] just outside the Pwllheli district. These lavas are overlain on the north limb by sandstones and mudstones, probably less than 50 m thick. Matley (1938) described the Mynydd Meilian rocks as spilites, but analyses (Table 7) indicate they are basaltic trachyandesites and comparable in composition to the 'mugearites' (Leat and Thorpe, 1986) of the Penmaen Formation at Moel-y-Penmaen [338 387]. Most of the basaltic trachyandesites seen on Mynydd Meilian are autobrecciated (Plate 12), flow-foliated, and, in the upper part, highly amygdaloidal [2971 3721 and 2940 3703], with the amygdales locally aligned at high angles to bedding, as also seen at the same levels on Moel-y-Penmaen. In the upper parts of the Penmaen Formation on Mynydd Meilian there are spectacular exposures of autobrecciated horizons [2765 3711 and 2745 3690]. The highest unit seen on Mynydd Meilian is a flow-foliated basaltic trachyandesite with abundant fresh augite similar to the basaltic trachyandesite sill at Bryn Crin (Chapter 5).

Petrologically, the extrusive rocks within this formation are typified by the porphyritic basaltic trachyandesite lavas exposed north of Pwllheli. These rocks occur associated with andesitic tuffs and the intrusive Bryn Crin Basaltic Trachyandesite sill, which overlies the mudstones and siltstones of the Plastirion Member in the area running north-east from Allt Salem. They are dominated by andesine phenocrysts in a microcrystalline, commonly flow-foliated and locally vesicular groundmass. They contain no primary pyroxene or amphibole (represented by green aggregates of secondary amphibole or chlorite) but locally show preserved biotite. Textural variation mainly reflects the grain size of the groundmass (fine to coarse microcrystalline) and the amount of flow alignment. Ubiquitous andesine phenocrysts range in size up to 4 mm, but are mostly less than 1 mm. Glomeroporphyritic clots of plagioclase and altered ferromagnesian minerals occur in several samples, and accessory minerals include apatite and sphene, with ore (possibly ilmenite) being common in all samples.

One of the best examples of this lithology is exposed at Penmaen [3620 3490] where a strongly porphyritic amygdaloidal lava contains andesine (up to 8 mm across; some zoned and fractured) and altered clinopyroxene (up to 0.8 mm) as single phenocrysts and in glomeroporphyritic clots in a dark, ore-rich, microcrystalline groundmass. Rare green biotite phenocrysts are up to 0.2 mm across. Chlorite-filled amygdales (up to 2 mm across) form up to 15% of the rock and are commonly rimmed by opaque minerals. The groundmass is rich in opaque minerals (ilmenite partially replaced by titanite), but crudely flow-aligned microlites of feldspar (0.05 to 0.1 mm) can be discerned.

Similar porphyritic basaltic trachyandesite lavas also occur on the north limb of the Llŷn Syncline, such as on Mynydd Meilian [2966 3708]. Typical lithologies show andesine and rarer augite phenocrysts within a dark green chloritic groundmass with flow-aligned plagioclase microlites. The andesine phenocrysts (0.5 to 3.0 mm) occur isolated as single crystals and in glomeroporphyritic clots, and commonly display 'sieve' textures infilled with fine chlorite. Several samples show amygdaloidal textures, with individual amygdales up to 1.3 mm across, and mostly infilled with chlorite (quartz also occurs). The trachydacitic lavas exposed around Llanbedrog are texturally similar to the basaltic trachyandesites described above. Andesine phenocrysts are again dominant, occurring as isolated crystals (up to 7 mm across) and in glomeritic clots within flow-aligned plagioclase microlites in a dark chloritic groundmass. Clinopyroxenes are mostly altered and rimmed with opaque minerals, and the typically dark,

Plate 11 Brachiopods and ostracods of the Cwm Eigiau and Dwyfach formations. All brachiopods ×2.5 (GS676).

i–v, viii *Howellites* sp. Plastirion Member, Dwyfach Formation.
i internal mould of brachial valve;
v external view of pedicle valve; ii, iii internal moulds of pedicle valves, Moel Caerau; iv, viii internal moulds of brachial valves, Moel Caerau.
vi, vii, ix *Sericoidea* cf. *abdita complicata*, upper Cwm Eigiau Formation.
x–xii, xiv, xv, xviii, xix *Sowerbyella* sp. Plastirion Member, Dwyfach Formation.
xiii, xvi *Dalmanella* sp. Plastirion Member, Dwyfach Formation.
xvii *Harperopsis scripta* Plastirion Member, Dwyfach Formation, ×5.
xx, xxi *Kjaerina* sp. Plastirion Member, Dwyfach Formation.

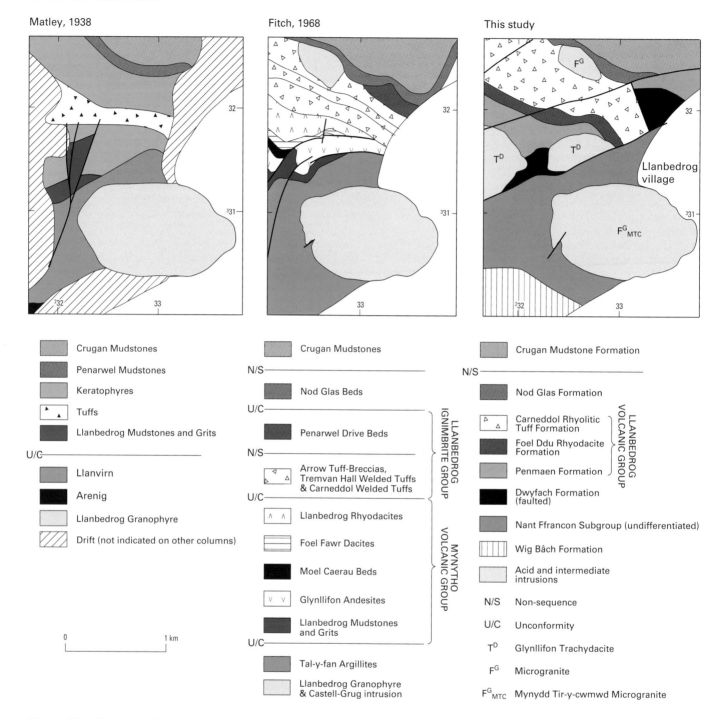

Figure 20   History of interpretations of the Llanbedrog area.

The interpretation of the succession and structure of the area around Llanbedrog village has been central to successive descriptions of the Caradoc volcanicity in Llŷn. The interpretation of Matley (1938) favoured a simple succession of extrusive lavas and tuffs, unconformable on the underlying mid-Ordovician mudrocks. Fitch (1967) interpreted the lack of lateral continuity within his 'Mynytho Volcanic Group' in terms of faulting and an unconformity generated by emplacement of a subvolcanic granophyre intrusion. The interpretation here invokes a faulted contact between the mid- and upper Ordovician successions and an intrusive, rather than an extrusive, origin for the Glynllifon Trachydacite. No intra-Caradoc unconformity is indicated. The Mynydd Tîr-y-cwmwd Granophyric Microgranite may indeed be associated with the eruption of the Carneddol Rhyolitic Tuff Formation. The complex nature of the stratigraphy may be attributed to proximity to the margin of the Llanbedrog caldera.

Plate 12 Autobrecciated basaltic trachyandesite, Penmaen Formation. Coed Mynydd Meilian [2943 3696] (GS679).

Compass is 10 cm long.

ore-rich groundmass of these lavas is strongly oxidised to give a reddened appearance.

Foel Ddu Rhyodacite Formation

The rhyodacitic lavas of this formation vary in thickness from less than 100 m to over 250 m. They occur in a belt parallel and adjacent to the Efailnewydd Fault (Figure 21), cropping out in the west around Foel Ddu, in the east near Pwllheli, and on the headland of Carreg-y-Defaid (Figure 22). Around Llanbedrog the formation is represented by rhyodacitic tuffs.

Between Garn Saethon [298 337] and Glan-y-gors [306 376] the formation typically comprises flow-foliated, porphyritic rhyodacite. At Glan-y-gors, where the lavas are only about 80 m thick, they show a flow-foliated, reddened, peperitic top [3042 3752]. In the Nant-y-Gledrydd area the unit thickens to about 120 m, and in the type area on Foel Ddu (and south of Nant Bodlas around Garn Saethon) the formation thickness has increased to over 275 m and is faulted against the Dwyfach Formation. The rhyodacite lavas exposed between Llanbedrog and Nant-y-Gledrydd have abundant sodic andesine phenocrysts (1 to 4 mm) and glomeroporphyritic clots set in a fine-grained, flow-aligned, partly amygdaloidal groundmass of grey plagioclase microlites and quartz. The primary texture of the groundmass is obscured by patchy recrystallisation, which produces a quartz mosaic texture that is characteristic of this lithology. The recrystallised patches are typically 0.2 to 0.3 mm in diameter. Zircon (up to 0.15 mm) and apatite are common accessories, and are well preserved, unlike the mafic phenocrysts which are altered to green or brown pseudomorphs (probably after clinopyroxene) and may show a rim of opaque minerals.

In the Pwllheli area, the same flow-foliated rhyodacites, with rare microdioritic enclaves, reach a maximum thickness (155 m) on Y-Garn [3620 3506],

where the upper part is extensively brecciated [3680 3530]. The outcrop continues west-south-west from Y-Garn to the Penmaen area (where it is about 125 m thick). To the east-north-east of Y-Garn, the outcrop is terminated by a fault which displaces the formation north-west [3727 3559], but farther north the formation thins and dies out in the vicinity of the Efailnewydd Fault. The Foel Ddu Rhyodacite Formation exposed both on Y-Garn and south of Garn Saethon, interpreted here as a flow-foliated lava, was previously interpreted as welded tuff (Roberts, 1979). In thin section, these rhyodacite lavas show oligoclase (up to 2.5 mm across) phenocrysts and glomeritic clots in a flow-foliated, amygdaloidal, microcrystalline, and strongly recrystallised groundmass. Some plagioclase phenocrysts show corroded, carious centres, and are enclosed by later alkali feldspar overgrowth. Accessory zircon and apatite are present, and all mafic minerals are completely pseudomorphed by green alteration products.

In the Mynytho and Llanbedrog areas, the formation is largely represented by rhyodacitic tuffs (approximately equivalent to the 'Llanbedrog Rhyodacites' of Fitch, 1967), and is at least 120 m thick on the hill between Foel Fawr and Foel Bach [306 323] and only slightly thinner in Llanbedrog. Dacitic lavas occur locally [3050 3245, 3282 3179] within the tuffs.

The 80 m of rhyodacitic rocks exposed at Carreg-y-Defaid [341 325], north-east of Llanbedrog, were described by Raisin (1889) and Harker (1889). Matley (1938) discussed the suggestion by Raisin that the rhyodacites should be correlated with the Pen-y-chain Rhyolitic Complex, and used graptolite evidence from the mudstones above the rhyolites to argue a possible earlier age than for the Llanbedrog Volcanic Group. Fitch (1967), instead correlated these mudstones with the Llanbedrog area, and this has been broadly supported by both mapping and graptolite revision during this survey (Figure 22). The grey rhyodacites

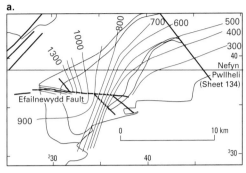

Strata between the Upper Lodge Fm and the
Nod Glas Fm (=Dwyfach Fm and Llanbedrog
Volcanic Group)

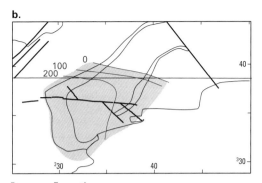

Penmaen Formation

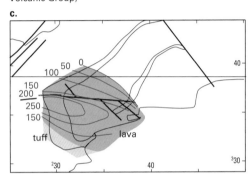

Foel Ddu Rhyodacite Formation

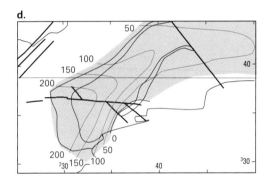

Carneddol Rhyolitic Tuff Formation
(Nant-y- Gledrydd Member)

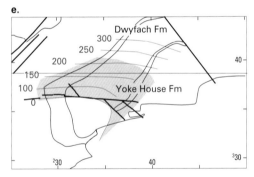

Strata between Bodgadle and Nant y Gledrydd members

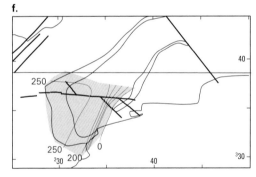

Carneddol Rhyolitic Tuff Formation (Bodgadle Member)

Figure 21 Evolution of the Llanbedrog Volcanic Group.

i   Approximately equivalent to the local Longvillian–Woolstonian succession

b–f   Woolstonian succession

exposed on the point of the headland (base not seen)
are correlated with the Foel Ddu Rhyodacite Formation.
They comprise grey/green locally autobrecciated, weakly
flow-foliated and generally rather massive lavas.

Carneddol Rhyolitic Tuff Formation

The Carneddol Rhyolitic Tuff Formation comprises
white-weathering, dominantly welded, rhyolitic ashflow
tuffs. The formation is subdivided into the
Nant-y-Gledrydd and overlying Bodgadle members, each
of which represents a separate major eruption of

rhyolitic tuff. The two members are contiguous in the
Llanbedrog area, but towards the north-east become progressively separated by a wedge of clastic rocks of the
Yoke House Formation and then of the Dwyfach
Formation. The contact between the two members is
exposed at Carreg-y-Defaid [34 32]. The Nant-y-Gledrydd
and Bodgadle members are based on type sections in
Nant-y-Gledrydd (north-west of the lane [294 366] and
south-west of Mochras Uchaf [299 365] respectively).

The two members are each 200 to 250 m thick between
Llanbedrog and Nant-y-Gledrydd, but eastwards they thin
rapidly between Carreg-y-Defaid and Pwllheli (Figure 21)

across a line that corresponds approximately to the western margin of the distribution of the Pitts Head Tuff Formation. A similar thinning takes place across the Efail-newydd Fault so that the eruptive centre is interpreted to have been south of this fault and west of Pwllheli. Outflow tuffs from this centre can be traced along the northern limb of the Llŷn Syncline into the Nefyn district as far as Trallwyn Hall [386 410], 6 km north of Pwllheli, and along the southern limb of the syncline, from Pwllheli eastwards to the Dwyfach valley at Llanystumdwy [466 397], over 17 km from the proposed site of the eruptions. Although the associated sedimentary rocks and fauna clearly indicate submarine emplacement of the outflow tuffs, it is not known whether the proximal tuffs between Llanbedrog and Nant-y-Gledrydd were emplaced in a submarine or subaerial environment.

The Carneddol Rhyolitic Tuff Formation is closely associated with the Mynydd Tir-y-Cwmwd microgranitic intrusion (just south of Llanbedrog), clasts of which occur in the tuffs. It is not possible to demonstrate with certainty that the Mynydd Tir-y-cwmwd Microgranite was intruded at the site of a vent of the Carneddol Rhyolitic Tuff Formation, but it seems likely that, at the very least, they shared a common magma source.

The formation crops out in three distinct areas within the north–south belt between Mochras and Llanbedrog: Mochras [29 36], Carneddol [30 33] to Bodgadle [30 35] and Llanbedrog [32 32]. It also crops out at Carreg-y-Defaid [341 326] and north-east of Pwllheli [376 366]. At Pwllheli, the formation is represented by a poorly exposed tuff, estimated as only 35 to 45 m thick, that overlies the Penmaen Formation in the north-eastern part of the district. These ignimbritic rocks have been identified in the fields south of Yoke House [3791 3542] where they are crystal-poor tuffs. Isolated phenocrysts of alkali feldspar and plagioclase (up to 2 mm across), and altered pumice clasts, lie within a fine, dusty, siliceous, faintly shardic and unwelded matrix. Much thicker and better exposed sequences are seen in the Mochras–Llanbedrog and Carreg y Defaid areas, and these are described below in more detail.

MOCHRAS TO LLANBEDROG

Nant-y-Gledrydd Member

The Nant-y-Gledrydd Member is well exposed in the north of the district, especially in Nant-y-Gledrydd [296 366] and in Gwinllan-y-Creigiau [304 374]. In Nant-y-Gledrydd, its type section, the member is approximately 200 m thick and lies on the oxidised, reddened top of rhyodacitic lavas belonging to the Foel Ddu Rhyodacite Formation, clasts of which occur abundantly at the base of the tuffs (e.g. at Nant-y-Gledrydd [295 3667] and Gwinllan-y-Creigiau [3045 3750]). The lowest 150 m of the member consist of pale grey, coarse, unwelded to poorly welded, shardic, crystal-lithic tuffs in a fine matrix. Clasts include dark pumice, siltstone, dacitic glomeroporphyritic clots, porphyritic dacite, brown oxidised vesicular flow-banded lava fragments; crystals consist of perthitic alkali feldspar and rarer plagioclase and quartz (Plate 13). The proportion of lithic fragments to crystals decreases upwards into unwelded, shardic rhyolitic crystal tuffs with abundant but faint shards.

The upper 50 m of the member become poorer in crystals, richer in shardic matrix, finer grained, and locally strongly welded (e.g. near Tremvan Hall [329 320]). In Nant-y-Gledrydd these primary tuffs can be traced upwards into the volcaniclastic rocks of the Yoke House Formation [2968 3660].

In the Bodgadle area, the Nant-y-Gledrydd Member comprises unwelded, crystal-rich rhyolitic tuffs with glomeroporphyritic clasts of granophyric microgranite (up to 6 mm across), alkali feldspar (up to 5 mm), plagioclase (up to 3 mm) and quartz (up to 1 mm) crystals in a recrystallised matrix. The Nant-y-Gledrydd Member is poorly exposed through much of the central part of the outcrop, but similar unwelded or poorly welded, shardic tuffs with rhyolitic and siltstone fragments, plagioclase and cryptoperthitic perthite crystals and siliceous nodules are seen in the lower part of the member at Seis [308 342] and Llanbedrog. At higher levels at Llanbedrog, where the total thickness of the member is reduced to 120 m there are strongly welded rhyolitic crystal tuffs, with locally parataxitic fabrics wrapping alkali feldspar and plagioclase crystals (up to 2 mm across), zircon (up to 0.5 mm), microgranite (up to 3 mm), and unwelded rhyolitic crystal tuff fragments.

Bodgadle Member

The Bodgadle Member is approximately 200 m thick at Llanbedrog, thickening to 250 m at Mochras. The base of the member, exposed around Llanbedrog and farther north near Bryn Gwyn [311 340], is marked by coarse, shardic, crystal-lithic tuffs, with plagioclase and alkali feldspar crystals (up to 5 mm across) characteristically rich in large dark pumice clasts (Plates 14, 15). The brown glassy pumice fragments in this lithology reach up to 14 mm in length, display ragged edges and spherulitic devitrification textures. They may be flattened to define a rough welding texture and can enclose individual plagioclase crystals. The shardic texture is very pronounced locally, with individual glass fragments commonly 0.5 mm long. These coarse tuffs are overlain by strongly welded crystal tuffs, which form a prominent scarp northwards past Carneddol [302 331] and Bodgadle [309 354] to Craig Wen [298 362]. In the Nant-y-Gledrydd area, a similar sequence shows a basal unwelded crystal-lithic tuff rich in alkali feldspar and flow-banded rhyolite clasts, with minor siltstone clasts, overlain by variably welded crystal tuffs with minor lithic fragments.

At higher levels in all areas the pumice, crystal and lithic fragments are less common, but the rocks remain strikingly shard-rich, variably welded, and fine upwards to grey, compact, ashy tuffs with few crystals and fine shards. At Llanbedrog these ashy, shard-rich tuffs are overlain by rhyolitic breccias and sandstones [3231 3255], interpreted as having been derived by erosion of the nearby Castell Crûg microgranite dome that obscures the original upper contact of this member. However, around Mochras [300 367], the tuff is overlain by volcaniclastic sandstones of the Yoke House Formation.

Carreg-y-Defaid

The Carneddol Rhyolitic Tuff Formation rests on the Foel Ddu Rhyodacite Formation on the headland of Carreg-y-Defaid (Figure 22), and it comprises two ash flows which are tentatively correlated with the two members of the formation. The lower part of the 'Carneddol Welded Tuffs' of Fitch (1967), together with his intrusion, are placed within the Nant-y-Gledrydd Member (approximately 70 m thick), and the upper part of Fitch's 'Carneddol Welded Tuffs' comprise the lower part of the Bodgadle Member (approximately 80 m thick). Fitch's 'Tremvan Hall Welded Tuffs' are interpreted as the secondarily

Plate 13 Welded crystal-lithic tuff from the lower part of the Nant-y-Gledrydd Member, Carneddol Rhyolitic Tuff Formation. The dark flattened pumice (fiammé) help define the welding fabric. Gwinllan-y-Craigiau [3044 3742] (GS654). Lens cap: 5.5 cm.

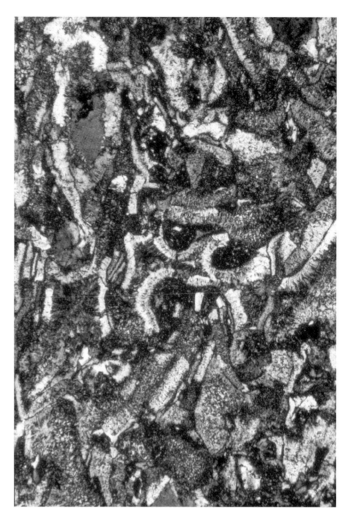

Plate 14 Highly shardic rhyolitic ashflow tuff from near the base of the Bodgadle Member, Carneddol Rhyolitic Tuff Formation (GS655). The bubble walls are clearly preserved in this virtually unwelded specimen from Llanbedrog [3247 3216]. Field of view: 1.2 mm. Crossed polarised light.

silicified upper part of this upper flow. The overlying reworked rhyolitic tuffs and breccias ('Arrow Tuff-Breccias' of Fitch) are placed in the upper part of the Bodgadle Member.

The base of the Nant-y-Gledrydd Member is exposed at Carreg-y-Defaid where approximately 5 m of thinly bedded fine-grained tuffs overlie the massive lavas of the Foel Ddu Rhyodacite Formation in a faulted and folded zone approximately 100 m north-west of the point. The basal tuffs are overlain by compact, poorly laminated, orange-weathering tuffs; the upper part of the tuffs are strongly altered, with a prominent zone of 'basket-of-eggs' siliceous nodules. Above this altered zone is 30 m of welded rhyolitic tuff with flattened pumice which represents the basal part of the Bodgadle Member at this locality. The lower part of this welded tuff contains contains large blocks (up to 0.5 m diameter) of tuff with siliceous nodules similar to those seen in situ in the underlying member. A similarly pumiceous tuff marks the base of the Bodgadle Member inland in the Llanbedrog area.

The uppermost levels of the basal welded tuff are intensely silicified, and the flow is overlain by at least 50 m of ash, breccias, and other volcaniclastic sediments. Some of the breccia horizons include clasts whose outlines suggest plastic deformation during hot emplacement, whereas towards the top of the succession sedimentary structures such as graded beds containing rounded boulders (up to 30 cm) indicate aqueous reworking. The top of these reworked beds is not exposed and they form a facies intermediate between that of the primary tuffs of the member and the more clearly sedimentary deposits of the Yoke House Formation.

Yoke House Formation

The Yoke House Formation comprises rhyolitic crystal-lithic tuffs, and tuffaceous sandstones and breccio-conglomerates. The formation crops out around Pwllheli and to the north and north-west of Cors Geirch. In both areas the lateral transition from the volcanic formations of the Llanbedrog Volcanic Group to the Yoke House Formation occurs at the Efailnewydd Fault. The lower

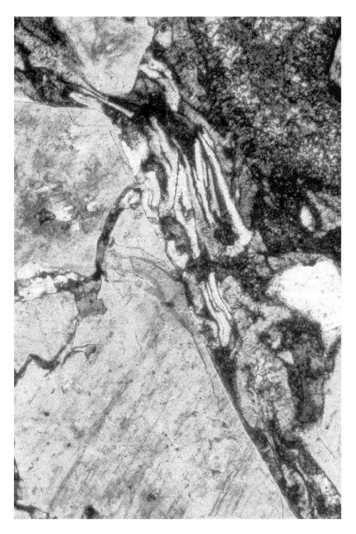

Plate 15   Shardic bubbles flattened against an alkali feldspar phenocryst in crystal tuff near the base of the Bodgadle Member, Carneddol Rhyolitic Tuff Formation Llanbedrog [3240 3218] (GS656). The shards display typical devitrification-induced axiolitic texture. Field of view: 1.2 mm. Crossed polarised light.

part of the formation is exposed in its type area near Yoke House [379 366] and the upper part near Caeau-gwynion-isaf [373 361]. The formation forms a clastic apron to the Llanbedrog Volcanic Group and passes laterally to the north-east into the finer grained siliciclastic rocks of the Dwyfach Formation (Figure 16). At least some of the sedimentary rocks of the Yoke House Formation were deposited under very shallow marine conditions.

The formation is approximately 130 m thick near Yoke House [379 367], where it rests on the Carneddol Rhyolitic Tuff Formation. It thins westwards to 50 to 60 m north of Penmaen [362 352], where it rests directly upon the Foel Ddu Rhyodacite Formation, which probably formed a locally upstanding feature. The exposures north of Penmaen comprise highly feldspathic, pale, medium-

to coarse-grained crystal-lithic tuffs, tuffaceous sandstones full of rhyolitic debris and tuffaceous lithic breccias with abundant rhyolite clasts. Clasts are dominated by spherulitic rhyolite, pumice (up to 20 mm across), and smaller crystal fragments of alkali feldspar and quartz. Similar tuffaceous breccias are well exposed north-west of the Garn [3692 3548], although here more mafic detritus is present in addition to the dominantly rhyolitic component seen farther north-east. Many clasts in thin section may be matched with the underlying Foel Ddu Rhyodacite Formation, whereas others are more mafic, and may be derived from the Penmaen Formation. Farther west, in the track leading to the Afon Ddwyryd [3680 3546], a series of bedded tuffaceous sandstones and siltstones are exposed at a higher stratigraphical level than the breccias. Clasts in these rocks are varied and include pumiceous acid volcanic detritus, spherulitic rhyolite, shardic ashflow tuff, rhyodacite and rare basalt. Exposures of volcaniclastic breccio-conglomerates occur at a similar stratigraphical level immediately south of the Afon Ddwyryd north-east of Caeau-gwynion-isaf [3749 3635]; they contain various clasts that include mudstones as well as abundant rhyolitic debris and oxidised basalt clasts. Exposures at a slightly higher level [3655 3543] show coarse tuffaceous rocks identical to those seen north of Yoke Farm [3790 3713], and record the same influx of abundant coarse alkali feldspar crystals from the Carneddol Rhyolitic Tuff.

These observations indicate that close to the Garn, where the Yoke House Formation rests directly on the Foel Ddu Rhyodacite Formation, the Yoke House Formation contains a range of lithic debris including abundant rhyodacite. Farther north-eastwards away from the local influence of the rhyodacites, and at higher stratigraphical levels in all areas, the detritus was dominated by an input from the Carneddol Rhyolitic Tuff Formation.

Farther west, around Nant-y-Gledrydd, the formation interdigitates with the Llanbedrog Volcanic Group. The Penmaen Formation in this area is overlain by a tongue of sedimentary rocks that comprise sandstones with minor siltstones. The most southerly occurrence of this tongue of the Yoke House Formation is a locality below Garn Saethon where Matley (1938) recorded fossils from the debris thrown out of a rabbit burrow. The Yoke House Formation is better exposed east of Carn Fadryn where it is coarser than the typical mud-rich sediments of the Dwyfach Formation, being more proximal to the Llanbedrog volcanic centre. Here, it is represented by thin-bedded tourmalinised sandstones [2875 3547] that lie on the Penmaen Formation, and are overlain by at least 60 m of more massive and locally fossiliferous sandstones exposed in a small quarry in the col between Moel Caerau and Carreg Dinas [2885 3554].This stratigraphically lowest tongue of the Yoke House Formation, lying between the Penmaen and Foel Ddu Rhyodacite formations, is traceable for over a kilometre from south of Wyddgrug [2862 3640] into Nant-y-Gledrydd where it is again locally fossiliferous [2924 3673].

The Yoke House Formation only indigitates with the higher, more evolved, parts of the Llanbedrog Volcanic Group north of the Efailnewydd Fault. For example,

Figure 22   Geological map of the Carreg y Defaid area. Geochemical evidence (Chapter 6) supports field evidence that the 'grey rhyodacites' belong to the Foel Ddu Rhyodacite Formation (although an alternative correlation with the Glynllifon Trachydacite intrusion is possible). The two rhyolitic tuff units correspond to the two members of the Carneddol Rhyolitic Tuff Formation. The reworked tuffs are similar to deposits at the top of the Carneddol Rhyolitic Tuff Formation north of the Castell Crûg intrusion. The small quarry exposing graptolitic mudstones was the source of the graptolite specimens from Carreg y Defaid in Figure 23.

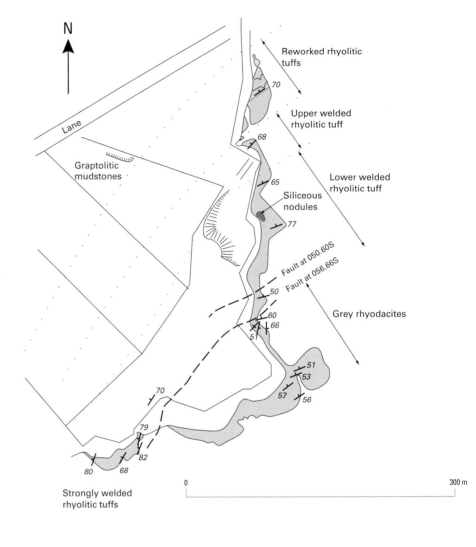

above the Nant-y-Gledrydd Member of the Carneddol Rhyolitic Tuff Formation, the Yoke House Formation is represented by 100 m of reworked volcaniclastic sedimentary rocks which fine upwards from poorly sorted conglomerates to sandstones [297 366]. The conglomerates contain angular to rounded clasts of lithic and crystal detritus within a grey cryptocrystalline matrix. Lithic clasts include mudstones and siltstones, brown oxidised lava fragments, shardic crystal tuff and devitrified spherulitic rhyolite. Crystal clasts are mostly angular alkali feldspar fragments and rounded to subrounded quartz, and the fine-grained siliceous matrix contains faintly preserved shardic debris. The overlying sandstones are compositionally similar but better sorted, with a typical grain size of around 0.5 mm. The 40 m of the Yoke House Formation that overlies the Bodgadle Member, comprises medium-grained sandstones which are well exposed south of Mochras Uchaf [302 366].

Localities within clastic sedimentary rocks above the prominent basaltic trachyandesite of Mynydd Meilian contain fossil assemblages including *Kjaerina* sp. and indeterminate graptolite fragments. Farther south-west, at Moel Caerau, there are richly fossiliferous sandstones with *Flexicalymene planimarginata*, *Broeggerolithus minor*, *Illaenus* (s.l.) sp., *Dalmanella* sp., *Howellites* sp., *Sowerbyella* sp., and *Kjaerina* sp., indicating a Longvillian/Woolstonian age. Similarly, highly fossiliferous conglomeratic sandstone fragments that are interpreted as having been derived from the formation were recovered from a ploughed field south-west of Yoke House [3791 3542]. The fauna included *Dinorthis* sp., *Dalmanella?* sp., *Encrinurus* sp. and *Kloucekia* sp. together with gastropods, bryozoans, and echinoderm fragments. This assemblage is similar to collections from the formation in the Boduan area of the Nefyn sheet [327 379] (Matley and Heard, 1930; Harper in Tremlett, 1962) and attributed to the Woolstonian. Sandstones from fossils in Penarwel Drive, Llanbedrog, described by Matley (1938) as lying at the top of the volcanic succession, have been reinterpreted as belonging to the Dwyfach Formation.

OGWEN GROUP: UPPER PART

Nod Glas Formation

The Nod Glas Formation, the uppermost part of the Ogwen Group, includes the 'Penarwel shales' and 'Ddwyryd shales' of Matley (1938), and is now employed as a formal lithostratigraphical term for the dark grey graptolitic mudstones formation which overlies much of the Caradoc volcanic sequences in North Wales (Rushton and Howells, 1999) (Figure 16). The term replaces previously defined units such as the 'Black slates of Dolwyddelan', 'Llanrhychwyn Slates' and the 'Cadnant Shales'. In the Bangor district, the formation was determined to be of *multidens* Biozone age, whereas in the Snowdonia district the *clingani* Biozone has been determined (Howells et al., 1985). In the Pwllheli district, sedimentary rocks of the Nod Glas Formation are 50 to 80 m thick, and the formation crops out around Pwllheli, Llanbedrog, and near Mochras. It varies in thickness, and includes tholeiitic basaltic rocks near Mochras (about 100 m thick) and Pwllheli (about 40 m). The volcanic activity appears to have been controlled at least to some extent by the Efailnewydd Fault.

The Nod Glas Formation is well exposed, apart from its base, in the neighbourhood of Penarwel House [3295 3235], the type area for Matley's 'Penarwel Shales', but there is little exposed ground between the highest tuffs of the Carneddol Rhyolitic Tuff Formation and the lowest black graptolitic mudstone. To the north, a thin conglomerate of microgranite pebbles is preserved on top of the Castell Crûg Porphyritic Microgranite dome [3261 3253], but again the actual contact with the overlying mudstones is not seen. The top of the formation is exposed immediately south of the Crugan Lane quarry [3327 3231] where black, laminated graptolitic mudstones are overlain by several metres of concretionary, pyrite-rich bioturbated mudstones and siltstones, referred to the overlying Crugan Mudstone Formation. Similar pyritised siltstones were recorded by Harper (1956) at a similar stratigraphical level in the Dwyfach valley, just outside the Pwllheli district.

Around Pwllheli, where the sedimentary rocks reach 80 m in thickness, a conformable contact with the Yoke House Formation occurs within an upwards-fining sequence [3736 3615]. The base of the formation has been positioned at the base of fine-grained sandstones overlying coarse-grained sandstones that are included in the Yoke House Formation. These sandstones fine upwards through micaceous grey siltstones with poorly preserved brachiopod fragments [3734 3610], and into monotonous, dark grey siltstones and silty mudstones that are well exposed in the bed of the Afon Ddwyryd north of Caeau-gwynion-isaf [3741 3633]. These silty mudstones locally host a thin vesicular, weakly porphyritic basalt [3740 3633], the Pensarn basaltic andesite sill [366 355], and are overlain by a 40 m-thick sequence of spilitised vesicular basalts [e.g. in the stream at 3737 3633] and dark grey-green, hyaloclastic, basaltic tuffs [e.g. by an old adit at 3685 3573]. Similar basalts, tuffs and tuffaceous sandstones are also seen in an old quarry just north of Caeau-gwynion-isaf [3728 3616]. Down-

stream from Pont-y-Ddwyryd, on the north bank of the stream [3693 3582], 5 m of grey porphyritic vesiculated basaltic tuffs and sandstones are overlain by 1 m of dark grey to black, splintery silty mudstones, and similar mudstones above basaltic tuffs near Caeau-gwynion-isaf [3727 3626] are rich in graptolites. The upward passage into the Crugan Mudstone Formation is not exposed in the vicinity of Pwllheli.

The formation around the Cors Geirch, near Bodgadle, includes basaltic pillow lavas and breccias in low, well defined outcrops along the west side of the marsh from north-east of Neuadd Bodgadle [314 359] to north-east of Graig-Wen [303 364]. The lower part of the Nod Glas Formation, and its contact with the Carneddol Rhyolitic Tuff Formation, are not exposed, but the features suggest that there are approximately 50 m of mudstones at the base of the formation, overlain by about 100 m of spilitised basaltic breccias, pumiceous and hyaloclastic tuffs and pillow lavas. The occurrence of basaltic rocks in the Nod Glas Formation at Pwllheli and Bodgadle suggests a spatial relationship between the basaltic volcanism and the Efailnewydd Fault.

At Mochras [302 365], the Yoke House Formation is overlain by about 40 m of dark siltstones and mudstones of the Nod Glas Formation, but the top is again not exposed. The siltstones contain thin laminae of volcaniclastic sand grains, together with small bioclasts, including ostracods.

At Mochras, Matley recorded a single unidentifiable graptolite specimen, but no further examples have been recovered. In contrast, the Nod Glas Formation near Penarwel yields abundant graptolites. These were identified by Elles (Matley, 1938), who concluded that the assemblage was from 'high up in the *clingani* Zone, probably at the base of the *linearis* Zone'. Re-examination of this collection by Rushton and Zalasiewicz (unpublished, 1991) determined *Climacograptus (Normalograptus) miserabilis*, *Climacograptus (Normalograptus)* aff. *mohawkensis*, *Climacograptus (Normalograptus) pollex* (Figure 23iii) *Corynoides curtus* (Figure 23ii), *Orthograptus* cf. *amplexicaulis*, *Amplexograptus* sp., *Diplograptus* sp. A (Figure 23vii, viii) and *Orthograptus* cf. *calcaratus* in the lower part of the formation, with small Normalograptids present in the uppermost levels. They concluded that a *clingani* Biozone age was most likely, although the formation may just possibly range up into the *linearis* Biozone.

Near Pwllheli, the lower part of the formation has yielded *Climacograptus (Normalograptus)?* sp., *Diplograptus* sp. A, *Corynoides?* sp., *Dicranograptus clingani resicis* (Figure 23i), *Diplograptus* cf. *foliaceus*, *Orthograptus calcaratus* (group) from localities below, and *Diplograptus* cf. *foliaceus?*, *Orthograptus calcaratus* (group) from above, the basaltic tuffs. These assemblages indicate the *clingani* Biozone, with *D. clingani resicis* suggesting the lower part of the zone.

The mudstones exposed near Carreg-y-Defaid [3402 3267] have long been interpreted as part of the Nod Glas Formation (Matley, 1938; Fitch, 1967; Roberts, 1979; Cattermole and Romano, 1981). Revision of the graptolite assemblage has shown the presence of *Climacograptus antiquus?*, *Diplograptus compactus* (Figure 23v) and *Orthograptus amplexicaulis* (group) (Figure 23iv) in

Matley's collections (BGS), with cf. *Amplexograptus arctus* (doubtful), *Dendrograptus* sp. and *Diplograptus* sp? in the G J Williams collection (National Museum of Wales). The two collections are very different in preservation, as well as faunal content, and may be from different horizons. The assemblage is not biostratigraphically diagnostic, but the doubtful presence of *Amplexograptus arctus* would, if confirmed, suggest the *multidens* rather than *clingani* Biozone (but see discussion of other records of *A. arctus* below).

The equivalent stratigraphical unit at Conwy (the 'Cadnant Shales' of Elles, 1909) was originally ascribed a largely *multidens* Biozone age, with only the upper 15 m referred to the *clingani* Biozone. The area was revised by Wood and Harper (1962), who instead referred the entire formation (over 120 m thick) to the *clingani* Biozone. Strachan (in Wood and Harper, 1962) suggested that the graptolites from the basal 10 m of the Cadnant Shales at Conwy compared closely with those from 'Gwynfryn near Pwllheli', referring to assemblages from the Nod Glas Formation north of Pwllheli. The Nod Glas Formation of the Bangor district has, however, also yielded *multidens* Biozone assemblages according to Howells et al. (1981, 1985). The persistence of *'D.* cf. *multidens'* into the *clingani* Biozone at Conwy, means their identification of the *multidens* Biozone must be treated with caution. Units in the Snowdon Volcanic Group as low as the Lower Rhyolitic Tuff and the Lower Crafnant Volcanic formations yield shelly faunas indicative of a Woolstonian age (Howells et al., 1991), but the Middle Crafnant Volcanic formation contains graptolitic faunas with *Amplexograptus arctus* (Howells et al., 1985). Although it is possible that the deposition of the Nod Glas Formation may have started in the *multidens* Biozone, a *clingani* Biozone age would appear more likely at Conwy, in parts of Snowdonia, and in the Pwllheli

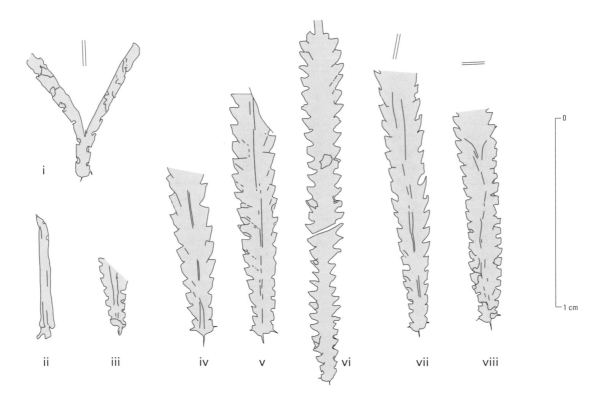

Figure 23   Graptolites from the Nod Glas Formation, all ×5.

All specimens are held in the Palaeontogical collection BGS, Keyworth.

The parallel lines indicate the trace of a weak cleavage.

i   *Dicranograptus clingani* Carruthers *resicis* Williams. The subspecies is characterised by a short biserial portion with only 2–3 thecal pairs. Caeau-gwynion-isaf, *clingani* Zone. BGS Zb 4110.

ii   *Corynoides curtus* Lapworth. South side of the Penarwel Dingle, *clingani* Zone?. Zb 4147.

iii *Climacograptus (Normalograptus) pollex* Rushton & Zalasiewicz, with bulbous virgellar structure. Top of south side of Penarwel dingle, *clingani* Zone. Ze 4755.

iv   *Orthograptus amplexicaulis* (Hall) [group]. Carreg y Defaid, *multidens* or *clingani* Zone. Ze 4656.

v   *Diplograptus compactus* Elles & Wood. Carreg y Defaid, *multidens* or *clingani* Zone. Ze 4645.

vi   *Orthograptus* sp., showing fluctuations in rhabdosomal width. Top of south side of Penarwel Dingle, *clingani* Zone. Ze 4759.

vii, viii   *Diplograptus* sp. A. The proximal end is narrower than that of *D. compactus* and the thecae are more closely spaced, especially proximally. Near path, boundary fence south of Penarwel Dingle, probably *clingani* Zone, Ze 4687, 4710.

district. The conventional correlation of the base of the *clingani* Biozone with the base of the Longvillian, would suggest that *Amplexograptus arctus* (if correctly identified in the Bangor district) would range up into the *clingani* Biozone. Although not yet certainly recorded from the Nod Glas Formation, its possible occurrence low in the formation at Carreg-y-Defaid would not be entirely incompatible with a *clingani* Biozone age.

It is likely, therefore, that the Llanbedrog Volcanic Group is Woolstonian in age. The overlying Nod Glas Formation is mainly of *clingani* Biozone age, although its top may be as young as *linearis* Biozone.

PALAEONTOLOGICAL DETAILS

For material from the Matley collections the old locality description is given, the revised faunal list of Rushton and Zalasiewicz and a revised lithostratigraphical horizon and interpreted National Grid reference.

1   Felin-fach: Matley collection. Zb 4104–4106 climacograptid indeterminate
    (Nod Glas Formation, below the basaltic tuffs [364 354])

2   Afon Ddwyryd, under churning wheel, 228.6 m (250 yards) south-east of Gwynfryn: Matley collection. Ze 4584–4601
    Climacograptus (*Normalograptus*)? sp., *Diplograptus* sp. A (Nod Glas Formation, below the basaltic tuffs [366 356])

3   Caeau-gwynion-isaf: Matley collection Zb 4107–4125
    Corynoides? sp., *Dicranograptus clingani resicis*, *Diplograptus* cf. *foliaceus*, *Orthograptus calcaratus* (group)

    (Nod Glas Formation, probably below the basaltic tuffs [3725 3615], lower part of *clingani* Zone)

4   Bank in lane above river, 91.4 m (100 yards) north of Caeau-gwynion-isaf: Matley collection. Ze 4602–4626
    Diplograptus cf. *foliaceus*?, *Orthograptus calcaratus* (group)
    (Nod Glas Formation, above the basaltic tuffs [3735 3615])

5   Penarwel Dingle, north of rhyolites (west end): Matley Collection. Zb 4159–4169
    Climacograptus sp., *Climacograptus* (*Normalograptus*) *miserabilis* (Nod Glas Formation [3245 3263] approximately)

6   South side of Penarwel Dingle, 15.2 m (50 to 60 feet) above rhyolites: Matley collection. Zb 4147–4158
    Climacograptus (*Normalograptus*) aff. *mohawkensis*, *Corynoides curtus*, *Orthograptus* aff. *amplexicaulis*
    (Nod Glas Formation [3284 3246] approximately)

7   Penarwel Dingle, top of S slope, 32m (35 yards) N of volcanic ridge: Matley collection. Ze 4747–4774
    Amplexograptus sp., *Climacograptus* sp., *Climacograptus* (*Normalograptus*) *pollex*, *Diplograptus* sp. A, *Orthograptus* sp.
    (Nod Glas Formation [3285 3242] approximately)

8   Penarwel, close to boundary fence path, S side of dingle: Matley collection. Ze 4733–4740
    Plectambonitacean indeterminate, *Schmidtites*? sp., *Climacograptus* (*Normalograptus*) aff. *mohawkensis*, *Orthograptus* cf. *amplexicaulis*
    (Nod Glas Formation [3287 3235] approximately.)

9   Penarwel, as locality 8, but 18.2 m (20 yards) east: Matley collection Ze 4684–4695, Ze 4706–4732
    Schizocrania sp., *Climacograptus* (*Normalograptus*) aff. *mohawkensis*, *Diplograptus* sp. A, *Orthograptus calcaratus* group. (Nod Glas Formation [3289 3235] approximately)

10 Path west of Penarwel House: Matley collection. Zb 4136–4146.
    Climacograptus sp., *Climacograptus* (*Normalograptus*) aff. *mohawkensis*, *Climacograptus* (*Normalograptus*) sp., *Diplograptus* sp. A, *Orthograptus amplexicaulis* group
    (Nod Glas Formation [3289 3245] approximately.)

11 Stream, south slope of Penarwel Dingle: Matley collection. Ze 4744–4746
    Diplograptus sp. A., *Orthograptus* cf. *calcaratus*.
    (Nod Glas Formation [3290 3243] approximately.)

12 22.8 m (25 yards) east of stream: Matley collection. Ze 4741–4743
    Climacograptus (*Normalograptus*) sp.
    (Nod Glas Formation [3292 3242] approximately.)

13 Near greenhouse, Penarwel gardens: Matley collection. Ze 4696–4705
    Climacograptus (*Normalograptus*) sp., *Corynoides* cf. *curtus*
    (Nod Glas Formation [3294 3235] approximately.)

14 Penarwel grounds: Matley collection. Ze 4681–4683
    Indeterminate graptolite fragments
    (Nod Glas Formation [3295 3235] approximately.)

15 Penarwel Drive: Matley collection. Ze 4627–4637, Ze 4673–4680.
    Diplograptids including *Pseudoclimacograptus*? sp.
    (Nod Glas Formation [3313 3237] approximately.)

16 Tremvan Drive: Matley collection. Zb 4126–4135
    Schmidtites? sp., *Climacograptus* (*Normalograptus*) sp.
    (Nod Glas Formation, probably from Penarwel Drive)

17 Topmost level of Nod Glas Formation [3327 3246 and 3330 3246]
    Schmidtites? sp., Plectambonitacean indeterminate. ?small normalograptids.

18 Carreg y Defaid [3405 3265]
    Matley collection. Ze 4638–4657; *Climacograptus antiquus*?, *Diplograptus compactus*, *Orthograptus amplexicaulis* (group) NMW 27.110 G 410, 411, 426, 427, 428 (G J Williams collection.); cf. *Amplexograptus arctus*?, *Dendrograptus* sp., *Diplograptus* sp?

STRATA ABOVE THE OGWEN GROUP

Crugan Mudstone Formation

The Crugan Mudstone Formation comprises over 600 m of brown-grey and green siliceous mudstones with carbonate concretions which may be small but abundant (e.g. at Crugan Lane quarry [33303240]), larger and rarer (e.g. Tan Rallt Quarry [3545 3608]), or sheet-like (e.g. near Gellidara [340 346]). The formation was defined by Price (1981) to formalise the 'Crugan mudstones' of Matley (1938). The contact with the underlying Nod Glas Formation is exposed in a bank above the small stream west of Crugan Farm [3326 3236] and is the basal stratotype for the formation. At least 4 m of weathered grey pyritous concretionary mudstones with abundant small burrows (including *Chondrites*) overlie the dark graptolitic mudstones of the Nod Glas Formation. The formation forms the core of the Llŷn Syncline and its top is not exposed. The outcrop of the Crugan Mudstone Formation corresponds closely with the extent of the Quaternary deposits of the Cors Geirch and the extensive gravel

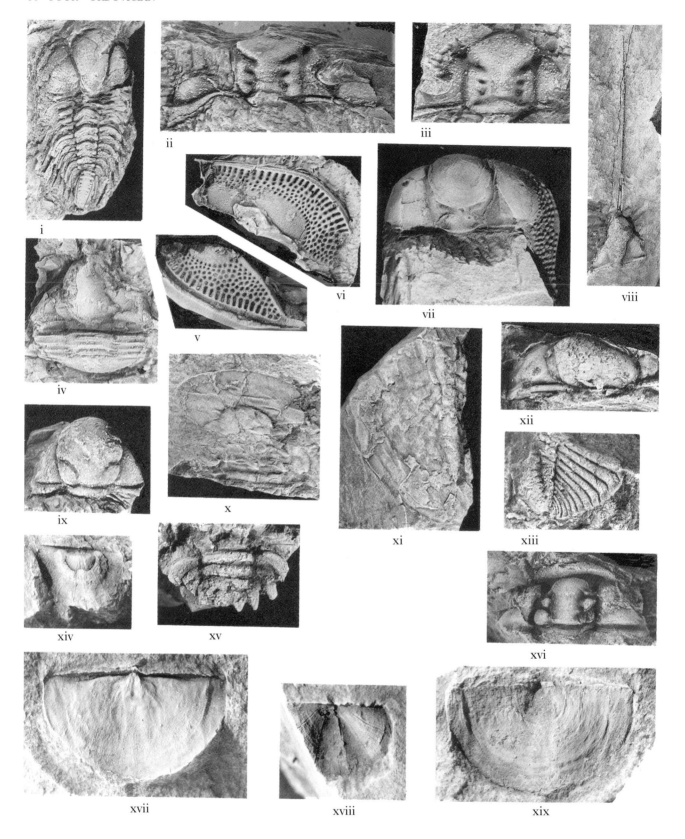

i

ii

iii

iv

v

vi

vii

viii

ix

x

xi

xii

xiii

xiv

xv

xvi

xvii

xviii

xix

terrace deposits between Llanbedrog and Llanor. Consequently, exposure is limited to the lower parts of the formation around the western margin of these Quaternary deposits, to small areas near Rhyd-y-clafdy [329 340], between Bron-y-Berth [337 343] and Gellidara [340 346] and, higher in the formation, at Efailnewydd [354 360] where mudstones in a quarry at Tan Rallt [3545 3608] had been claimed to be of Llanvirn age (Matley, 1938), but have yielded an Ashgill fauna (see below).

The faunas of the Crugan Formation include both trilobites (Price, 1981) and brachiopods (Cocks and Rong, 1988) and suggest rather deep water environments, being referred to the Nankinolithus–Opsimasaphus association (Price, 1981) and Foliomena Fauna (Sheehan, 1973) respectively. Price (1981) attributed an age of Rawtheyan Zone 5 or 6 to the fauna from localities 1 to 3 below, mainly on the basis of the species of *Tretaspis* present. The Crugan Lane quarry [3330 3240], locality 1 below, the lowest fossiliferous locality recorded in the Crugan Mudstone Formation (less than 30 m above the base of the formation) is constrained by *Tretaspis carita* which ranges upwards from the base of the Rawtheyan. Locality 2 yields *Tretaspis hadelandica brachysticus*, restricted to Rawtheyan Zones 5 and 6.

Plate 16 Fauna of the Crugan Mudstone Formation (GS677).

i *Dindymene longicaudata* Kielan. Crugan quarry, NMW.83.19G.376, ×4.

ii, iii *Cybeloides (Paracybeloides) girvanensis* (Reed). Crugan quarry. ii, cranidium, NMW.27.110G.483, ×2.5; iii cranidium, NMW.27.110G.483a, ×4.

iv *Raphiophorus* cf. *tenellus* (Barrande). Crugan quarry, NMW.83.19G.305, ×4.

v–vii *Tretaspis carita* Price. Between Bachellyn and Crugan. Latex casts of cephalic fringe fragments and internal mould of cephalon, all ×2.5. v. BGS Zl.8385; vi, Zl.8383; vii, Zl.8384.

viii *Lonchodomas* cf. *drummockensis* (Reed). Crugan quarry. Cranidium, NMW 27.110G.472, ×2.5.

ix, xv *Pseudosphaeexochus seabornei* Price. Crugan quarry. ix, cranidium, NMW 92.23G.1, ×2; xv, pygidium, NMW 92.23G.2, ×3.

x, xi *Opsimasaphus radiatus* (Salter). Crugan quarry. x, compressed cranidium, NMW 92.23G.3, ×2; xi, pygidium, NMW 92.23G.4, ×3.

xii, xiii *Dionide* cf. *richardsoni* Reed. Crugan quarry. xii, latex cast of incomplete cranidium, NMW 92.23G.5 x2.5; xiii, incomplete pygidium, NMW 92.23G.6, ×4.

xiv, xviii *Leptestiina prantli* (Havlicek), Crugan quarry. xiv, external mould of brachial valve; xviii external mould of conjoined pedicle valve.

xvi *Flexicalymene* sp. Bachellyn Lane. Cranidium, BGS Zb. 4390, ×3.

xvii, xix *Foliomena folium* (Barrande), Crugan quarry. xvii internal mould of pedicle valve; xix, external mould of pedicle valve.

PALAEONTOLOGICAL DETAILS

1 Crugan Lane Quarry [3330 3240]
This quarry exposes cleaved grey mudstones with bands of large discoidal concretions. The exposed sequence is estimated to lie around 26 m above the base of the formation which is exposed in the valley side to the south [3326 3236]. The fauna (Plate 16) includes the brachiopods (after Cocks and Rong, 1988) *Leptestiina prantli*, *Christiania nilssoni*, *Foliomena folium*, *Dedzetina* sp., *Anoptambonites?* sp., *Eostroeodonta* sp. *Leangella* sp., *Zygospira* sp., *Durranella?* sp. and *Orbiculoidea* sp. and the trilobites (after Price, 1981) *Nankinolithus* cf. *granulatus*, *Opsimasaphus radiatus*, *Dindymene longicaudata*, *Gravicalymene* aff. *pontilis*, *Raphiophorus* cf. *tenellus*, *Pseudosphaerexochus seabornei*, *Dionide* cf. *richardsoni*, *Tretaspis carita*, *Lonchodomas* cf. *drummuckensis*, *Arthrorhachis tarda*, *Cybeloides (Paracybeloides) girvanensis*, *Duftonia geniculata*, *Phillipsinella parabola aquilonia*, *Amphitryron radians*, *Panderia* cf. *megalophthalma*, *Cyclopyge* sp., *Encriuroides sexcostatus*, *Liocnemis recurvus*, *?Platylichas glenos*, *Ceraurinella intermedia* and *Microparia?* sp.

2 Berllan Cottage [3248 3365]
Brachiopods after Cocks and Rong (1988) locality 3
Leptestiina prantli, *Foliomena folium*, *Dedzetina* sp., *Cyclospira* sp., *Eopholidostrophia* sp., *Leptaena* sp., *Anisopleurella* sp., *Glyptorthis* sp., *Christiania nilssoni* and *Holtedahlina?* sp.
Trilobites after Price (1981) *Tretaspis hadelandica brachysticus*, *Cybeloides (Paracybeloides) girvanensis*, *Dindymene longicaudata*, *Liocnemis recurvus*, *Opsimasa phus radiatus*, *Panderia* cf. *megalophthalma*, *Phillipsinella parabola aquilonia*, *Raphiophorus* cf. *tenellus* and *Arthrorhachis tarda*

3 'Afon Penrhos' [3345 3250]
Brachiopods after Cocks and Rong (1988) locality 4
Leptestiina prantli, *Foliomena folium*, *Dedzetina* sp., *Christiania nilssoni* and *Leptaena* sp. Trilobites after Price (1981) locality B *Nankinolithus* cf. *granulatus*, *Opsimasaphus radiatus*, *Gravicalymene* aff. *pontilis*, *Raphiophorus* cf. *tenellus*, *Pseudosphaerexochus seabornei*, *Dionide* cf. *richardsoni*, *Lonchodomas* cf. *drummuckensis*, *Arthrorhachis tarda*, *Duftonia geniculata*, *Phillipsinella parabola aquilonia*, *Amphitryron radians*, *Cyclopyge* sp., *Liocnemis recurvus?*, *Platylichas glenos* and *Stenopareia?* sp.

4 155 m from the south end of lane to Bachellyn farm [3313 3256]
Trilobites after Price (1981) locality C
Nankinolithus cf. *granulatus*, *Opsimasaphus radiatus*, *Dindymene longicaudata*, *Gravicalymene* aff. *pontilis*, *Raphiophorus* cf. *tenellus*, *Lonchodomas* cf. *drummuckensis*, *Arthrorhachis tarda*, *Phillipsinella parabola aquilonia*, *Amphitryron radians*, *Cyclopyge* sp. and *Liocnemis recurvus*

5 Tan Rallt quarry, Efailnewydd [3545 3608]
Foliomena folium, *Raphiophorus?* sp. and inarticulate brachiopod indeterminate

6 Coed-y-wern [327 366]
Trilobites after Price (1981)
Cybeloides (Paracybeloides) girvanensis, *Dindymene longicaudata*, *Liocnemis recurvus?*, *Opsimasaphus radiatus*, *Panderia* cf. *megalophthalma*, *Phillipsinella parabola aquilonia*, *Raphiophorus* cf. *tenellus* and *Arthrorhachis tarda*

FIVE

Igneous intrusions

Within the Pwllheli district there is a wide variety of intrusions, most of which are directly associated with the Caradoc volcanism. However, a few basic sills in the western part of the district are considered to belong to an earlier, Llanvirn, phase of magmatism that involved intrusion into unconsolidated wet sediment; these occur in the area west of the Cefnamwlch–Rhiw Fault and extend into the Aberdaron district (Gibbons and McCarroll, 1993). Most of the acid and intermediate high-level intrusions below and within the Caradoc succession are regarded as subvolcanic to the Llanbedrog Volcanic Group. Two suites of these intrusions are particularly prominent. The Carn Fadryn Suite of dacitic to quartz microdioritic intrusions occurs in the area around Carn Fadryn and Nant Saethon. The Nanhoron Suite of steeply dipping peralkaline, commonly riebeckite-bearing, microgranitic intrusions forms a linear feature from Bodlas [282 340] to Foel Gron [301 309]. The large Mynydd Tîr-y-cwmwd Granophyric Microgranite near Llanbedrog [33 31] is notable for the similarity of its chemical composition with that of the rhyolitic tuffs of the Llanbedrog Volcanic Group. Basic igneous intrusions are also represented, both by minor dolerite intrusions and by the major tholeiitic sills of Mynydd Penarfynydd and Carreg-yr-Imbill, intruded near the faults marking the north-west and south-east margins of the Llŷn Syncline respectively, and are probably coeval with the deposition of the Nod Glas Formation.

BASIC INTRUSIONS OF LLANVIRN AGE

Basalt and dolerite sills of Mynydd Rhiw and Sarn

These sills intrude Arenig and lower Llanvirn strata west of the Cefnamwlch–Rhiw Fault (Figure 24) and farther west into the sill complex of the Aberdaron area (Gibbons and McCarroll, 1993). The stratigraphically lowest intrusions and the greatest aggregated thickness occur in the area between Maen Gwenonwy [201 259] and Sarn [23 32]. On the west side of Mynydd Rhiw the lowest dolerite sill intrudes the Wig Bâch Formation of probable Moridunian age. On Mynydd Rhiw, there at least four sills within the Trygarn Formation below the Mynydd Rhiw Rhyolitic Tuff, and at least one further intrusion higher within the Nant Ffrancon Subgroup, above the north-east sector of the later Mynydd Penarfynydd layered intrusion. In Nant-y-Carw, near Sarn [235 323], six sills (including the Sarn Hill Basalt, see below) total over 150 m in thickness, forming 35% of the succession between the base of the Bryncroes Formation and the top of the Trygarn Formation. In the Sarn area, where Moridunian strata are absent, the lowest sill, exposed near Ty Ruttan [231 321], intrudes the Fennian-

age Bryncroes Formation. All higher sills of this suite in the Bryncroes area intrude the early Llanvirn Trygarn Formation.

The sill complex ends in the vicinity of the Ty Mawr Fault, with only a few minor basic intrusions in the Soch valley north of Sarn, as far north as a point south-east of Pen-yr-Orsedd [2450 3500]. The dolerites are fine to medium grained, and heavily altered. They comprise albitised plagioclase laths, locally up to 2 mm long, anhedral clinopyroxene up to 0.5 mm, and secondary chlorite, actinolite, sphene, calcite and quartz. Chlorite, calcite and quartz amygdales up to 1.5 mm in diameter are abundant.

Although these sills crop out close to the Mynydd Penarfynydd Layered Intrusion, together forming the 'Mynydd Rhiw Igneous Complex' of Cattermole (1969) and assumed by previous authors to be related (Cattermole, 1969, 1976; Hawkins, 1970), the interpretation adopted here is that, whereas the dolerite sill complex is of Llanvirn age, the layered intrusion belongs to the Caradoc suite. Many of the sills (but not the layered intrusion) show evidence for intrusion into unconsolidated wet sediment (Gibbons and McCarroll, 1993); margins of sills commonly show convoluted contacts, with fine-grained apophyses and separated blebs. Such features are more common in the intrusions lying at higher stratigraphical levels, such as in Nant Carw [2365 3225] and on the coast near Hen Felin [2386 2806]. A good example of a transgressive sill is exposed to the west of Mynydd Rhiw where it transgresses the sequence to the south-west from Moridunian strata near Maen Gwenonwy [201 259], through Whitlandian at Ogof Lleuddad [190 256], passing up through rocks of probable Fennian age east of Ebolion [190 251], before appearing as a concordant peperitic body on Ynys Gwylan-fawr [184 246] (Gibbons and McCarroll, 1993).

Another example of the high level of this intrusive suite is provided by the spilitic, pillowed and peperitic Sarn Hill Basalt which crops out southwards for 7 km, from north of Sarn [2356 3326] along strike in the Rhiw area. This basalt is typically highly vesicular, with albitised plagioclase laths (up to 0.8 mm) lying within interstitial chlorite, sphene, albite, quartz and iron oxide. At Sarn Hill quarry [2342 3245] the top of the basalt is in contact with a thin veneer (0.05 m) of ooidal ironstone with phosphatic oncoids, and, in the stream to the south [2340 3233], the lower contact of the basalt lies immediately on a similar lithology. The sensitive environmental requirements for the generation of an ooidal ironstone would make continuity of ironstone formation after the emplacement of a basaltic lava flow unlikely, so that the basalt is therefore interpreted as an

Figure 24 Map of the basic sill complex in western Llŷn. The Arenig/Llanvirn complex is intruded by the later Mynydd Penarfynydd layered intrusion, believed to be of Caradoc age.

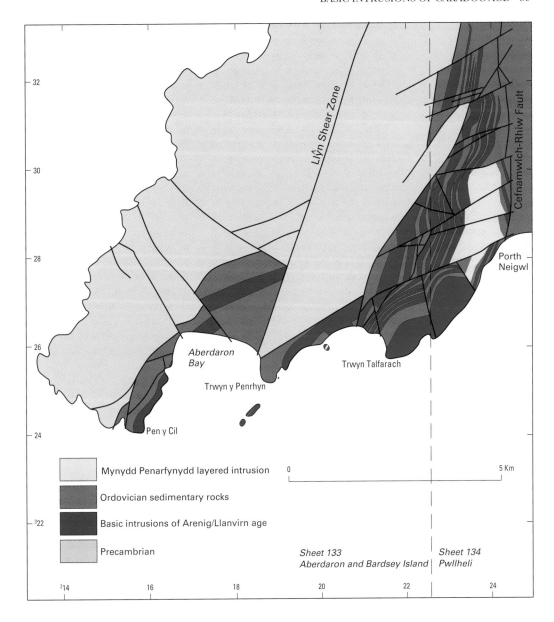

Mynydd Penarfynydd layered intrusion

Ordovician sedimentary rocks

Basic intrusions of Arenig/Llanvirn age

Precambrian

Sheet 133
Aberdaron and Bardsey Island

Sheet 134
Pwllheli

0   5 Km

intrusion into wet sediments at the horizon of the ooidal ironstone. On Mynydd Rhiw, the Sarn Hill Basalt crops out around the western side of the hill. Northwards from north of Conion Uchaf [2262 2882] it is faulted, reappearing [at 2295 2952] to continue for 300 m north-east. The basalt also coincides with the base of the Trygarn Formation, but in boreholes (Brown and Evans, 1989) [2290 2950] the basalt overlies an ooidal ironstone body. In the manganese mining belt (Gibbons and McCarroll, 1993) to the south-west of Mynydd Rhiw, a similar pillowed basalt occurs in the hanging wall of the manganese ore zone, again associated with lithologies indicative of the base of the Trygarn Formation. There is reasonable stratigraphical evidence, therefore, that the Sarn Hill Basalt occurs at a discrete stratigraphical horizon from Sarn to the manganese mining district, and that, like the sill on Ynys Gwylan-fawr, it is an intrusion into unconsolidated wet sediment.

Lower Ordovician intrusive activity was accompanied by volcanicity in both the Arenig (minor volcaniclastic sediments of Fennian and Whitlandian age occur in the Aberdaron area) and, more significantly, in the early Llanvirn. Tuffitic beds are widespread in the early Llanvirn of the Aberdaron area and form an important component of the lower part of the Trygarn Formation of the area from Rhiw to Sarn with exposures on Mynydd Rhiw [2313 2961] and in Nant Carw [2353 3233]. On Mynydd Rhiw, the Mynydd Rhiw Rhyolitic Tuff lies near the top of the Trygarn Formation (Chapter 4).

BASIC INTRUSIONS OF CARADOC AGE

Major basic sills

The **Mynydd Penarfynydd Layered Intrusion** is an easterly dipping transgressive gabbroic sill within

Llanvirn sedimentary rocks (Hawkins, 1970; Figure 25). At Mynydd Penarfynydd it is intruded into the Nant Ffrancon Subgroup, at least 200 m above the top of the Trygarn Formation, but lies entirely within the Trygarn Formation to the north. On Mynydd-y-Craig [23 27] the sill is almost 400 m thick, and this thickness is maintained for 3 km to the north, before terminating abruptly north-west of Tyddyn Corn. On Mynydd-y-Graig, the gabbro typically contains brown intercumulus hornblende, commonly enclosing augitic clinopyroxene, altered plagioclase and up to 10% ore minerals (magnetite, ilmenite, pyrite and pyrrotite). The texture and mineralogy are similar to the type hornblende cumulate gabbros well exposed on Mynydd Penarfynydd [22 26] just beyond the western boundary of the district (Gibbons and McCarroll, 1993), although layering is much less well developed. On Mynydd Rhiw the intrusion is less well exposed, but shows a similar lithology, although the gabbro is commonly more pegmatitic.

The **Carreg-yr-Imbill Dolerite** intrusion forms an extensively quarried rocky headland (Figure 25) that commands the south-eastern entrance to Pwllheli Harbour [3865 3428]. It is seen for 375 m along the north-east-orientated promontory, and over a cross-strike width of 115 m, but neither base nor top of the intrusion is exposed. A faint north-north-west-dipping igneous layering is discernable, and there are both petrographical and geochemical similarities between this intrusion and the Mynydd Penarfynydd Layered Intrusion, suggesting similar and simultaneous emplacement. The south-westernmost exposures of Carreg-yr-Imbill are cut by a prominent south-west-dipping fault [3865 3430] with moderately south-westward-plunging mineral slickenlines that indicate dip-slip movement. The dolerite south-west of this fault is coarse-grained with patches of gabbroic pegmatite (Plate 17). Large poikilitic clinopyroxenes produce a distinctive blotchy texture on weathered surfaces. The main exposure of the intrusion lies north-east of the fault, where the dominant lithology is coarse-grained dolerite with numerous patches of gabbroic pegmatite and a range of ultramafic to leucocratic lithologies. These highly heterogeneous patches, commonly up to a metre across, show lobate, rounded

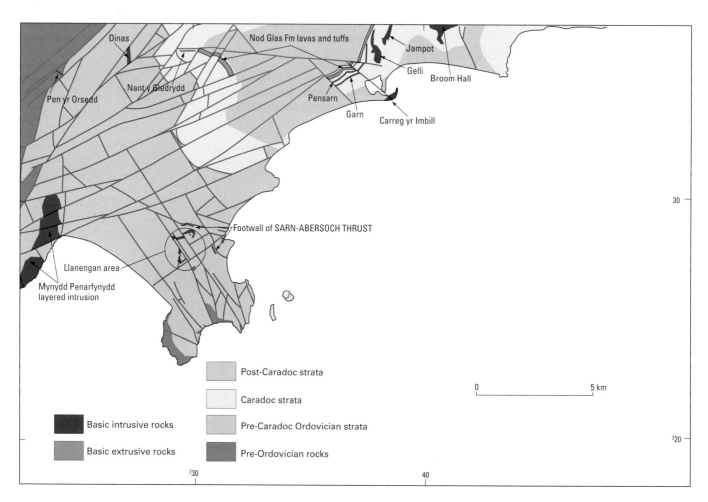

Figure 25 Location of basic intrusions of Caradoc age, and the basaltic volcanism associated with the Nod Glas Formation. The minor intrusions of the Llanengan area, including the Pen-y-gaer Dolerite, may be associated with the earlier, Llanvirn, phase of magmatism.

Plate 17 Gabbroic pegmatite patch within the Carreg-yr-Imbill Dolerite. Typically, the pegmatites show lobate margins and display an irregular pipe-like form within the enclosing dolerite from Carreg-yr-Imbill [3883 3435] (GS660).

margins with some pegmatites displaying pipe-like forms. Some ultramafic and gabbroic patches are faintly layered with olivine-rich zones. The ultramafic lithologies are, petrographically, olivine meladolerites (picrobasalt in chemistry). In addition to the normal augite-plagioclase assemblage, these rocks are rich in small (less than 1 mm) altered olivine crystals, and both phlogopite and secondary actinolite are conspicuous. In contrast, the leucocratic patches are dominated by equant albite crystals with interstitial quartz. Mafic phases are reduced to minor actinolite and magnetite, with abundant small zircons reflecting the high zirconium content of these evolved rocks. The transition from the normal dolerites to these albitites is characterised by dolerites rich in accessory apatite crystals, reflecting the high P_2O_5 revealed by geochemical analysis (Chapter 6) Commonly, the albite-rich segregations are spatially associated with ultramafic areas and are dominated by albite,

with rare vugs containing quartz, pectolite, apophyllite, analcime and prehnite [e.g. 3882 3437] (Chapter 8).

Basic intrusions associated with the basaltic volcanism within the Nod Glas Formation

In the vicinity of Pwllheli, the Nod Glas Formation is intruded by the Pensarn Basaltic Andesite and the Gelli and Garn dolerites (Figures 25, 26). A thin basaltic sheet within the Nod Glas Formation, exposed in the Afon Ddwyryd [3740 3633], may also be intrusive. In the north-western part of the district, in Nant-y-Gledrydd [2956 3652], a basaltic dyke intrudes the Carneddol Rhyolitic Tuff Formation above which the Nod Glas Formation is rich in basaltic tuffs and pillow lavas. This dyke has a similar west-north-west orientation to both the Efailnewydd Fault and to doleritic dykes cutting the granite of the Sarn Complex at Pen-yr-Orsedd [2422 3534], and in the Gwna Melange on the coast near Tudweiliog.

The **Gelli** and **Garn dolerites** crop out north-north-east of Pwllheli, and are petrographically similar amygdaloidal dolerites; locally they are coarse enough to be described as ophitic microgabbros, such as east of Gelli Farm [3773 3611]. Despite the presence of fresh clinopyroxene, the dolerites are altered and contain common secondary chlorite and prehnite. The Gelli Dolerite sill (Figures 25, 26) forms a north–south scarp running for 1.4 km from the north of Yoke House Farm [3780 3700] to the south-east of Gelli Farm [3780 3600] to where it terminates against the Bryn Crin Basaltic Trachyandesite [3873 3583] and the east–west fault and fold belt running west from Plastirion [3870 3582]. The sill is thickest (235 m) east of Gelli Farm but thins markedly 400 m south of Yoke House [3790 3635] to become only 115 m thick at Yoke House Farm. The sill also transgresses up sequence northwards from within the Penmaen Formation to near the top of the Yoke House Formation.

To the west of Pwllheli [3630 3515 to 3707 3547] the Garn Dolerite sill forms a prominent scarp above the Foel Ddu Rhyodacite Formation and has been quarried [3652 3526 and 3665 3532]. A thin dolerite exposed in the Afon Ddwyryd [3746 3636] may be the transgressive north-eastern continuation of this intrusion. The sill is 80 m thick north of the Garn, but , like the Gelli Dolerite, it thins north-eastward as it transgresses up the sequence, from the base of the Yoke House Formation to within the overlying Nod Glas Formation.

The **Pensarn Basaltic Andesite**, a feldspar porphyritic (crystals up to 1 mm across) and highly vesicular sill, lies at the base of the Nod Glas Formation in the area north-west of Pwllheli (Figures 25, 26). It is up to 40 m thick, dips steeply towards the north-north-west, and can be traced for over 700 m along strike from just south of Pont Pensarn [3168 3523] to near Pont Ddwyryd [3670 3559]. The andesite is highly altered with abundant secondary chlorite and calcite (especially infilling vesicles), although the original texture is still well preserved.

The two north-west-striking **Pen-yr-Orsedd dykes,** exposed in a quarry [2421 3535], are up to 9 m wide, and

Figure 26   Efailnewydd Fault and adjacent igneous intrusions.

Many of the intrusive igneous rocks of the Pwllheli area are spatially associated with the Efailnewydd Fault and its branches. This is particularly true of the high level Bryn Crin Basaltic Trachyandesite, which was emplaced with a transgressive portion coincident with the fault during the eruption of the Llanbedrog Volcanic Group. Later, during the magmatism of Nod Glas Formation times, the Gelli and Garn dolerites show an abrupt termination and a change in rate of transgression across the fault respectively. The Pensarn Basaltic Andesite occurs only south of the fault, and the basaltic extrusive activity is centred around the position of the fault.

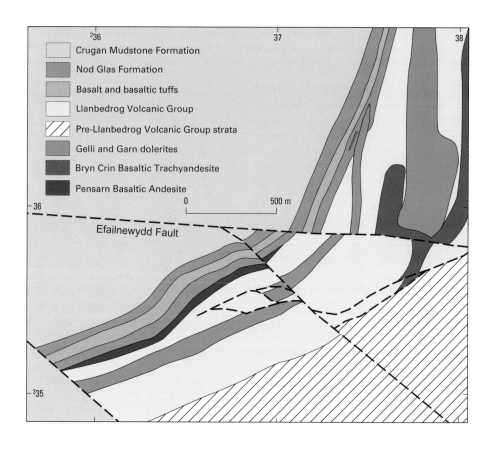

Crugan Mudstone Formation
Nod Glas Formation
Basalt and basaltic tuffs
Llanbedrog Volcanic Group
Pre-Llanbedrog Volcanic Group strata
Gelli and Garn dolerites
Bryn Crin Basaltic Trachyandesite
Pensarn Basaltic Andesite

0   500 m

Efailnewydd Fault

intrude the Sarn Granite (Figure 25). A small north-east-trending offshoot from the more north-easterly dyke occurs at the north-western end of the quarry. Crystals of magnetite and augitic clinopyroxene (up to 2 mm across) show ophitic and subophitic relationships with variably altered plagioclase (up to 2.5 mm across). Clinopyroxene, in places, forms up to 50% of the rock, and olivine is locally abundant (up to 30%); this is an unusual feature for dolerite dykes in the Pwllheli district, and one reminiscent of the olivine-rich rocks near the base of the Mynydd Penarfynydd Sill. Phlogopitic mica forms a minor phase, and apatite is a common accessory mineral. The dykes are locally porphyritic (plagioclase crystals are up to 5 mm across), and strongly altered in most samples to secondary chlorite, sericite, actinolite and calcite.

A minor, amygdaloidal (chlorite-calcite), basalt dyke is exposed on the south side of Nant-y-Gledrydd (Figure 25), from the top of the valley behind the cottages [2956 3652] to the floor of the valley east of the lane [2966 3651]. Although of very limited outcrop, this dyke is significant as it is intruded into the Carneddol Rhyolitic Tuff Formation, suggesting association with the basalts of the overlying Nod Glas Formation. It is the only basic intrusion recorded close to the basaltic volcanics of the Nod Glas Formation in the western area of outcrop. The dyke is aligned parallel to the fault extending eastwards from Nant-y-Gledrydd to Pwllheli, and the basaltic volcanism of the Nod Glas Formation occurs in only two areas (Nant-y-Gledrydd to Bodgadle and north-west of Pwllheli) both of which are near to this fault.

Other basic intrusions

The **Jampot Dolerite** (Figure 25) forms a prominent scarp on which is situated the 'Jampot' folly [3859 3711]. The intrusion transgresses up sequence to the south-west, through the Allt Fawr Rhyolitic Tuff Formation into the overlying Dwyfach Formation, and near its south-western termination a thin upper protrusion further transgresses up into the base of the Penmaen Formation. The main body of the dolerite, where it cuts the Allt Fawr Tuff Formation, is approximately 195 m thick and forms a marked ridge which terminates in a prominent exposure [3845 3680]. The intrusion continues above and to the west as a thinner body (90 m thick) that is equally well featured in the rocky ridge 350 m east of Yoke House [3830 3670]. The chilled, vesicular top of this intrusion is exposed on the west side of this ridge [3823 3665] where it intrudes contact-altered siltstones and cherty tuffites. This second dolerite ridge shows another enlarged southern termination [3825 3655], mimicking that formed below and to the north-east. The pattern of intrusion is repeated once more on a still smaller scale by a minor intrusion that emerges from the upper intrusion. This runs as a thin porphyritic basalt sill exposed at the western end of a quarry [3822 3672] where it is 2 m thick, porphyritic and vesicular; it intrudes grey siltstones interbedded with cherty tuffites. This thin dolerite has fresh ophitic clinopyroxenes and is petrographically distinct from other dolerites in the district in displaying a porphyritic texture with plagioclase phenocrysts (up to 10 mm) which is especially marked within the upper part and along the margins of the intrusion ([3823 3652, 3824 3664].

The **Broom Hall dolerites** are fine to medium grained, grey, altered dolerites that intrude the Pen-y-chain Rhyolitic Complex in the Broom Hall estate (Figure 25). They are exposed on either side of the valley west of Ty'n-lon [4070 3660, 4070 3666], as a series of low, ice-smoothed exposures south-west [4068 3700] and north-west [4074 3750] of Broom Hall, and around Gwinllan Craig [4135 3750] where the dolerites show much textural variation and locally coarsen to ophitic micro-gabbros. In places, such as south-west of Broom Hall, the dolerites are porphyritic, vesicular and show abundant fresh clinopyroxene with green olivine phenocryst pseudomorphs. The extent of these small dolerite exposures suggests that a large part of the unexposed ground east of Abererch may be underlain by basic intrusives.

The **Dinas Dolerite** intrudes siltstones of the Nant Ffrancon Subgroup and is exposed on either side of the valley south-west of Cefn-madryn Farm (Figure 25). On the north side, some 100 m thickness is exposed, as are contact altered near-vertical siltstones close to the western margin [2722 3619]. On the south side of the valley, the dolerite has been extensively quarried [2726 3590], and terminates against a fault. The dolerite has been intensely altered: olivine crystals are pseudomorphed by fine-grained aggregates of green secondary amphiboles, plagioclase is replaced by fine sericite and epidote-group aggregates. In contrast, the clinopyroxene is relatively fresh with large poikilitic crystals (up to 4.5 mm) showing well-preserved ophitic and subophitic texture and small crystals of pale brown mica are also reasonably well preserved.

Minor doleritic sills occur in the footwall of the **Sarn–Abersoch Thrust** (Figure 25), and are exposed in several places (but never more than 20 m below the fault) such as in old quarries near Llangian [2968 2910, 2975 2908], in old workings on the north side of the Soch valley near Abersoch [3092 2930], and farther south near the playing field [3094 2902, 3093 2908]. These sills are all very heavily weathered, and were all intruded at the level of ooidal ironstones and/or debris flow deposits which are exposed at all of these localities.

The **Pen-y-gaer Dolerite** (Figures 25, 55), up to 50 m thick, forms a topographical feature around Pen-y-gaer and the western end of the Soch Gorge at about 70 m above the Hen-dy-capel Ironstone (Young, 1991b). It has been quarried above Bont Newydd [295 282] and north-east of Pen-y-gaer on the eastern limb of the anticline [3003 2842]. Highly altered vesicular dolerite in the adit [2982 2823] intrudes the Hen-dy-capel Ironstone and shows fresh primary clinopyroxene (up to 6 mm across) ophitically enclosing plagioclase, and abundant secondary chlorite, calcite and albite.

Minor intrusions occur elsewhere in the Pen-y-gaer Anticline: below the Hen-dy-capel Ironstone in an adit on Pen-y-gaer, two intrusions within Arenig sedimentary rocks north of Llanengan, and more persistently on the east side of the anticline north-east of Llanengan at about the same stratigraphical horizon as the Pen-y-gaer Dolerite farther north (Figure 55). It is not known whether this group of basaltic intrusions is of Caradoc age or is associated with the Arenig/Llanvirn basic magmatism of the Sarn/Rhiw area.

ACID AND INTERMEDIATE INTRUSIONS OF CARADOC AGE

Carn Fadryn Suite

The Carn Fadryn Suite comprises intermediate intrusions within the Caradoc succession and the underlying Nant Ffrancon Subgroup. They are commonly sill-like, with the notable exception of the discordant, circular outcrop of the Carn Fadryn intrusion. One group of intrusions is chemically similar to the Penmaen Formation (Carn Fadryn Porphyritic Quartz-microdiorite and minor intrusions in Nant Saethon) and a second, more evolved, group chemically resembles the Foel Ddu Rhyodacite Formation (including the Garn Bach Dacite and the Glynllifon Trachydacite). The Garn Bach intrusion, near what is interpreted to be the centre of the caldera, lay at a relatively deep level within the Nant Ffrancon Subgroup, but the Glynllifon Trachydacite farther south-east intruded near the base of the Caradoc succession, before becoming markedly discordant towards the south-east margin of the caldera and cutting up sequence as far as the Foel Ddu Rhyodacite Formation.

The **Carn Fadryn Porphyritic Quartz-Microdiorite Intrusion** (Figure 27) forms a prominent hill [278 352], subcircular in plan and approximately 800 m in diameter, which dominates the topography of the northern part of the Pwllheli district. The contact with host siltstones of the Nant Ffrancon Subgroup is not exposed, and both the northern and south-eastern margins are modified by faults. The quartz-microdiorite contains equant plagioclase (up to 3 mm across) and quartz (up to 0.4 mm) phenocrysts, accessory apatite and zircon in a finer grained, highly altered groundmass with abundant secondary chlorite and calcite. A suite of related microdiorite dykes crop out on Nant Saethon [2941 3411] (where it was designated as an andesite by Matley, 1938), in a roadside quarry [2915 3351] whence it can be traced up the hillside [to 2928 3325] (where it was designated a spilite by Matley, 1938). These dykes are petrographically similar to the nearby Carn Fadryn intrusion. They are mostly porphyritic, with phenocrysts of altered plagioclase (thin crystals up to 4 mm) and smaller quartz (0.4 mm) lying in a fine-grained quartzo-feldspathic groundmass.

The **Garn Bach Dacite** intrusion is well exposed about Garn Bach [285 345] (Figure 27), and similar dacites crop out in the Horon valley to the south-east of Garn Bach [2995 3458] and in several small exposures on the west side of the valley, around Clogwyn [2972 3450] and Nant-y-pwdin [2968 3430]. The dacite is strongly porphyritic, with abundant andesine phenocrysts and glomeroporphyritic plagioclase clots (up to 5 mm), rare microdioritic xenoliths, minor zircon, apatite, and altered mafics that include ore-rimmed amphibole pseudomorphs, and a finely recrystallised, felsitic groundmass that is flow aligned in places.

The **Glynllifon Trachydacite** intrusion is around 350 m thick and crops out in two areas (Figure 27), separated by a thin zone of deformed sedimentary rocks of the Dwyfach Formation seen in the valley at Glynllifon [322 215], and bounded to the south-east by a north-east-trending fault. To the east of the valley the intrusion transgresses from the Dwyfach Formation to the tuffs of the Foel Ddu Rhyodacite Formation, whereas to the west of the Glynllifon area it appears more sill-like and its top lies within the lower part of the Penmaen Formation. The southern margin is obscured by drift and is interpreted to be faulted because the only records of solid geology beneath the drift are of Nant Ffrancon Subgroup (Matley 1938). The overall form of the intrusion is suggestive of intrusion along an east–west normal fault running between Mynytho Common [299 316] and Llanbedrog [330 316], later modified by a fault running south-west from Llanbedrog village towards Mynytho. The most westerly outcrops are at the north-west end of Mynytho Common [2974 3204], giving an observed length to the intrusion of about 3 km, but an unexposed continuation for a farther kilometre towards Nanhoron quarry is likely. The

trachydacite is porphyritic, with sodic andesine phenocrysts, glomeroporphyritic clots and mafic pseudomorphs (all less than 5 mm), and accessory zircon and apatite, lying within a weakly flow-aligned microcrystalline groundmass of plagioclase, alkali feldspar and quartz similar to, but coarser than, that of the Foel Ddu Rhyodacites.

The **Bwlch Groes Porphyritic Microgranite** intrusion crops out on the hill north-west of Bwlch Groes Farm [278 337] (Figure 27). Contact with the country rock (Nant Ffrancon Subgroup) is not exposed, and the outcrop is probably truncated by faults to both north and south. A minor intrusion in Nant Bodlas [2901 3329] is petrographically similar. In the microgranite, euhedral to subhedral quartz, with rounded, resorbed margins and hexagonal basal sections, and altered feldspar phenocrysts are set in a very fine, siliceous, equigranular, recrystallised, spherulitic groundmass.

Nanhoron Suite

The strongly peralkaline intrusions of the Nanhoron Suite comprise three distinct major bodies: the Nanhoron Granophyric Microgranite, the Mynytho Common

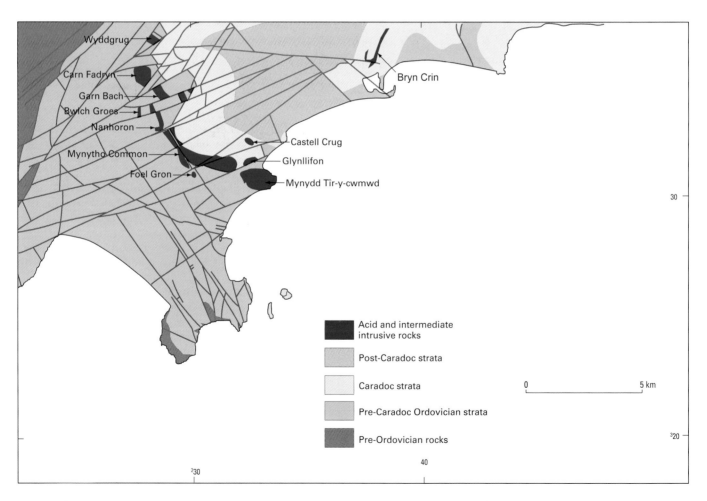

Figure 27   Distribution of acid and intermediate intrusions associated with the Llanbedrog Volcanic Group.

Riebeckite Microgranite and the Foel Gron Granophyric Microgranite. Minor intrusions in Nant Gaseg are probably offshoots of these main bodies. The **Nanhoron Granophyric Microgranite** is exposed in Nanhoron Quarry [287 329] and to the north in a small quarry near Penbodlas [2835 3278]. Contacts with the mudstones of the Nant Ffrancon Subgroup are mainly faulted. The microgranite is nonporphyritic and comprises anhedral quartz (up to 6 mm) and alkali feldspar (up to 1.0 mm), with less common subhedral oligoclase (up to 0.2 mm). A granophyric texture is variably overprinted by secondary alteration. The margin of this intrusion is fine grained, pervasively devitrified, weakly porphyritic (rare quartz, oligoclase and alkali feldspar phenocrysts up to 0.3 mm across), and crowded with spherulites.

The **Mynytho Common Riebeckite Microgranite** is well exposed on Mynytho Common (Figure 27) where its southern edge [2988 3133] is marked by the development of a flow-folded marginal rhyolitic facies. The northernmost exposure of the microgranite is in the quarry by Pont Llidiard-y-dwr [2886 3290] where a brecciated, fine-grained, locally sulphide-rich facies is truncated northwards by a fault. A small quarry in Nant Gaseg [2908 3296] exposes rhyolitic rocks similar to the marginal facies from which Matley (1938) determined riebeckite and is interpreted as a small offshoot from the main intrusion. The typical microgranite comprises an equigranular, locally granophyric, aggregate (0.3 to 1.0 mm) of quartz and feldspar with some spherulitic recrystallisation, rare phenocrysts of perthite (1.2 mm), and accessory zircon. The deeply pleochroic riebeckite occurs mostly as aligned, poikilitic crystals up to 3 mm in length, enclosing small feldspar and quartz and defining a crude fabric in hand specimen. The rhyolitic marginal facies is fine grained (up to 0.03 mm), strongly flow banded, and spherulitic, with rare, aligned perthitic phenocrysts, skeletal aggregates of iron oxide and altered mafic minerals, and brown xenoliths of contact-altered mudstone which show new biotite growth.

The **Foel Gron Granophyric Microgranite** is the southernmost of the peralkaline intrusions [301 310], and is similar to the Nanhoron Microgranite. It is subcircular in plan and intruded into mudstones of the Nant Ffrancon Subgroup (Figure 27). This fine-grained, aplitic, pale microgranite comprises an equigranular groundmass of anhedral quartz (0.4 mm), subhedral oligoclase (0.4 mm), subhedral alkali feldspar laths (up to 1.4 mm), altered biotite, and 1 mm clusters of granophyrically intergrown quartz and alkali feldspar.

Other acidic and intermediate intrusions

The strongly porphyritic **Bryn Crin Basaltic Trachyandesite**, a transgressive sill up to 100 m thick (Figures 26, 27), is well exposed at the type locality of Bryn Crin [3788 3587] and forms a strong feature northwards for some 1.4 km. Similar rocks are exposed to the west, but are separated from the main sill by the Gelli Dolerite. The main part of the sill is intruded into the Penmaen Formation, but higher offshoots, as seen west of Gelli Farm [3763 3614], may have intruded levels as high as the

Carneddol Rhyolitic Tuff Formation. The rock is characterised by abundant euhedral to subhedral, rarely zoned, calcic andesine phenocrysts and glomeroporphyritic clots (up to 7 mm across), augitic clinopyroxene and apatite in a microcrystalline groundmass (Plate 18). The rock is locally amygdaloidal and variously altered to secondary chlorite, titanite, sericite and epidote group minerals.

The **Castell Crûg Porphyritic Microgranite** [325 325] forms a dome-like intrusion through the upper part of the Bodgadle Member of the Carneddol Rhyolitic Tuff Formation (Figure 27), and represents the youngest acidic magmatism identified in the Llanbedrog area. The top of the intrusion, at its contact with the overlying Nod Glas Formation, is covered with a thin conglomerate of microgranite pebbles, and formed a slight topographical feature prior to deposition of the Nod Glas Formation. The pale-weathering, faintly flow-foliated microgranite locally contains more basic, porphyritic enclaves, and small phenocrysts of euhedral to anhedral perthite (up

Plate 18   Glomeroporphyritic cluster of andesine and augitic clinopyroxene within the Bryn Crin Basaltic Trachyandesite, south-east of Yoke House [3813 3652] (GS663). Field of view 5 mm. Crossed polarised light.

to 3 mm) occur with much rarer quartz (0.7 mm) and oligoclase (1 mm) in a felsitic recrystallised patchy mosaic of groundmass plagioclase, quartz, iron oxides, and chloritised mafics.

The pale-weathering and massive **Wyddgrug Porphyritic Microgranite** [285 367], intruded into the Nant Ffrancon Subgroup, is structurally isolated in a highly faulted area within the overturned northern limb of the Llŷn Syncline (Figure 27). It has been extensively quarried immediately north-east of Wyddgrug House [2857 3660]. The microgranite comprises isolated phenocrysts and glomeroporphyritic clusters of oligoclase and perthitic alkali feldspar (up to 3 mm across), with oligoclase mantling alkali feldspar in places, as also seen in the Foel Ddu Rhyodacite Formation. The fine-grained groundmass comprises an equigranular aggregate of quartz and feldspar with accessory zircon.

The **Mynydd Tîr-y-cwmwd Porphyritic Granophyric Microgranite** intrusion forms Llanbedrog Head (Figures 20, 27), and is elliptical in plan (1.5 km × 0.9 km) with major radial and concentric joint sets which are well exposed in the quarries around the southern margin. The joint pattern suggests that the present level of erosion is close to the exhumed top of the intrusion. At one point in the south-west of the intrusion, a small fault allows downward displacement of part of the roof of the intrusion so that baked mudrocks are exposed in contact with the microgranite [3242 3072]. The microgranite is dominated by perthite phenocrysts (up to 4 mm across) with lesser plagioclase (0.7 mm), and minor green biotite. Quartz is abundant in the equigranular, unfoliated groundmass, and abundant granophyric aggregates (Plate 19) commonly nucleate around feldspar phenocrysts.

Plate 19   Granophyric texture typical of the Mynydd Tîr-y-cwmwd Porphyritic Granophyric Microgranite. South side of Mynydd Tîr-y-cwmwd [334 305] (GS680). Field of view: 1.2 mm. Crossed polarised light.

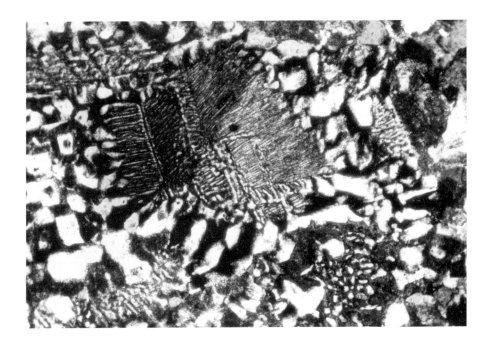

SIX

Igneous geochemistry

Chemical data from some 90 samples of lavas, pyroclastic rocks and related high-level intrusions from the Pwllheli district have been assembled from a database of new analyses, together with previous, published (Tremlett, 1972; Croudace, 1982; Leat and Thorpe 1986) and unpublished investigations. In addition, the following discussion draws upon previously published analyses from the neighbouring parts of the Nefyn and Aberdaron districts. Analyses have been determined by XRF, with rare earth element (REE) concentrations of selected samples determined by ICP and chondrite-normalised according to Nakamura (1974). Analyses are presented in Tables 2 to 19.

The interpretation of these geochemical data recognises the fact that the Lower Palaeozoic rocks of Llŷn have been affected by low-grade regional metamorphism at sub-greenschist facies levels (Roberts, 1981; Bevins and Rowbotham, 1983; see also Chapter 8). This metamorphic overprint involved the breakdown of primary igneous minerals such as olivine, pyroxene, feldspar and Fe–Ti oxide, the growth of metamorphic minerals such as epidote, prehnite and pumpellyite, and the ubiquitous development of a mafic phyllosilicate (chiefly chlorite). It was accompanied by element migration, with some elements, notably the large ion lithophile (LIL) elements Rb, Sr, K and Ba, being more susceptible to migration than relatively immobile minor and trace elements such as Zr, Y, Nb, Ti, P and the REE (Merriman et al., 1986). Interpretations of the igneous geochemistry outlined below are based primarily on data relating to these immobile elements.

MAGMATISM OF LLANVIRN AGE: THE BASIC INTRUSIONS AND ACID TUFF OF MYNYDD RHIW AND SARN

Analyses of the basalts and dolerites of Mynydd Rhiw and Sarn (Table 3) plot in the subalkaline basalt and andesite/basalt fields on the Zr/TiO_2 vs Nb/Y diagram (Winchester and Floyd, 1977; Figure 28a). REE patterns for three samples show relatively flat profiles (Figure 28b); La_N/Yb_N is 1.78 for the Sarn Hill Basalt, with values of 1.88 and 1.73 recorded for the dolerite sill immediately above the Sarn Hill Basalt. These profiles are broadly similar to N-type MORB, indicating a tholeiitic character, but show relative enrichment, suggesting that the rocks are the result of fractionation processes. Ni and Cr contents are high and those of incompatible elements generally low. On a multi-element diagram normalised against MORB (Figure 28c) the generally flat pattern again indicates an affinity with N-type MORB, but a minor subduction zone influence is suggested by, for example, the consistent Th enrichment relative to Nb and Ta.

The Mynydd Rhiw Rhyolitic Tuff Member of the Llanvirn Trygarn Formation of the Rhiw area is represented by two analyses (Table 4), both of which plot in the subalkaline rhyodacite/dacite field of the Zr/TiO_2 v Nb/Y diagram (Figure 28a), with one in the rhyolite and one the trachydacite field (presumably showing alkali-enrichment during alteration) of the TAS diagram (Figure 30). The samples have markedly lower Nb/Y (0.25 to 0.26) values than the Caradoc subalkaline rhyolites of the Pen-y-chain complex (compare Figures 28a and 29).

MAGMATISM OF CARADOC AGE

The wide variety of geochemical characteristics shown by the Caradoc igneous rocks is illustrated by Figure 29 which, for comparison, also shows a field representing the range of extrusive rocks of the Llewelyn and Snowdon Volcanic groups of Caradoc age from Snowdonia (Howells et al., 1991). The Pen-y-chain Rhyolitic Complex is subalkaline, and plots within the field of these analyses from Snowdonia. In contrast, the Llanbedrog Volcanic Group shows minimal compositional overlap with the Llewelyn and Snowdon Volcanic groups and are marginally alkaline. Tholeiitic volcanic rocks of the Nod Glas Formation are also distinctive, plotting only partially within the field occupied by the more mafic rocks of the Snowdon Volcanic Group (Howells et al., 1991).

Despite the effects of later alteration, TAS (Figure 30) and AFM (Figure 31) diagrams document the present composition of the rocks, and provide some evidence for the former major element geochemistry of these rocks. The scatter of data from individual units on the TAS diagram gives an indication of the degree of alkali mobility. The AFM (Figure 31) diagram reveals the early iron-enrichment trend of the major basic intrusions and of the Nod Glas Formation volcanism and the overall tholeiitic signature of the Caradoc magmatism.

Pen-y-chain Rhyolitic Complex, including Pitts Head Tuff Formation

Analysed acid igneous rocks of the Pen-y-chain Rhyolitic Complex are subalkaline (Table 5), with a trace element geochemistry similar to the Pitts Head Tuff in Snowdonia. The subalkaline character of these rhyolites and tuffs with Nb/Y ratios of less than 0.50 (range = 0.26 to 0.49; Figure 32), distinguishes them from all the other acid igneous rocks of the Pwllheli district. Samples of the

Table 3   Analyses of rocks from the Llanvirn basic sills of Mynydd Rhiw and Sarn.

%	Clip area			Mynydd Rhiw area				Sarn area			
	1	2	3	4	5	6	7	8	9	10	11
SiO_2	50.06	53.28	48.61	48.90	51.64	51.89	49.41	49.29	52.49	43.05	43.82
TiO_2	2.92	3.29	2.95	3.25	2.09	1.66	2.79	2.00	2.21	2.59	3.05
Al_2O_3	13.34	13.77	13.39	14.47	14.38	15.10	13.63	15.20	13.95	12.95	16.65
Fe_2O_3	13.65	11.82	13.84	14.15	12.99	10.26	14.42	11.75	11.83	13.21	16.47
MnO	0.24	0.25	0.26	0.35	0.15	0.17	0.21	0.23	0.16	0.37	0.09
MgO	4.77	3.06	3.81	4.02	6.55	6.43	4.86	7.24	6.05	5.55	8.61
CaO	7.17	5.72	8.59	8.65	5.51	8.67	6.36	7.18	5.02	9.80	2.86
Na_2O	4.55	5.20	3.83	2.85	3.25	3.13	3.11	3.18	3.36	2.51	2.69
K_2O	0.02	0.26	0.39	0.29	0.06	0.27	0.44	0.05	0.03	0.02	0.02
P_2O_5	0.51	1.02	0.80	0.99	0.24	0.24	0.36	0.20	0.26	0.29	0.43
ppm											
Ba	27	101	184	152	58	149	141	52	62	81	95
Cr	23	5	18	46	115	151	35	148	91	91	125
Cu	nd	nd	nd	<	15	33	<	43	25	13	12
Ga	nd	nd	nd	17	17	15	16	17	18	15	16
Hf	5.79	5.77	4.79	nd	nd	nd	nd	nd	nd	nd	nd
Nb	7	10	8	6	3	3	4	3	7	4	6
Ni	13	6	11	23	41	45	18	40	38	27	36
Pb	nd	nd	nd	<	<	<	12	<	<	<	<
Rb	<	4	9	12	7	15	13	11	9	9	9
S	nd	nd	nd	587	88	125	1756	163	1098	1110	669
Sr	141	250	345	258	124	255	94	77	138	186	82
Ta	0.39	0.75	0.59	<	<	<	<	<	<	<	<
Th	2.02	1.89	1.51	<	<	<	<	<	<	<	<
U	nd	nd	nd	<	<	<	<	<	<	<	<
V	nd	nd	nd	254	348	267	441	362	351	403	537
Y	54	67	59	56	35	35	43	32	36	33	41
Zn	nd	nd	nd	112	76	86	112	92	97	73	99
Zr	240	222	178	153	114	117	144	103	124	103	118
La	13.43	17.12	15.37	<	<	<	<	<	<	<	<
Ce	32.84	40.22	35.26	<	<	<	<	73	65	<	<
Pr	nd	nd	nd	32	<	<	<	25	<	<	<
Nd	22.20	34.29	26.52	29	<	<	<	<	<	<	<
Sm	6.84	10.18	8.36	nd	nd	nd	nd	nd	nd	nd	nd
Eu	2.54	4.16	3.08	nd	nd	nd	nd	nd	nd	nd	nd
Gd	7.87	12.44	10.43	nd	nd	nd	nd	nd	nd	nd	nd
Tb	1.50	2.33	1.81	nd	nd	nd	nd	nd	nd	nd	nd
Tm	0.92	1.22	0.97	nd	nd	nd	nd	nd	nd	nd	nd
Yb	5.18	6.43	5.47	nd	nd	nd	nd	nd	nd	nd	nd
Lu	0.86	1.04	0.90	nd	nd	nd	nd	nd	nd	nd	nd
Zr/TiO_2	0.008	0.007	0.006	0.005	0.005	0.007	0.005	0.005	0.006	0.004	0.004
Nb/Y	0.13	0.15	0.14	0.11	0.09	0.09	0.09	0.09	0.19	0.12	0.15
La_N/Yb_N	1.73	1.78	1.88	nd	nd	nd	nd	nd	nd	nd	nd

Key to analyses

1   Sarn Hill Basalt, Clip, KB392 [2236 2841] analysis information from R Bevins
2   Sarn Hill Basalt, S of Clip, KB390 [2232 2827], analysis information from R Bevins
3   Sill above Sarn Hill Basalt, S of Clip, KB391 [2238 2835], analysis information from R Bevins
4   Base of first sill above Sarn Hill Basalt, Mynydd Rhiw, A4b [2297 2954], XRF analysis by C Lewis
5   Upper part of first sill above Sarn Hill Basalt, Mynydd Rhiw, A4t [2312 2962], XRF analysis by C Lewis
6   Base of second sill above Sarn Hill Basalt, Mynydd Rhiw, A5b [2314 2962], XRF analysis by C Lewis
7   Third sill above Sarn Hill Basalt, Mynydd Rhiw, A6 [2327 2961], XRF analysis by C Lewis
8   First sill above Sarn Hill Basalt, Nant Carw, Sarn, ANYC4 [2348 3236], XRF analysis by C Lewis
9   Second sill above Sarn Hill Basalt, Nant Carw, Sarn, ANYC5 [2358 3230], XRF analysis by C Lewis
10   Third sill above Sarn Hill Basalt, Nant Carw, Sarn, ANYC6 [2364 3226], XRF analysis by C Lewis
11   Fourth sill above Sarn Hill Basalt, Nant Carw, Sarn, ANYC7 [2366 3224], XRF analysis by C Lewis

nd   not detected
<   less than detection limit
NOTE   Total iron expressed as Fe_2O_3

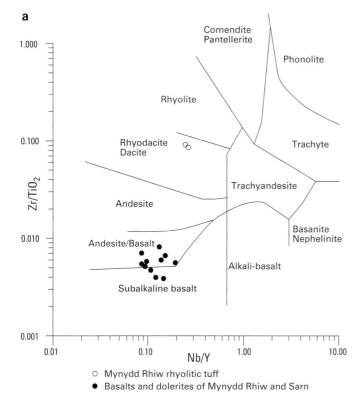

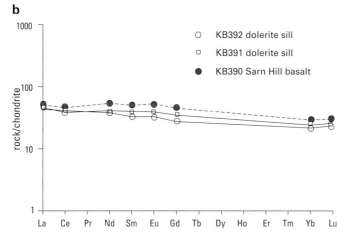

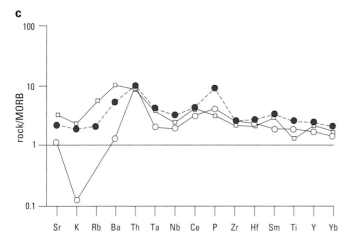

○ Mynydd Rhiw rhyolitic tuff
● Basalts and dolerites of Mynydd Rhiw and Sarn

○ KB392 dolerite sill
□ KB391 dolerite sill
● KB390 Sarn Hill basalt

rhyolites mainly lie within the rhyodacite/dacite field and the Pitts Head Tuff sample within the rhyolite field on the Zr/TiO_2 v Nb/Y diagram (Figure 32). The latter sample, from the rheomorphic tuffs of the Pitts Head Tuff Formation of Porth Fechan [4354 3579], plots with the Lower Outflow and Intracaldera tuffs on the discriminant diagrams (Y v TiO_2 ; Nb v Zr) of Howells et al. (1991, figs. 42,43) as well as within the field of analyses from the Pitts Head Tuff Formation on two discriminant diagrams (Y–Zr–Nb ternary plot; Y v Zr) employed by Orton (1992) for the Pitts Head Tuff Formation of Llwyd Mawr and Snowdonia (Figures 33, 34).

The geochemical similarity of the rhyolites to the tuffs of the Pitts Head Tuff Formation strongly suggests that they are genetically related. Penecontemporaneous rhyolitic intrusions have been recorded elsewhere within the Pitts Head Tuff Formation, particularly within the intracaldera facies around Llwyd Mawr (Roberts, 1967; Howells et al., 1991).

Allt Fawr Rhyolitic Tuff Formation

The Nb/Y ratios of samples (Table 6, columns 3–5) from the Allt Fawr Rhyolitic Tuff Formation are high (range = 0.67 to 1.03), indicating its alkaline nature. The discriminant diagrams of Figures 33 and 34 both indicate that the Allt Fawr Rhyolitic Tuff Formation differs in its trace element geochemistry from the tuffs of the Llanbedrog Volcanic Group (the Allt Fawr Tuff is richer in Zr and Nb than the Carneddol Tuff Formation). They also support the preliminary field correlation of the Allt Fawr Rhyolitic Tuff Formation with the rhyolitic tuffs of Moel Bromiod [41 45], Moelfre [39 44] and Pen-y-Gaer [43 45] in the Llanaelhaearn area of the Nefyn district (Leat and Thorpe unpublished analyses, 1992, Open University).

The problematic facies seen at the base of the Allt Fawr Tuff Formation at Tan-y-graig [3894 3724] (see above, Chapter 4) is unusual, not only in being less evolved, but also in having a high level of Zr (723 ppm) compared with the main body of the Allt Fawr Rhyolitic Tuff. It is broadly similar in chemistry to some trachydacites in the Penmaen Formation, but has a higher Zr content, similar to some samples from the Foel Ddu Rhyodacite Formation, with which it plots on the Zr/TiO_2 vs Nb/Y diagram. There are no obvious close affinities between this rock and any others of the Pwllheli district, but the trace element geochemistry of the tuffs of the Moel Bromiod area, interpreted as a proximal or intracaldera facies of the Allt Fawr Rhyolitic Tuff Formation, provides intermediate compositions between Tan-y-graig and the more usual composition of the Allt Fawr Tuff in

Figure 28 Geochemical features of the Llanvirn magmatism.

a Zr/TiO_2 vs Nb/Y diagram (Winchester and Floyd, 1977).
b Chondrite-normalised REE distribution.
c MORB-normalised multi-element plot (this and subsequent multi-element plots following Pearce, 1983).

Table 4 Analyses of rocks from the Mynydd Rhiw Rhyolitic Tuff.

%	1	2
SiO_2	71.06	68.20
TiO_2	0.51	0.57
Al_2O_3	13.71	15.29
Fe_2O_3	5.77	5.84
MnO	0.10	0.07
MgO	0.90	0.82
CaO	0.42	0.25
Na_2O	3.39	1.90
K_2O	2.75	5.97
P_2O_5	0.07	0.08
ppm		
Ba	906	1220
Cr	34	20
Cu	nd	<
Ga	nd	22
Nb	20	25
Ni	14	20
Pb	nd	10
Rb	68	107
S	nd	540
Sr	166	86
Ta	nd	<
Th	nd	<
U	nd	<
V	42	48
Y	77	101
Zn	nd	66
Zr	nd	519
La	nd	48
Ce	nd	<
Pr	nd	<
Nd	nd	56
Zr/TiO_2	0.085	0.092
Nb/Y	0.26	0.25
La_N/Yb_N	nd	nd

Key to analyses

1 Mynydd Rhiw, float, KB393, XRF analysis by C Lewis

2 Mynydd Rhiw, float, RIG, analysis information from R Bevins

nd not detected

< less than detection limit

NOTE Total iron expressed as Fe_2O_3

average increase in Nb/Y ratio with degree of fractionation. The most basic members of the suite plot in the field of subalkaline basalt, and the most evolved lithologies plot in the comendite/pantellerite field. Compared with similar data for the Snowdon Volcanic Group (Howells et al., 1991, Figure 36) intermediate rocks are more common in the Llanbedrog Volcanic Group, which does not show the marked bimodality seen in the Llewellyn and Snowdon volcanic groups. The volcanostratigraphy of the Llanbedrog Volcanic Group suggests that the magmas evolved from older, more basic forms to younger, rhyolitic ones.

Despite the geochemical coherence of the Llanbedrog Volcanic Group indicated by the plot of Zr/TiO_2 v Nb/Y (Figure 36), more complex relationships are suggested by a plot of Log Nb v Log Zr (Figure 37). Four broad geochemical groups can be identified, three of which plot as discrete linear clusters suggesting that they represent groups of rocks related by similar fractionation processes. A fourth group (Group Ib, see below) does

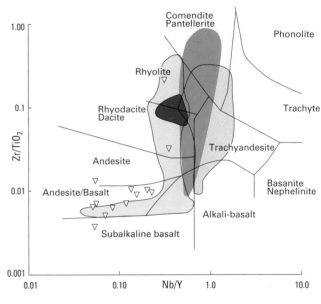

Figure 29 Zr/TiO_2 v Nb/Y diagram (Winchester and Floyd, 1977) showing fields occupied by analysed rocks from the various phases of Ordovician magmatism in the Llŷn and Snowdonia.

the Pwllheli area (Figure 34). The Tan-y-graig rhyodacite is therefore interpreted as an integral part of the Allt Fawr Rhyolitic Tuff Formation.

The Wyddgrug Porphyritic Microgranite (Table 12) is a problematic intrusion which may be geochemically related to either the Upper Lodge Formation or Llanbedrog Volcanic Group (Figures 35, 37, 38, 39). Its high Nb/Y ratio (0.66) suggests possible association with the Upper Lodge Formation, since the major intrusions of northern Llŷn typically have higher Nb/Y ratios than those associated with the Llanbedrog Volcanic Group elsewhere. In view of the uncertainty, however, this intrusion features on diagrams relating to both centres.

Llanbedrog Volcanic Group

The Llanbedrog Volcanic Group and associated intrusions form a geochemically coherent suite of rocks which plot along the alkaline/subalkaline divide of the Zr/TiO_2 v Nb/Y diagram (Figure 36), with a slight

Figure 30 Total alkali-silica (TAS) diagram for the Ordovician igneous rocks of the Pwllheli district.

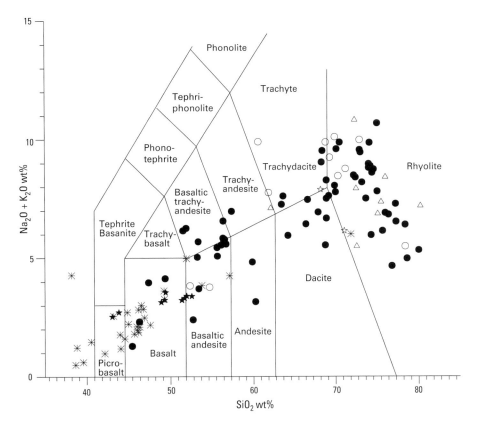

* Major basic intrusions of Caradoc age
★ Llanvirn intrusions
☆ Llanvirn tuffs
● Llanbedrog Volcanic Group and associated intrusions
○ Upper Lodge and Allt Fawr formations and associated intrusions
△ Pen-y-chain Rhyolitic Complex

not represent rocks directly related by simple fractionation, but shows similar ranges of Nb and Zr contents (Figure 37).

These four groups are illustrated by plotting various parameters (Y, Nb, Zr, TiO_2, ΣREE, La_N/Yb_N) against an index of fractionation Zr/TiO_2 (Figure 38) and Zr, TiO_2 and Zr/TiO_2 plotted against SiO_2 (Figure 39). The four groups represent the products of distinct fractionation processes within different compositional ranges.

Group Ia   Samples included in Group Ia include those from the basic intrusions associated with the Llanbedrog Volcanic Group (Dinas and Jampot dolerites; Table 7), the Bryn Crin Basaltic Trachyandesite (Table 9), the Carn Fadryn Quartz Microdiorite (Table 11 columns 1–3) and the more basic parts of the Penmaen Formation (Table 8). With increasing fractionation, these rocks ($Zr/TiO_2 < 0.065$), show increasing Y (from 25 to 80 ppm), Nb (from <10 to 60 ppm), Zr (from 60 to 660 ppm) and ΣREE, accompanied by increasing La_N/Yb_N (Figure 38). A value of $Zr/TiO_2 = 0.065$ (Figure 39) corresponds approximately with a rock containing 62% SiO_2. Using the international classification based on the TAS diagram, and assuming a transitionally alkaline composition,

this is approximately the boundary between trachyandesites and trachydacites. Thus Group Ia rocks vary from basaltic to trachydacitic compositions. REE plots from samples from Group Ia rocks (Figure 40) show an increase in light REEs (LREE) (La_N/Yb_N range 4.13 to 8.03), and the most evolved rocks show a small negative Eu anomaly (Carn Fadryn Quartz Microdiorite, Figure 40).

Group Ib   This group includes the more evolved rocks of the Penmaen Formation, the Foel Ddu Formation and the more evolved intrusions of the Carn Fadryn Suite (including the Garn Bach Dacite and the Glynllifon Trachydacite). It overlaps with Group 1a, and hence the position of the boundary is somewhat arbitrary. Analyses show only slightly increasing values of Y (range = 40 to 80 ppm) and ΣREE, but slightly decreasing contents of Nb (range = 30 to 58 ppm) and Zr (range = 0 to 725 ppm), with increasing Zr/TiO_2 (Figure 38). The increasing Zr/TiO_2 index (from 0.03 to 0.22) is due entirely to systematically and rapidly falling concentrations of TiO_2 (from 1.8 to 0.2%). SiO_2 contents increase from 60% to 74% in this group (Figure 39), and assuming transitional alkaline compositions, this embraces the fields of trachyandesites,

Figure 31 Ordovician magmatic rocks from the Llŷn plotted on an Alkali-Iron-Magnesium (AFM) diagram.

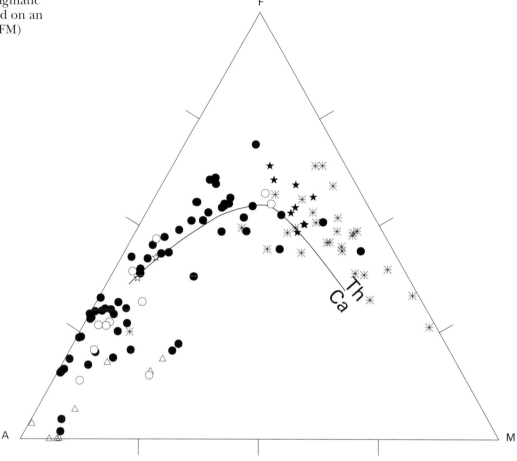

Llanvirn
★ Basic sill
☆ Mynydd Rhiw rhyolitic tuff

Caradoc
△ Pen-y-chain Rhyolitic Complex
○ Upper Lodge and Allt Fawr formations, and associated intrusions
● Llanbedrog Volcanic Group and associated intrusions
✳ Nod Glas Formation volcanism, related intrusions and major basic intrusions

trachydacites and rhyolites (Figure 30). Slight differential changes in Nb and Y causes the Nb/Y ratio to be very slightly lower in the more evolved members of the group. The Log Nb v Log Zr plot (Figure 37) clearly shows Group Ib to include several units of distinct composition, some of which shows evolution subparallel to the trends of Groups Ia and III, but with limited extent. The REE pattern from the Glynllifon Trachydacite (Figure 40) shows a small negative Eu anomaly and a slope similar ($La_N/Yb_N = 13$) to the most evolved rocks in Group 1a.

Group II   Group II includes samples from the Carneddol Rhyolitic Tuff Formation and from the Mynydd Tîr-y-cwmwd Granophyric Microgranite. Although data for this group do not form an extension of trends shown by Groups 1a and 1b, they show overlap in many geochemical characteristics with the more evolved rocks of

Group Ib (Figure 38). This includes the range of Zr/TiO_2 values (from 0.1 to 0.2), as well as the contents of Y, Nb and ΣREE. TiO_2 contents are generally lower than those of Group Ib rocks (range 0.11 to 0.25%; average of 11 samples = 0.17%), whereas silica content is slightly higher, in the range 72 to 78% (Figure 39). Group II rocks are relatively depleted in Zr (around 300 ppm) compared with the more evolved Group Ib rocks (typically approximately 600 ppm), and, because of this samples plot below the general trend of correlation between Zr/TiO_2 and SiO_2 for other groups (Figure 39) REE data for Group II is limited to two samples from the Mynydd Tîr-y-cwmwd Granophyric Microgranite. They have La_N/Yb_N ratios of 7.06 and 7.53, rather less than for the most evolved Group Ib rocks, and are characterised by a large negative Eu anomaly (Figure 40).

Table 5 Analyses of rocks from the Pen-y-chain Rhyolitic Complex.

| | Pen-y-chain rhyolites | | | | | tuff | Broom Hall | |
| | | | | | | | rhyolite | ?tuff |
%	1	2	3	4	5	6	7	8
SiO$_2$	72.57	75.10	76.00	75.50	72.30	80.22	72.50	62.10
TiO$_2$	0.32	0.26	0.24	0.22	0.27	0.26	0.35	0.12
Al$_2$O$_3$	10.59	16.06	10.36	10.24	11.81	10.57	11.73	10.41
Fe$_2$O$_3$	1.49	2.35	<	0.66	<	0.30	0.01	1.94
MnO	nd	nd	nd	nd	nd	<	nd	nd
MgO	1.66	2.34	0.70	0.70	0.70	0.05	0.70	0.92
CaO	<	<	<	<	<	0.05	<	<
Na$_2$O	0.30	2.42	3.11	0.30	0.30	2.00	0.30	0.90
K$_2$O	5.19	4.44	5.30	7.06	10.51	5.19	7.62	6.20
P$_2$O$_5$	nd	nd	nd	nd	nd	0.03	nd	nd
ppm								
Ba	nd	nd	nd	nd	nd	647	nd	nd
Cr	nd	nd	nd	nd	nd	<	nd	nd
Cs	nd	nd	nd	nd	nd	<	nd	nd
Cu	5	5	3	6	8	22	5	7
Ga	nd	nd	nd	nd	nd	14	nd	nd
Nb	21	24	19	17	20	27	20	27
Ni	nd	nd	nd	nd	nd	9	nd	nd
Pb	17	19	16	12	10	15	7	32
Rb	154	169	143	196	184	102	135	158
S	nd	nd	nd	nd	nd	<	nd	nd
Sr	33	64	33	32	35	66	40	30
Ta	nd	nd	nd	nd	nd	10	nd	nd
Th	16	17	14	12	12	16	13	20
U	3	<	6	6	<	<	4	6
V	nd	nd	nd	nd	nd	15	nd	nd
Y	43	61	72	35	44	57	47	58
Zn	18	nd	20	22	12	15	23	43
Zr	225	228	209	184	199	298	251	161
La	nd	nd	nd	nd	nd	58	nd	nd
Ce	nd	nd	nd	nd	nd	<	nd	nd
Pr	nd	nd	nd	nd	nd	<	nd	nd
Nd	nd	nd	nd	nd	nd	35	nd	nd
Zr/TiO$_2$	0.070	0.088	0.087	0.084	0.074	0.114	0.072	0.134
Nb/Y	0.49	0.39	0.26	0.49	0.45	0.47	0.43	0.47
La$_N$/Yb$_N$	nd	nd	nd	nd	nd	nd	nd	nd

Key to analyses:

1   PC1, flow foliated rhyolite, Leat and Thorpe (1986)
2   PC2, grey felsite, Leat and Thorpe (1986)
3   PC3, Leat and Thorpe (1986)
4   PC4, Leat and Thorpe (1986)
5   PC5, Leat and Thorpe (1986)
6   P110, rhyolitic tuff, Porth Fechan [4352 3577], analyst C Lewis
7   PW3, ?rhyolitic lava in Broom Hall complex
8   PW5, ?andesite in Broom Hall complex
nd   not detected
<   less than detection limit

NOTE: Total iron expressed as Fe$_2$O$_3$

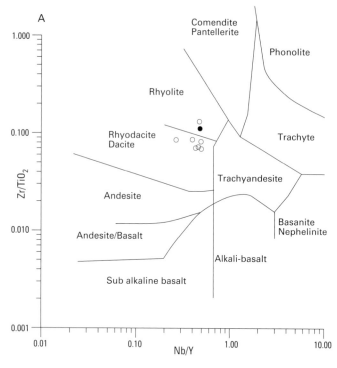

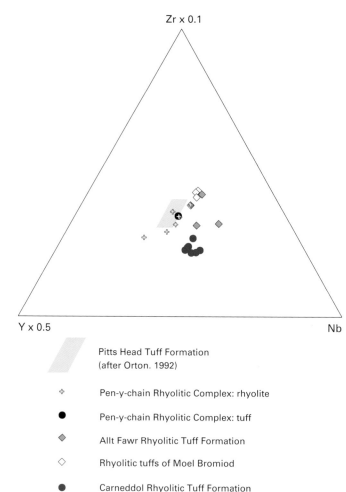

○ Pen-y-chain Rhyolitic Complex: Rhyolites
● Pen-y-chain Rhyolitic Complex: Pitts Head Tuff Formation

Figure 32 Zr/TiO_2 v Nb/Y diagram (Winchester and Floyd, 1977) for analysed rocks from the Pen-y-chain Rhyolitic Complex.

Pitts Head Tuff Formation
(after Orton. 1992)

✤ Pen-y-chain Rhyolitic Complex: rhyolite

● Pen-y-chain Rhyolitic Complex: tuff

◆ Allt Fawr Rhyolitic Tuff Formation

◇ Rhyolitic tuffs of Moel Bromiod

● Carneddol Rhyolitic Tuff Formation

Figure 33 Y–Zr–Nb ternary diagram (Orton, 1992) showing discrimination of Pen-y-chain Rhyolitic Complex, Allt Fawr Rhyolitic Tuff Formation and Carneddol Rhyolitic Tuff Formation.

Group III   Group III is represented by the Nanhoron Suite of acid intrusions and are the most evolved rocks in the Pwllheli district. Y, Nb, Zr, and ΣREE are all greatly increased from the more evolved rocks of groups Ib and II (Figure 38), while SiO_2 contents lie between 74 and 80% (Figure 39). These rocks are peralkaline and have Zr contents up to 1524 ppm, Nb to 151 ppm, Y to 222 ppm and La_N/Yb_N ratios up to 12.28. However, a sample from the less evolved part of the suite, the Nanhoron Microgranite has a La_N/Yb_N ratio of only 5.63 — less than the values from some samples from groups Ib and II. Zr/TiO_2 values range from 0.3 to 0.8, and the TiO_2 contents are between 0.13 and 0.26% (average of 10 samples = 0.22%), a little higher than for Group II. REE plots of Group III rocks have La_N/Yb_N values ranging from 5.63 to 12.28; they show a large negative Eu anomaly, and a progressive development of a negative Ce anomaly in the more evolved samples (Figure 40).

These four groups appear to form a discontinuous series, with compositional discontinuities largely related to the behaviour of Zr in the rhyolitic rocks. Leat and Thorpe (1986) proposed that there were two unrelated magmas involved in the generation of what is now the Llanbedrog Volcanic Group. One evolved to produce intermediate lavas (now the Penmaen Formation, mainly Group Ia)

together with 'high-Zr, originally peralkaline, trachytes and rhyolites' (now the Foel Ddu Formation and Nanhoron Suite, Groups Ib and III), whereas the other gave rise to a 'low-Zr, originally high-K, subalkalic group of rhyolites' (now the Carneddol Formation and Pen-y-chain Rhyolitic Complex). Whilst the present study supports the distinction of the Pen-ychain rocks as the product of a distinct subalkaline magma, the Carneddol Formation (Group II) has the same Nb/Y ratio as groups Ia, Ib and III, and is transitionally alkaline. Instead of a continuous fractionation series relating the most basic rocks of Group Ia to the most evolved of Group III, as envisaged by Leat and Thorpe (1986), the present dataset indicates evolution through Groups Ia and Ib to compositions approaching that of Group II (Figures 37, 38, 39).

The relationship of Group II to other rocks of the Pwllheli area is problematical. The group has high Nb/Y ratios (mean = 0.60), close to the subalkaline/alkaline boundary, similar to rocks of Group I. The REE pattern of

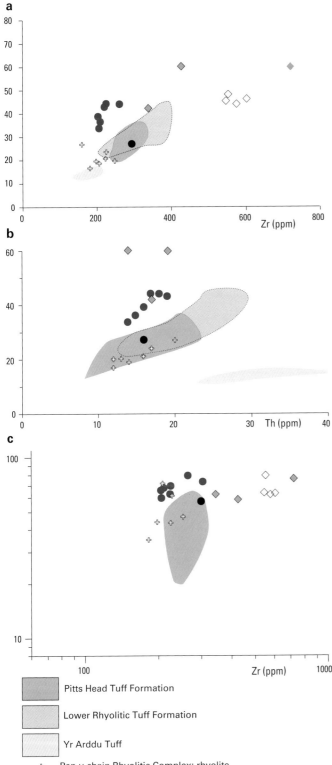

Pitts Head Tuff Formation

Lower Rhyolitic Tuff Formation

Yr Arddu Tuff

⊕ Pen-y-chain Rhyolitic Complex: rhyolite

● Pen-y-chain Rhyolitic Complex: tuff

◆ Allt Fawr Rhyolitic Tuff Formation

◇ Rhyolitic tuffs of Moel Bromiod

● Carneddol Rhyolitic Tuff Formation

the Mynydd Tîr-y-cwmwd intrusion is also similar to rocks of Group Ib, with a La_N/Yb_N ratio of 7.07, and a marked negative Eu anomaly possibly relating to the extensive removal of feldspars during crystal fractionation. It seems possible, therefore, that Group II rocks have been derived from the same magma source as the transitionally alkaline suite of Group Ib, but have been subject to the preferential removal of Zr, possibly by fractionation of zircon.

In summary, the Llanbedrog volcanic centre erupted and intruded more evolved rocks through time. These initially formed a continuous series of compositions, but then further evolved into Zr-poor rhyolitic magma, emplaced as the Mynydd Tîr-y-cwmwd intrusion and erupted as the Carneddol Rhyolitic Tuff Formation, and a Zr-enriched peralkaline magma, intruded as the Nanhoron Suite of intrusions.

DETAILS

Basic intrusions associated with the Llanbedrog Volcanic Group

The Jampot and Dinas dolerites have higher La_N/Yb_N ratios (> 4.0; Figure 40; Table 7) than the tholeiitic basic rocks of the Nod Glas Formation (Table 15). The analyses plot well away from the Nod Glas Formation field on the Zr/TiO_2 vs Nb/Y diagram (compare Figures 36 and 41), falling within Group Ia, towards the mafic end of the alkalic suite. It is probable that these rocks represent the more mafic component of the alkaline–peralkaline suite, although the Nb/Y ratios appear slightly lower, and the compositional gap between the samples and the most mafic analyses from the Penmaen Formation makes correlation difficult.

The Dinas Dolerite has relatively high Ni, Cr and V contents, and low contents of incompatible elements. A REE profile (Figure 40) shows a relatively steep slope of LREE enrichment (La_N/Yb_N = 4.13) compared with those for the basic rocks associated with the tholeiitic volcanism within the Nod Glas Formation (Figure 41; 1.56 < La_N/Yb_N < 2.84), and is more like those for the transitionally alkaline suite. The origin of the marked positive Ce anomaly is uncertain, possibly being related to selective enrichment during alteration.

The Jampot Dolerite, like the Dinas Dolerite, has Group Ia geochemical characteristics, with relatively high Ni, Cr and V and low concentrations of the incompatible elements. Concentrations of Nb are relatively high compared to tholeiitic rocks associated with the volcanism within the Nod Glas Formation, and accordingly Nb/Y ratios are high (see the Zr/TiO_2 vs Nb/Yb diagram Figure 36). The dolerite also shows a relatively steep LREE enrichment (Figure 40), with a La_N/Yb_N ratio of 4.91.

Penmaen Formation

The various components of this formation (Table 8) show a transitional range of compositions from subalkaline basalt

Figure 34 Discriminant binary diagrams comparing Pen-y-chain Rhyolitic Complex with Pitts Head Tuff Formation of Snowdonia. Analyses of Allt Fawr Rhyolitic Tuff Formation and Carneddol Rhyolitic Tuff Formation also shown.

a Nb v Zr
b Y v Nb
c Y v Zr

Table 6 Analyses of rocks from the Upper Lodge and Allt Fawr formations.

	Upper Lodge basaltic trachyandesites		Allt Fawr Rhyolitic Tuff Formation		
%	1	2	3	4	5
SiO_2	52.29	54.66	61.83	71.20	70.32
TiO_2	2.71	2.77	0.67	0.31	0.33
Al_2O_3	14.31	13.72	17.76	14.46	15.42
Fe_2O_3	2.97	3.05	8.43	5.38	3.56
FeO	7.92	8.15	nd	nd	nd
MnO	0.17	0.19	0.11	nd	0.07
MgO	4.79	4.25	0.84	1.45	0.38
CaO	7.77	4.99	0.16	<	0.08
Na_2O	2.93	2.71	6.95	3.64	3.17
K_2O	0.90	1.06	0.80	5.12	5.29
P_2O_5	0.42	0.44	0.13	nd	0.05
ppm					
Ba	441	758	267	nd	695
Cr	45	40	<	nd	<
Cu	16	16	<	6	9
Ga	nd	nd	25	nd	27
Nb 24	29	60	42	60	
Ni	15	8	10	nd	10
Pb	11	16	25	25	12
Rb	21	20	21	114	142
S	nd	nd	<	nd	62
Sr	658	583	101	75	117
Th	<	4	14	17	19
U	<	3	<	5	<
V	nd	nd	<	nd	13
Y	34	41	76	63	58
Zn	84	101	185	87	137
Zr	289	371	723	342	425
La	nd	nd	92	nd	79
Ce	nd	nd	102	nd	163
Pr	nd	nd	<	nd	28
Nd nd	nd	94	nd	79	
Zr/TiO_2	0.011	0.013	0.108	0.110	0.129
Nb/Y	0.71	0.71	0.79	0.67	1.03
La_N/Yb_N	nd	nd	nd	nd	nd

Key to analyses

1 Leat and Thorpe (1986), LL142
2 Leat and Thorpe (1986), LL143
3 Allt Fawr Rhyolitic Tuff Formation, basal trachydacite facies, Tan-y-graig, sample P92 [3896 3728], analyst C Lewis
4 Allt Fawr Rhyolitic Tuff Formation, Leat and Thorpe (1986), PW2 [385 357]
5 Allt Fawr Rhyolitic Tuff Formation, Pont-y-Garreg-fechan, [3632 3478], analyst C Lewis
nd not detected
< less than detection limit

NOTE: Total iron expressed as Fe_2O_3 unless otherwise stated

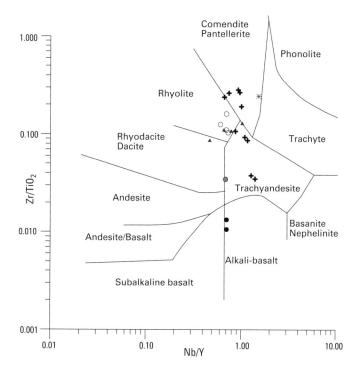

Pwllheli district

▲ Allt Fawr Rhyolitic Tuff Formation
✳ Wyddgrug Porphyritic Microgranite

Nefyn district

● Basaltic trachyandesites of Upper Lodge Formation
○ Tuffs of Moel Bromiod (=Allt Fawr Rhyolitic Tuff Formation?)
◉ Moelfre trachyandesite
✚ Major intrusions of northern Llŷn

Figure 35 Zr/TiO_2 v Nb/Y diagram (Winchester and Floyd, 1977) for analyses from the Upper Lodge and Allt Fawr formations and associated intrusions.

through andesite to trachyandesite (Zr/TiO_2 vs Nb/Y: Figure 36). Most analyses fall into Group Ia as defined above, but the most evolved are in Group Ib (Figures 37, 38).

The most basic sample of this formation (Table 8 column 1) is from near Penmaen House and plots just inside the subalkaline basalt field (Nb/Y = 0.57) on the Zr/TiO_2 vs Nb/Y diagram (Figure 36), and in the basaltic trachyandesite field on the TAS diagram (Figure 30). Basaltic trachyandesitic tuffs from near Ffridd (Table 8 column 3) are similarly slightly subalkaline on the Zr/TiO_2 vs Nb/Y diagram (Figure 36), plotting in the andesite field (Nb/Y = 0.53). Nonetheless, they also lie on the main trend of the Group Ia rocks on the log Nb vs Log Zr plot (Figure 37).

The basaltic trachyandesite of Mynydd Meillian (Table 8, columns 2, 4) falls within the trachyandesite field on the Zr/TiO_2 vs Nb/Y diagram (the Nb/Y ratio averages 0.77; Figure 37). On the log Zr vs log Nb plot (Figure 37) it can be seen to belong to the more evolved part of Group 1b. Concentrations of most incompatible elements, including Zr, Y, Nb and P, are high.

Analyses from the trachydacites of the Penmaen Formation from Foel Fawr (Table 8, columns 5, 7) indicate affinity with

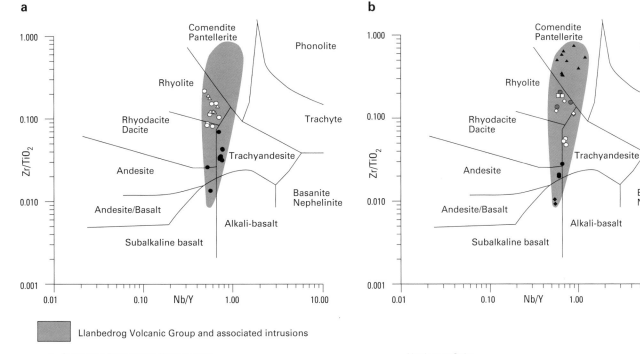

Figure 36 Zr/TiO$_2$ v Nb/Y diagrams (Winchester and Floyd, 1977).

a Llanbedrog Volcanic Group.
b from associated intrusions.
c data for northern Llŷn from Croudace (1982).

Group Ib. They plot in the trachyandesite field of the Zr/TiO$_2$ vs Nb/Y diagram (Figure 37) and within the field of Group Ib analyses on the log Nb vs log Zr diagram (Figure 36). The REE pattern of one sample (Figure 40; Table 8 column 5) shows a shallower profile (La$_N$/Yb$_N$ = 4.85) than other analysed samples of similar composition. This sample also shows lower Zr, Y, and Nb contents than the more evolved members of Group Ia (Figures 38, 39).

Bryn Crin Basaltic Trachyandesite

The Bryn Crin Basaltic Trachyandesite belongs to Group Ia (Table 9), having an average Nb/Y ratio of 0.62 for the three samples. Analyses plot in the lower part of the trachyandesite and andesite fields of the Zr/TiO$_2$ vs Nb/Y diagram (Figure 36). The REE data shows a steep LREE enrichment profile (Figure 40), with La$_N$/Yb$_N$ = 6.65. The characteristics of this intrusion are very close to those of the more basic members of the Penmaen Formation.

Foel Ddu Rhyodacite Formation

The rocks of this formation straddle the subalkaline/alkaline boundary on the Zr/TiO$_2$ vs Nb/Y diagram (Figure 36),

plotting in the rhyodacite/dacite and rhyolite fields. Most of the analyses (Table 10) have Nb/Y < 0.6, and reflect the relative depletion of Nb with respect to Y in the more evolved rocks of Group Ib (Figure 38).

Carn Fadryn Suite

The Carn Fadryn Suite includes the Carn Fadryn Quartz Microdiorite, a related minor intrusion in Nant Saethon, the Garn Bach Dacite and the Glynllifon Trachydacite (Table 11). The suite therefore includes the intrusive components of a wide range of the transitionally alkaline series, from trachyandesitic to rhyolitic composition according to the Zr/TiO$_2$ vs Nb/Y diagram (Figure 36). The Carn Fadryn and Nant Saethon Intrusions are similar in composition to parts of the Penmaen Formation, while the Garn Bach and Glynllifon intrusions are similar to the Foel Ddu Formation.

The two analyses from Carn Fadryn plot in the trachyandesite field of the Zr/TiO$_2$ vs Nb/Y diagram (mean Nb/Y = 0.69). The samples show high Zr, Nb and Y, and are among the most evolved rocks in Group 1a (Figures 37, 38, 39). A REE profile (Figure 40) shows LREE enrichment (La$_N$/Yb$_N$ = 8.03) very similar to the much more evolved Glynllifon Trachydacite. An analysis of the minor intrusion in Nant Saethon indicates a

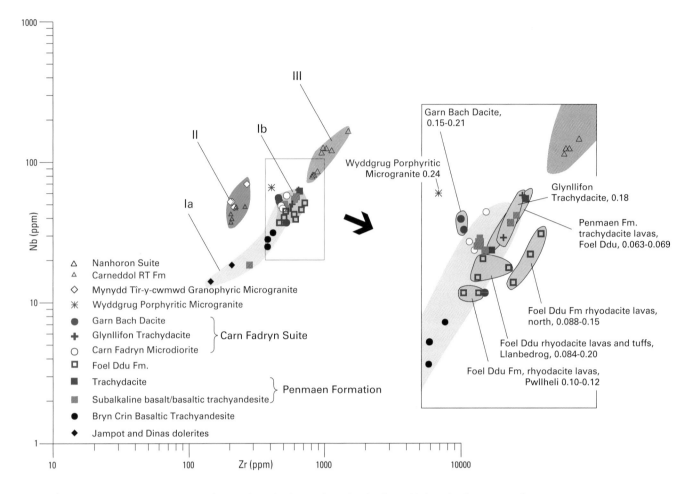

Figure 37   Log Nb v Log Zr for analyses of rocks from the Llanbedrog Volcanic Group and associated intrusions. The inset diagram shows the details of the various trachydacite and rhyodacite units, which exhibit parallel trends. These units are also distinguished by their Zr/TiO_2 ratios, quoted after unit label, a differentiation index, which indicates that a simple single evolving magma cannot have been responsible for the variation observed.

Group Ia association. It plots in the trachyandesite field on Figure 36, with a Nb/Y ratio of 0.73 typical of alkaline rocks, and contains low concentrations of MgO, Ni and Cr and high concentrations of Zr, Nb and Y. On the Nb vs Zr diagram (Figure 37), the Zr versus element and SiO_2 versus element variation diagrams (Figures 38, 39) and on the Zr/TiO_2 vs Nb/Y diagram (Figure 38) the analysis plots very close to those from the Carn Fadryn Intrusions, with which it is spatially associated.

The Garn Bach Dacite has high Zr, Nb and Y contents and plots in the rhyolite field of the Zr/TiO_2 vs Nb/Y diagram (Figure 36). Samples from Garn Bach (Leat and Thorpe, 1986, sample CBACH), from north of Clogwyn (Leat and Thorpe, 1986, NB1) and from Clogwyn (Leat and Thorpe, 1986, NB2) are very similar, and have Nb/Y ratios of 0.82, 0.58 and 0.62 respectively. They have much higher Zr/TiO_2 ratios (range = 0.16–0.21) than the Carn Fadryn Quartz Microdiorite (0.05).

Analyses of the Glynllifon trachydacite plot in the rhyolite field of the Zr/TiO_2 vs Nb/Y diagram (Figure 36) and belong to Group Ib (average Nb/Y = 0.63). The REE profile shows a steep slope of REE enrichment (La_N/Yb_N = 8.14) with a moderate negative Eu anomaly, and is very similar to the REE profile for the Carn Fadryn Quartz Microdiorite. The Garn

Bach Dacite is very similar in composition to the Glynllifon Trachydacite, so the two intrusions may be closely related. They both share a similar physical form, being apparently sill-like bodies transgressing up the section from north to south.

Wyddgrug Porphyritic Microgranite

The Wyddgrug Porphyritic Microgranite is geochemically intermediate between Groups II and III (Figure 37; Table 12). A

Figure 38   Variation of 'immobile' elements Y, Nb, Zr and of chondrite-normalised La_N/Yb_N, ΣREE and TiO_2 against Zr/TiO_2, a differentiation index, for analyses of rocks from the Llanbedrog Volcanic Group and - associated intrusions.
See Figure 37 for key to individual symbols.
Grey shading indicates field of Group II rocks.
Vertical line indicates division between groups Ia and Ib (see text).

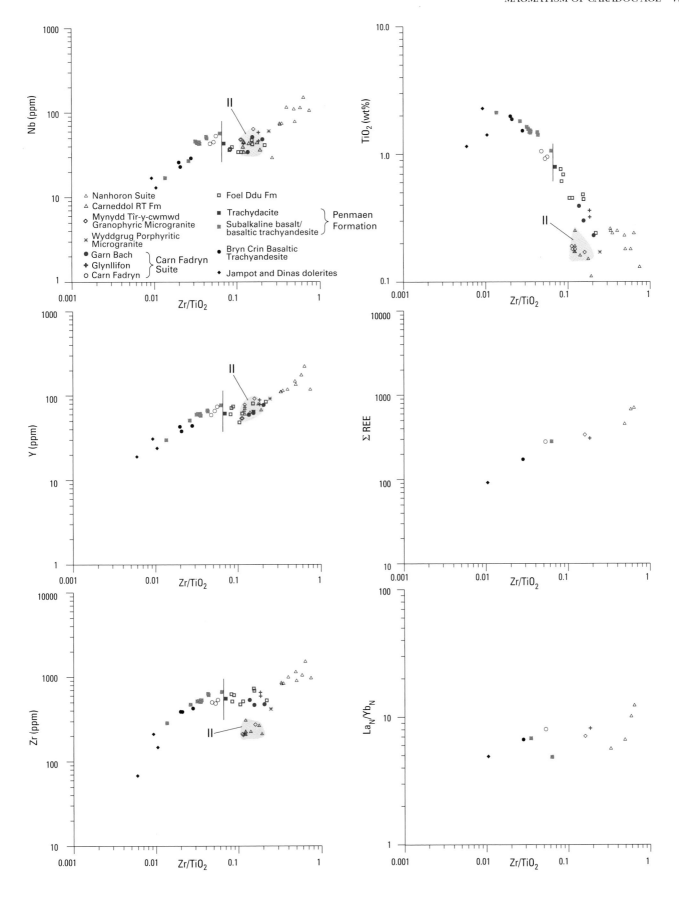

high Nb/Y ratio identifies this as an alkaline intrusion, but the contents of Zr and Ti are lower than for Group III rocks of similar silica content, and higher than for Group II. Nb and Y are present in larger amounts than is typical for the Group Ib and II rocks, although almost in comparable amounts to some analyses from Group III rocks. The significance of this intrusion is uncertain. It may represent one of the most evolved Group Ib rocks, but may equally belong to the earlier magmatism associated with the Upper Lodge Formation.

Carneddol Rhyolitic Tuff Formation

The Carneddol Rhyolitic Tuff Formation samples fall into Group II. They have Nb/Y ratios close to those of the Group I suite, but differ in having much lower Zr contents. The concentrations (Table 13) of the immobile elements Zr, Th, Nb and Y (Figures 33, 34) clearly distinguish the Carneddol tuffs from the other rhyolitic tuffs of the Pwllheli district. The Carneddol Formation has higher Nb/Zr and Y/Zr ratios than the Penychain and Allt Fawr tuffs and Nb/Y and Nb/Th ratios intermediate between them. The Nb/Y ratio (mean 0.60) is close to the subalkaline/alkaline boundary on the Zr/TiO_2 vs Nb/Y diagram, and it is possible that these rocks may be related to the transitionally alkaline suite by fractionation involving removal of Zr.

Mynydd Tir-y-cwmwd Granophyric Microgranite

This low-Zr microgranite belongs to Group II (Table 14). Although it plots close to the Carneddol Rhyolitic Tuff Formation on a log Nb vs log Zr diagram (Figure 37), the Nb/Y ratio is much higher (mean 0.74). Despite this difference, the Carneddol Tuff Formation and the Mynydd Tîr-y-cwmwd intrusion have overlapping fields on a plot of Y v Zr and closely related fields on plots of Nb v Th and Y v Zr. Taken overall, the trace element concentrations support a relationship between the two units. The REE profile shows a steep slope of LREE enrichment (La_N/Yb_N = 7.07 to 7.53), and a marked Eu anomaly (Figure 41). It is suggested that the intrusion is related to the transitionally alkaline suite, with Zr having been depleted by zircon fractionation (Plate 19).

Nanhoron Suite

This suite of strongly peralkaline intrusions forms a discontinuous series of steeply inclined bodies trending north-north-west, west of the Llŷn Syncline. These rocks have an average Nb/Y ratio of 0.73 and represent the most evolved members of the Llanbedrog Volcanic Group (Figure 36; Table 15), with samples plotting in the comendite/pantellerite field. They have very high concentrations of the incompatible elements, Y, Zr, Th and Nb and the REE, very low P_2O_5 contents, and plot in the most evolved portion of the log Zr vs log Nb diagram (Figure 37). The REE data show steep profiles of LREE enrichment (Figure 40; La_N/Yb_N = 5.63 and 6.61 from Nanhoron; 10.10 from Mynytho Common and 12.28 from Foel Gron). The steepening of the profiles may be due to zircon removal, which would preferentially deplete the HREE. The REE profiles show marked negative Eu anomalies, suggestive of an extensive plagioclase fractionation, whereas the negative Ce anomaly is peculiar, and may be due to fractionation of monazite. Regional geochemical variation, including increasing enrichment in LREEs and increases in Zr/TiO_2 ratios and SiO_2 content from north to south, suggest that the Nanhoron Microgranite shows the lowest degree of fractionation and the Foel Gron Microgranite the greatest. Nevertheless, the rocks are closely related and are placed together in Group III.

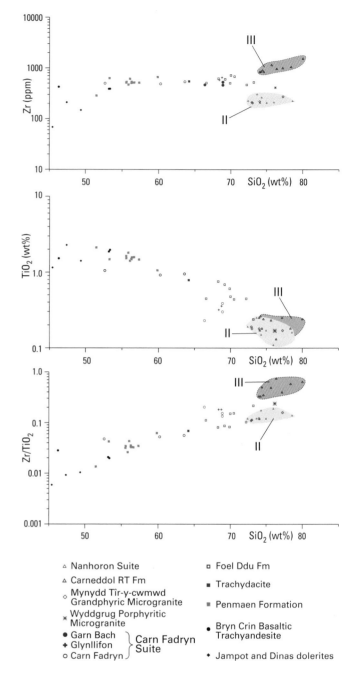

Figure 39 Diagrams showing variation of the differentiation index (Zr/TiO_2) as used in Figure 38 against SiO_2, and the variation of Zr and TiO_2 against SiO_2, for analyses of rocks from the Llanbedrog Volcanic Group and associated intrusions.

Key as Figure 37. Pale grey shading indicates field of Group II rocks, dark grey shading indicates Group III field.

Nod Glas Formation basaltic volcanism and associated intrusions

The lavas of the Nod Glas Formation and associated high-level intrusions comprise subalkaline basalts and dolerites, characterised by low Nb/Y ratios (< 0.2; Figure 41a). REE

Table 7 Analyses of basic intrusions associated with the Llanbedrog Volcanic Group.

%	1	2	3
SiO_2	45.42	47.37	49.36
TiO_2	1.15	2.28	1.41
Al_2O_3	17.94	16.06	19.09
Fe_2O_3	9.33	12.11	8.70
MnO	0.13	0.36	0.14
MgO	9.38	5.87	5.64
CaO	11.08	5.58	8.77
Na_2O	1.01	3.37	2.51
K_2O	0.28	0.60	1.63
P_2O_5	0.11	0.29	0.20
ppm			
Ba	38	198	136
Cr	199	153	96
Cu	81	66	55
Ga	14	19	16
Nb <	17	13	
Ni	177	44	42
Pb	<	<	<
Rb	14	19	42
S	366	nd	nd
Sr	319	295	397
Th	<	<	<
U	<	<	<
V	169	295	143
Y	19	31	24
Zn	59	82	65
Zr	68	211	147
La	8.84	<	14.85
Ce	77.71	<	32.59
Pr	2.39	<	4.42
Nd 10.19	<	18.29	
Sm 2.76	nd	4.64	
Eu	1.01	nd	1.37
Gd 3.54	nd	4.61	
Tb	0.53	nd	0.71
Dy	2.85	nd	3.99
Ho 0.59	nd	0.84	
Er	1.58	nd	2.25
Tm 0.28	nd	0.37	
Yb	1.43	nd	2.02
Lu	0.26	nd	0.32
Zr/TiO_2	0.006	0.009	0.010
Nb/Y	<	0.55	0.54
La_N/Yb_N	4.13	nd	4.91

Key to analyses

1   Dinas Dolerite, Dinas quarry, sample RB10 [2724 3588], XRF
     C Lewis, ICP Chalmers, Aberystwyth
2   Jampot Dolerite, AG605, locality P36 [3825 3671], offshoot from
     main sill, XRF analyst C Lewis
3   Jampot Dolerite, AG606, Clogwyn Llwyd [3861 3704], XRF
     analyst C Lewis, ICP Chalmers, Aberystwyth
nd   not detected
<   less than detection limit

NOTE: Total iron expressed as Fe_2O_3

patterns for these rocks (Figure 41b) are relatively flat-lying (La_N/Yb_N range = 1.55–2.78), indicating a tholeiitic character. The geochemical character of these rocks is similar to that of the major basic intrusions of Carreg-yr-Imbill and Penarfynydd (Nb/Y less than 0.35; La_N/Yb_N ratio for typical Carreg-yr-Imbill dolerite 2.86; see below).

EXTRUSIVE ROCKS

Analyses of the basaltic lavas of the Nod Glas Formation (Table 16, columns 1, 2) plot within the subalkaline andesite/basalt field on the Zr/TiO_2 vs Nb/Y discrimination diagram (Figure 41a). They are characterised by low concentrations of incompatible elements (e.g. Zr, Nb, Y, P, Ti and the REE) and high concentrations of Ni, Cr and V, reflecting their mafic character. A multi-element plot of the basalt from Bodgadle (LL156, Leat and Thorpe, 1986; Figure 41c) shows chemical features broadly similar to MORB, although the low Nb (2 ppm and below detection limit) content is typical of marginal basin basalts, reflecting a minor subduction zone influence. Leat and Thorpe (1986) discussed the significance of this basalt (the 'upper andesite series' of Tremlett, 1969), indicating that it has island arc tholeiite affinities, but with high Cr and Ni contents suggesting that it is transitional to MORB.

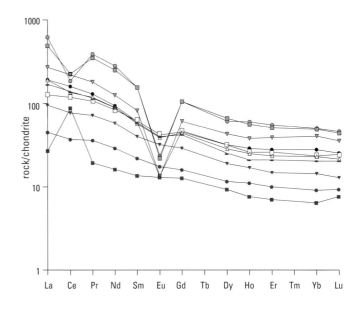

⊙	Foel Gron Porphyritic Microgranite	
▣	Mynytho Common Porphyritic Microgranite	Group III
▽	Nanhoron Porphyritic Microgranite	
●	Mynydd Tir-y-cwmwd Granophyric Microgranite	Group II
△	Glynllifon Trachydacite	
□	Penmaen Fm, Foel Fawr	Group Ib
▬	Carn Fadryn Quartz Microdiorite	
▼	Bryn Crin Basaltic Trachyandesite	
●	Jampot Dolerite	Group Ia
■	Dinas Dolerite	

Figure 40 Chondrite-normalised REE plots for analyses of rocks from the Llanbedrog Volcanic Group and associated intrusions.

Table 8 Analyses of rocks from the Penmaen Formation.

%	1	2	3	4	5	6	7
SiO_2	51.47	53.28	55.87	56.08	59.86	62.97	64.20
TiO_2	2.11	1.48	1.81	1.41	1.06	0.72	0.79
Al_2O_3	14.29	15.64	16.93	15.14	18.62	16.42	15.60
Fe_2O_3	10.76	3.27	10.40	3.16	8.38	2.33	8.81
FeO	nd	8.73	nd	8.42	nd	3.76	nd
MnO	0.16	0.34	0.10	0.27	0.16	0.17	nd
MgO	1.61	2.17	1.85	1.73	1.83	1.16	1.61
CaO	7.32	4.51	0.94	3.70	1.51	2.69	5.96
Na_2O	5.99	4.19	3.53	4.19	3.31	5.88	4.83
K_2O	0.16	1.50	2.43	1.36	1.52	1.38	1.12
P_2O_5	0.50	0.64	0.70	0.58	0.44	0.29	nd
ppm							
Ba	248	686	695	712	479	nd	nd
Cr	41	27	<	13	<	nd	nd
Cu	26	6	9	8	27	nd	10
Nb	17	52	27	50	57	nd	43
Ni	22	3	11	<	11	nd	nd
Pb	7	10	12	23	12	nd	15
Rb	12	30	46	26	34	nd	27
Sr	257	775	131	732	213	nd	667
Th	<	3	<	9	<	nd	5
U	<	<	<	3	<	nd	<
V	171	nd	157	nd	<	nd	nd
Y	30	67	51	65	77	nd	61
Zn	64	208	137	166	202	nd	134
Zr	286	632	472	612	665	nd	551
La	<	nd	nd	nd	43.62	nd	nd
Ce	<	117	nd	115	107.46	nd	nd
Pr	25	nd	nd	nd	13.81	nd	nd
Nd	7	nd	nd	nd	56.65	nd	nd
Sm	nd	nd	nd	nd	12.72	nd	nd
Eu	nd	nd	nd	nd	3.44	nd	nd
Gd	nd	nd	nd	nd	12.99	nd	nd
Tb	nd	nd	nd	nd	1.95	nd	nd
Dy	nd	nd	nd	nd	11.33	nd	nd
Ho	nd	nd	nd	nd	2.13	nd	nd
Er	nd	nd	nd	nd	6.21	nd	nd
Tm	nd	nd	nd	nd	0.94	nd	nd
Yb	nd	nd	nd	nd	6.01	nd	nd
Lu	nd	nd	nd	nd	0.91	nd	nd
Zr/TiO_2	0.014	0.043	0.026	0.043	0.063	nd	0.070
Nb/Y	0.57	0.78	0.53	0.77	0.74	nd	0.70
La_N/Yb_N	nd	nd	nd	nd	4.85	nd	nd

Key to analyses

1 Basaltic trachyandesite lava, P84 [361 349], analyst C Lewis

2 Basaltic trachyandesite lava, Leat and Thorpe (1986) LL154, Mynydd Meilian [2972 3725]

3 Basaltic trachyandesite tuff, sample P8F, Ffridd, Pwllheli [3768 3578]

4 Basaltic trachyandesite lava, Leat and Thorpe (1986) LL155, Mynydd Meilian [2972 3725]

5 Trachydacite lava, sample RB6, Foel Fawr [3061 3217], analyst C Lewis, ICP Chalmers, Aberystwyth

6 Trachydacite lava, Fitch (1967) 'D', Llanbedrog [315 388]

7 Trachydacite lava, Leat and Thorpe (1986) MY3, Foel Fawr [305 321]

nd not detected

< less than detection limit

NOTE: Total iron expressed as Fe_2O_3 except for samples 2, 4 and 6

INTRUSIVE ROCKS

Analyses of two dolerites (the Gelli and Garn Dolerites) spatially associated with the basaltic rocks of the Nod Glas Formation plot in the subalkaline field (Figure 41a; Nb is below detection in some samples) and show relatively high contents of MgO, Ni and Cr and low concentrations of incompatible elements. The REE patterns of two samples (Figure 41b) are relatively flat (La_N/Yb_N of 2.43 and 1.56), suggesting that the intrusions are tholeiitic in character. The origin of the marked positive Ce anomaly in one sample is unclear, possibly being related to alteration.

The Pensarn Basaltic Andesite (a sill intruding the Nod Glas Formation) is broadly similar to other tholeiitic rocks of the Nod Glas Formation and associated intrusions, plotting in the subalkaline andesite/basalt field on the Zr/TiO_2 vs Nb/Y discrimination diagram (Figure 41a), but has relatively high SiO_2 and very low CaO, probably related to alteration. A REE plot (Figure 41b) has a slightly enriched LREE pattern (La_N/Yb_N = 2.78), reflecting the subalkaline, tholeiitic character of this intrusion.

The geochemical features of the Garn and Gelli dolerites, together with the Pensarn Basaltic Andesite, are very close to those of the extrusive basalt from Bodgadle described above. The intrusive and extrusive rocks are clearly very closely related, with the geological evidence suggesting that the strongly transgressive basic intrusions may have been feeders for the basaltic volcanism.

Table 9 Analyses of rocks from the Bryn Crin Basaltic Trachyandesite.

%	1	2	3
SiO_2	46.28	53.35	53.18
TiO_2	1.52	1.97	1.87
Al_2O_3	16.43	17.89	16.70
Fe_2O_3	11.67	9.34	9.62
MnO	0.16	0.21	0.14
MgO	7.83	3.28	4.08
CaO	10.10	8.23	4.04
Na_2O	2.26	2.25	4.38
K_2O	0.06	1.46	0.66
P_2O_5	0.12	0.51	0.44
ppm			
Ba	488	416	209
Cr	19	14	19
Cu	49	35	35
Ga	19	20	20
Nb 29	26	23	
Ni	18	17	16
Pb	<	<	<
Rb	24	29	18
S	nd	nd	nd
Sr	720	626	154
Th	<	<	<
U	<	<	<
V	158	150	165
Y	44	43	38
Zn	122	98	103
Zr	426	390	388
La	32	31.42	31
Ce	<	67.96	<
Pr	<	8.85	<
Nd 53	37.08	<	
Sm nd	8.18	nd	
Eu	nd	2.50	nd
Gd nd	8.15	nd	
Tb	nd	1.15	nd
Dy	nd	6.41	nd
Ho nd	1.30	nd	
Er	nd	3.33	nd
Tm nd	0.50	nd	
Yb	nd	3.16	nd
Lu	nd	0.44	nd
Zr/TiO_2	0.028	0.020	0.021
Nb/Y	0.66	0.60	0.61
La_N/Yb_N	nd	6.64	nd

Key to analyses

1 East of locality P39 [3810 3705], analysis AG602, analyst C Lewis.
2 North-east of locality P39 [3812 3708], analysis AG603, XRF analyst C Lewis, ICP Chalmers Aberystwyth.
3 West of locality P18 [3764 3614], analysis AG608, analyst C Lewis.
nd not detected
< less than detection limit

NOTE Total iron expressed as Fe_2O_3

Analyses from the basic dykes of Pen-yr-Orsedd (Table 17) show low Zr, Y and Nb contents. The dykes are probably tholeiitic in character, but the incomplete analyses make this uncertain. Field relationships do not constrain the age of the dykes well, and it is possible that they may be associated with the Llanvirn phase of tholeiitic volcanism, rather than the Nod Glas Formation volcanism. They do, however, have an orientation close to that of the Efailnewydd Fault and to a basic dyke cutting the Carneddol Formation in Nant-y-Gledrydd, suggesting they, too, may be associated with activity during Nod Glas Formation times.

Major basic intrusions

The major basic intrusions of Mynydd Penarfynydd and Carreg-yr-Imbill are both subalkaline and tholeiitic in character. Because of their relatively deep level of intrusion there is little stratigraphical evidence for their age. The position of the Carreg-yr-Imbill intrusion on the line of the Efailnewydd Fault, and the existence, at only slightly higher stratigraphical horizons, of strongly transgressive tholeiitic minor intrusions associated with the Nod Glas Formation extrusive basaltic volcanism argues in favour of the association of the Carreg-yr-Imbill intrusion with these late basalts.

The Mynydd Penarfynydd intrusion is remote from the other vestiges of the Caradoc volcanism, so its relationship with those other features remains speculative. As already noted, in both its petrology and geochemistry it resembles the Carreg yr Imbill intrusion, so a connection with the Nod Glas Formation tholeiitic volcanism is not unlikely, although the Mynydd Penarfynydd intrusion presently lies far from the Efailnewydd Fault which appears to control this volcanism elsewhere in the district (there is, however, a possibility of significant sinistral strike-slip faulting on the Cefnamwlch–Rhiw Fault, see Chapter 8).

The mafic rocks of the Carreg-yr-Imbill intrusion have low Nb/Y ratios, indicating their subalkaline character (Figure 41a). On a normalised REE diagram (Figure 41b) the typical lithology exhibits a relatively flat pattern (La_N/Yb_N = 2.84). The analyses (Table 18) show high MgO, Ni and Cr, with low concentrations of the incompatible elements. The albite-rich segregations have lower MgO, Ni and Cr concentrations, higher incompatible elements and a steeper slope of LREE enrichment, with marked Eu depletion. These segregations plot in the rhyodacite and rhyolite fields, and probably represent highly fractionated magmas.

The Mynydd Penarfynydd gabbros are characterised generally by very low concentrations (Table 19) of incompatible elements (Zr, Nb, Y) and high total Fe, MgO, Ni, Cr and V, features especially marked in the picritic cumulates, reflecting olivine and/or pyroxene accumulation. Two samples of melagabbro have relatively low Ni and Cr and markedly higher concentrations of TiO_2 and V, indicative of high modal proportions of an Fe-Ti oxide. On the Zr/TiO_2 vs Nb/Y diagram (Figure 41a) they plot in the subalkaline basalt and andesite/basalt fields. Accordingly they comprise a suite of tholeiitic picrites and gabbros.

Table 10   Analyses of rocks from the Foel Ddu Rhyodacite Formation.

| | Pwllheli area lavas | | Cors Geirch area lavas | | | Llanbedrog area | | |
| | | | | | | lava | tuffs | |
%	1	2	3	4	5	6	7	8
SiO_2	66.62	72.20	70.01	70.50	68.30	73.20	69.90	69.20
TiO_2	0.45	0.45	0.48	0.44	0.76	0.24	0.61	0.69
Al_2O_3	14.61	13.94	15.46	15.36	13.85	14.33	14.46	15.36
Fe_2O_3	5.87	4.62	3.94	3.43	4.46	3.85	8.32	7.56
MnO	0.09	nd	0.04	0.03	nd	nd	nd	nd
MgO	0.72	0.96	0.31	0.07	0.70	1.15	1.61	1.25
CaO	1.40	0.04	0.13	0.12	2.02	0.16	0.71	0.18
Na_2O	4.68	4.22	7.69	4.90	5.93	4.02	6.05	4.28
K_2O	2.78	4.27	0.09	4.97	3.11	4.17	2.00	3.34
P_2O_5	0.12	nd	0.12	0.06	nd	nd	nd	nd
ppm								
Ba	511	nd	211	837	nd	nd	nd	nd
Cr	<	nd	<	<	nd	nd	nd	nd
Cu	5	5	6	6	5	2	5	4
Nb	34	34	47	42	36	41	37	39
Ni	8	nd	9	10	nd	nd	nd	nd
Pb	7	11	9	9	17	17	15	7
Rb	54	89	11	110	66	90	43	70
Sr	107	136	96	126	447	60	116	97
Th	10	11	13	14	10	12	10	12
U	<	3	<	<	3	3	<	3
V	8	nd	13	<	nd	nd	nd	nd
Y	61	48	80	64	60	84	71	74
Zn	111	83	63	19	108	194	173	75
Zr	512	471	725	683	621	525	510	605
La	56	nd	83	55	nd	nd	nd	nd
Ce	122	nd	90	<	nd	nd	nd	nd
Pr	<	nd	<	<	nd	nd	nd	nd
Nd	63	nd	108	53	nd	nd	nd	
Sm	nd	nd	nd	nd	nd	nd	nd	
Eu	nd	nd	nd	nd	nd	nd	nd	nd
Gd	nd	nd	nd	nd	nd	nd	nd	
Tb	nd	nd	nd	nd	nd	nd	nd	nd
Dy	nd	nd	nd	nd	nd	nd	nd	nd
Ho	nd	nd	nd	nd	nd	nd	nd	
Er	nd	nd	nd	nd	nd	nd	nd	nd
Tm	nd	nd	nd	nd	nd	nd	nd	
Yb	nd	nd	nd	nd	nd	nd	nd	nd
Lu	nd	nd	nd	nd	nd	nd	nd	nd
Zr/TiO_2	0.113	0.105	0.152	0.155	0.082	0.219	0.084	0.088
Nb/Y	0.56	0.71	0.59	0.66	0.60	0.49	0.52	0.53
La_N/Yb_N	nd	nd	nd	nd	nd	nd	nd	nd

Key to analyses

1   Lava, sample P67, Garn [3695 3536], analyst C Lewis
2   Lava, Leat and Thorpe (1986) PW1, Garn [370 354]
3   Lava, sample 90.045, Madryn [2899 3661], analyst C Lewis
4   Lava, sample 90.052, Foel Ddu [2923 3617], analyst C Lewis
5   Lava, Moel-y-Penmaen, Leat and Thorpe (1986) MP1
6   Lava, Leat and Thorpe (1986) CD3, Carreg-y-Defaid
7   Tuff, Leat and Thorpe (1986) MY4, Foel Fawr [306 323]
8   Tuff?, Leat and Thorpe (1986) LB1, Llanbedrog [328 318]
nd   not detected
<   less than detection limit

NOTE   Total iron expressed as Fe_2O_3.

Table 11   Analyses of rocks from the Carn Fadryn Suite of alkaline intrusions.

%	Carn Fadryn		Saethon	Garn Bach			Glynllifon	
	1	2	3	4	5	6	7	8
SiO$_2$	63.60	60.25	52.64	68.90	66.40	68.90	68.77	68.40
TiO$_2$	0.95	0.92	1.05	0.30	0.23	0.39	0.36	0.32
Al$_2$O$_3$	13.40	14.51	18.73	14.90	14.98	15.24	16.06	15.19
Fe$_2$O$_3$	8.69	7.54	2.86	4.07	5.80	6.81	4.31	5.34
FeO	nd	nd	7.62	nd	nd	nd	nd	nd
MnO	0.32	0.21	0.38	0.27	nd	nd	0.17	nd
MgO	1.11	1.14	2.17	0.27	0.70	0.70	0.60	0.70
CaO	2.22	5.11	9.69	2.16	3.00	0.14	1.23	0.88
Na$_2$O	4.65	1.04	0.79	5.11	5.25	3.88	3.11	3.77
K$_2$O	2.96	2.12	1.61	3.17	1.18	2.79	2.43	5.75
P$_2$O$_5$	0.33	0.34	0.61	0.06	nd	nd	0.08	nd
ppm								
Ba	1005	476	277	105	nd	nd	796	nd
Cr	<	<	25	<	nd	nd	<	nd
Cu	nd	27	5	<	7	5	34	7
Ga	nd	22	nd	<	nd	nd	25	nd
Nb 53	45	43	51	48	34	58	46	
Ni	<	11	2	<	nd	nd	11	nd
Pb	18	9	7	3	nd	9	15	17
Rb	79	69	59	63	37	75	57	133
S	nd	129	nd	nd	nd	nd	109	nd
Sr	183	167	136	105	110	69	188	264
Th	6	9	<	8	10	11	<	7
U	nd	<	<	nd	4	2	<	<
V	nd	<	nd	nd	nd	nd	10	nd
Y	74	66	59	62	77	59	88	78
Zn	nd	134	139	nd	135	109	132	122
Zr	535	487	501	464	472	531	653	588
La	62	54.63	nd	60	nd	nd	62.46	nd
Ce	118	114.08	99	117	nd	nd	118.67	nd
Pr	nd	14.14	nd	nd	nd	nd	14.56	nd
Nd 61	56.25	nd	50	nd	nd	56.46	nd	
Sm nd	11.88	nd	nd	nd	nd	11.63	nd	
Eu	nd	3.11	nd	nd	nd	nd	3.00	nd
Gd nd	11.74	nd	nd	nd	nd	12.17	nd	
Tb	nd	1.53	nd	nd	nd	nd	1.71	nd
Dy	nd	8.65	nd	nd	nd	nd	9.83	nd
Ho nd	1.61	nd	nd	nd	nd	1.96	nd	
Er	nd	4.76	nd	nd	nd	nd	5.49	nd
Tm nd	0.74	nd	nd	nd	nd	0.80	nd	
Yb	nd	4.55	nd	nd	nd	nd	5.13	nd
Lu	nd	0.68	nd	nd	nd	nd	0.74	nd
Zr/TiO$_2$	0.056	0.053	0.048	0.155	0.205	0.136	0.183	0.184
Nb/Y	0.72	0.68	0.73	0.82	0.62	0.58	0.66	0.59
La$_N$/Yb$_N$	nd	8.02	nd	nd	nd	nd	8.13	nd

Key to analyses

1   Carn Fadryn, Croudace (1982), CFAD [280 348]
2   Carn Fadryn, sample RB9 [277 351], majors/traces XRF analyst C Lewis, REE Chalmers, Aberystwyth
3   Carn Fadryn, Leat and Thorpe (1986), LL153
4   Minor intrusion in Nant Saethon, Croudace (1980), CBACH [288 345]
5   Garn Bach Dacite, Clogwyn, Leat and Thorpe (1986), NB2 [297 343]
6   Garn Bach Dacite, Clogwyn, Leat and Thorpe (1986), NB1 [300 347]
7   Glynllifon Trachydacite, Mynytho Common [298 317], RB4, majors/traces XRF analyst C Lewis, REE Chalmers, Aberystwyth
8   Glynllifon Trachydacite, Mynytho Common, Leat and Thorpe (1986) MY2
nd   not detected
<   less than detection limit

NOTE   Total iron expressed as Fe$_2$O$_3$ except for analyses 3 and 6

Table 12   Analysis of Wyddgrug Microgranite.

%	Sample 90.015
SiO_2	76.21
TiO_2	0.17
Al_2O_3	13.02
Fe_2O_3	1.73
MnO	0.01
MgO	0.06
CaO	0.17
Na_2O	4.04
K_2O	4.15
P_2O_5	0.01
ppm	
Ba	343
Cr	<
Cu	16
Ga	26
Nb	60
Ni	9
Pb	28
Rb	125
S	<
Sr	42
Ta	7
Th	29
U	5
V	5
Y	91
Zn	53
Zr	416
La	65
Ce	122
Pr	50
Nd	84
Zr/TiO_2	0.245
Nb/Y	0.66
La_N/Yb_N	nd

Analysis of sample 90.015, Wyddgrug [283 368], by C Lewis

nd   not detected
<   less than detection limit

NOTE   Total iron expressed as Fe_2O_3

Table 13 Analyses of rocks from the Carneddol Rhyolitic Tuff Formation.

%	1	2	3	4	5	6	7
SiO_2	73.67	74.10	72.40	78.60	75.00	76.00	74.30
TiO_2	0.25	0.19	0.17	0.16	0.17	0.11	0.15
Al_2O_3	13.59	12.20	10.72	15.30	15.03	13.69	18.88
Fe_2O_3	1.88	0.57	0.18	1.98	0.06	2.41	2.66
MnO	0.06	nd	nd	nd	nd	nd	nd
MgO	0.55	0.70	0.70	1.87	0.70	1.34	2.39
CaO	0.78	<	<	<	<	<	<
Na_2O	3.80	3.50	2.68	0.30	9.26	6.46	1.22
K_2O	3.70	6.36	5.72	4.67	1.42	0.44	4.75
P_2O_5	0.04	nd	nd	nd	nd	nd	nd
ppm							
Ba	847	nd	nd	nd	nd	nd	nd
Cr	<	nd	nd	nd	nd	nd	nd
Cu	11	6	2	6	6	6	6
Ga	23	nd	nd	nd	nd	nd	nd
Nb 45	44	39	43	34	36	44	
Ni	9	nd	nd	nd	nd	nd	nd
Pb	21	24	14	17	16	7	13
Rb	130	127	124	105	27	13	120
S	20	nd	nd	nd	nd	nd	nd
Sr	151	28	67	39	153	72	56
Ta	<	nd	nd	nd	nd	nd	nd
Th	19	18	16	19	14	15	17
U	<	7	3	6	3	5	4
V	12	nd	nd	nd	nd	nd	nd
Y	73	69	66	63	60	67	79
Zn	74	20	16	39	59	124	71
Zr	305	226	206	224	207	210	264
La	91	nd	nd	nd	nd	nd	nd
Ce	178	nd	nd	nd	nd	nd	nd
Pr	<	nd	nd	nd	nd	nd	nd
Nd 76	nd	nd	nd	nd	nd	nd	
Zr/TiO_2	0.122	0.121	0.119	0.140	0.122	0.191	0.176
Nb/Y	0.62	0.59	0.64	0.68	0.57	0.54	0.56
La_N/Yb_N	nd	nd	nd	nd	nd	nd	nd

Key to analyses

1   Nant-y-Gledrydd Member, sample 91.006 [3042 3741]
2   Nant-y-Gledrydd Member, Leat and Thorpe (1986) LB2 [327 321]
3   Bodgadle Member, Leat and Thorpe (1986) NB3 [3105 3523]
4   Y Ffôr, Leat and Thorpe (1986) FC2 [403 396]
5   Leat and Thorpe (1986), CD1 Carreg-y-Defaid [342 324]
6   Leat and Thorpe (1986), CD2 Carreg-y-Defaid [342 324]
7   Leat and Thorpe (1986), CD4 Carreg-y-Defaid [342 324]
nd   not detected
<   less than detection limit

NOTE   Total iron expressed as Fe_2O_3

Table 14   Analyses of rocks from the Mynydd
Tîr-y-cwmwd Porphyritic Granophyric Microgranite.

%	1	2	3	4
SiO_2	77.26	72.90	73.00	74.00
TiO_2	0.17	0.19	0.18	0.18
Al_2O_3	13.34	14.20	14.60	13.70
Fe_2O_3	1.69	2.00	2.00	1.97
MnO	0.05	0.13	0.12	0.13
MgO	0.08	0.08	0.08	0.11
CaO	0.55	0.01	0.01	0.60
Na_2O	1.84	4.37	4.23	3.97
K_2O	4.69	5.19	5.23	5.00
P_2O_5	0.02	0.04	0.04	0.02
ppm				
Ba	531	512	523	495
Cr	<	<	<	<
Cu	45	nd	nd	nd
Ga	24	<	<	<
Nb 64	48	48	44	
Ni	13	<	<	<
Pb	29	25	23	28
Rb	176	183	181	161
S	194	nd	nd	nd
Sr	43	30	29	46
Th	17	19	17	16.6
U	6	nd	nd	2.85
V	6	nd	nd	nd
Y	92	54	54	78
Zn	73	nd	nd	nd
Zr	274	211	205	219
La	65.77	nd	nd	73
Ce	139.48	nd	nd	186
Pr	16.19	nd	nd	nd
Nd 59.99	nd	nd	74	
Sm 12.53	nd	nd	16.93	
Eu	1.04	nd	nd	1.25
Gd 12.80	nd	nd	nd	
Tb	1.86	nd	nd	2.37
Dy	11.21	nd	nd	nd
Ho 2.21	nd	nd	nd	
Er	6.35	nd	nd	nd
Tm 0.96	nd	nd	nd	
Yb	6.22	nd	nd	6.48
Lu	0.88	nd	nd	0.86
Zr/TiO_2	0.159	0.111	0.114	0.122
Nb/Y	0.70	0.89	0.89	0.56
La_N/Yb_N	7.06	nd	nd	7.53

Key to analyses

1   Sample RB1, south side of headland [334 305], XRF analyst
    C Lewis, ICP Chalmers
2   Croudace (1980) IC37i, top of headland [329 309]
3   Croudace (1980) IC37ii, top of headland [329 309]
4   Croudace (1982) LLANB, south side of headland [326 305]
nd   not detected
<   less than detection limit

NOTE: Total iron expressed as Fe_2O_3

Table 15 Analyses of rocks from the Nanhoron Suite of peralkaline intrusions.

%	Foel Gron		Mynytho Common					Nanhoron		
	1	2	3	4	5	6	7	8	9	10
SiO$_2$	80.01	74.60	78.36	76.37	77.21	75.02	74.40	75.66	74.20	74.00
TiO$_2$	0.24	0.24	0.18	0.13	0.25	0.24	0.18	0.23	0.26	0.25
Al$_2$O$_3$	11.97	12.20	11.50	11.31	11.27	11.43	10.91	11.29	12.40	12.40
Fe$_2$O$_3$	1.09	3.89	2.94	1.82	1.30	0.79	2.56	3.39	3.89	4.21
FeO	nd	nd	nd	0.93	0.83	2.89	nd	nd	nd	nd
MnO	0.01	0.21	0.05	<	0.02	0.07	nd	0.09	0.22	0.21
MgO	0.04	0.10	0.00	0.81	0.56	0.47	1.22	0.04	0.09	0.11
CaO	0.01	0.39	0.01	0.03	0.13	0.87	0.00	0.22	0.27	0.26
Na$_2$O	2.13	4.68	2.05	4.00	4.15	3.73	2.90	1.92	4.35	4.81
K$_2$O	3.20	4.06	4.35	2.83	3.13	4.08	5.70	4.22	4.53	4.00
P$_2$O$_5$	0.01	0.01	<	0.01	0.01	<	nd	0.01	0.02	0.02
ppm										
Ba	189	51	198	<	<	nd	nd	205	17	73
Cr	<	<	<	nd	nd	nd	nd	<	<	<
Cu	50	<	40	nd	nd	nd	5	42	nd	nd
Ga	36	<	29	25	24	nd	nd	29	nd	nd
Nb	151	74	114	106	115	nd	78	110	74	72
Ni	13	<	10	nd	nd	nd	nd	11	<	<
Pb	16	19	33	nd	nd	nd	12	22	25	20
Rb	146	155	215	175	182	nd	208	188	140	141
S	225	nd	76	nd	nd	nd	nd	280	nd	nd
Sr	17	7	18	10	15	nd	5	27	8	9
Th	36	27	27	nd	nd	nd	23	30	27	25
U	7	nd	6	nd	nd	nd	8	7	4	nd
V	7	<	6	nd	nd	nd	nd	7	nd	nd
Y	222	114	175	118	114	nd	135	148	110	110
Zn	89	<	199	nd	nd	nd	114	180	nd	nd
Zr	1524	833	1043	965	990	nd	898	1141	850	826
La	202.12	84	163.34	145	200	nd	nd	89.65	91	90
Ce	156.65	166	195.08	245	255	nd	nd	184.76	183	184
Pr	47.43	nd	42.18	nd	nd	nd	nd	21.92	nd	nd
Nd	176.36	72	152.66	nd	nd	nd	nd	80.35	77	78
Sm	31.59	nd	31.30	nd	nd	nd	nd	16.90	18.55	nd
Eu	1.84	nd	1.69	nd	nd	nd	nd	1.06	1.06	nd
Gd	27.99	nd	29.58	nd	nd	nd	nd	16.85	nd	nd
Tb	3.87	nd	4.07	nd	nd	nd	nd	2.55	2.62	nd
Dy	20.60	nd	22.52	nd	nd	nd	nd	15.03	nd	nd
Ho	4.59	nd	4.34	nd	nd	nd	nd	2.88	nd	nd
Er	12.41	nd	11.84	nd	nd	nd	nd	8.88	nd	nd
Tm	1.86	nd	1.72	nd	nd	nd	nd	1.34	nd	nd
Yb	11.00	nd	10.80	nd	nd	nd	nd	9.07	10.80	nd
Lu	1.57	nd	1.51	nd	nd	nd	nd	1.21	1.64	nd
Zr/TiO$_2$	0.635	0.347	0.579	0.742	0.396	nd	0.499	0.488	0.327	0.330
Nb/Y	0.68	0.65	0.65	0.89	1.01	nd	0.58	0.74	0.67	0.65
La$_N$/Yb$_N$	12.28	nd	10.10	nd	nd	nd	nd	6.61	5.63	nd

Key to analyses

1 Sample RB2, Foel Gron [301 309], XRF C Lewis, ICP Chalmers
2 Croudace (1982) FOELG, Foel Gron [301 309]
3 Sample RB3, Mynytho [2966 3182], XRF C Lewis, ICP Chalmers
4 Tremlett (1972) T798, Mynytho, microgranite
5 Tremlett (1972) T493, Mynytho, rhyolitic margin

6 Tremlett (1972) J, Mynytho Common, rhyolitic margin
7 Leat and Thorpe (1986) MY1, Mynytho Common
8 RB11, Nanhoron [2865 3295], XRF C Lewis, ICP Chalmers
9 Croudace (1982), NANTB, Nanhoron Quarry [287 329]
10 Croudace (1980), NANTBi, Nanhoron Quarry, [287 329]
nd   not detected
<   less than detection limit

NOTE   Total iron expressed as Fe$_2$O$_3$ except for anayses 4, 5 and 6

Table 16 Analyses of igneous rocks from the Nod Glas Formation and associated high-level intrusions.

%	Extrusive basalts		Pensarn basaltic andesite	Garn and Gelli dolerites		
	1	2	3	4	5	6
SiO$_2$	46.16	38.18	53.74	51.87	46.50	49.22
TiO$_2$	1.81	1.61	1.36	2.14	2.21	1.57
Al$_2$O$_3$	15.24	17.95	16.56	17.37	14.43	15.58
Fe$_2$O$_3$	3.44	15.14	10.33	9.47	14.54	11.28
FeO	9.18	nd	nd	nd	nd	nd
MnO	0.15	0.48	0.17	0.19	0.21	0.17
MgO	8.01	5.86	6.10	3.72	7.19	6.72
CaO	9.86	5.99	1.63	4.59	8.69	8.66
Na$_2$O	2.44	3.45	2.40	4.03	2.46	2.39
K$_2$O	0.38	0.83	1.44	0.94	0.56	1.23
P$_2$O$_5$	0.15	0.14	0.13	0.52	0.16	0.16
ppm						
Ba	328	137	445	87	272	871
Cr	422	236	233	145	170	273
Cu	79	51	81	75	86	133
Ga	nd	17	17	19	15	14
Nb	2	<	5	<	2	<
Ni	168	114	111	80	41	46
Pb	7	<	<	<	1	<
Rb	11	13	21	7	23	24
S	nd	611	nd	nd	nd	nd
Sr	477	139	128	403	342	496
Th	<	<	<	<	3	<
U	<	<	<	<	<	<
V	nd	309	255	210	314	233
Y	24	22	25	24	29	28
Zn	88	74	91	70	82	73
Zr	114	101	139	87	113	117
La	nd	<	8.16	8.12	7.54	<
Ce	9	<	20.46	72.51	19.03	<
Pr	nd	<	2.87	2.59	3.05	37
Nd	nd	<	13.24	12.37	15.91	<
Sm	nd	nd	3.27	3.56	4.87	nd
Eu	nd	nd	0.90	1.30	1.73	nd
Gd	nd	nd	3.65	4.59	5.66	nd
Tb	nd	nd	0.58	0.67	0.99	nd
Dy	nd	nd	3.42	4.27	5.90	nd
Ho	nd	nd	0.68	0.88	1.25	nd
Er	nd	nd	2.03	2.39	3.43	nd
Tm	nd	nd	0.30	0.38	0.54	nd
Yb	nd	nd	1.96	2.23	3.24	nd
Lu	nd	nd	0.30	0.38	0.52	nd
Zr/TiO$_2$	0.006	0.006	0.010	0.004	0.005	0.004
Nb/Y	0.08	<	0.20	<	0.07	<
La$_N$/Yb$_N$	nd	nd	2.78	nd	1.55	2.43

Key to analyses

1   Basalt, Bodgadle, Leat and Thorpe (1986) LL156
2   Basalt, Caeau-gwinion-isaf, sample P21x [3740 3632], analyst C Lewis
3   Pensarn Basaltic Andesite, AG610 (loc. P73) [3670 3559], XRF C Lewis, ICP Chalmers
4   Garn Dolerite, AG601 [3663 3531], XRF C Lewis, ICP Chalmers
5   Garn Dolerite, AG609 [3665 3531] XRF C Lewis, ICP Chalmers
6   Gelli Dolerite, AG607 [3777 3605], XRF C Lewis
nd   not detected
<   less than detection limit

NOTE   Total iron expressed as Fe$_2$O$_3$ except for sample 1

Figure 41   Geochemical characteristics of the magmatism associated with the Nod Glas Formation and of the major basic intrusions (Carreg yr Imbill and Penarfynydd).

a   Zr/TiO$_2$ vs Nb/Y diagram (Winchester and Floyd, 1977).
b   Chondrite-normalised REE distribution.
c   MORB normalised multi-element plot.

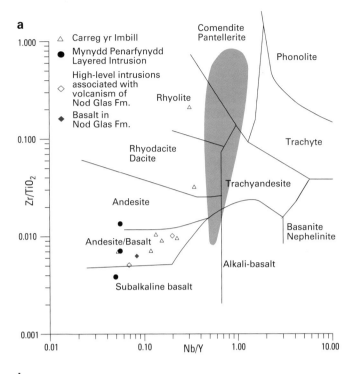

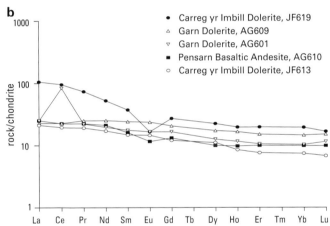

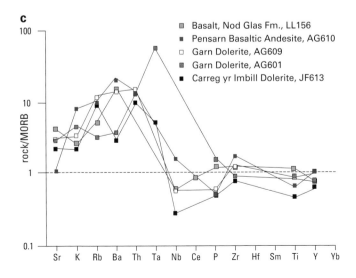

Table 17 Analyses of rocks from the Pen-yr-Orsedd dykes.

%	1	2	3	4	5	6
SiO_2	42.14	43.96	44.85	44.99	43.18	44.05
TiO_2	0.84	1.63	1.68	1.23	0.72	1.85
Al_2O_3	13.10	14.86	16.06	15.58	16.52	13.59
Fe_2O_3	12.97	13.33	11.98	12.74	10.48	15.70
MnO	0.17	0.20	0.17	0.18	0.15	0.22
MgO	16.73	9.36	7.75	9.87	12.32	8.50
CaO	7.78	10.30	9.81	9.55	6.96	10.05
Na_2O	0.61	0.90	1.12	1.15	0.66	1.08
K_2O	0.37	0.87	1.59	1.07	1.90	0.10
P_2O_5	0.07	0.10	0.18	0.08	0.07	0.13
ppm						
Ba	107	195	271	<	140	123
Cr	719	321	166	320	455	225
Cs	nd	nd	nd	nd	nd	nd
Cu	nd	nd	nd	nd	nd	nd
Ga	nd	nd	nd	nd	nd	nd
Nb nd	nd	nd	nd	nd	nd	
Ni	415	148	88	173	295	124
Pb	nd	nd	nd	nd	nd	nd
Rb	26	50	72	61	127	47
S	nd	nd	nd	nd	nd	nd
Sc	nd	nd	nd	nd	nd	nd
Sr	183	213	349	183	158	152
Ta	nd	nd	nd	nd	nd	nd
Th	nd	nd	nd	nd	nd	nd
U	nd	nd	nd	nd	nd	nd
V	159	266	239	258	138	328
Y	15	17	18	14	13	28
Zn	nd	nd	nd	nd	nd	nd
Zr	45	54	102	48	45	66
La	nd	nd	nd	nd	nd	nd
Ce	nd	nd	nd	nd	nd	nd
Pr	nd	nd	nd	nd	nd	nd
Nd nd	nd	nd	nd	nd	nd	
Sm nd	nd	nd	nd	nd	nd	
Zr/TiO_2	0.005	0.003	0.006	0.004	0.006	0.004
Nb/Y	nd	nd	nd	nd	nd	nd
La_N/Yb_N	nd	nd	nd	nd	nd	nd

Key to analyses

1	North-east side of main dyke, north end of quarry, SE12, analyst C Lewis
2	North termination of dyke outcrop, SE13, analyst C Lewis
3	Small dyke to south-west, SE14, analyst C Lewis
4	South-east of exposure of main dyke, SE15, analyst C Lewis
5	Fresh rock near fault, SE16, analyst C Lewis
6	South-west part of main dyke, SE17, analyst C Lewis
nd	not detected
<	less than detection limit

NOTE   Total iron expressed as Fe_2O_3

Table 18   Analyses of rocks from the Carreg-yr-Imbill Intrusion.

%	1	2	3	4	5	6	7	8	9
SiO$_2$	44.55	45.98	46.07	46.16	46.31	46.87	49.26	57.07	71.85
TiO$_2$	1.81	1.11	1.74	1.81	1.01	1.17	2.24	1.75	0.50
Al$_2$O$_3$	9.12	17.27	10.03	9.79	17.75	17.69	15.19	14.31	14.64
Fe$_2$O$_3$	16.76	10.31	15.45	16.26	9.61	10.42	8.20	8.07	2.60
MnO	0.23	0.05	0.21	0.21	0.05	0.15	0.16	0.23	0.05
MgO	14.28	9.19	13.30	13.77	8.90	8.48	6.26	4.81	0.98
CaO	6.83	9.92	6.42	6.45	10.40	9.08	12.15	7.39	3.81
Na$_2$O	1.17	1.71	1.51	1.37	1.73	2.30	2.91	4.04	5.98
K$_2$O	0.43	0.40	0.43	0.49	0.36	0.18	0.36	0.21	0.03
P$_2$O$_5$	0.13	0.14	0.16	0.14	0.12	0.14	0.28	0.11	0.06
ppm									
Ba	107	61	74	102	61	38	92	126	77
Cr	247	158	224	275	135	129	142	68	2
Cu	122	65	109	128	71	75	91	42	42
Ga	13	14	14	13	16	16	17	19	26
Nb	<	1	4	4	<	2	9	17	23
Ni	207	123	206	226	13	125	74	72	15
Pb	<	5	3	4	3	4	1	2	14
Rb	20	18	20	22	18	13	15	16	10
S	nd	nd	nd	nd	nd	nd	nd	nd	nd
Sr	109	281	127	127	291	260	209	155	66
Th	<	<	<	<	<	<	<	9	17
U	<	<	<	<	<	<	<	<	<
V	279	148	228	257	135	166	243	146	34
Y	25	19	30	26	17	17	40	49	74
Zn	82	62	80	82	62	65	67	38	17
Zr	163	77	181	163	73	83	215	562	1063
La	<	6.92	<	<	<	<	<	<	34.75
Ce	<	16.52	<	<	<	<	<	<	83.05
Pr	<	2.31	<	<	<	<	<	<	8.96
Nd	<	10.85	<	<	<	<	<	<	33.51
Sm	nd	3.04	nd	nd	nd	nd	nd	nd	7.67
Eu	nd	1.12	nd	nd	nd	nd	nd	nd	1.27
Gd	nd	3.32	nd	nd	nd	nd	nd	nd	7.62
Tb	nd	0.52	nd	nd	nd	nd	nd	nd	1.33
Dy	nd	3.04	nd	nd	nd	nd	nd	nd	7.57
Ho	nd	0.64	nd	nd	nd	nd	nd	nd	1.51
Er	nd	1.72	nd	nd	nd	nd	nd	nd	4.34
Tm	nd	0.27	nd	nd	nd	nd	nd	nd	0.68
Yb	nd	1.63	nd	nd	nd	nd	nd	nd	4.24
Lu	nd	0.23	nd	nd	nd	nd	nd	nd	0.57
Zr/TiO$_2$	0.009	0.007	0.010	0.009	0.007	0.007	0.010	0.032	0.211
Nb/Y	0.05	0.05	0.13	0.15	<	0.12	0.23	0.35	0.31
La$_N$/Yb$_N$	nd	2.86	nd	nd	nd	nd	nd	nd	5.48

Key to analyses

All samples from coast west of Carreg-yr-Imbill caravan park [3883 3438]

1   F615; 2 JF613; 3 JF616; 4 JF617; 5 JF611; 6 JF618; 7 JF622; 8 JF620; 9 JF619.
      XRF analyses by C Lewis, ICP for REE by Chalmers, Aberystwyth

nd   not detected
<   less than detection limit

NOTE   Total iron quoted as Fe$_2$O$_3$

Table 19   Analyses of rocks from the Mynydd Penarfynydd layered intrusion.

%	1	2	3	4	5	6	7	8	9
SiO_2	46.73	39.58	38.65	47.58	45.68	38.82	40.52	50.41	48.18
TiO_2	1.19	0.52	0.48	1.01	0.53	2.42	2.26	2.18	2.75
Al_2O_3	14.91	5.79	5.60	11.73	18.59	12.85	14.16	15.71	17.47
Fe_2O_3	11.37	12.53	15.65	10.57	6.20	18.28	16.56	13.56	12.73
MnO	0.17	0.18	0.23	0.17	0.10	0.20	0.18	0.26	0.27
MgO	9.15	31.08	27.30	13.04	9.73	7.99	6.90	4.74	2.51
CaO	8.90	4.28	5.45	10.52	13.70	14.35	14.31	6.23	8.84
Na_2O	2.69	0.43	0.34	1.35	1.44	0.75	0.99	4.87	4.28
K_2O	0.16	0.18	0.16	0.83	0.36	0.47	0.47	0.24	0.05
P_2O_5	0.13	0.05	0.06	0.10	0.07	0.17	0.11	0.23	0.26
ppm									
Ba	82	54	43	302	61	131	142	294	39
Cr	402	2309	1581	2003	266	61	43	<	<
Cu	21	43	9	56	44	5	<	<	<
Ga	15	11	10	13	14	14	15	16	18
Nb <	<	<	<	<	<	<	<	2	
Ni	111	764	485	202	102	20	11	7	7
Pb	<	<	<	9	<	<	<	<	<
Rb	11	14	10	29	29	15	18	14	9
S	827	898	176	112	138	5274	2240	<	<
Sr	197	84	70	179	179	73	165	266	76
Th	nd	nd	nd	<	nd	nd	nd	<	<
U	nd	nd	nd	<	nd	nd	nd	<	<
V	242	118	132	213	213	848	745	90	159
Y	22	12	10	18	18	18	18	69	39
Zn	88	62	70	62	39	52	57	73	71
Zr	74	36	26	72	72	37	38	141	114
La	<	<	<	<	<	<	<	<	<
Ce	<	<	<	68	<	<	81	<	<
Pr	28	<	<	<	29	26	<	<	<
Nd <	<	<	<	<	<	27	51	<	
Zr/TiO_2	0.006	0.007	0.005	0.007	0.014	0.002	0.002	0.008	0.004
Nb/Y	<	<	<	0.06	0.06	<	<	<	0.05
La_N/Yb_N	nd	nd	nd	nd	nd	nd	nd	nd	nd

Key to analyses

1   Lower chilled margin, M1, analyst C Lewis
2   Picrite, Penarfynydd, M2, analyst C Lewis
3   Picrite, Penarfynydd, M3, analyst C Lewis
4   Base of intrusion, Mynydd Rhiw, AL1, analyst C Lewis
5   Leucogabbro, Penarfynydd, M4, analyst C Lewis
6   Melagabbro, Penarfynydd, M5, analyst C Lewis
7   Melagabbro, Penarfynydd, M6, analyst C Lewis
8   Leucogabbro, Penarfynydd, RLG, analyst C Lewis
9   Leucodiorite, Penarfynydd, RLD, analyst C Lewis
nd   not detected
<   less than detection limit

NOTE   Total iron expressed as Fe_2O_3

SEVEN

Quaternary

During the Quaternary, the Pwllheli district has been affected by successive ice sheets from two sources; 'Welsh ice' from the mountains of North Wales moved westwards out of the Vale of Ffestiniog into Cardigan Bay and 'Irish Sea ice' moved southwards down the basin of the Irish Sea. As these powerful ice sheets became established across Llŷn, subglacial meltwater carved spectacular steep-sided meltwater channels, most of which are now either dry or occupied by diminutive misfit streams. During the last (Late Devensian) glaciation the Welsh and Irish Sea ice sheets were confluent in the Pwllheli district and the widespread glacigenic 'drift' deposits of the area record their uncoupling and final movements prior to melting. During and after the melting of the glaciers the region suffered periglacial conditions, with widespread solifluction and redistribution of tills by debris flows. The hills have been largely denuded of drift whilst the areas of low ground, particularly the large embayments, support thick and complex sequences of diamicton (till or boulder clay), sand and gravel. Uncoupling of the ice sheets resulted in local ponding, with lake levels falling as the ice melted. Extensive terraces of sand and gravel in central Llŷn and on the south coast were probably laid down in these ice-dammed lakes. During the Flandrian (Holocene) there have been only minor modifications to the Llŷn landscape. The sea has eroded into the glacigenic deposits of the major embayments, forming the sand and gravel beaches of the region, and blown sand has formed dune ridges. One of the larger streams, the Soch, has diverted away from its original course to the sea at Porth Neigwl to flow through a subglacial gorge towards Abersoch.

Because the Quaternary deposits are unlithified and lie largely in the position in which they were deposited, sediments and landforms are intimately related. Although they are well exposed in many places at the coast, inland exposures are rare and shallow excavations reveal only the top metre of sediments, which has almost inevitably been disturbed during the Flandrian. The most useful way to classify the 'drift' deposits is, therefore, using landform/sediment assemblages. In general, the sediments are seen only at the coast and inland mapping is based largely on morphology. A brief discussion of the pre-Quaternary landscape and of landforms produced by glacial and fluvioglacial erosion is given, followed by descriptions of five glacigenic landform/sediment assemblages. Two of these are dominated by diamicton and three by sand and gravel. By convention, and for ease of comparison with other maps, the landform/sediment assemblages are translated into established, mainly lithological, drift categories such as 'till' and 'glaciofluvial sheet deposits'. It is unfortunate that some of these terms have specifically genetic denotations, since there is considerable disagreement about the origin of many of the 'drift' deposits of the Pwllheli district. However, even if the genetic interpretations used here prove erroneous, the division of the landscape and drift deposits according to landform/sediment assemblages should remain useful.

PREVIOUS WORK

The first detailed work on Llŷn was that of Jehu (1909), who described sections throughout the region, including Porth Neigwl, Porth Ceiriad, Afon Wen and Glanllynnau. He devised a tripartite sequence of upper and lower boulder clays separated by sands and gravels. Although accepting that they could have been produced by a retreat and minor readvance of the same ice sheet, Jehu preferred the concept of two separate glaciations. Nicholas (1915) discussed in detail the drift deposits of the St Tudwal's Peninsula; he suggested that following withdrawal of the Irish Sea glacier, ice advanced westwards out of the mountains of North Wales into Cardigan Bay and on to southern Llŷn.

Synge (1964) described sections from throughout Llŷn, including Porth Neigwl and Llanbedrog. From the nature of the drift morphology, the degree of weathering of deposits and the nature of periglacial formations he inferred evidence for three distinct glaciations. The earliest was recognised only on the basis of striated clasts incorporated in solifluction deposits at Porth Neigwl and Llech Lydan. All of the glacial deposits of the Pwllheli district are attributed to the intermediate glaciation and the last, Late Devensian, limit of the Irish Sea ice is placed along the north coast. This is the limit proposed earlier by Carvill Lewis (1894). Subsequent workers have rejected this interpretation, placing the Late Devensian ice limit in south Wales (John, 1970; Bowen, 1991).

Saunders (1968a) used clast fabric measurements to suggest that most of the glacial diamictons of Llŷn were deposited by Irish Sea ice which crossed the peninsula from north-west to south-east, despite the fact that striations in western Llŷn are aligned north-east–south-west, parallel to the direction of ice movement suggested by Jehu (1909) and Synge (1964). Saunders also proposed that a second readvance of Irish Sea ice moving from north-east to south-west only reached the north coast of Llŷn, while ice moving out of the mountains of North Wales extended westwards as far as the St Tudwal's Peninsula. The landforms and deposits around the Cors Geirch were studied in detail by Saunders (1968b), who attributed them to an ice-dammed lake, following Matley (1936) who had used the name Lake Bodfean. Matley (1936) and Whittow (1965) discussed marine deposits of the south coast.

The glacial history of Llŷn was summarised by Whittow and Ball (1970), based largely upon the work of Saunders (1968a, 1968b). They assigned deposits to two glacial phases (Figure 42). In the earlier phase Irish Sea Advance(1b), ice from the north-west, moved over northern and western Llŷn while Welsh ice of the Criccieth Advance (1a) moving from the north-east had its westward boundary on St Tudwal's Peninsula. In the later phase, Irish Sea ice of the Main Anglesey Advance moved from the north-east to encroach upon the north coast of Llŷn and extend into the area of the Cors Geirch [310 365]. Welsh ice of the Arvon Advance moved from northern Snowdonia south-westwards through the Pant Glas col and along the flanks of Yr Eifl towards Bodfean. Welsh ice from the Vale of Ffestiniog moved westwards across Cardigan Bay to reach as far as the St Tudwal's Peninsula and into the eastern end of Porth Neigwl. During this later phase much of Llŷn is interpreted as ice-free. The sand and gravel features of central Llŷn are interpreted as kame terraces formed on the flanks of a dead ice tongue which stagnated in the Cors Geirch hollow.

The drift section exposed on the coast at Glanllynnau [4580 3728] includes Late-glacial organic sediments and is amongst the most intensively studied Quaternary sites in Wales (Jehu, 1909; Matley, 1936; Saunders, 1968a, 1968b, 1968c, 1968d, 1973; Synge, 1964, 1970; Whittow and Ball, 1970; Simpkins, 1968, 1974; Coope and Brophy, 1972; Bowen, 1973, 1974, 1977; Boulton, 1977a, 1977b; Campbell and Bowen, 1989; Harris and McCarroll, 1990). The interpretation of the glacial and postglacial history of the site remains contentious. A triangular area of eastern Llŷn, between Penygroes in the north and Criccieth and Pwllheli in the south has been investigated for sand and gravel resource potential (Crimes et al., 1988, 1992). This involved geomorphological and lithological mapping of a small area of the Pwllheli sheet. Thomas et al. (1990) interpreted the landforms and deposits in terms of the advance, coalescence and subsequent retreat and uncoupling of Welsh and Irish Sea ice sheets.

A fundamental re-interpretation of the Quaternary landforms and deposits of Llŷn has been proposed by Eyles and McCabe (1989a,b, 1991). They interpreted most of the deposits as glacimarine, deposited during retreat of the Irish Sea glacier. The sand and gravel terraces surrounding the Cors Geirch were interpreted as marine deltas. The diamictons, sands and gravels exposed in the coastal sections to the south and west were interpreted as prodelta marine deposits and as glacimarine sediments which have been re-deposited by a variety of mass flow processes.

Figure 42 Glacial phases in north-west Wales as recognised by Whittow and Ball (1970).
Reprinted by permission of the publishers, from Whittow and Ball, 1970 (figs, 2.1, 2.2). In the earliest phase, Irish Sea ice (1a) moved over northern and western Llŷn from the north-west to meet Welsh ice (1b) moving from the north-east. The Irish Sea ice withdrew and readvanced (2a) from the north, reaching the north Llŷn coast and extending into the Cors Geirch. Welsh ice continued to extend on to southern Llŷn as far west as St Tudwal's peninsula.

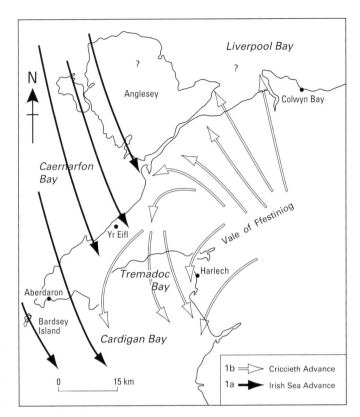

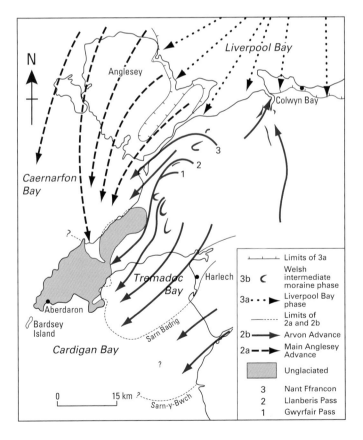

Within the Pwllheli district, three sites (Porth Neigwl, Porth Ceiriad and Glanllynnau) are considered sufficiently important to be included in the Joint Nature Conservancy Council's Geological Conservation Review of the Quaternary of Wales (Campbell and Bowen, 1989).

PREGLACIAL LANDSCAPE EVOLUTION

The large-scale bedrock topography of Llŷn, dominated by isolated hills and broad plains (Plate 20), was considered by Brown (1960) to form part of the 'coastal plateaux' of Wales. He suggested that the isolated hills may be remnants of an upland plain rising towards Snowdonia. The rest of the landscape he attributed to marine erosion during the Pleistocene. Whittow (1957) recognised evidence for several periods of high sea level on Llŷn. However, modern process studies have questioned the ability of marine erosion to cut broad plains (King, 1963; Ollier, 1981), and the uniform erosion of landscapes under humid temperate conditions is also in doubt (Twidale, 1976; Brunsden, 1980; Bradshaw, 1982).

The similar topography of Anglesey, with its broad plain and isolated hills, previously interpreted as the products of two episodes of Cainozoic (Tertiary) marine planation (Brown, 1960; Embleton, 1964), has been re-interpreted as the result of deep tropical weathering (Battiau-Quenney, 1984). Deep chemical weathering under humid tropical or subtropical conditions followed by removal of the saprolite (weathered products) reveals the weathering front as an 'etchplain'. Etchplanation surfaces need not be related to a stable base level and are unlikely to be flat. Differential resistance of bedrock to weathering, either because of lithology or structure, and differential removal of saprolite can lead to the formation of inselbergs (isolated hills), broad plains, closed hollows and broad valleys.

It is possible to interpret the large-scale topography of Llŷn in terms of etchplanation. The acidic rocks around Garnfadryn and Mynytho would be more resistant to chemical weathering than the cleaved mudrocks that form much of the (now drift-covered) lowland. Deep weathering may have begun as early as the Triassic, since Anglesey and probably Llŷn must have emerged at that time to supply sediment to the area of the Mochras borehole, near Harlech (Harrison, 1971; Allen and

Jackson, 1985). The topography of Llŷn may, therefore, have been formed over a much longer timescale than has traditionally been supposed. However, during the Pleistocene, the area was inundated, probably on several occasions, by glaciers flowing down the Irish Sea basin and issuing from the mountains of Snowdonia, and much of the direct evidence of the previous landforming processes is likely to have been eroded or covered by drift. Moreover, the differences in lithology and structure which may lead to differential resistance to chemical weathering are in many cases likely to provide similar resistance to glacial and glaciofluvial erosion.

The large drift-filled embayment at Porth Neigwl, the smaller embayment of Porth Ceiriad and probably the drift-filled area between Mynydd Tîr-y-cwmwd and Abersoch must predate at least the last (Late Devensian) glaciation. Their age is uncertain and they may have been occupied by the sea and progressively excavated by marine erosion during several interglacials.

PLEISTOCENE GLACIATION

EROSIONAL EVIDENCE

Striations

The clearest evidence of glacial erosion in the Pwllheli region is in the form of striations and grooves produced by clasts at the base of the glacier. Inland, such features are generally obscured by a cover of drift, or have been removed by weathering. They are visible, however, on the coast in the north-west of the area, near Porth Ysglaig, and in the south on the St Tudwal's Peninsula (Figure 43). Those in the north-west are aligned at 050° (south-west) and conform to the pattern recognised along the coast of south-western Llŷn (McCarroll, 1991). The striations of the St Tudwal's Peninsula are not

Plate 20 Carn Fadryn (371 m above OD) rises abruptly above the surrounding drift-covered lowlands. It may represent an inselberg isolated because of its resistance to deep weathering (GS664).

confined to the coast, but are also found on exposures (particularly of the Arenig sandstones of the Trwyn-yr Wylfa Member) inland. Most of the striations fall in the range 54° to 75°/234° to 255° (i.e. north-east–south-west). One site at the extreme east end of Porth Neigwl [2911 2548] retains clear striations aligned almost due west (271°). At Trwyn Llech-y-Doll [2992 2345] striations are aligned between 260° and 289°, suggesting ice moving onshore from Cardigan Bay. No striations were found on the St Tudwal's Islands.

Glacial meltwater channels

Large steep-sided valleys, now occupied by markedly underfit streams, are among the most spectacular features of the Llŷn landscape (Figure 43). Nant Saethon, the imposing valley of the Afon Horon has steep sides reaching 70 m high in places. The valley of the Afon Soch, north of Sarn, though smaller, is still much too large to have been cut by the diminutive stream which now occupies it. Nant Llaniestyn is wider than the others (300 m) with steep sides reaching 50 m. The valley at Sarn is aligned north-south, and Nant Llaniestyn and Nant Saethon swing round to the north-east.

The area around Abersoch and the St Tudwal's Peninsula is also dissected by steep-sided valleys. The most spectacular of these is aligned east–west and joins Abersoch and Llangian. It is occupied by the Afon Soch, which has diverted from its original course to the sea towards the east end of Porth Neigwl. Farther south, a

valley aligned north-east, runs from Sarn Bach [3043 2658] to Pen y Gogo [2942 2592]. At Llanbedrog a valley runs west from the village before turning south-south-west, isolating Mynydd Tîr-y-cwmwd. South-east of Mynytho, a similar steep-sided valley runs south-westwards to Oerddwr [3091 3037] before turning southwards to Bryn Ceithyn [3078 2895]. Smaller steep-sided valleys, which might be interpreted as subglacial chutes (Mannerfelt, 1945) lie north-east of Llangian, between Bachwared [2988 2526] and Pant Farm [2940 2552], and north of Porth Ceiriad at Nant-y-big [3082 2509] and at Nant Farm [3082 2509]. The bedrock north of Pwllheli is also dissected by several channels. The largest enters the town from the north-east and the A499 follows this channel. Smaller valleys incise the northern and western flanks of the outcrop.

The meltwater channels of Llŷn were discussed by Saunders (1968b), who suggested that four distinct types could be recognised: subglacial channels, direct channels, marginal/submarginal channels and overflow channels. The rationale behind this classification is unclear and all of the channels could be subglacial in origin, though some may have provided routeways for proglacial meltwater during and following retreat.

GLACIGENIC DEPOSITS

In this study, bedrock was regarded as outcropping where the cover of drift was seen to be, or interpreted to

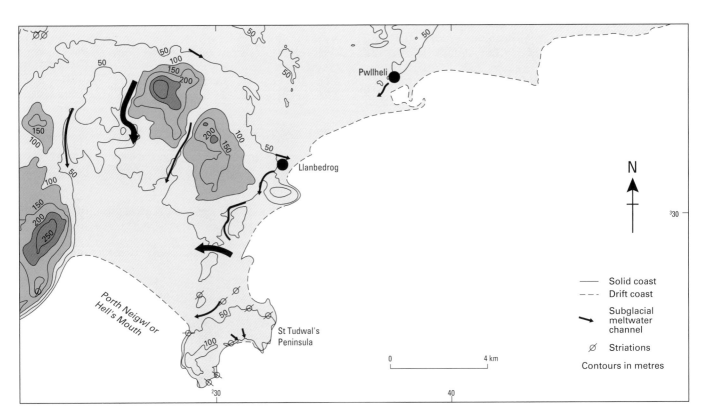

Figure 43 Erosional evidence of ice movement direction (striae and meltwater channels).

be, less than 1 m thick. The remainder of the glacigenic deposits are divided into five units, two of which are dominated by diamictons (boulder clay) and three by sand and gravel. Although classified, by convention, on the basis of lithology and inferred origin, the units were mapped as landform/sediment assemblages, and in interpreting their origins the geomorphological evidence is often just as important as the sedimentary evidence. Some of the units can be further subdivided on the basis of morphology.

Diamicton-dominated landform/sediment assemblages

Till

Given the uncertainty and current debate concerning the origin of many of the glacigenic deposits surrounding the Irish Sea basin, it is unfortunate that the term till, used here by convention, has an explicitly genetic denotation. Till is properly defined as a deposit formed directly by or from glacier ice without subsequent reworking by meltwater (Lowe and Walker, 1984). The term is used here in a looser sense to refer to diamictons that mantle the landscape but where bedrock remains the dominant control on topography. This landform/sediment approach facilitates mapping of deposits that are typically very poorly exposed, and more importantly distinguishes these deposits from superficially similar facies that form part of much thicker and more heterogeneous drift sequences. Those parts of the district dominated by 'till' include the eastern flanks of Mynydd Rhiw and Mynydd Cefnamwlch, the gentle slopes between Wyddgrug [2857 3672] and Brynodol [2507 3634], much of the high ground between Carn Fadryn [2788 3518] and Abersoch [3133 2820] and some of the terrain north of Pwllheli and east of Abererch.

The 'till' deposits are rarely exposed, other than in shallow pits (less than 1 m), which are almost exclusively in mud-rich diamicton with variable clast contents. The origin of such near-surface diamictons is, however, difficult to interpret. They could represent lodgement tills or meltout tills. However, because they are so near the surface, they are likely to have been remobilised to some extent during or after deglaciation, and therefore fabric studies, which may distinguish meltout, lodgement and flow tills (Dowdeswell and Sharp, 1986), are of little value. It also has been argued that the diamictons are proglacial subaqueous deposits (Eyles and McCabe, 1991). The few sites where the bedrock/drift contact is exposed suggest active erosion by warm-based ice (not frozen to the bed) with subsequent downslope remobilisation of diamictons.

DETAILS

At Nanhoron Quarry [2864 3200], high on the side of Nant Saethon meltwater channel, bedrock is overlain by broken bedrock, with little matrix, aligned parallel to the valley. This is overlain by diamicton, dominated by the local lithology, but with more matrix, grading up into a more matrix-rich diamicton with larger clasts. The clasts in the diamictons are aligned downslope, at 90° to the underlying glacially tectonised bedrock clast fabric.

This section suggests that the site was covered by glacier ice moving from the north-north-east which crushed and aligned the bedrock, and deposited diamicton on the surrounding slopes, possibly as meltout till. During and following deglaciation the tills were remobilised, first as debris flows and perhaps later under periglacial conditions, and their clasts aligned downslope. A site on the valley side, near the base of the quarry [2875 3289], reveals a similar section with 1 m of comminuted bedrock aligned down-valley, and is overlain by 1 m of similar material but showing angular clasts with more rounded edges and a silty matrix. This is overlain by 1.5 m of diamicton with larger clasts, some of which are striated, and which are orientated down-slope into the valley, at about 90° to the fabric of the underlying comminuted bedrock ('comminution till').

Glacial deposits undifferentiated

Where they are exposed on the coast, these deposits display considerable heterogeneity. Most of the sections comprise complex sequences dominated by diamicton, associated with sand and gravel. These sections hold the key to interpreting the Quaternary history of Llŷn and the development of the present landscape. As they are only exposed on the coast, inland mapping of these deposits is based largely on morphology. Generally, they fill depressions in the subdrift topography and the bedrock does not control the morphology of the drift surface. In interpreting these deposits it is useful to subdivide them on the basis of surface morphology and probable thickness, though the boundary is usually difficult to place. In this report, the very thick deposits that fill major rock-bound embayments are distinguished from thinner sequences elsewhere. The latter may have irregular, undulating topography with enclosed depressions interpreted as kettle holes.

Undulating topography with many kettle holes is common in western Llŷn (Gibbons and McCarroll, 1993), where it forms much of the agricultural land between isolated bedrock hills. It includes the thick drift which fills some of the main meltwater channels, such as Nant Llaniestyn and Nant Saethon, and it extends south of Nanhoron, where enclosed depressions, some forming small pools, can be interpreted as kettle holes formed by the melting of buried ice. The sediments comprising this assemblage are poorly exposed in the region.

Kettled drift topography also occurs in a low (less than 10 m OD) coastal strip around Afon Wen [4388 3755]. Coastal sections west of the outlet of the Afon Wen are characterised by diamicton overlain by poorly sorted, commonly cryoturbated gravel. The best exposure in these sediments lies near the eastern boundary of the district, near Glanllynnau (Figures 44, 45, 46; Plate 21).

GLANLLYNNAU [4580 3728]

A ridge of clay-rich, dense grey (lower) diamicton is overlain by sand and gravel and by cryoturbated gravelly (upper) diamicton. The surface of the lower diamicton is incised by inclined wedge-shaped fractures which are stained brown. Contorted laminated clays separate lower diamicton from the overlying sand and gravel. The sequence has been interpreted as the result of two separate advances, with the wedge-shaped fractures and contorted clays representing intermediate periglacial conditions. However, it is simpler to interpret the whole sequence in terms of the in situ decay of a single ice sheet (Boulton, 1977). The ridge of lower diamicton may represent a drumlin-like glacial bedform, and the inclined fractures are best interpreted as simple tensile cracks discoloured by water percolating from the overlying brown clays. They lack some of the characteristic features of true ice wedge casts. The upper, gravelly diamicton can be interpreted as flow till derived from the melting of dead ice ridges.

DETAILS

At the section exposed on the coast near Glanllynnau [4580 3728], coastal erosion has dissected an irregular inland topography of enclosed peat-filled hollows and ponds separated by ridges of gravel. (Figure 45). The section which has attracted most interest (Campbell and Bowen, 1989) is more than 360 m long and reaches 10 m high (Figure 44). A ridge of clay-rich, dense grey diamicton is overlain by sand and gravel and by a cryoturbated gravelly diamicton. The lower diamicton and the sand and gravel are separated by an irregular layer of brown

diamicton (variously interpreted as a weathering horizon and as a separate deposit) and by a layer of brown deformed laminated clay. Inclined wedge structures cut the upper surface of the lower diamicton. At the western end, the section shows incised kettle depressions bounded by normal faulting in the surrounding sand, gravel and upper diamicton. Organic sediments in the kettle depressions date from the Late-glacial and Holocene.

The origin of the glacigenic sediments at Glanllynnau is disputed. On the basis of clast fabrics, Saunders (1968a, 1968b) suggested that the lower diamicton was deposited by ice flowing from north-east to south-west. He interpreted the wedges as ice wedge pseudomorphs and the brown diamicton as a lower diamicton which had been weathered and soliflucted. The sands and gravels were interpreted as outwash; the upper gravelly diamicton, was interpreted as the result of another glacial advance, this time from the east. Thus the section indicates two Late Devensian advances separated by a cold interstadial.

This interpretation was accepted by Whittow and Ball (1970) who ascribed the lower diamicton to the 'Criccieth Advance' and the upper diamicton to the 'Arvon Advance'. This subdivision was retained by Bowen et al. (1986) who proposed a 'Gwynedd readvance' of both the Welsh and Irish Sea glaciers.

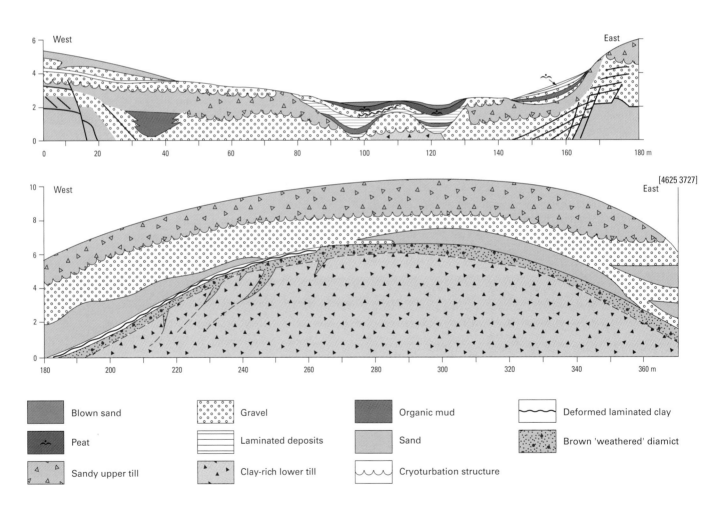

Figure 44 Quaternary deposits exposed on the coast at Glanllynnau (after Harris and McCarroll, 1990). Late-glacial and Holocene organic-rich deposits are preserved in kettleholes at the western end of the section. To the east, two diamictons (clay-rich lower till and sandy upper till) are separated by water-laid clay, sand and gravel.

a

b

Plate 21 Glanllynnau [4580 3728] (GS667).

a A ridge of dense grey (lower) diamicton is overlain by sand and gravel and by a cryoturbated (upper) diamiction.

b The surface of the lower diamicton is incised by inclined wedge-shaped fractures which were previously interpreted as ice wedge casts.

c To the west, kettle depressions contain organic and inorganic sediments recording environmental changes following deglaciation.

c

More recently, Bowen (in Campbell and Bowen, 1989) has raised the possibility that the lower diamicton may be Early Devensian (before 50 000 BP), the zone of weathering and ice wedges Middle Devensian, and the upper diamicton Late Devensian, in age.

An alternative explanation was proposed by Boulton (1977) who suggested that the whole sequence could be interpreted as the product of a single glacial episode. He interpreted the lower diamicton as a subglacial till and the upper diamicton as flow till. The model involves burial of debris-rich glacier ice which formed ridges. Fluvioglacial gravels occupied the hollows and flow tills were derived from the surrounding dead ice. When flow tills entered active fluvial channels they were disaggregated, but when meltwater supply was terminated the gravels were covered by flow till. During melting, the topographic expression was reversed, with the gravels forming ridges and the areas of buried ice forming depressions (kettle holes) (Figure 45). Melting of buried ice accounts for the normal faulting surrounding the organic-filled hollows, and associated deformation of organic sediment in the kettles suggests that melting of buried glacier ice may have continued well into the Late-glacial. Boulton (1977) recognised that the zone of weathering and the ice wedge pseudomorphs, interpreted by others as indicating a period of nonglacial conditions, was problematic.

The cliff at Glanllynnau is actively eroding, and the section recorded in 1989 (Figure 44) differs in detail from those described by earlier workers (Saunders, 1968a, 1968b; Whittow and Ball, 1970; Boulton, 1977; Campbell and Bowen, 1989). In particular, Boulton recorded a lower diamicton beneath a gravel lens (his lens A) at the western end of the section, but in 1989 laminated silts underlain by gravels were observed. These probably represent local ponding due to melting of buried ice during early deglaciation, so that the site was buried by outwash before any

accumulation of organic muds. The section is discussed by Harris and McCarroll (1990); they accepted that the sequence can be interpreted in terms of a single glacial episode, but rejected the evidence that has been proposed for a period of nonglacial conditions with associated weathering and ice-wedge formation.

Close inspection of the wedge forms in the surface of the basal diamicton (Plate 21) shows that they lack some of the diagnostic features of ice-wedge casts (Watson, 1981). In particular, there is no evidence for the upturning of adjacent strata, though there is some downward slumping of fill material. The fill material is derived from the overlying brown diamicton and granulometrically is very similar to the lower diamicton. Also, clasts cross the wedge boundary, as defined by colour change, with no modification in their orientation or dip. A striking feature of the wedges is that they all dip, commonly steeply, towards the west, and a crack extends from the base of the wedge down into the underlying diamicton, and in some cases can be traced across the beach. Harris and McCarroll (1990) concluded that the wedge forms are not ice wedge pseudomorphs, but probably originated as tensile cracks on the lee side of the drumlin-like ridge of basal diamicton and were infilled by the overlying diamicton.

The interpretation of the brown diamicton as a weathered horizon is also in doubt. Gray (in Harris and McCarroll, 1990) suggested that it may represent a subglacial meltout till or flow till deposited in the early stages of ice wastage. Alternatively, it could represent lower diamicton which has been stained brown

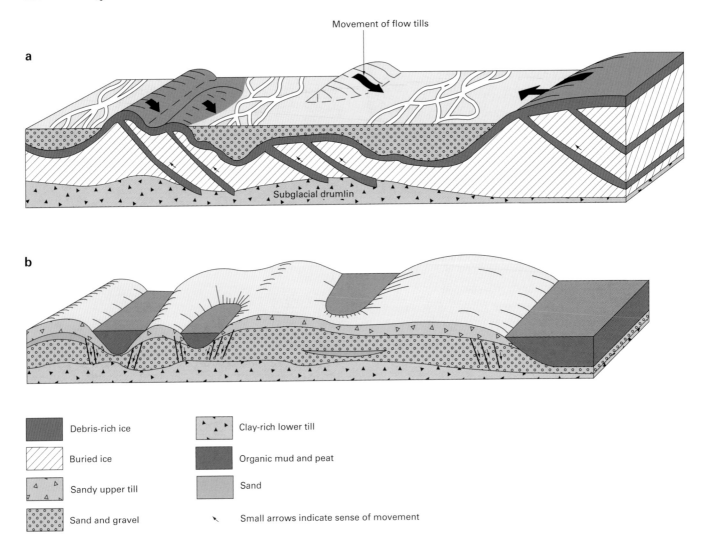

Movement of flow tills

a

Subglacial drumlin

b

▓ Debris-rich ice	▨ Clay-rich lower till
▨ Buried ice	▓ Organic mud and peat
△ Sandy upper till	Sand
∘ Sand and gravel	↖ Small arrows indicate sense of movement

Figure 45 Cartoon showing (a) deglaciation phase and (b) present-day coastal exposure and inland topography at Glanllynnau (after Harris and McCarroll, 1990).

because of its close contact with the overlying brown clay. Given this reinterpretation of the wedge forms and brown diamicton at Glanllynnau, there seems to be little evidence for a model involving two glacial episodes. Boulton's (1977) model of a supraglacial landform system and sediment assemblage appears preferable (Figure 45).

The provenance of the clasts at Glanllynnau remains problematic. Saunders (1968a, 1968b) suggested that the lower diamicton is dominated by slaty erratics 'which have probably been derived from the Bethesda to Nantlle slate belt', while the outwash sands and gravels and the upper till 'contain an erratic suite diagnostic of derivation from south Snowdonia, the Vale of Ffestiniog and the Harlech Dome'. Boulton (1977) suggested that the change in erratic content occurs within the lower diamicton, but presented no evidence. Similarly, Gray (in Harris and McCarroll, 1990) suggested differences in lithology between the lower diamicton and the overlying brown 'weathered' diamicton but presents no evidence. He rejected the Nantlle–Bethesda slate belt as a source for the slaty erratics. The most likely provenance for the erratics seems to be the area to the east.

The organic sediments preserved in the kettle holes at Glanllynnau record changes in climate since deglaciation. Two

kettle basins are exposed in section and these join behind the cliff. The sedimentary sequence in the kettles is displayed in Figure 46. Basal, grey, silty clay grades laterally into diamicton and contains some fine gravel layers near its base. The overlying mud, rich in organic detritus, grades upwards into a grey inorganic clay which contains angular clasts, particularly near the edges of the basin. The overlying peat may be traced over the ridge which separated the two basins (see also Figure 44), and above this peat layer, blown sand and stony slope deposits form the parent material for the modern soil.

Simpkins (1968) studied pollen from the site and recognised the three pollen zones of the Late Devensian Late-glacial. The basal grey clay revealed only sparse, mainly far-travelled pollen, but in the organic-rich detritus mud a marked increase in *Juniperus* sp. and *Rumex* sp. suggests amelioration of climate at the beginning of Zone 1 (Older Dryas). About 10 cm above the base of the organic mud, the more significant warming of Zone II (Windermere Interstadial) is indicated by the sharp increase in *Betula* sp. Return to the cold conditions of Pollen Zone III (Younger Dryas or Loch Lomond Stadial) is indicated by the transition into inorganic clay. Macrofossils of the arctic alpine *Salix herbacea* (least willow) are associated with this horizon.

Three radiocarbon dates (Figure 46) suggest that the area was deglaciated prior to 14 468 ± 300 BP (the oldest minimum date in Wales).

Investigation of coleopteran assemblages from the kettle holes provided a different interpretation of Late-glacial climatic change at this site (Coope and Brophy, 1972). Beetles provide excellent palaeoclimatic indicators because many (stenothermic) species are extremely sensitive to climate, particularly summer temperature. Beetles are also much more mobile than plants and therefore provide a more precise indication of the timing of climatic changes.

The coleopteran evidence suggests that the maximum mean July temperature (17°C) was achieved towards the end of Pollen Zone I, and that when the more extensive vegetation of Pollen Zone II was becoming established, the climate had already begun to deteriorate. The extremely rapid changes in climate recognised at Glanllynnau have been confirmed at several other Late-glacial sites in Britain (Coope and Pennington, 1977; Coope and Joachim, 1980), and may represent changes in the position of the North Atlantic Polar Front (Ruddiman et al., 1977; Sissons, 1979). The sands and gravels and the upper diamicton at Glanllynnau display clear cryoturbation features associated with cold conditions following deglaciation and during the Loch Lomond Stadial (Harris and McCarroll, 1990).

PORTH NEIGWL

The main outcrop of very thick drift filling rock-bound embayments occurs in the Porth Neigwl (Hell's Mouth) area (Figure 47). It extends from the base of Mynydd Rhiw in the west to the bedrock escarpment between Llanengan and Llangian in the east. The inland boundary extends from Llangian north-west to Sarn Meyllteyrn [2398 3247]), and here a borehole proving a drift cover in excess of 110 m has been reported, although the location is unfortunately not clearly recorded (Saunders 1968a). The area is characterised by gently undulating topography and is crossed by the Afon Soch and its tributaries.

Seismic reflection and refraction surveys were undertaken in the intertidal area of the beach at Porth Neigwl beach near Rhiw [242 283], Punt Gwynedd [273 271] and Nant [287 258] (Figures 48, 49), and on inland sites close to the farms of Gelliwig [246 295], Llawr-y-dref [279 286] and Towyn [282 272]. At each of these survey sites glacigenic sediments exhibiting a seismic velocity of 1600 to 1780 m/s are underlain by a higher velocity refractor of 3200 to 3950 m/s which is interpreted as bedrock. At the inland sites, this bedrock lies at a constant elevation of around 35 m below OD whereas at the coast a gently westerly dipping bedrock surface declines from around 30 m below OD at Nant, to a maximum depth of 45 m below OD at the western end of the bay where the Quaternary sediments dip towards the scarp face of Mynydd Rhiw. Such bedrock depth estimates suggest a total drift thickness of 80 m at the coast. The seismic reflection results from the beach are of a sufficiently high quality to reveal a tripartite density stratification (Figure 49). Although in the absence of borehole control the Quaternary lithostratigraphy remains unknown, these data reveal the interesting possibility that some of the buried sediments predate the Late Devensian.

For most of the Porth Neigwl section, the deposits display little variation; clay-rich diamicton dominates and is characterised by a muddy matrix with scattered,

commonly striated, clasts of mixed lithology. Broken marine shell fragments are common, and compressed wood also occurs. Some crude stratification is apparent, particularly near the western end of the bay. Layers and lenses of sand and gravel are uncommon generally, but where present they occur towards the top of the section. In places towards the top of the section (e.g. 2447 2852), there are deformation structures where small lenses of gravel appear to have slumped into the underlying muddy diamicton. These could represent soft-sediment deformation immediately following deposition or the melting of permafrost much later.

The eastern end of Porth Neigwl is more complex and includes laminated muds and bedded sands and gravels, some of which are clearly water-laid (Plate 22). Jehu (1909) described a tripartite sequence of upper and lower tills, of Irish Sea derivation, separated by sands and gravels. The upper till occurs only at the south-eastern end of the bay, and Nicholas (1915) interpreted it as the product of a Welsh glacier which advanced from the east following withdrawal of the Irish Sea ice. Synge (1964) proposed a glacial phase predating the lower till, citing as evidence the presence of a 'soliflucted local till' overlying head in the south-eastern corner of the bay.

Whittow and Ball (1970) followed Saunders (1968a, 1968b) in interpreting the sequence in terms of Irish Sea glaciation followed by an advance of Welsh ice. They interpreted the dominant calcareous diamicton as the product of the 'Irish Sea Advance' of ice from the northwest, and the gravelly Welsh Till as having been deposited by the later 'Arvon Advance' of Welsh ice from the east (Figure 42). The Arfon Advance ice is supposed to have reached St Tudwal's Peninsula, whereupon an ice-tongue crossed the low valley from Sarn Bach to Nant, Porth Neigwl, but failed to reach Porth Ceiriad.

Sand and gravel overlying Irish Sea diamicton at the eastern end of Porth Neigwl has generally been regarded as fluvial outwash, and the associated laminated muds as lacustrine. Eyles and McCabe (1989a, b) have reinterpreted the sequence in terms of a glacimarine model of deglaciation. They suggested that the Irish Sea diamicton was deposited by a 'wide variety of mass flow processes' in a proglacial marine environment, and referred to an exposure of a 'regional mud drape', which presumably is the laminated mud.

A detailed survey of the eastern 2 km of the coastal section revealed a complex record of changing sedimentary environments and evidence of glaciation from both the north and the east (Figure 47). The section is dominated by a ridge of clay-rich matrix-supported massive to very crudely stratified calcareous diamicton ('Irish Sea till'). This lacks some diagnostic features of basal meltout till, and is more likely to be subglacial deformation or advection till. The upper surface of this ridge slopes to the east where it is overlain by water-laid sands and laminated silts and muds (Plate 22; Figure 47, 0–390 m). They are interpreted as the result of local ponding on the surface of stagnant Irish Sea ice. The main source of sediment supply in the sands seems to have been from the east, and in the laminated muds from a dead ice ridge to the west.

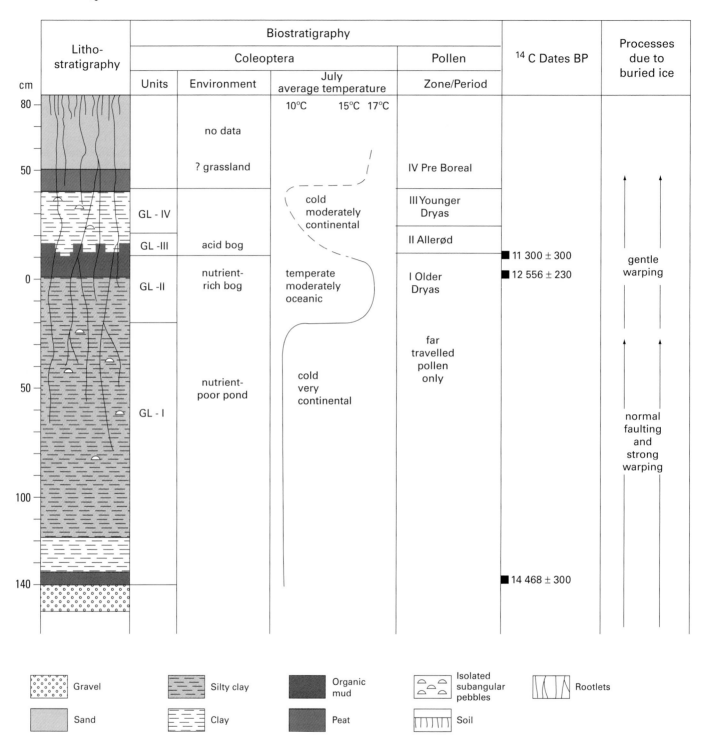

Figure 46 Lithostratigraphy, biostratigraphy and chronostratigraphy of the kettle hole deposits at Glanllynnau, with inferred changes in local environment and regional climate. Based on Coope and Brophy (1972), Boulton (1977) and Harris and McCarroll (1990).

Figure 47
Quaternary
sediments
exposed at the
eastern end of
Porth Neigwl
(Hell's Mouth)
[between
2720 2710 and
2911 2550].

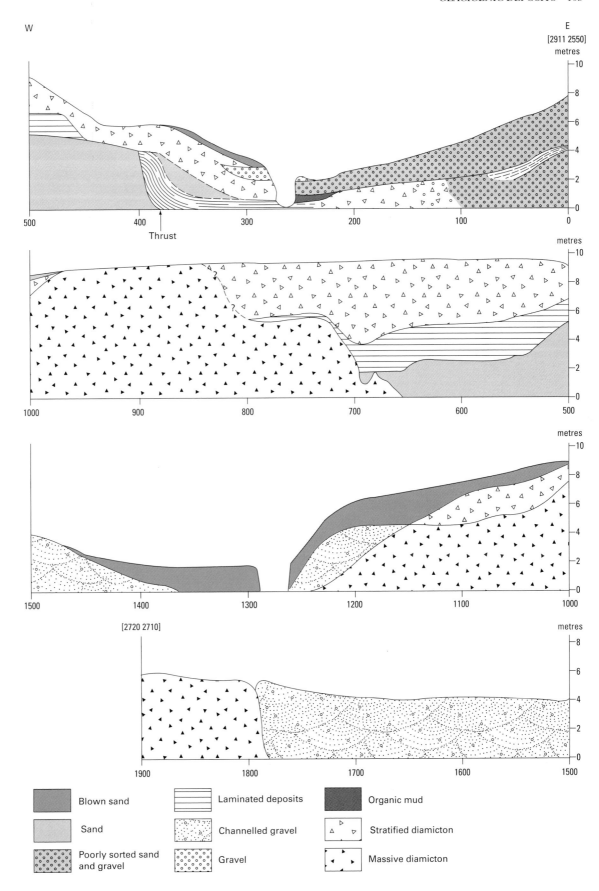

Figure 48 Location of survey lines (a) and the results of seismic refraction studies (b) from the thick drift behind Porth Neigwl.

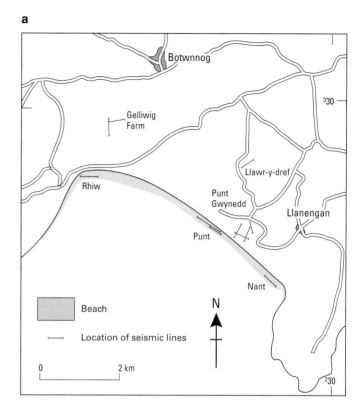

b   Travel time graphs

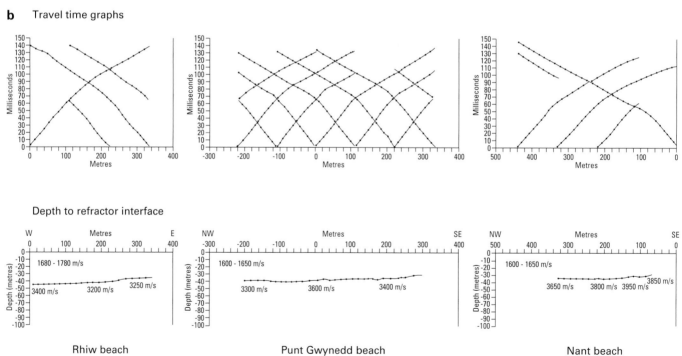

Depth to refractor interface

Rhiw beach

Punt Gwynedd beach

Nant beach

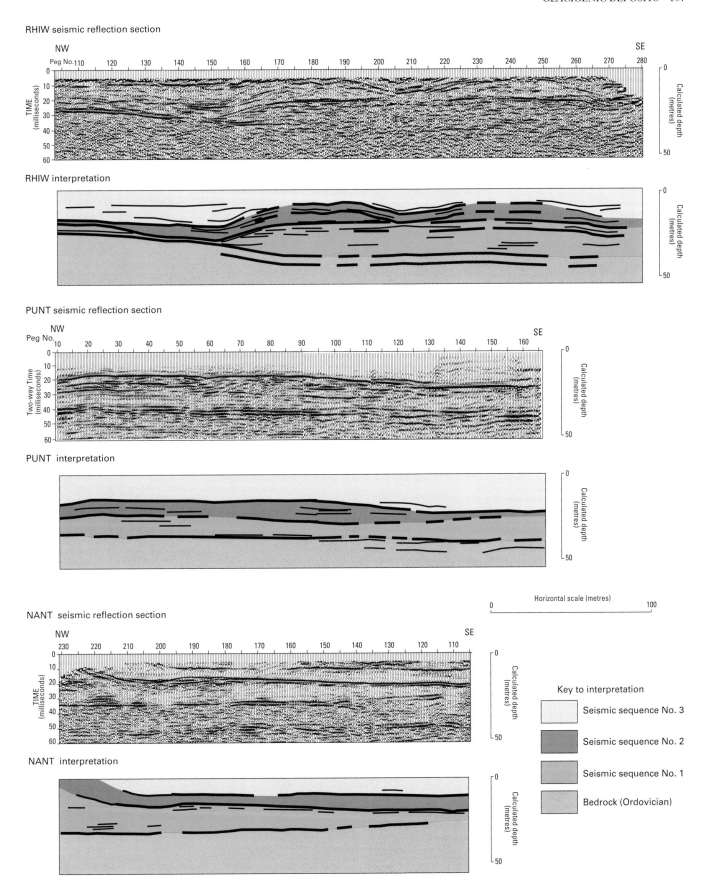

Figure 49 Results of high resolution shallow seismic reflection surveys from the beach at Porth Neigwl.

Plate 22 Porth Neigwl (GS669).

a   Towards the eastern end of Porth
    Neigwl [2835 2522], laminated muds
    and fine-grained sands overlie
    bedded sand and gravel.
b   These deposits are clearly water-laid.
    Formerly they were interpreted as
    glacimarine. Here, they are
    re-interpreted as lacustrine.

a

b

About 400 m west of the end of the
section a wedge of stratified diamicton has been thrust from east to
west up and over sands. This is interpreted as marking the limit of an
advance of Welsh ice which postdates
the stagnation of Irish Sea ice in the
Porth Neigwl embayment. The Irish
Sea glacier may have been effectively
holding back the less powerful Welsh
ice, and as the former became
pinned north of the hills, and
stagnated to the south, the latter was
able to advance over St Tudwal's
Peninsula and on to the dead ice in
the Porth Neigwl embayment. The
sequence of events during deglaciation is dealt with in more detail
under 'Quaternary history'.

The melting and retreat of the
Welsh ice is marked by two facies
dominated by clasts of eastern derivation. The lower unit comprises laminated silts and sands displaying post-
depositional deformation on the
eastern flank of the thrust wedge,
and coarsening and thickening to
the east, where the laminated
deposits grade into stratified diamicton and then into poorly sorted
steeply dipping gravels. At the
eastern end of the section, an alluvial
fan of sand and gravel slopes to the
west and grades into stream channel
deposits with organic detritus that
includes hazelnuts.

Following retreat of the Welsh ice back on to
St Tudwal's Peninsula, the ridge of dead Irish Sea ice to
the west continued to melt producing flow tills (stratified
diamicton) which buried the water-laid sequence to the
east. To the west, the flow tills would have flowed into
and been disaggregated by a substantial river which
drained to the south-west. This would have carried
meltwater from the decaying ice in the Porth Neigwl
embayment, from melting ice on the surrounding hills
via the large meltwater channels and also from the Welsh
ice when it extended at least as far west as St Tudwal's

Peninsula. Sands and gravels deposited by this river
extend along the coast for over 400 m before banking up
against the massive diamicton. The eastern end of the
Porth Neigwl section is described in more detail below.

The thick deposits exposed in the embayment of Porth
Ceiriad have been eroded back so that only a restricted
terrace of drift survives (Plate 23). At the time of survey,
the section was very badly slumped, but the general
sequence of head overlain by 'Welsh till' and solifluction
deposits was confirmed. A lens of soliflucted Irish Sea till
reported from the western side of the section (Whittow
and Ball, 1970) was not visible in situ, but eroded

fragments of calcareous diamicton were present on the beach.

If the report of Irish Sea till at Porth Ceiriad is correct, it suggests that the Irish Sea glacier must have extended over St Tudwal's Peninsula, holding the Welsh ice back to the east. The Welsh ice was able to advance as the Irish Sea ice retreated and stagnated. The sediments exposed in the bay were probably delivered, largely as debris flows, via the two small meltwater channels to the north.

DETAILS

The section presently exposed at the eastern end of Porth Neigwl (Figure 47) differs markedly from the sketches which have been figured previously (Saunders, 1968b; Synge, 1964; Eyles and McCabe, 1989a, b). The bedrock exposed at the eastern end provides a convenient datum and locations are described in meters west of this.

East of a small stream at 260 m, the section can be divided into two sedimentary units which display considerable lateral changes. Striations on the bedrock are aligned 091–271°, supporting the probability of ice flow from the Welsh mountains to the east. The junction between bedrock and drift is obscured by slumping. The lowest undisturbed drift unit clearly exposed above sea level (0 to 250 m on Figure 47) is a matrix-supported, poorly sorted gravel, dominated by clasts derived from the east, and including boulders up to 1m in diameter. The long axes of clasts are aligned east–west, parallel with the striae. This unit includes 'clasts' of mud and sand, many of which are angular in outline, suggesting that they were incorporated while frozen. This poorly sorted but clearly bedded gravel thins and grades westwards into a matrix-supported stratified diamicton and then into laminated muddy sand and laminated mud. At the eastern end, the gravel reaches 5 m above the beach and is overlain by 50 cm of laminated silty mud, but farther west the latter grades into and becomes indistinguishable from the underlying laminated deposits.

At this eastern end of the section, the lowest unit is overlain by 3.5 m of sands and gravels sloping and thinning to the west. Clasts are derived mainly from the east and long axes are aligned down-slope. This unit is clearly cryoturbated in places. As it thins westwards the bedded sand and gravel grades into a series of channelled sands, gravels and muds adjacent to the small stream at 260 m. These channel sediments include abundant sorted plant remains. Between 230 and 260 m the glacigenic deposits are overlain by a peaty sand palaeosol (20 cm) and by blown sand (10 to 50 cm thick).

Although the base of the poorly sorted sand and gravel is not exposed east of the stream at 260 m, there is evidence that it is underlain by sediments of northern derivation. At 25 m, there is a mound about 1 m in diameter of dense, blue-grey muddy calcareous diamicton exposed on the beach 6 m in front of the drift section. This 'Irish Sea till' is similar to the sediments which dominate the section farther west.

Between 270 and 100 m, the section can be divided into four units (muddy diamicton, water-laid sediments, laminated deposits and statified diamicton), locally overlain by blown sand. The lowest unit is a dense muddy diamicton with scattered clasts. This is 'Irish Sea till', dominated by mud and rich in broken shell fragments and foraminifera. It is similar to the lower diamicton unit at Aberdaron (Gibbons and McCarroll, 1993; McCarroll and Harris, 1992) but lacks the compressionally deformed fine sand and silt bodies, and the convex-upwards lenses of gravel that are indicative of a meltout till. It is probably a subglacial deformation till. It is assumed

that this unit underlies all of the sediments exposed at Porth Neigwl, including those of eastern derivation, but is exposed only to the west of 655 m.

From 379 to 800 m, this Irish Sea till is overlain by a westward-thinning development of water-laid deposits, including massive, planar bedded and rippled sands, laminated silts and muds that reach at least 5 m in thickness at 500 m, where their base is concealed. The lower part of these deposits is sand, which in places displays large-scale cross-bedding suggesting current flowing from east to west. The sands are overlain by laminated mud and silt, which locally (at 600 m) reach 3 m in thickness. These laminated deposits impede drainage through the drift, causing widespread waterlogging and slumping, so these are typically very poorly exposed.

The water-laid sequence is truncated to the east by a thrust (between 379–400 m) bringing laminated deposits over the water-laid sands. These laminated muds, silts and sands are laterally continuous with the gravels to the east (at 100 m), which are dominated by easterly derived clasts, but which also include shell fragments that were probably derived from sediments of northern derivation. The thrust is marked by a thin (10 cm) band of sheared mud, and the sand beneath is eroded but not deformed. The sediment that has been thrust up has a friable texture produced by intersecting mud layers, interpreted as a result of displacement during thrusting. Where the laminated unit lies upon the water-laid sands, the lamination dips steeply south-south-west, and at 372 m they were observed to have a strike at 106° and a dip of 13°. The deposits have clearly been deformed after deposition.

The water-laid sediments are overlain (between 400–800 m) by another diamicton of northern derviation, which varies laterally from massive to poorly stratified and contains channels of sorted gravel. Like the upper diamicton at Aberdaron (Gibbons and McCarroll, 1993), it is interpreted as comprising flow tills from the melting of ridges of dead ice within the Porth Neigwl embayment and debris flows from dead ice on the surrounding hills. Eastwards from 460 m, this upper diamicton truncates both the water-laid sediments and the thrust. To the west of 800 m, the contact between the two diamictons is obscure, but is visible as a west-dipping contact to the west of 980 m. Several large rotational slides dissect the cliff in this area. The top of the Irish Sea till continues to dip west, until it passes below beach level at 1230 m. To the west of 1160 m, the Irish Sea till is overlain by sands and gravels with cross-cutting channels, which thicken to the west above the declining surface of the till, reaching 4 m in thickness at 1220 m, but they are dipping beneath the beach at 1260 m, where they are overlain by 2 m of blown sand.

The cliff section is broken between 1260 and 1290 m by a small stream. On the beach directly seaward of this stream, a submerged forest bed is occasionally exposed from beneath a cover of beach gravel. In February 1993, this bed and associated organic deposits were exposed on the beach 68 m south-west of the channel mouth. The exposed section was 27 m wide and 47 m long and was eroded on the north-west, south-west and north-east sides, so that these represent its maximum dimensions in these directions. Towards the land, the organic deposits continued beneath the beach. The thickest section through the organic sediments was at the southern end of the exposure and revealed a series of channels filled with silt, sand, gravel and sorted plant remains (up to 70 cm) overlain by an in situ peat layer with tree stumps and fallen trees. Hazelnuts and acorns were conspicuous, and the largest log, at the northern end of the exposure, measured 86 cm in diameter. The development of peat and the growth of trees in this palaeochannel probably represents the diversion of the Soch stream to flow north-east, away from the sea, and through the gorge to Abersoch.

West of the small stream at 1260 m, the section comprises blown sand up to 2 m thick which from 1360 m is underlain by sands and gravels. The blown sand thins westwards to be replaced by up to 4 m of cross-bedded channelled sands and gravels. These sediments were deposited by the river that drained the Porth Neigwl area during and following deglaciation. This substantial river would have been fed by melting ice on the surrounding hills, via the meltwater channels at Sarn Meyllteyrn, Nant Llaniestyn and Nant Saethon and from active and later stagnant ice to the east via the Soch gorge and the channel south of Nant Farm. West of 1800 m, the sands and gravels are banked against a steeply inclined surface of Irish Sea till.

The drift sequence described here from the eastern end of Porth Neigwl can be interpreted in terms of the stagnation and in situ decay of the Irish Sea glacier. The Welsh ice, which had been held back to the east by the stronger Irish Sea glacier was able to advance to the west and extend beyond St Tudwal's Peninsula. Where it extended onto the decaying Irish Sea sheet it thrust a block of Irish Sea till, or perhaps debris-rich Irish Sea ice, up to the west over water-laid sands and laminated sediments. As the Welsh ice melted and withdrew, water-laid sediments were deposited.

As the stagnant ice in the Porth Neigwl embayment melted, water flowed towards the sea in a substantial braided river system, the position of which is now marked by a width of over 400 m of channel sands and gravels exposed at the coast. The postglacial course of the Soch river originally followed the eastern margin of these gravels, but was later diverted to flow away from the coast and through the gorge towards Abersoch. The submerged forest bed occasionally exposed on the beach represents the silting up and development of vegetation upon the original course of the Soch.

Porth Ceiriad

At Porth Ceiriad, a narrow terrace of drift at the back of a rock-bound embayment is incised to reveal a section 800 m long and 30 m high (Plate 23). The section was described by Whittow and Ball (1970) who recognised blocky head and shale head overlain by a grey-brown,

non-calcareous Welsh till. This was overlain by a soliflucted till containing, on the western side, a lens of soliflucted calcareous Irish Sea till. The whole sequence was overlain by stratified local head, cryoturbated towards the top. They correlated the Welsh till with the lower till exposed farther east (e.g. Glanllynnau), attributing it to the earlier of their two proposed advances, the Criccieth Advance (Figure 42). During the second, Arvon Advance a lobe of ice is supposed to have reached Porth Neigwl via the channel leading west from Sarn Bach, leaving Porth Ceiriad ice-free. The presence of soliflucted Irish Sea till in the sequence is taken as evidence that during the earlier glacial phase in this area the northern Irish Sea Advance ice was confluent with Welsh Criccieth Advance ice moving in from the north-east.

During the period of this survey, the section at Porth Ceiriad was badly slumped and the key part of the sequence on the western side was obscured. However, the general stratigraphy was confirmed, comprising local scree and head, overlain by a gravelly brown diamicton, followed by poorly sorted gravel and sand, and overlain in turn by local angular head. The lens of calcareous diamicton reported from the western side of the section was not exposed.

In interpreting the section at Porth Ceiriad it is important to consider its position in relation to the surrounding topography. The drift deposits of the rock-bound embayment have been eroded so that only a narrow platform at the back of the bay remains. Two short, steep meltwater channels descend into the embayment from the north. There seems to be no clear justification for interpreting any of the deposits at Porth Ceiriad as lodgement tills. All of the sediments could have been supplied via the two meltwater channels. Whether the material was supplied subglacially or as flow tills and debris flows during and following deglaciation is unclear.

Plate 23 The drift deposits of Porth Ceiriad form a narrow platform at the back of the bay (GS670). Much of the sediment may have been supplied by two small meltwater channels, both subglacially and following deglaciation.

Sand and gravel-dominated landform–sediment assemblages

Deposits dominated by sand and gravel occur in three landform-sediment assemblages: as constructional drift topography probably associated mainly with ice-marginal environments (hummocky glacial deposits), as terraces (glacial sand and gravel undifferentiated), and as extensive low-level spreads (glaciofluvial sheet deposits). With the possible exception of a few isolated ridges and mounds, some of which may have been deposited sub-glacially, the sand and gravel dominated landform-sediment assemblages are interpreted as proglacial, deposited as the last ice sheet retreated northwards.

Hummocky glacial deposits

This landform/sediment assemblage includes sands and gravels, including some diamicton, arranged as ridges and mounds. Extensive tracts occur in three areas of the sheet: in the north-west near Tudweiliog, in the Mynydd Cilan area of St Tudwal's Peninsula and in the area north of Pwllheli. Isolated ridges and mounds of sand and gravel, that may have quite different origins are treated separately.

The constructional drift topography of the north-west is part of a broad band of ridges and mounds of drift, dominated by sand and gravel, which extends along the north coast of Llŷn from Tudweiliog in the west to Penygroes in the east. In places [e.g. 2952 3750] peaty enclosed hollows and small pools may represent kettle holes formed by the melting of buried ice. The sediments associated with this area of constructional topography are poorly exposed. The ridge on which Tudweiliog is situated is interpreted as part of this constructional topography. Although there are no sections, Jehu (1909) reported a boring made for water at Ty-issa, which revealed 1.8 m (6 feet) of sand, 8.2 m (27 feet) of stiff bluish grey boulder clay and 0.9 m (3 feet) of coarse sand, the base of which was not reached. At the County School he reported a boring which passed through 4.9 m (16 feet) of sandy clay and 0.6 m (2 feet) of 'pure sand', the base of which was not reached. 'A little further down the slope of the same hill' a borehole passed through 3 m (10 feet) of 'pure sand'.

The best exposure has been described from the refuse disposal site, just north of the Pwllheli district, at Maesoglan [3018 3787]. Edge (1990) considered the sedimentary associations consistent with an origin as a Gilbert-type delta. It is not clear whether it prograded into fresh or sea water, though no marine fauna have been reported. The best exposures at this site are now obscured. Because the site lies in a gap in the line of hills of the north coast, at the northern margin of the Cors Geirch, it is questionable to what degree the facies are representative of similar topography elsewhere.

Irregular mounds and ridges of drift also characterise the area around Mynydd Cilan, west of Porth Ceiriad. Exposures are rare, but at Bryn Rodyn [2952 2407], which lies at the eastern end of a prominent ridge, a 3 m section revealed massive, matrix-supported muddy diamicton with scattered clasts. Fabric analysis suggests ice movement from the east, which accords with the direction of striations in the area.

The area north of Pwllheli is characterised by east–west bedrock ridges curving inland to north-east, and by ridges of drift which follow that curve. Some of the features are bedrock-cored and probably have only a thin cover of drift. Thomas et al. (1990) interpret the landforms in this area as ice-marginal ridges of an active ice front retreating to the north-west, surrounded by proglacial sandur deposits. The alignment of the drift ridges is more likely to be controlled by the alignment of the nearby bedrock ridges and by drainage adapted to that alignment. For example, one of the features identified by Thomas et al. (1990) as a 'dead ice ridge', at Bryn Tan [3720 3689], comprises sand and gravel.

Isolated mounds and small ridges of sand and gravel occur at Bryn Bugail [3071 3123], north of Sarn Bach [3048 2708], at Muriau on Mynydd Gilan [3010 2424], on the north side of Carn Fadryn [2882 3594] and near Cefn Madryn [2770 3652]. The features at Bryn Bugail and Sarn Bach are elongate and dominated by gravel. They may have been deposited by subglacial or englacial streams in the same way as eskers. The term esker, however, is generally reserved for much larger features (Gray, 1991), and these examples are perhaps best termed elongate kames. Mounds of sand and gravel at Muriau, Carn Fadryn and Cefn Madryn may represent small kames formed by the local ponding of meltwater at the ice margin during deglaciation. A promontory of sand at Nanhoron may represent a delta prograding south from the end of Nant Saethon.

DETAILS

At **Bryn Bugail** a small elongate (north–south) mound of gravel lies on a thinly drift-covered ridge extending south from Foel Fawr. The feature is about 5 m high with dimensions about 45 × 70 m. On the south-west side, behind Bryn Bugail, a temporary section, 6 m wide, revealed 2.4 m of bedded gravel dominated by clasts in the range 1 to 3 cm, but with some larger clasts up to 12 cm long. Lithologies are mixed, with roundness ranging from subangular to subrounded with a few rounded pebbles. Some clasts retain striations. Beds dip 8° west at the east end of the section and 22° west at the western end. An ice-wedge pseudomorph, 35 cm wide at the top and extending 1.5 m into the gravels, was recorded at the eastern end of the section. Clasts dip into the centre of the wedge and it is cut off 30 cm from the surface. The origin of the mound is uncertain, but it may represent part of an esker formed where an englacial stream reached the glacier sole. Coarse, freely draining gravel on the crest of a ridge may remain stable, even under the periglacial conditions following deglaciation (Paul and Eyles, 1990).

North of **Sarn Bach**, an isolated ridge aligned north–south extends for 580 m [3043 2693 to 3052 2748]. It is up to 130 m across and up to 9 m high. The southern section has been exploited for sand and gravel, but the excavations are degraded and the sediments poorly exposed; the deposit appears to be dominated by gravel. There are no exposures in the northern section of the ridge and it is possible that this section may be bedrock-cored. The origin of this feature is problematic, since it lies almost normal to the direction of ice movement as indicated by striations. Such an isolated feature, dominated by gravel, is unlikely to represent a terminal moraine. It is more likely to have been deposited by a subglacial or englacial stream. The movement of englacial and subglacial meltwater need not parallel the movement of basal ice, but can be adjusted to the local bedrock topography. There is a band of high ground to the west of the ridge, so meltwater may have turned south to flow towards Sarn Bach and cut through the high ground via the channel south of Ty Newydd. It is notable that the gravel ridge is directly in line with the north-eastern section of the meltwater channel, which is now partly infilled with diamicton and supports an underfit stream. This feature was probably formed during retreat when the ice margin extended over the site of the Cors Llyferin but did not reach as far west as Llanengan.

At **Nanhoron** [2810 3150], a 'promontory' of sand extends southwards from the bedrock slope which swings to the west at the southern end of Nant Saethon. The feature is up to 300 m wide and extends 250 m south of the bedrock scarp. The surface of the feature lies up to 25 m above the diamicton-filled base of the valley. A temporary exposure east of the house revealed 70 cm of upwards-fining, medium- to fine-grained, rippled sand. Climbing ripples indicate a palaeocurrent towards 196°, which is parallel with Nant Saethon. This is overlain by 40 cm of diamicton, with a silty sand matrix. A disused sand pit lies on the southern side of the feature, but it is much degraded and no sections are exposed. A 2 m auger boring revealed fine- to medium-grained sand throughout the pit, with no evidence of gravel. The feature may represent a delta that prograded into standing water trapped by stagnant ice in the area now occupied by thick drift.

Other glacial sand and gravel landform–sediment assemblages

Extensive terraces of sand and gravel surround the Cors Geirch depression (Figure 50) between Pwllheli and Carn Fadryn [314 364]. More restricted terraces occur between Carreg y Defaid and Llanbedrog [334 321] and near the Warren, between Mynydd Tir-y-cwmwd and Castellmarch [320 330].

The Cors Geirch is an elongate, north-west-orientated area of wetland at less than 30 m above OD, lying between Pwllheli and Carn Fadryn. The north-western end encroaches upon a gap in the hills that parallel the north coast of Llŷn. The gap is now blocked by ridges and mounds of sand and gravel which are exposed in the waste disposal site at Maesoglan (described above). The Cors Geirch is surrounded to the south-west and north-east by sand and gravel deposits. To the south-west, a flat-topped terrace of sand and gravel at about 50 m above OD abuts the bedrock and thinly diamicton-covered slopes around Ty Isaf [3154 3458]. On the same slope nearer the coast, a similar terrace around Coed Cae-rhos [322 330] and Cefn Llanfair [320 338] lies at about 45 m above OD. To the north-east of Cors Geirch a ridge of sand and gravel, reaching as high as 86 m OD, extends from near Pen y bryn [3136 3804] south-east to Cefn Mine [338 359], continuing southwards at a lower altitude (less than 52 m above OD) as far as Pont Rhyd-John [3402 3340]. Around Bryn Bodvel [3345 3643], the surface of the deposit forms a flat terrace at about 50 m above OD and farther south near Penrhos Home [335 336] a similar flat surface lies at about 15 m above OD. For much of its length, both sides of the gravel ridge are steep. Near Gallt

y Beren [3208 3524] and south of Rhyllech Uchaf [3392 3564], the sand and gravel probably overlies diamicton. Although diamictons are not exposed in section, the soils are heavy and clay-rich, and the ground is poorly drained indicating their probable presence.

Exposures in the terrace deposits are rare. A disused sand pit near Traian [3301 3621] is now degraded, but Synge (1964) recorded horizontally bedded sand and gravel containing typical Irish Sea erratics that include flint and coal, as well as 'numerous Welsh erratics'. In the same pit, Whittow and Ball (1970) recorded a large fossil ice wedge. In 1990, an archaeological excavation near Bryn Bodvel [336 363] revealed sand and gravel with northern erratics including flint and coal. Near Penrhos Camp [3314 3402], a small pit dug in the ridge extending south of Rhyd-y-clafdy proved 1.5 m of bedded sand and gravel with evidence of normal faulting as described below.

The terrace between Carreg y Defaid and Llanbedrog lies at a similar altitude (about 16 m above OD) to that near Penrhos. The deposits are exposed at the seaward end of Nant Iago [3312 3138], where 4 m of horizontally bedded gravel with a coarse sand matrix is overlain by 2 m of medium-grained sand. A smaller section on the north side of Carreg y Defaid reveals 2 m of bedded sand and gravel overlain by 2 m of fine, horizontally bedded gravel. The latter probably represents slope wash from the hill.

Near the Warren, there are two clear terrace features. The higher terrace, which reaches 37 m at Talgoed [3205 3056], has a steep eastern scarp that curves round from a bedrock outcrop in the meltwater channel near Tan-y-mynydd [3215 3084] south and south-west to Trewarren [3190 3035], where the scarp grades into a gentle slope. The sediments of the upper terrace are exposed in road cuttings at Talgoed [3198 3057] and opposite Trewarren, where they comprise poorly sorted very coarse gravel with a sandy matrix. On the scarp slope of the terrace near Tal-y-fan, small temporary exposures reveal sandy diamicton rather than gravel. The lower terrace extends to the south and east and slopes from about 17 m above OD in the north to 11 m OD in the south. The deposits are exposed at The Warren [319 299] where they comprise well-sorted bedded sands and gravel, with ripples indicating a palaeocurrent from the north. The section is described below.

The features surrounding the Cors Geirch were originally interpreted as the remnants of an ice-dammed lake (Matley, 1936). In a detailed study, Saunders (1968b) suggested that terraces surrounding the Cors Geirch can be interpreted as shorelines, and that their altitude accords closely with the intake levels of associated overflow channels. He recognised terraces at 84 m, 70 m and 49 m above OD, associated with channels at Nant Bodlas (Nant Saethon) [2988 3452], Llanbedrog [3228 3162] and Penarwel [3264 3256], suggesting that the lake level fell to each of these levels as the ice to the south and east retreated. Saunders' 'terraces' included bedrock and till-covered surfaces and the sand and gravel to the east of the Cors Geirch was interpreted as deltaic, prograding into the lake from ice to the east. The origin of similar

Figure 50 Drift deposits of the area around Cors Geirch.

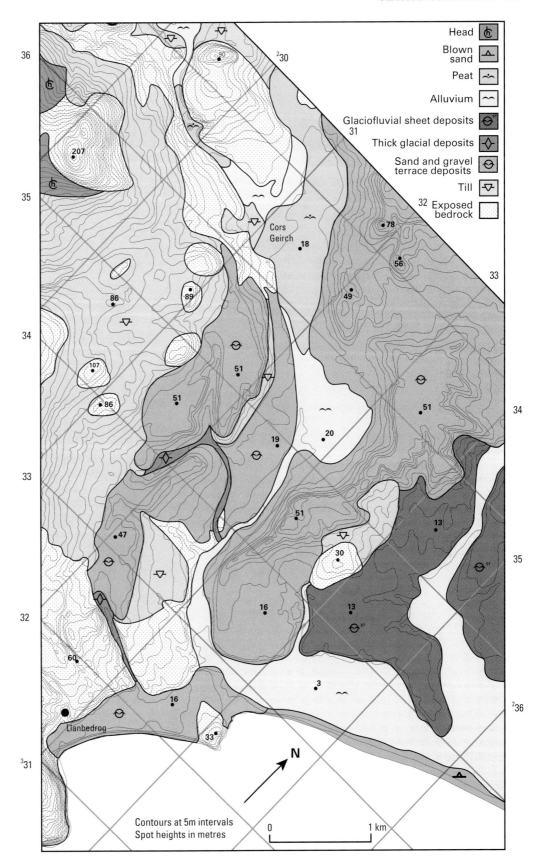

Head

Blown sand

Peat

Alluvium

Glaciofluvial sheet deposits

Thick glacial deposits

Sand and gravel terrace deposits

Till

Exposed bedrock

N

Contours at 5m intervals
Spot heights in metres

0   1 km

terraces of sand and gravel on the opposite side of the Cors Geirch was not made clear.

Whittow and Ball (1970) rejected the concept of an ice-dammed lake because there is no evidence of lacustrine deposits. They interpret the sand and gravel terraces as kames formed around a lobe of Irish Sea ice which occupied the Cors Geirch during the second, Main Anglesey Advance. This would account for the terraces to the west of the Cors Geirch, which are banked against a line of hills. To explain the eastern terraces, which are steep-sided, requiring some support to the east, Whittow and Ball (1970) suggested that contemporaneous (Arvon Advance) ice from northern Snowdonia passed through the Pant Glas col and swung south-westwards towards the area of Bodfel [343 365].

An alternative explanation has been provided by Eyles and McCabe (1989a,b) who interpreted them as Gilbert-type deltas which record the lowering of sea level due to rapid isostatic recovery. If this interpretation is correct, then these features provide a valuable indication of the rate of isostatic rebound. The terraces to the east of the Cors Geirch do not now receive any drainage, they are isolated from the bedrock slopes to the north by a deep channel. These features could, therefore, only have formed when the ice was in direct contact. As soon as the ice withdrew to the north and east the supply of meltwater and sediment would have been removed. Since the highest terrace remnants are at 86 m above OD and the lowest terrace surface lies below 15 m above OD, there must have been a fall in relative sea level of more than 70 m while the ice margin remained in this part of Llŷn. The highest rate of isostatic recovery reported by Eyles and McCabe (1989a,b), from the margins of the much larger Laurentide ice sheet of North America, was nearly 50 m within 1000 years of deglaciation. Even taking this maximum rate, the ice margin would have had to remain virtually stationary on Llŷn for 1400 years. It is extremely unlikely that a tidal ice margin could have remained stationary for so long, so an origin as marine Gilbert-type deltas must be rejected.

The interpretation favoured here is that the sand and gravel terraces were laid down in fresh water and that the different surfaces reflect falls in the lake level as the confining glaciers melted and withdrew. All of the features can be accommodated within a single retreat phase and there is no need to invoke a substantial readvance of northern and eastern ice as envisaged by Whittow and Ball (1970). The highest terrace remnants, to the north-east of the Cors Geirch, may represent the earliest stages in the uncoupling of northern ice that became pinned behind the hills of the north Llŷn coast and ice that extended into central Llŷn from the east. Active ice would have continued to extend through the gap in the hills west of Garn Boduan and onto the site of the Cors Geirch. The lower terraces and those along the coast to the south and west would have formed after a drop in the water level as the lake was ponded against Welsh ice to the south. If it is assumed that the sands and gravels were deposited in ice-dammed lakes, then the height of the terraces provides a minimum estimate of the height of the ice surfaces. This can be used to reconstruct possible positions of the ice fronts during deglaciation. This evidence is discussed in more detail under 'Quaternary history'.

DETAILS

Near **Penrhos Home** [3314 3402], a small refuse pit dug in the gravel ridge at 40 m above OD provided a section which showed a bed of very coarse-grained sand in gravels, with extensive small-scale normal faulting. The faults dip south-south-west, suggesting extension towards the Cors Geirch depression. The faulting is consistent with an origin as a kame terrace banked against ice occupying the Cors Geirch depression.

In the car-park of **The Warren** caravan park, a section [3205 3002] near the southern margin of the lower terrace, aligned 210°, revealed 2 m of bedded gravel (base not seen) dipping at 28° to the east (foresets) overlain by 40 cm of similar gravel dipping only 12° to the east (topsets). The section is topped by 30 cm of sandy soil. This sequence suggests that the lower terrace may represent a delta which prograded eastwards. A 1m section, 30 m to the south revealed medium-bedded sand, with abundant pebbles up to 3 cm, dipping south-south-west at 20°. To the north-west, this facies is overlain by 2 m of horizontally bedded coarse gravel including clasts up to 30 cm.

Glaciofluvial sheet deposits

A low spread of sand and gravel extends southwards between the thinly drift-covered bedrock extending north of Pwllheli to Llanor and the eastern boundary of the sand and gravel terraces surrounding the Cors Geirch. The best exposures occur along the Afon Rhyd-hir, beyond the Holocene river alluvium. West of Felin Llanor [3490 3678], 6 to 10 m sections reveal horizontally bedded, poorly sorted, cobble gravel with a coarse sand matrix and thin beds of well-sorted, coarse- to very fine-grained sand and very sandy diamicton. To the south-west of Gellidara, augering proved 2 m of well-sorted medium sand. The southern boundary of the sand and gravel spread forms a low scarp between Pont Rhyd-John [3402 3340] and Castell [3534 3412]. This landform sediment assemblage can be interpreted as a sandur produced by braided meltwater streams, probably following the present course of the Afon Rhyd-hir.

POSTGLACIAL DEPOSITS

Head

The term head is restricted here to locally derived material which has been transported and deposited in a periglacial environment. It does not include glacigenic deposits that have been transferred downslope after deposition in a glacial environment; many of the glacigenic deposits of the Pwllheli district have been remobilised in this way. Head is a highly heterogeneous mixture of upslope lithologies, and with variable grain and clast size.

In the west of the district, deposits of head more than 1 m thick extend along the eastern side of Mynydd y Graig north to Ffynon Aelrhiw [2339 2848] and Plas yn Rhiw [2374 2835], north of Mynydd Rhiw around Glan Delyn [2382 3055], and along the foot of the steep bedrock slope at Bronllwyd Bach [2430 3001]. In the north of the district, thick and extensive head occurs on the southern and eastern sides of Garn Fadryn. Near Caerau-Uchaf [2924 3516], a cutting exposes 2.5 m of local angular to subangular head, with a coarse sandy matrix. A smaller (1 m) exposure to the west [2910 3515] includes some striated, foreign clasts. Thinner deposits of local angular to subangular material, which has probably been solifluicted, mantle many of the remaining hills but are of insufficient thickness to be included on the map. In a few localities, thin head deposits display a manganese-rich cement of variable hardness, as on the northern side of Garn Bach [2884 3496].

Scree

Although many of the steeper bedrock slopes are mantled by a thin cover of rockfall material it has not accumulated sufficiently to form scree slopes. Good examples are the higher slopes of Garn Fadryn, Garn Bach and Garn Saethon. The thickest accumulation of scree occurs on the eastern side of Nant Saethon near Pont Llidiard-y-dwr [2887 3238], where stratified, angular local debris 15 m thick is quarried for aggregate. A similar accumulation of scree extends along the southern side of Mynydd Tir-y-Cwmwd, cropping out on the coast east of Plas Nimmo [3297 3035]. In both areas the deposits are vegetated and clearly inactive. They probably date from the periglacial conditions following deglaciation and during the Loch Lomond Stadial.

Alluvial fan

Two alluvial fans occur in the district, both lying on the eastern margin of the thick drift that fills the Porth Neigwl embayment. The village of Llanengan sits on the larger of these but the sediments are not exposed. The smaller fan is incised at the coast in the eastern corner of Porth Neigwl. It comprises beds of sand and gravel dipping and thinning to the west. The long axes of clasts are aligned downslope, and the deposits are clearly cryoturbated. The fans probably formed mainly during the cold conditions following deglaciation and during the Loch Lomond Stadial, when vegetation would have been sparse and surface flow would have been generated by snow melt over frozen ground. At the eastern end of Porth Neigwl, the fan deposits grade laterally into stream deposits which include the remains of temperate vegetation, including hazelnuts. This suggests that the fans may have been reactivated occasionally, perhaps by large storm events, during the Holocene.

Alluvium

Deposits of silt, sand and gravel occur along the courses of the principal streams in the region including the Afon Soch, Afon Rhyd-hir and Afon Erch, but are absent in the major meltwater channels of Nant Llaniestyn and Nant Saethon. Sandy alluvium also occurs in parts of the Cors Geirch and along the stream draining to the south. Gravelly alluvium is exposed in a section at the eastern end of Porth Neigwl and includes some organic-rich horizons. Marine alluvium,

protected by coastal sand dunes, occurs along the coast east of Pwllheli as far as Pen-ychain and west of Pwllheli as far as Pont Rhyd-John, where it merges with river alluvium. Its thickness is not known. Although the deposits could record a Holocene sea level slightly higher that at present, they may simply represent the seaward migration of dune ridges.

Peat

Peat deposits occur in several areas within the Pwllheli district. The thickest and most extensive lie within the Cors Geirch depression, where they overlie glacigenic deposits and alluvium, and in Cors Llyferin, south of Abersoch, where they overlie marine alluvium. The only peat deposits which have been studied in detail are those exposed by the coastal incision of kettle holes at Glan-llynnau. These contain rich pollen and coleopteran assemblages which have been used to reconstruct environmental changes during the Lateglacial and Holocene (Simpkins, 1968; Coope and Brophy, 1972).

Blown sand

Well-developed sand dunes occur on top of the thick drift of Porth Neigwl to the west of Tai-morfa [284 265], and blown sand extends inland to the north of Porth Ceiriad. Much of the south coast of Llŷn is marked by linear ridges of blown sand, including the seaward boundary of Cors Llyferin south of Abersoch, The Warren south of Mynydd Tîr-y-cwmwd, between Carreg y Defaid and Pwllheli, and between Pwllheli and pen-ychain. The deposits of blown sand exposed above the glacigenic deposits of Porth Neigwl are stratified and contain abundant terrestrial gastropod shells.

Shoreface and beach deposits

Long sandy beaches produced by erosion of the widespread glacigenic deposits provide one of the most important economic resources of the region. Beach deposits dominated by cobble gravels are also common, comprising a rich variety of lithologies, again derived primarily from erosion of the glacigenic deposits.

Marine deposits undifferentiated

Marine deposits, dominated by intertidal muds and fine-grained sands occur at the mouths of the larger streams, including Pwllheli harbour and around Abersoch. The areas of low ground between Pwllheli and Pen-ychain to the east, and between Pwllheli and Carreg y Defaid to the west consist mainly of marine alluvium. Although these could represent a slight fall in sea level late in the Holocene, they may simply reflect aggradation of land due to the migration of dune ridges.

QUATERNARY HISTORY

The large-scale landforms of the Pwllheli district probably predate the Pleistocene glaciations, but their origin and the timescale involved in their evolution is the subject of debate (see above *Preglacial landscape evolution*). The general consensus is now that the major bedrock landforms of the Pwllheli district have been formed over a much longer timescale than has been formerly assumed. The hills of the district, formed mainly on acid intrusive rocks, may have emerged as inselbergs, preserved because of their greater resistance to chemical weathering. However, during the Pleistocene the area has been inundated, probably on several occasions, by ice sheets moving southwards down the basin of the Irish Sea, and most of the direct evidence of previous land-forming processes has been removed or covered by drift. Moreover, the differences in relative resistance which are likely to lead to differential relief under tropical weathering are, in many cases, likely to provide similar resistance to glacial and fluvioglacial erosion.

Within the Pwllheli district, no direct evidence of the timing of the onset of glacial conditions is available. Detailed oxygen isotope studies of deep sea cores, however, record numerous glacial/interglacial cycles over the last 2.4 million years (Shackleton and Opdyke, 1973, 1976). On land the record is less complete, but there is evidence in Wales for three glacial advances which would have inundated the Llŷn peninsula. The earliest, which reached Fremington on the north coast of Devon (Bowen, 1969) and deposited northern erratics in South Wales (Strahan and Cantrill, 1904), has been correlated with the Anglian glaciation of England and the Munsterian glaciation of Ireland (Bowen et al., 1986). It has been assigned to Oxygen Isotope Stage 12 (428 to 480 ka), which is the period of the major Elster glaciation of Europe.

In Wales, evidence for the intermediate advance is restricted to Paviland in Gower, where a ridge of diamicton has been interpreted as a moraine predating the interglacial raised beaches of Minchin Hole, which are ascribed to Oxygen Isotope Stage 7 (Bowen et al., 1986). The Paviland glaciation has been correlated with the Kirkhill till of Scotland (Connel and Hall, 1984) and with the post-Hoxnian but pre-Ipswichian deposits of England (the term Wolstonian is inappropriate since the 'type' deposits at Wolston are considered to be Anglian in age: Rose, 1987; Rice and Douglas, 1991). It has been assigned to Oxygen Isotope Stage 8 (252 to 302 ka), which is the stage of the Drenthe (Saale) of Europe (Bowen et al., 1986) but may be older.

Although some of the erosional landforms of Llŷn may have developed during successive glaciations, all of the exposed glacigenic deposits of the Pwllheli district can be assigned to the last, Late Devensian (Irish Midlandian or Fenitian; Hoare, 1991; Warren, 1991) cold stage. Known as the Dimlington advance in England (Rose, 1985), it has been assigned to Oxygen Isotope Stage 2 (10 to 26 ka).

The maximum extent of Late Devensian ice in the Irish Sea basin, and the timing and mode of deglaciation have all been subject to considerable debate. Mitchell (1960, 1972) and Synge (1964) placed the limit along the north coast of Llŷn, leaving much of the Pwllheli district and the southern Irish Sea unglaciated. Their methodology involved mapping moraine ridges, counting the number of diamicton (till) units in coastal sections and assessing the degree of weathering of tills and the 'freshness' of drift landforms. This methodology was criticised by Bowen (1973), who presented a simpler explanation of glacial deposits around the Irish Sea, using inter-glacial raised beach deposits as stratigraphical markers. The southern limit of Irish Sea ice was placed south of Cardigan Bay. Although some 'beaches' may have been misidentified (Gibbons and McCarroll, 1993), this interpretation has subsequently been supported by amino acid geochronology (Bowen, 1991; Bowen et al., 1985; Bowen et al., 1986; Bowen and Sykes, 1988).

The timing of the Dimlington advance is well constrained at the type site on the Yorkshire coast (Rose, 1985), where glacial diamictons directly overlie silts which contain moss and coleoptera with glacial affinities, and which have yielded radiocarbon dates of $18\,500 \pm 400$ BP and $18\,240 \pm 250$ BP (Penny et al., 1969). Lake deposits which overlie glacial deposits at two sites have yielded radiocarbon dates of $16\,713 \pm 340$ BP and $13\,045 \pm 270$ BP (Jones, 1977; Keen et al., 1984). The maximum age is supported by a thermoluminescence date of $17.5 \pm 1.6 \times 10^3$ years from a solifluction deposit underlying diamicton of the Dimlington advance at Eppleworth in Yorkshire (Wintle and Catt, 1985).

The timing of the Dimlington advance in the Irish Sea basin is not so well constrained. Five radiocarbon dates in the range 18 400 to 18 900 BP from the base of kettle holes developed on glacigenic deposits in the Isle of Man (McCarroll, 1990) were initially used as evidence that ice in the Irish Sea basin had retreated substantially before the ice on the east coast had reached its maximum extent (Mitchell, 1972; Thomas, 1976, 1977). However, these dates are now regarded as unreliable (Lowe and Walker, 1984) and a maximum age for the Dimlington advance is provided by a radiocarbon date of 18 000 (+1400, -1200) obtained from a mammoth bone from a till-sealed cave in the Vale of Clwyd (Rowlands, 1971). A minimum age is provided by a radiocarbon date of $14\,468 \pm 300$ BP from the base of a kettle hole overlying glacigenic deposits at Glanllynnau on Llŷn (Coope and Brophy, 1972). The evidence suggests, therefore, that Late Devensian ice probably covered Llŷn soon after 18 000 BP and that the region was deglaciated by about 14 500 BP.

The erosional and depositional evidence suggests that the Pwllheli district was inundated by ice from two distinct sources (Figure 51a). Ice moving down the basin of the Irish Sea carved striations and grooves now exposed by the erosion of drift on the north and west coasts of Llŷn and delivered Scottish erratics, including riebeckite-eurite from Ailsa Craig. Striations and grooves in the north-west of the Pwllheli district are aligned at 230°, suggesting ice flow from the north-east. This conforms with erosional and depositional evidence of ice flow direction in western Llŷn presented by McCarroll (1991). The Irish Sea ice was also responsible for the formation of the spectacular meltwater channels of central Llŷn, including Nant Llani-estyn and Nant Saethon.

The striations and evidence of subglacial meltwater demonstrate that at some stage the Irish Sea ice over Llŷn must have been warm-based (i.e. it was not frozen to

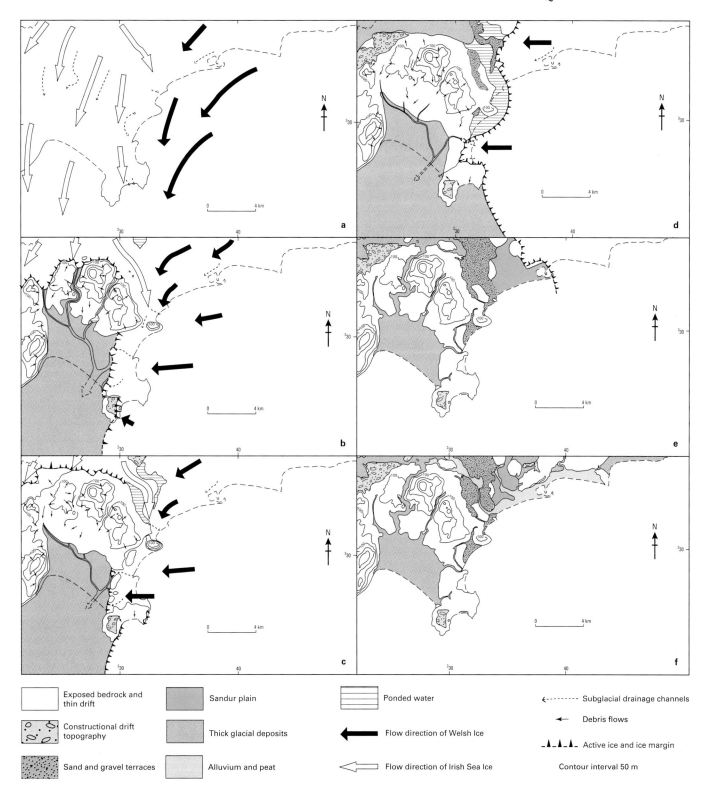

Figure 51   Reconstruction of the sequence of events during deglaciation (see text for details).

its bed). Such conditions are likely to have prevailed when the ice was thick, with high subglacial pressure raising the melting point of the basal ice. This warm-based ice was probably responsible for distorting the bedrock described from the side of Nant Saethon, producing 'comminution till' with clasts aligned down-valley, at right angles to the local slope. Some of the thin diamicton, where bedrock remains the dominant control on topography, may have been lodged under warm-based ice, but the exposures are too shallow and disturbed to be interpreted with confidence. The small elongate mound of gravel at Bryn Bugail, near Mynytho, was probably deposited by an englacial stream which reached or approached the glacier sole at this point.

Ice flowing westwards from the Vale of Ffestiniog similarly carved striations and subglacial meltwater channels indicative of a warm-based thermal regime. These erosional features provide evidence of the maximum extent of the Welsh ice. Striations on St Tudwal's Peninsula suggest that the ice moved from between east-north-east and due east, and on the coast at Trwyn Llech-y-Doll there is evidence of ice moving onshore from Cardigan Bay. Although the Porth Neigwl embayment is now filled with glacigenic sediments of northern derivation, striations at the eastern end of Porth Neigwl are aligned almost due east–west, suggesting that, at some time, Welsh ice extended west of St Tudwal's Peninsula (Figure 51b). This is supported by the east–west alignment of meltwater channels, including the gorge of the Afon Soch, which dissect the western side of St Tudwal's and have been cut to below the level of the drift filling the Porth Neigwl embayment.

The ridge of clay-rich, dense grey diamicton exposed in the section at Glanllynnau may represent a buried drumlin-like feature formed by subglacial lodgement and deformation. There is little evidence to support the contention that it represents an earlier advance than the overlying facies. The isolated ridge of sand and gravel at Sarn Bach, south of Abersoch, may represent an esker fragment formed by subglacial meltwater that was diverted by high ground to the west to flow towards the head of the meltwater channel south of Ty Newydd Farm.

Although the erosional and some of the depositional evidence suggests that at some stage both the northern and Welsh ice streams covering the Pwllheli district must have been warm-based, this in no way implies that all of the sediments were deposited under such conditions. On the contrary, most of the glacigenic deposits of the Pwllheli district were probably laid down during deglaciation, when the basal thermal regime of the glacier, and therefore the dominant processes of deposition, may have been quite different.

At Aberdaron, in western Llŷn, a thick sequence of glacigenic sediments has been interpreted in terms of the stagnation and in situ decay of northern ice (Austin and McCarroll, 1992; McCarroll and Harris, 1992; Gibbons and McCarroll, 1993). Flow-tills derived from the melting of stagnant ice on surrounding hills buried ice in a fault-bounded embayment, allowing slow melting and the release of basal meltout tills. In order to explain the incorporation of subglacial sediments into the ice, this model requires cold-based conditions over Llŷn. Such conditions are likely to have pertained as the ice retreated and thinned, and permafrost extended north-wards. In the Pwllheli district, there is clear evidence of permafrost conditions following glacier retreat in the form of ice wedge casts at Bryn Bugail and near Traian (Whittow and Ball, 1970). Similar features have been recorded from several sites in eastern Llŷn (Thomas et al., 1990). Stagnation of glacier ice in western Llŷn is attributed to the influence of topography on glacier dynamics, with active ice pinned against the hills of the north Llŷn coast and widespread stagnation south-west of this limit (McCarroll, 1991). This model of deglaciation, with topographical obstructions causing pinning of the ice margin and widespread stagnation of debris-rich ice on the lee side, can be extended to explain many of the Quaternary landforms and sediments of the Pwllheli district.

In the east of the district, the decay of the Welsh ice resulted in a low coastal strip of kettled drift topography. The sediments are exposed in coastal sections around Afon Wen, the best example being Glanllynnau. The sediments exposed at this site have been interpreted as the result of two glacial advances, with tills separated by a zone of weathering and periglacial disturbance suggesting nonglacial conditions. However, there appears to be little evidence to support this interpretation, and the sequence is more easily interpreted as resulting from the in situ stagnation and decay of cold-based ice (Boulton, 1977). Buried, debris-rich glacier ice formed ridges, with fluvioglacial gravels occupying the hollows and flow tills descending from the decaying ice ridges. During melting the topography was reversed, with the gravels forming ridges and the areas where ice was buried forming depressions (kettle holes). Deformation of organic sediments in the kettles suggests that buried ice melted very slowly, perhaps persisting well into the Late-glacial.

Many of the landforms and sediments produced by the northern ice can also be interpreted in terms of the in situ decay of cold-based debris-rich ice. Kettled topography similar to that around Afon Wen is rare however, mainly because of the greater relief of much of the district.

The very thick sequence of glacigenic sediments exposed in Porth Neigwl can be interpreted in a similar way to that at Aberdaron in western Llŷn. Most of the deposits exposed above beach level can be interpreted as subglacial in origin. They may represent in situ melt-out till, but they lack some of the diagnostic features that are so prominent at Aberdaron, including the convex-upward lenses of gravel. Flow tills are less prominent than at Aberdaron, presumably because the Porth Neigwl coastal section incises a much larger drift-filled embayment, so the source area for the supply of flow tills derived from the melting of stagnant ice on the surrounding hills is farther away. Ponding of meltwater on the dead ice surface, with supply of sediment via flow tills from the surrounding dead ice ridges, is clearly demonstrated towards the eastern end of the section. Seismic reflection results suggest that beneath beach level a tripartite division of the sediments is possible, based on laterally persistent differences in density. Some of the unexposed sediments could predate the Late Devensian.

The drift deposits exposed at Porth Ceiriad can similarly be interpreted largely in terms of the accumulation of flow tills and debris flows derived from the melting of buried ice, much of the material being supplied via the small meltwater channels to the north.

The hills and slopes surrounding the sediment sinks of the major embayments now support only a thin drape of drift or are largely denuded. Even on gentle slopes the high porewater pressures which are produced by the melting of debris-rich ice render the preservation of meltout tills unlikely. Downslope movement and realignment of clast fabrics is well displayed in the diamicton overlying glacially tectonised bedrock on the side of Nanhoron.

Areas of constructional drift topography in the Pwllheli district record the pinning of active ice fronts at topographical highs. The most impressive area of constructional topography, comprising ridges and mounds dominated by sand and gravel, is banked against the hills of northern Llŷn. Synge (1964) termed this the 'Clynnog-fawr moraine' and interpreted it as the maximum limit of the Late Devensian Irish Sea ice sheet. He suggested that the more subdued topography to the south reflects periglacial conditions beyond the glacier margin. Whittow and Ball (1970) interpreted it as a readvance limit of the Devensian ice, and this was retained by Bowen et al. (1986) as the 'Gwynedd readvance'. However, by considering the influence of bedrock topography on glacier dynamics it is possible to interpret the landforms and sediments in terms of a single glacial episode (McCarroll, 1991).

When the Irish Sea ice was at its maximum extent it would have covered even the highest summits of Llŷn. However, as the ice retreated and thinned a threshold would be reached where the surface gradient was no longer sufficient to allow the ice to cross the hills of the north coast. Ice to the south and south-west would then stagnate and melt in situ, while active ice would continue to press against the northern side of the hills and extend through major gaps such as that at Pant Glas in eastern Llŷn and north of Cors Geirch in the Pwllheli district. The subdued drift topography of much of southern and western Llŷn can be interpreted as representing the redistribution as flow tills of sediment released from stagnant ice, and the constructional topography of the 'Clynnog-fawr moraine' as accumulation of sediment at a topographically (rather than climatically) controlled stillstand position. It is not necessary, therefore, to invoke a 'Gwynedd readvance' of the last Irish Sea glacier.

The constructional drift topography of Mynydd Cilan may record a similar, though smaller scale stillstand of active marginal Welsh ice banked against the ridge forming the west coast of the headland. North of Pwllheli, the topography is dominated by a bedrock ridge curving inland from east–west to north-east. Drift topography immediately to the north is dominated by ridges curving in the same direction. They may also represent accumulation at a topographically controlled stillstand of active marginal ice. Although Thomas et al. (1990)

interpreted the landforms of this area as ice-marginal ridges marking the retreat of an ice front moving from the north-west, the alignment is more likely to be due to meltwater routes following the curve of the bedrock.

The uncoupling of the northern and Welsh ice streams, and the juxtaposition of stagnant ice and active ice fronts, produced a complex proglacial environment over much of the Pwllheli district. Isolated mounds of sand and gravel record the ponding of water between ice and bedrock on the north side of Garn Fadryn and near Cefyn Madryn in the north of the district, and at Muriau in the south. The most useful information on the position of the ice fronts during deglaciation comes from the area surrounding the Cors Geirch. The sand and gravel terraces of this area can be divided into three groups on the basis of altitude, and they probably represent falls in the level of ponded meltwater as the ice sheets withdrew.

When the Irish Sea glacier became pinned at the 'Clynnog-fawr Moraine', much of the Pwllheli district would have been covered by stagnant northern ice, while active ice would have extended through the gap in the hills west of Garn Boduan to occupy the site of the Cors Geirch. Farther east, active northern ice together with ice from Snowdonia would have extended through the Pant-Glas col and onto central Llŷn. Ice from the Vale of Ffestiniog would still have extended at least as far west as St Tudwal's Peninsula.

The first direct evidence of the uncoupling of ice streams from different directions is provided by the highest terrace remnants north-east of the Cors Geirch around Bryniau. They reach 82 m above OD in the district and 86 m above OD 500 m to the north. These sands and gravels were probably laid down in fresh water trapped between the lobe of ice occupying the Cors Geirch and ice to the east which may have stagnated or may still have been fed from the east. Not all of the ponded water body need necessarily have received a great thickness of sand and gravel, and some of the sediment deposited during this phase may have been eroded as the lake level fell, so the present extent of these high sands and gravels provides only a minimum estimate of the extent of uncoupling at this stage (Figure 51b).

Since the water level must have reached at least 86 m above OD, the level of the surrounding ice sheets must have exceeded this. Ice from the Cors Geirch would, therefore, have extended into the northern end of the Nanhoron meltwater channel. A delta at the southern end of this channel, with a maximum elevation of 45 m above OD, may represent local ponding against lower level stagnant ice filling the Porth Neigwl embayment (Figure 51b).

If the ice flowing eastward from the Vale of Ffestiniog reached a similar altitude to that in the Cors Geirch (over 86 m above OD) it would still have extended over much of St Tudwal's Peninsula, leaving only the Mynydd Gilan area exposed. Part of the hummocky topography of this headland may represent in situ decay of dead ice at this time. The mound of sand and gravel at Muriau may also have formed at this stage in ponded water as active ice pressed against the western side of the Porth Ceiriad embayment. At this stage Mynydd Tîr-y-cwmwd, south of

Llanbedrog, would have stood above the ice as a nunatak.

The drift stratigraphy at the eastern end of Porth Neigwl shows Irish Sea till, of northern derivation, overlain by a diamicton of Welsh origin which thickens to the east. This suggests that following stagnation of the northern ice in the Porth Neigwl embayment, the Welsh ice, moving from the Vale of Ffestiniog, may have been free to extend farther west, beyond the St Tudwal's Peninsula and onto dead ice in the Porth Neigwl embayment.

The most extensive of the Cors Geirch terraces lie at a height of around 50 m above OD. They occur on both sides of the Cors Geirch depression. The Penarwel channel, near Llanbedrog, would have provided an overflow for water trapped at about this level (Saunders, 1968), though this need not have been the case because glacier-dammed lakes can also drain via conduits within the ice. Since the level of the supporting ice at this stage must have exceeded 54 m above OD, it would have covered Llanbedrog and curved around Mynydd Tîr-y-cwmwd (Figure 51c). The hill west of Castellmarch may have been isolated at this time as ice entered both ends of the 'Rhandir channel' which bounds it to the north and west.

Assuming that altitude of the Welsh ice was declining at a comparable rate, at this stage the southern part of St Tudwal's Peninsula would have stood above the active ice front (Figure 51c). Decaying ice in this area would have released flow tills which filled the depression south of Bwlch Tocyn and would have flowed south along the small channels at Nant-y-big and south of Pant farm. These would represent the upper part of the sequence exposed in the drift cliff at Porth Ceiriad. The lower part of the sequence may represent earlier deposition, perhaps in a subglacial cavity, and may also have been supplied via the channels. Active ice would have continued to stream eastward across central St Tudwal's, though some of the hills on the western margin may have protruded as nunataks. Outlet glaciers from the main ice front would probably have extended along the Soch gorge and the gorge south of Ty Newydd, and may have formed piedmont lobes over slowly decaying sediment-covered ice to the west (Figure 51c).

As the Welsh ice retreated further from this position, ice would have failed to extend west of Bwlch farm while still extending along the valley west of Sarn. Subglacial meltwater moving towards the ice front in central St Tudwal's would therefore be deflected southwards, so the north–south-orientated ridge of sand and gravel in this area, interpreted as an esker fragment (elongate kame) may have formed at this time. As the ice started to withdraw from the area between Mynydd Tîr-y-cwmwd and Abersoch, it may have retreated first from the north-east end of the Rhandir channel, so that meltwater would have flowed from south to north, ponding between Castellmarch and Mynyth Tîr-y-cwmwd and forming a small sand and gravel terrace reaching 35 m above OD.

The lowest terraces around the Cors Geirch lie at less than 20 m above OD. By this stage ice that had occupied the Cors Geirch must have retreated at least as far north as Mathan isaf and may have stagnated. Ice to the east would have retreated as far as Llannor, while to the south

the ice must have been offshore off Carreg-y-defaid to allow ponding of water north-east of Llanbedrog (Figure 51d). Water was also ponded between Mynydd Tîr-y-cwmwd and to the north of Abersoch, forming a terrace at about 16 m above OD. However, there is no similar terrace south of Abersoch, so the ice front may have extended over the site of the Cors Llyferin as far west as Sarn Bach (Figure 51d). Meltwater would have flowed south-west along the channel south of Ty Newydd. Ice would also have entered the eastern end of the Soch gorge, which would have carried meltwater westwards, in the opposite direction to the present flow. The main route for meltwater was probably then south-west along the present course of the Soch, in the opposite direction to its present flow. Channelled gravels deposited by this substantial braided meltwater river, which would also have received drainage from the north and west, are exposed for more than 500 m towards the eastern end of the Porth Neigwl cliff section (Figure 47).

After the formation of the lowest terraces, the Cors Geirch may have continued to act as a route-way for meltwater passing through the northern hills, but the ice to the south and east must have withdrawn sufficiently to prevent ponding. Ice to the east may have become pinned for a time to the north of Pwllheli (Figure 51e). This would account for the constructional topography of this area. Active ice banked against the hill at Llannor would have supplied the braided outwash streams that deposited the fluvioglacial sheet deposits of the south and west. Stagnation of the ice north and east of Pwllheli explains the occurrence of thick drift east of Llannor and south of Abersoch and accords with the preferred interpretation of the section at Glanllynnau in terms of in situ melting.

An alternative interpretation of most of the Quaternary landforms and sediments of the Pwllheli district is that the band of constructional topography to the north (the 'Clynnog-fawr moraine') represents a grounding line of the last Irish Sea glacier as it retreated rapidly due to an isostatically raised sea level relatively higher than today (Eyles and McCabe, 1989a,b, 1991). The sand and gravel terraces around Cors Geirch would then be regarded as marine, Gilbert-type deltas, and the thick sequence of drift exposed at Porth Neigwl as glacimarine in origin. Glacigenic deposits elsewhere around the Irish Sea have similarly been interpreted as glacimarine (Colhoun and McCabe, 1973; Eyles and Eyles, 1984; Eyles et al., 1985; Eyles and McCabe, 1989a, 1989b; McCabe, 1986a, 1986b, 1987; McCabe et al., 1984, 1987; McCabe and Eyles, 1988; McCabe et al., 1986; McCabe and Hirons, 1986). This model requires massive isostatic depression (about 280 m above OD), even close to the edge of a relatively thin ice sheet, and extremely rapid readjustment following deglaciation. Around the Cors Geirch, for example, the terraces could only have formed in contact with the ice front, so the difference in height between the highest and lowest terraces (more than 70 m) would have to be explained by isostatic uplift while the ice front remained stationary. Even taking the fastest reported rate of isostatic recovery of 50 m above OD within 1000 years, for the much larger Laurentide ice sheet, the ice margin would have had to remain stable on

Llŷn for 1400 years (McCarroll, 1995). Such a long period of stability is extremely unlikely, particularly for a tidal ice margin. The glacimarine hypothesis is also difficult to reconcile with the clear evidence of buried ice and kettle formation at Glanllynnau and elsewhere.

Evidence for conditions following the withdrawal of the glaciers is provided by ice wedge casts and other indicators of periglacial conditions in sandy and gravel-rich deposits both within and to the north of the district. The ice wedge pseudomorphs are particularly useful palaeoenvironmental indicators because ice wedges only form in areas of permafrost. The head deposits of the region, which mantle the hills, and the scree deposits on the east side of Nant Saethon were probably formed largely during the periglacial conditions following the melting of the glaciers and the cold conditions of the Loch Lomond Stadial.

Organic sediments exposed in a kettle hole at Glanllynnau suggest that the region was deglaciated prior to 14 500 BP (Figure 44). Coleopteran (beetle) assemblages investigated by Coope and Brophy (1972) provided evidence for rapid warming, with mean July temperatures reaching 17°C, followed by more gradual cooling and the re-establishment of periglacial conditions lasting for about 1000 radiocarbon years (Loch Lomond Stadial or Younger Dryas). The latter episode is also recorded in the cryoturbation of sediments. At the beginning of the Holocene (10 000 BP), the coleopteran record suggests there was abrupt warming. As with other Lateglacial sites, the pollen record at Glanllynnau suggests a considerable lag in the response of vegetation to rapid climatic change.

During the Holocene, natural processes have probably effected little alteration of the Llŷn landscape. Alluvium has been deposited along the stream courses, and some blown sand has accumulated along the coast. Blown sand may also have been responsible for blocking the former course of the Afon Soch towards the eastern end of Porth Neigwl, diverting it to flow northwards and through the Soch gorge, which would have drained originally form east to west. Peat has developed in low lying areas. The major Holocene effect has probably been coastal erosion of the thick Quaternary sequences exposed in the bays and, in the east, the accretion of land protected by sand dunes. However, the fertile agricultural land, expanse of seashore and the security afforded by the hills has made the district an attractive home since Mesolithic times. The agricultural landscape of today, despite its beauty, must bear little resemblance to the natural, largely woodland landscape, that predated human activity.

EIGHT

Structure and metamorphism

The disrupted sediments and lavas belonging to the Gwna Mélange in the extreme north-west of district are characterised by pervasive lower greenschist facies metamorphism, a strong cleavage and evidence for polyphase deformation. In contrast with this, the Cambro-Ordovician cover south-east of the Llŷn Shear Zone has suffered only anchizonal (broadly sub-greenschist facies) metamorphism and generally retains original sedimentary and igneous textures. Although the cover sedimentary rocks (especially the mudstones) are commonly cleaved, the distribution of strain across the district is highly variable. Both the attitude and intensity of cleavage development is closely related to proximity to local folds and faults.

The most influential tectonic line in north-west Wales is the Menai Strait Fault System (Figure 52), running south-west from the Menai Strait area through the north-western margin of the Llŷn Peninsula (Gibbons, 1987). Many of the prominent faults that dissect the Pwllheli district form part of this fault system, the most notable structures being the Llŷn Shear Zone, and the Cefnamwlch–Rhiw Fault. In addition, however, broadly east–west cross faulting, similar to that seen at the north-western margin of the Harlech Dome, has produced structures such as the Efailnewydd Fault and the Sarn–Abersoch Thrust. These two sets of structures have had the effect of compartmentalising deformation into several distinct fault-bounded blocks which are interpreted to have controlled both the subsidence pattern during early Palaeozoic sedimentation and magmatism, as well as strain distribution during Acadian (early Devonian) fold and cleavage development. The influence of basement structures in localising Acadian deformation and metamorphism within the cover sequence is in fact a dominant theme of the geology in the Pwllheli district, as it is elsewhere in North Wales (Wilkinson and Smith, 1988). A further, more arcane, effect of Acadian metamorphism was to reset the isotope systematics to produce, for example, Devonian Rb–Sr ages from several of the Caradoc intrusions such as Mynydd Tîr-y-cwmwd, Nanhoron and Carn Fadryn (Evans, 1990; Howells et al., 1991).

This chapter deals firstly with structures within the Gwna Mélange exposed within the district along the north-western coast of the peninsula, and secondly with the folds and fault systems present within the cover sequence. Finally, the distribution of cleavage and the metamorphic grade across the district are discussed.

GWNA MÉLANGE

The Gwna Mélange has undergone several deformation phases. The first of these (D_1) is expressed as the initial disruption of the original succession to form a mélange. This disruption appears to have involved break-up of marine sediments and pillow lavas along planes (S_1) approximately parallel to bedding (S_0), leaving some relatively coherent slabs preserved within chaotic sediment. More massive lithologies such as quartzite, limestone and igneous clasts are commonly thoroughly brecciated. The second event (D_2) was the dominant deformation, and produced an anastomosing slaty foliation (S_2) which, in the Pwllheli district, is orientated approximately parallel to bedding, but is refracted through a low angle to bedding in alternating pelitic and psammitic beds. S_2 is defined by flattened clasts and growth of new orientated chlorite and muscovite. This anchizonal to epizonal (lower greenschist facies) metamorphism imposed during D_2 is typical of the Gwna Mélange in the district. Asymmetric F_2 'Z' folds display a geometry consistent with a position on a steep overturned limb of a south-easterly verging antiform plunging gently south-west and with a north-westerly dipping axial planar S_2 fabric. Farther south-west in the Llŷn Peninsula, around the hinges (and on the north-west limbs) of large F_2 folds, the S_2 cleavage can clearly be seen to cut the earlier S_1 fabric at high angles (Gibbons and McCarroll, 1993). In the Pwllheli district, however, it is commonly difficult to separate S_1 and S_2.

The S_2 foliation is crenulated by a moderate to gently north-west-dipping pressure solution cleavage (S_3), defined primarily by trails of insoluble iron oxides. F_3 folds plunge gently south-west and are abundantly displayed on the coastal exposures west of Porth Towyn (Plate 24). The polyphase geometry of these F_2/F_3 structures is reminiscent of that displayed on steep overturned south-east-verging folds elsewhere in the Monian Supergroup, such as on the south-eastern limb of the Rhoscolyn Anticline on Holy Island, Anglesey.

The steeply inclined fabrics in the mélange (i.e. $S_0/S_1/S_2$) are locally warped into more gentle north-west dips by late monoclinal folds (F_4). These structures are well displayed at several exposures immediately west of the beach at Porth Towyn, especially where they fold white quartzite lenses. The F_4 monoclines show moderately south-eastward dipping axial surfaces, and are associated with minor box-folds and kinks.

Several brittle faults cut the Gwna Mélange: these are exposed only at the coast. One prominent north-north-east-striking vertical fault [2292 3747] lies adjacent to an F_4 monocline that was probably produced by upthrow movement on the western side of the fault. A zone of gently west-dipping faults occurs along the southern corner of Porth Towyn, and the associated shattering and deep weathering is presumably, at least partly, responsible for the origin of the bay. Although one of these

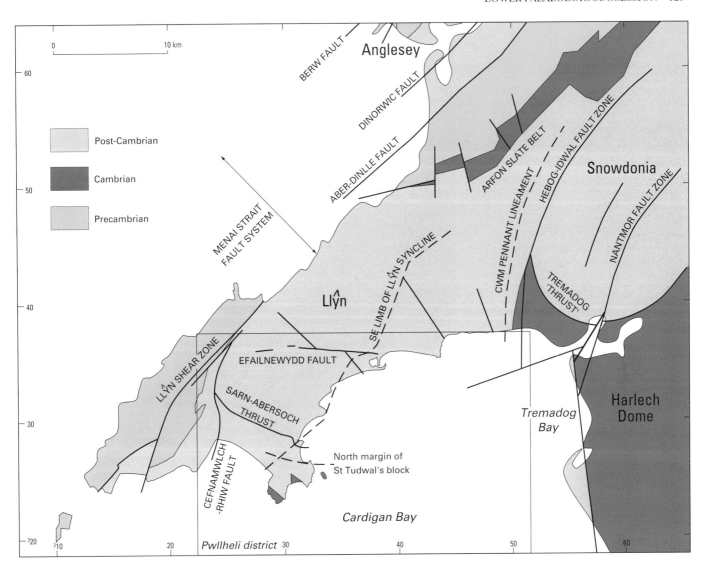

Figure 52   Major structures of north-west Wales.

faults displays asymmetric cataclastic fabrics indicating normal displacement, movement direction data are not present along most faults cutting the mélange.

LOWER PALAEOZOIC SUCCESSION

Some of the structures in the Lower Palaeozoic cover show evidence for having been influenced by basement structures. In the north-west of the district, the pre-Arenig Llŷn Shear Zone (part of the north-east-trending Menai Strait Fault System) juxtaposes the Gwna Mélange and Precambrian Sarn Complex, but associated brittle faulting extends up into the Ordovician cover (Gibbons, 1989). The southwards deflection of the Llŷn Shear Zone in the Aberdaron area (Gibbons and McCarroll, 1993) shows a similar orientation to the curving Cefnamwlch–Rhiw Fault and the south-east limb of the Llŷn Syncline in the Pwllheli district (Figure 52) which may also be rooted in major basement faults. There are several examples of localised folds, faults and associated strong cleavage, commonly with the folds assuming a sharp, kink-like geometry, that are consistent with deformation above basement faults.

The dominant structural grain of the district trends north-east to east-north-east, as defined by the axis of the Llŷn syncline, regional cleavage, and several faults. In addition, there exists a prominent series of east-south-east-striking cross faults (locally with associated cleavage) that include the Efailnewydd Fault, interpreted as influencing Caradocian volcanicity, the Sarn–Abersoch Thrust (a relatively low-angle reverse fault) (Figure 53b), and the northern limit of the St Tudwal's Block (Figure 52). Another fault set, best developed in the south of the peninsula, comprises north-west-orientated, dominantly north-east-dipping reverse faults.

Although most of the folds and faults in the Pwllheli district are interpreted as Acadian and therefore late in the Palaeozoic evolution of the area, the well documented angular unconformity between Cambrian and

Plate 24 F₃ chevron folding of strong S₂ fabric in Gwna metasediment. Coast west of PorthTowyn [2277 3755] (GS672). The F₃ axial surfaces dip north-west, deforming S₂ fabric on the steep, slightly overturned limb of a south-east-verging regional fold. The earliest fabric (bedding parallel S₁) is transposed by S₂.

shallow marine Arenig strata on St Tudwal's Peninsula records a phase of deformation prior to the deposition of the Gwynedd Supergroup (Woodcock, 1990) and local inversion of the Cambrian sedimentary basin. The overall deformation style of the tilted Cambrian, with a lack of any pre-Arenig cleavage, suggests the uplift of the Cambrian succession by movements along faults such as the east-south-east structures mentioned above, leading to the development of a 'St Tudwal's structural high' in the south of the district.

Folds

Llŷn Syncline

The structure of the Llŷn Peninsula is perhaps best known for the synclinal outcrop pattern of the Lower Palaeozoic strata. Matley (1938) described the structure as 'a large asymmetrical and broken synclinal fold or syn-clinorium' and it has since become generally known as the Llŷn Syncline (Roberts, 1979). As Matley observed, in the Pwllheli district this structure is by no means a simple syncline. Even allowing for the previously mistaken attri-bution to the Llanvirn of the Ashgill (Crugan Mudstone Formation) rocks at Efailnewydd (Matley, 1938), the 'Llŷn Syncline' has a distinctive hour-glass shape in plan. It is relatively broad in the central part of the Pwllheli district, where a 5 km distance separates the Caradoc strata of the north and south limbs between Carreg-y-Defaid and Boduan, and the core of the syncline contains rocks of Ashgill age. The syncline narrows con-siderably north-eastwards, with the Ashgill strata absent north-east of a point near Y Ffôr, where less than 3 km separates the outcrop of the Allt Fawr Rhyolitic Tuff Formation on the opposing limbs. Farther north-east, the syncline apparently opens again in the poorly exposed area of the Nefyn district centred on Glasfryn. Although a north-east strike is most characteristic, the steep limbs

of the syncline can be seen to change strike abruptly across the Efailnewydd Fault (see below), which runs from the southern limb of the syncline at Pwllheli, through the core of the syncline, to the zone of overturn-ing on the north limb of the syncline between Nant-y-Gledrydd and Dinas.

Although apparently typically 'Caledonian' in being south-eastward verging, the outcrop pattern of the Llŷn Syncline is not only strongly modified by numerous faults, but also displays a peculiar geometry of its 'hinge zone', the outcrop of which shows a wide area of gentle dips bounded by steep limbs; a vertical to overturned north-western limb, and a steep north-west-dipping south-eastern limb (Figure 53). Another unusual charac-teristic of the hinge zone is that the rocks here are not especially strongly cleaved, with the deformation being concentrated instead on the limbs, especially the north-western limb, rather than in the core. The hinge area has clearly been protected during deformation relative to the limbs. This pattern of folding is interpreted as the effect of Acadian south-eastwardly directed compression acting upon a block-faulted basement and cover. The steeper zones correspond to existing tectonic lineaments which are linked to sediment facies and thickness changes (see Chapter 4; Figure 21) that suggest the Llŷn Syncline was generated on the site of a Caradoc basin.

St Tudwal's Peninsula

The Cambrian and Ordovician rocks of the St Tudwal's Peninsula are folded into a series of open folds with axes plunging gently north-north-east. The folds increase in amplitude and tightness northwards, with the tightest fold being the anticline traceable north-north-east from Llanengan towards Pen-y-gaer (Pen-y-gaer Anticline; Figure 55). This northwards increase in intensity of folding is also well exemplified by the change between the anticline seen between Ty Newydd and Tan Rallt

Figure 53 Elements of the structural geology of the Lower Palaeozoic rocks of the district.

a   Cleavage, strike and dip direction. Dashed line is the 0.40° Δ2Θ isocryst (see Figure 54), which is the value below which Merriman and Roberts (1985) suggested cleavage becomes prominent in pelites of Llanvirn age in north Wales. Shaded area indicates Δ2Θ values below this threshold.

b   Faults (Lineament east of Efailnewydd Fault after McDonald et al., 1992)

c   Folds

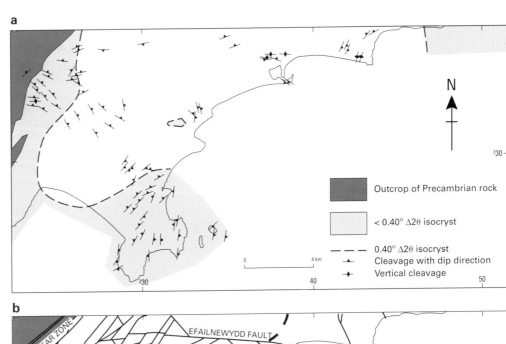

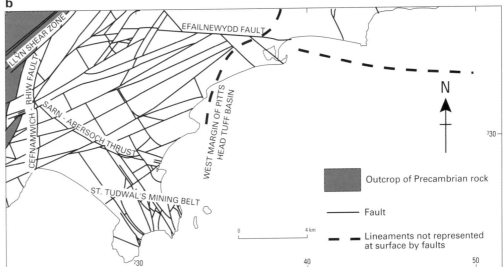

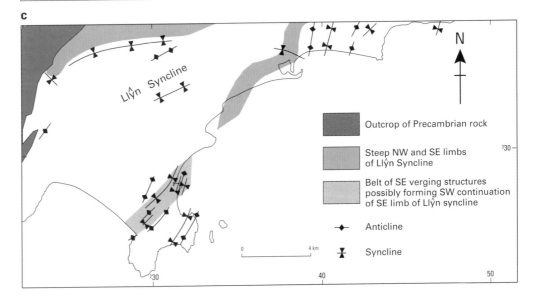

[295 265] and that north of Llanengan [295 275]. The north-north-east-trending folds have been overprinted by later north-west to north-north-west-trending reverse faults and associated minor folds, such as at Pistyll Cim [248 324] where a prominent hanging-wall anticline is associated with a north-north-west-trending reverse fault and associated with north-north-west-trending folds.

Pwllheli to Pen-ychain

The outcrop pattern of the Ordovician rocks exposed in the north-eastern corner of the district is dominated by the presence of four folds (Figure 19). Eastwards from Pwllheli, in an area to the south of Broom Hall, extensive exposures of the Pen-y-chain Rhyolite Complex on the eastern limb of the north-north-east-plunging Abererch Anticline (Roberts, 1979) indicate that a wide zone towards Pwllheli without exposure conceals Nant Ffrancon Subgroup mudstones in the core of the anticline. Most of the Broom Hall exposures dip gently north-west or north as they curve around a poorly exposed syncline complimentary to the Abererch Anticline.

Eastwards from Broom Hall, the rhyolitic rocks are faulted out in place of strongly cleaved Nant Ffrancon mudstones, apparently in the core of another anticline. The rhyolites occur again in the vicinity of Pen-y-chain where they dip gently north-east. Despite the poor exposure above and below the rhyolites, another synclinal fold hinge may be traced north of Tal-y-bont [4280 3710] just beyond where the Pen-y-chain rhyolites thin towards the north-west. This fold swings the overall strike from north-west to north-north-east and is associated with a north-east striking steeply north-west-dipping cleavage. Farther east again, the trace of the Llanystumdwy Syncline passes out to sea on the edge of the Pwllheli district (Figure 53). No solid rocks are exposed, however, within this part of the Pwllheli district.

Faults

Menai Strait Fault System and associated faults

The Menai Strait Fault System, a major north-east-trending tectonic boundary intermittently active since late Precambrian times (Gibbons, 1987), is represented in the Pwllheli district by the Llŷn Shear Zone, which separates the Sarn Complex from the Gwna Mélange, and by abundant post-Ordovician faults produced by later brittle reactivations. The Llŷn Shear Zone is a near-vertical belt of greenschist facies mylonitic rocks derived from lithologies found within both the Gwna Mélange and the Sarn Complex, and overlain unconformably by Arenig strata (Gibbons, 1983). The age and movement history of the shear zone are not well constrained, but correlation with the similarly near-vertical mylonitic schists of the Berw Shear Zone in Anglesey suggests that the earliest movement on the shear zone was latest Precambrian and involved sinistral strike-slip displacement of unknown amounts (Gibbons, 1987; Gibbons et al., 1995; Gibbons and Horák, 1996). Although not exposed

in the district, mylonitic rocks in the Llŷn Shear Zone are exposed in the Aberdaron area to the west (Gibbons and McCarroll, 1993) and in the Nefyn district to the north (Gibbons, 1983). Brittle faulting parallel to, but south of, the Llŷn Shear Zone, can be observed cutting the granite of the Sarn Complex on Mynydd Cefnamwlch, and bounds the small faulted block of Ordovician strata lying unconformably on the Sarn Complex in Mountain Cottage quarry [230 347]. Uplift and south-east-directed compression of the rocks to the north of the Llŷn Shear Zone is responsible for the generation of the steep north limb of the Llŷn Syncline.

Matley (1928) postulated that the contact between the Ordovician cover and the Precambrian basement is a thrust. Although thrusting has been demonstrated west of Aberdaron (Gibbons, 1989), farther eastwards in Llŷn there is no indication of significant thrusting of the Sarn Complex over the Ordovician strata. The contact is only exposed in the Pwllheli district at Mountain Cottage quarry [230 347], where an unconformable junction is seen beneath Ordovician strata (Matley and Smith, 1936). Farther south, along the ridge between Sarn Meyllteyrn and Mynydd Cefnamwlch, small outcrops of highly sheared mudstones associated with the eastern-most outcrops of the Sarn Complex, suggest that here the contact may be steeply faulted, as it is west of Mynydd Rhiw.

North-east-trending faults, parallel to the strike of near-vertical bedding on the northern limb of the Llŷn Syncline, are common in the north-west of the Pwllheli district. The most prominent of these passes through Dinas and Sarn and appears to be a continuation of the fault separating the Sarn Complex and the Ordovician cover on the western side of Mynydd Rhiw. Movements on similar faults near Bodgaeaf have produced a narrow horst of Sarn Complex granite, exposed near Muriau [231 311]. The Bodgaeaf area lies close to the lateral transition from the Wig Bâch Formation into the Bryncroes Formation, so these faults may have had an extensional synsedimentary phase.

Cefnamwlch–Rhiw Fault

The Cefnamwlch–Rhiw Fault (Figures 52, 53) forms one of the more prominent structural features of the Pwllheli district, although the fault plane is nowhere exposed, and its course is estimated from rather sparse outcrops. South of Sarn Meyllteyrn, there are no constraining outcrops to the east whereas to the west of the fault the topography is dominated by the Mynydd Penarfynydd Layered Intrusion. The sedimentary rocks exposed in the roof of this intrusion between Treheli [242 286] and Bronllwyd [242 302] all show moderately strong cleavage and jointing, suggesting close proximity of the fault to the east. To the north of Sarn Meyllteyrn the fault juxtaposes both Arenig and Llanvirn rocks to the east, with a fairly constant horizon just above the top of the Trygarn Formation (lower Llanvirn) to the west. The fault is not observed cutting the Sarn Complex basement, but as it appears to splay from the Llŷn Shear Zone (Figure 52) it may be a reactivated ancient structure.

Direct lithostratigraphical correlation of Ordovician rocks across the fault is not possible, and there is a strong likelihood, but no proof, of significant strike-slip displacement. It is considered likely that the fault formed the north-western margin of the Wig Bâch sedimentary basin, together with the faults in the manganese ore zone, the Parwyd Fault west of Aberdaron (Gibbons and McCarroll, 1993) and possibly the faulting along the Sarn Complex/Ordovician junction west of Mynydd Rhiw. The fault may also have been a significant feature during the Caradoc, when the Mynydd Penarfynydd Layered Intrusion was emplaced nearby.

West-north-west–east-south-east fault set

EFAILNEWYDD FAULT

Post-Ordovician movements on the Efailnewydd Fault (Figure 52) appear to have been obliquely compressional, and can be clearly identified near its western end at Nant-y-Gledrydd and at its eastern end at Pwllheli. The eastern termination of the fault at surface near Pwllheli is marked by a syncline; there is a pronounced swing in strike direction of the rocks across the syncline on either side of the fault from east-north-east to north-north-east (Figures 26, 53). This kink-like synclinal fold plunges moderately towards the north-west and is associated with several minor faults. The hinge zone of the syncline defines a belt of east–west cleavage development in rocks which are otherwise relatively undeformed. This cleavage is particularly well developed in the more argillaceous lithologies but is traceable in all formations above the Allt Fawr Tuff west of Plastirion [3800 3608] up to and including the Nod Glas Formation, beyond which exposure is lost.

Farther west the fault defines the boundary between the gently dipping core of the Llŷn Syncline and its steeply dipping overturned northern limb, so that beyond Nant-y-Gledrydd, the structure splits into two distinct faults which pass to the north of Garn Fadryn. Beyond these western limits the Efailnewydd Fault loses its identity and passes into folded rocks along the north-western margin of the Llŷn Syncline.

The Efailnewydd Fault is associated with north-west-trending splay faults such as, in the east, the Crochan Berw Fault which emerges at the coast in a gully (Crochan Berw) eroded into the Carreg yr Imbill dolerite. The fault dips south-west at 60–65°, and shows mineral slickenfibres plunging moderately south-west and indicating oblique-slip displacement. This fault is closely associated with the development of a spaced cleavage in the adjacent dolerite. This cleavage decreases in intensity away from the fault and shallows to an increasingly more gentle south-westerly dip in the cliff-top north-east of the gully. Inland, the fault continues beyond Pwllheli as a landform feature, especially where it displaces the Garn Rhyodacite [3720 3544]. It is interpreted to be one of a family of such faults, the most prominent of which is that responsible for the termination of the Caradoc outcrop at Pont-y-Garreg-fechan [3633 3473].

Another prominent splay fault, in this case towards the western end of the Efailnewydd Fault, passes north-westwards into the Nefyn district between Penhyddgan and Garn Boduan; it corresponds to the western limit of the field of major Ordovician intrusions of northern Llŷn.

The position of the Efailnewydd Fault and its north-west-trending branches is well imaged on the Euler solution plots for regional gravity data (McDonald et al., 1992). The plots indicate anomalies due to discontinuities at depths of 2 to 3 km. Such depths agree well with estimates for depths at which the Efailnewydd Fault would form the southern boundary of the Upper Lodge Formation below the core of the Llŷn Syncline. The Euler solution plots also indicate that the features associated with the faulting continue beyond the termination of the Efailnewydd Fault, running offshore and parallel to the coast past Pen-ychain to link with faults forming the northern margin to the Tremadog Bay Mesozoic basin. The solutions for this extension are at 3 to 4 km depth, suggesting the presence of a basement feature not extending up into the cover.

The early history of the Efailnewydd Fault has been discussed above (Chapter 4; Figures 18, 21). It is interpreted as having formed the southern margin of a basin in which the Upper Lodge volcanic rocks were generated. Subsequent subsidence of the area south of the fault was associated with the eruption of the Llanbedrog Volcanic Group. The fault zone appears to have been utilised as a route for magma ascent: the Broom Hall, Jampot and Dinas dolerites emplaced during Llanbedrog Volcanic Group activity are spatially associated with the fault, as are the tholeiitic intrusions (Garn, Gelli and Carreg yr Imbill dolerites, a minor intrusion in Nant-y-Gledrydd and the Pensarn Basaltic Andesite) as well as extrusive rocks (at Pwllheli and Bodgadle) of the volcanic episode associated with the Nod Glas Formation.

SARN–ABERSOCH THRUST

This structure is a west-north-west-trending low-angle reverse fault which brings rocks of Tremadoc and Arenig age southwards over the Nant Ffrancon Subgroup of probable Llanvirn age (Figures 53, 57). The Nant Ffrancon Subgroup below the fault is deformed down to the level of the Hen-dy-capel Ironstone, showing polished and lineated bedding-parallel or slightly curved surfaces which are folded around the Pen-y-gaer Anticline, and which predate the steep north-east regional cleavage. The rocks adjacent to the hanging wall of the thrust belong to the Dol-cyn-afon Formation, which is generally very deformed near the thrust-plane, and is generally difficult to distinguish from the mudstones of the upper part of the underlying Nant Ffrancon Subgroup. Characteristic rocks, including ooidal ironstones and thin doleritic sills, occur in the footwall at several places in the Abersoch and Llangian areas (Chapter 4). These occurrences suggest that the observed footwall is constrained stratigraphically. The occurrences of ooidal ironstones at Crugeran, near Sarn

Meyllteyrn [242 321], a locality also interpreted as lying in the footwall of the fault, suggest that this feature may be maintained over the whole exposed length of the fault. The rocks of the hanging-wall block include a considerable thickness of the Dol-cyn-afon Formation, particularly around Abersoch, but the base of the formation is not preserved. It is possible that the Sarn–Abersoch Thrust has utilised a décollement at the stratigraphical level of the black shales of the Dolgellau Formation, on which the Dol-cyn-afon Formation rests elsewhere in North Wales.

Previous interpretations have also recognised the requirement of a major reverse structure to explain the presence of rocks of the Dol-cyn-afon Formation in the Abersoch area, but have generally (e.g. Crimes, 1969a) interpreted its orientation as north-east, passing offshore through Porth Neigwl. The locality at Crugeran is important for it suggests that the subcrop of the thrust continues to the west-north-west, below the thick drift behind Porth Neigwl. Such an interpretation is supported by the west-north-west strike of the Arenig Wig Bâch Formation in the hanging wall from Abersoch to Sarn Meyllteyrn. The age of the main thrust movements is interpreted as post-Ordovician but prior to the regional cleavage (i.e. early Acadian).

NORTHERN MARGIN OF THE ST TUDWAL'S BLOCK

The northern edge of St Tudwal's Peninsula, between Llanengan and Penrhyn Du, is marked by an abrupt northwards increase in dip (Figure 57), an increase in intensity and plunge of folding (although this is partially due to the belt of folding running south-west from Abersoch to Llanengan, discussed above), and a marked increase in cleavage intensity. The southern part of the St Tudwal's Peninsula is gently folded and faulted, but the sub-Arenig unconformity is constrained to within 140 m above OD and 100 m below OD over several square kilometres. Within 1 km north of the line between Llanengan and Penrhyn Du, the unconformity is interpreted to be at approximately 1000 m below OD (Figures 56, 57). These features suggest that the line marks a monoclinal fold above a basement fault. Whereas there are few direct surface indications of faulting, this zone is marked by a belt of mineralised Pb–Zn–Cu–Ag veins running across the St Tudwal's Peninsula (Chapter 9).

East-north-east–west-south-west fault set

Some of the youngest of the faults in the Pwllheli district form a set trending east-north-east. Despite their considerable apparent lateral continuity across the district, their throws are generally fairly small. They are rarely exposed and most have been inferred from offsets in outcrop patterns. One exposure of a fault of this set is present in the track leading to Trefaes [252 328], where quartz veining and brecciation can be seen cutting mudstones of the Nant Ffrancon Subgroup. The most important fault of this group is that lying between Rhiw and Llanbedrog, and which truncates the upper Ordovician volcanic succession at Llanbedrog, induces an abrupt change of strike at Rhiw, and continues as a prominent structure into the neighbouring Bardsey Island district.

North-west–south-east fault set

This fault set is particularly influential on the geology of the southern part of the district, especially the St Tudwal's area, but also in the area from Aberdaron to Llanystumdwy. On the St Tudwal's Peninsula, several of these faults are exposed, particularly at Pistyll Cim [247 323], in the north-western corner of Porth Ceiriad [304 247] and below Pared-mawr [308 248]. They are typically high-angle reverse faults, upthrowing to the north-east, and show well developed associated hanging-wall anticlines with axial planar cleavage. Arcuate lines of concretions in the wall rock of a fault on the east side of Porth Ceiriad [319 247] and a common association with carbonate concretions (e.g. a fault on the western side of St Tudwal's Island West), suggest passage of fluids along the fault planes during burial diagenesis. Palaeocurrent data for the St Tudwal's Formation is consistent with a north-east-facing palaeoslope controlled by early extension on this fault set.

A subset of this group of faults are exceptional in showing downthrow to the north-east. These faults run across Mynytho Common, parallel to the belt of peralkaline intrusions, and between the Upper Lodge Group and the Nant Ffrancon Subgroup; they occur also to the east of Carn Fadryn, between the Dwyfach Formation and the Foel Ddu Rhyodacite Formation. There is a close relationship between these faults and the peralkaline and Glynllifon Trachydacite intrusions, suggesting that their origin may be connected with volcano-tectonic subsidence.

Cleavage

Well-cleaved sedimentary rocks occur across three areas: the St Tudwal's Peninsula, near Cefnamwlch and near Pen-ychain. These areas correspond to regions with white mica crystallinity indices from pelitic rocks close to or below $0.40° \Delta°2\vartheta$, the value at which Roberts and Merriman (1985) indicated that cleavage becomes prominent in Llanvirn pelites. The area through the central part of the Pwllheli district that is characterised by very low grades of metamorphism on the basis of white mica crystallinity values generally shows only poor development of cleavage, except near major faults such as the Efailnewydd Fault.

Cleavage in the St Tudwal's Peninsula is approximately axial planar to the north-north-east-orientated folding described above. Towards the west of the peninsula, in Cambrian strata of the Hell's Mouth Grit Formation, the cleavage is steeply east-dipping and strikes approximately north-east. Farther east, in rocks of Ordovician age, the strike swings to be closer to north–south. In the north of the peninsula, the folding becomes more intense (see above) and the cleavage becomes north-west-dipping. The same cleavage orientation is observed above and below the Sarn–Abersoch Thrust. In the highly sheared strata of the footwall to the thrust, however, the dominant foliation is a polished north-east-dipping foliation, approximately parallel to the fault. This is interpreted as the foliation associated with southward-thrusting of the Llŷn Syncline prior to the imposition of the regional cleavage.

Cleavage in the north-east of the district near Pen-ychain is, like that of the St Tudwal's Peninsula, associated with Caledonian north-east or north-north-east-trending folds. The intensity of the cleavage is surprising, in view of the white-mica crystallinity isocryst map (Figure 54), which suggests relatively low grades in this area. However, data points are few, and it is likely that the belt of very low-grade pelites extending north-north-east from Abererch may be significantly narrower than the isocryst map indicates, and the 0.42° Δ°2θ isocryst may be plotted too far to the east (Figures 53, 54).

METAMORPHISM

Metabasite secondary mineralogy

Mineral assemblages of basic igneous rocks have been widely used to investigate the grade of metamorphic terranes. Although some metabasites in the Pwllheli district contain undiagnostic mineral assemblages, especially carbonate-rich lithologies which are common in high-level intrusives such as the Llanvirn sills and the Nod Glas Formation, the majority of samples have assemblages diagnostic of the prehnite–pumpellyite facies. Both prehnite and pumpellyite are commonly present, along with abundant chlorite, but epidote is rare. Only

samples from an outcrop of the Broom Hall Dolerites close to the crest of the Abererch Anticline have indications of sub-prehnite–pumpellyite facies assemblages, with the presence of a mixed-layer chlorite/smectite phyllosilicate (Bevins et al., 1991; Merriman and Roberts, 1985).

Several samples of more mafic rocks from Carreg yr Imbill, Mynydd Penarfynydd, Dinas and Pen-yr-Orsedd yielded a contrasting mineral assemblage, including actinolite, brown ± green amphibole and, locally, fresh plagioclase. This assemblage is of only local development within these intrusions, and contrasts with the regional metamorphism, in which the plagioclase has been altered to albite and amphiboles are absent. It is likely, therefore, that this assemblage (except the brown amphibole which is probably late magmatic) is the product of early alteration by hydrothermal activity rather than the result of regional metamorphism. The hydrothermal assemblage was largely unaffected by the later regional low-grade metamorphism. At Carreg yr Imbill (Gimlet Rock) the albite-rich segregations include rare vugs containing quartz, pectolite, apophyllite, analcime and prehnite [e.g. 3882 3437]. Specimens of minerals associated with these pegmatitic vugs within the dolerite were collected by G J Williams, Inspector of Mines and Quarries for North Wales, when the quarry was active early last century (*Frontispiece*).

Unfortunately, there are no metabasites suitable for metamorphic grade determination over the region between the Efailnewydd and Sarn–Abersoch faults, so there is no confirmation that this area of low mica crystallinity (Roberts, 1981; Merriman and Roberts, 1985;

Figure 54 Variation in white mica crystallinity values in the Pwllheli district and adjoining areas. Data from Merriman and Roberts (1985) recontoured using kriging. The contouring of the western half of the district and the general features of the area north-north-east of Pwllheli are reasonably reliable, but in other areas the limited data make contouring susceptible to changes in contouring parameters.

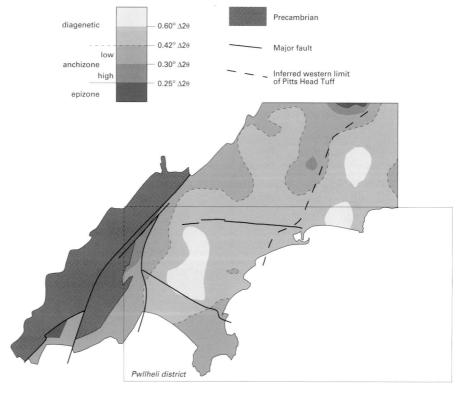

Howells et al., 1991) is accompanied also by low-grade metabasites.

White mica crystallinity index values

A study of white mica crystallinity in Snowdonia and Llŷn by Merriman and Roberts (1985) and Roberts and Merriman (1985) included some 70 samples from the Llŷn Peninsula. These data have been recontoured in the present study (Figure 54), using the contour intervals employed by Merriman, Roberts and Hirons (1992), except that the diagenetic grade has been subdivided at 0.60 rather than 0.55° $\Delta°2\vartheta$. Extreme caution must be taken in the interpretation of such contoured data, for not only is the data set rather restricted with large regions containing few control points, but Robinson et al., (1990) have highlighted problems of variation within such datasets. However, the major features of the map are robust, even under fairly demanding approaches to contouring. These major features are:

- an area of very low-grade metamorphism running northwards from Broom Hall, corresponding to the area where some sub-prehnite–pumpellyite facies metabasites have been recovered (see above)

- an area of high anchizonal grade running along, or immediately to the west of, the western margin of the Pitts Head Tuff basin, parallel to and to the west of the above feature. The high-grade belt is not traceable south-west of Pwllheli

- an area of very low-grade extending through the area between the Sarn–Abersoch Thrust and the Efailnewydd Fault, to the west of the crop of the Caradoc volcanic succession

- an area of relatively intermediate and variable grade north of the Efailnewydd Fault and west of the Pitts Head Tuff basin

- an area of relatively intermediate-high grade adjacent to, and south of, the Sarn–Abersoch Thrust, with grade decreasing slightly to the south on St Tudwal's Peninsula

- a belt of high anchizonal grade, with grade increasing westwards, north-west of the Cefnamwlch–Rhiw Fault

The map confirms other evidence for higher grade rocks around the margins of distinct fault blocks, with some of those fault blocks characterised by cores with relatively very low grades. Indeed, it is a significant feature of the map that the area of the Llŷn Syncline includes the largest area of low grade anchizonal and late diagenetic zone rocks in North Wales.

Interpretation of white mica crystallinity data from the Welsh Basin has followed two separate paths. Roberts and Merriman (1985) have argued that the white mica crystallinity of the Ordovician sedimentary rocks is dependant on Caledonian regional metamorphism and particularly on strain. In contrast, Bevins and Rowbotham (1983) and Robinson (1987) argued that the low pressure metamorphism was produced during burial and predated tectonic deformation. Roberts et al. (1991) and Merriman et al. (1992) have, however, demonstrated that in some areas of the Welsh Basin both burial and strain are factors. The present data are equivocal. The high grades associated with some of the tectonic lineations and faults are likely to be associated with high strain, but it could be argued that they could equally be due to enhanced fluid flow near basin-bounding faults during subsidence. The coincidence of higher grade metapelites with the distribution of cleavage may be because both features originated during Acadian deformation, or that both features were controlled by the same basement structures, but at different times in basin evolution.

NINE

Economic geology

Iron

The ooidal ironstone of the Hen-dy-capel Ironstone (Figure 55) was mined during the 19th century (Cantrill and Sherlock, 1920) in the northern part of the St Tudwal's Peninsula. The age of this ironstone has long been debated. A correlation of the ironstone with that at Tremadog (Caradoc, *Nemagraptus gracilis* Biozone) has been proposed (Crimes, 1969a), but more recently a slightly earlier age (Llandeilo, *Nemagraptus gracilis* Biozone) age (Trythall et al., 1987; Trythall, 1989a, 1993), supported by the biostratigraphical data presented by Nicholas (1915) and by study of acritarch assemblages. This age has now been challenged by Young (1991a, 1991b, 1993), who has demonstrated an even earlier (Llanvirn) age for the deposit (see Chapter 4).

The exploitation of iron in the St Tudwal's area dates to at least the second quarter of the 19th century. The main quarry was at Hen-dy-capel [300 270], with another smaller quarry at Llanengan [294 272] and trial workings at Pen-y-gaer [298 282]. Hen-dy-capel quarry received its name from an adjacent chapel which had to be replaced in 1828 after the persistent damage to its roof during blasting at the quarry. This quarry was linked to the coast by a railway, built by the Llanengan Ironstone Company in 1842. The mining operation and the railway closed in 1885.

The three principal sites of exploitation, or attempted exploitation, coincide with areas in which the ironstone body has become thickened. At Pen-y-gaer the trials are on the crest of an anticline, at Llanengan there is faulted repetition of the ironstone and at Hen-dy-capel the ironstone is folded and repeated by faulting.

Recent description of the Pen-y-gaer locality is to be found in Young (1991a, 1991b). A brief description of the Hen-dy-capel locality was given by Trythall (1989a). The Hen-dy-capel area has been reinterpreted as a highly faulted north-north-east-plunging, south-east-verging anticline, apparently a small-scale parasitic anticline on the south-east limb of the Llanengan Syncline, with an approximately similar attitude to the Pen-y-gaer Anticline to the north-west (Figure 55b). The deformation in the quarry appears to relate to a single tectonic episode, with a cleavage (poorly developed in the massive ironstone itself) axial planar to the folds and approximately parallel to the north-east-trending reverse faults. The reverse faulting and the folding have combined to produce a locally thickened body of ironstone, within which the quarry was dug.

The sedimentary rocks also show evidence of pre-cleavage deformation, with polished curved fracture surfaces and abundant indicators of soft-sediment folding. The polished surfaces are interpreted as being related to similar surfaces seen in higher levels of the

Nant Ffrancon Subgroup in the footwall of the Sarn–Abersoch Thrust, associated with early, compressional, movement on that fault. The soft-sediment folding may be syndepositional. Many of the (accessible) higher beds of ironstone showing such soft-sediment deformation are also highly impure, with ooid-rich lithologies chaotically intermixed with clastic silt- and sand-dominated laminae and beds. This strongly suggests that the ironstone was, at least partially, a reworked deposit, probably comprising a succession of debris-flow units. This suggestion is even more strongly indicated at Pen-y-gaer quarry B (Young, 1991b; Trythall, 1989a), where debris flows in the upper part of the Hen-dy-capel Ironstone exposed in the low north face of the quarry contain cobble-grade exotic metavolcanic clasts, in addition to finer grained clastic material, ferruginous ooids and phosphatic oncoids (Plate 25).

The lower, more ooidal, parts of the Hen-dy-capel Ironstone in both areas are more iron-rich, and were presumably the main worked horizon. These ironstones are very poorly sorted, and comprise ferruginous ooids and pisoids, as well as phosphatic oncoids ('Bolopora'). The iron-bearing minerals are dominantly siderite (as a cement) and chamosite (in the ooids and pisoids). The ironstones are locally rich in hematite, contain significant quantities of secondary sulphide minerals in places, and in some beds (particularly low in the ironstone at the Llanengan Rectory quarry) are rich in manganese, though the manganese-bearing beds are now highly weathered. No complete section of the Hen-dy-capel Ironstone survives, but sections on Pen-y-gaer and Ty Fry [296 271] suggest that it was probably approximately 6 m thick.

No information is available concerning output from these workings. The ore is likely to have been of mostly inferior quality on account of its high content of phosphorus, sulphur and silica (Cantrill and Sherlock, 1920). An analysis of a sample of ore from the Hen-dy-Capel quarry is given in a report by Groves (1952) where the Fe content is stated to be 33.80%.

Manganese

Manganese enrichment and replacement of ooidal ironstone occurs in the Llanengan quarry [294 272] in the Hen-dy-capel Ironstone. The presence of this manganese ore was recorded by Cantrill and Sherlock (1920). A similar ore bed has been referred to Hen-dy-capel quarry, but this may possibly be in confusion with the Llanengan occurrence. It is not known whether any of the quarrying of the ironstone at Llanengan was particularly to exploit this manganese ore.

a

b

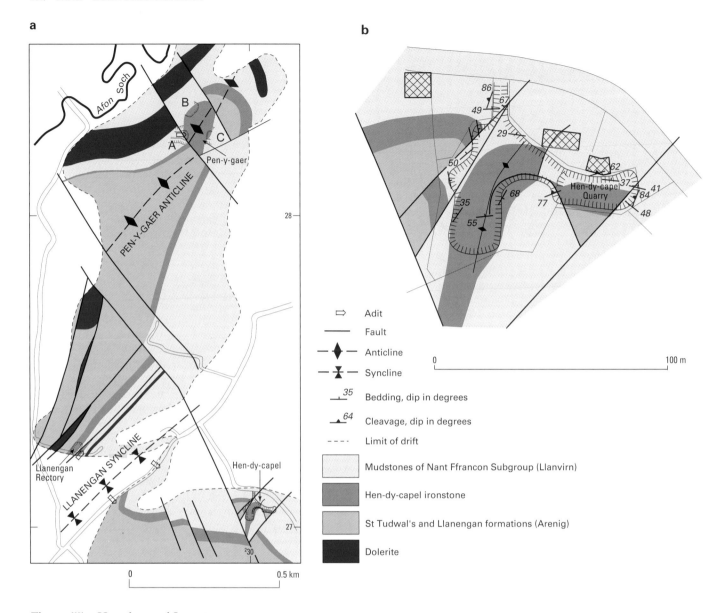

Adit

Fault

Anticline

Syncline

35 Bedding, dip in degrees

64 Cleavage, dip in degrees

---- Limit of drift

Mudstones of Nant Ffrancon Subgroup (Llanvirn)

Hen-dy-capel ironstone

St Tudwal's and Llanengan formations (Arenig)

Dolerite

Figure 55 Hen-dy-capel Ironstone.

a Outcrop of the Hen-dy-capel Ironstone in the Llanengan area, showing the main quarries and trials. Quarries A, B, and C at Pen-y-gaer after Young (1991b).

b Geological sketch map of the Hen-dy-capel quarry. The quarry is now largely infilled to the level of the minor road to the north. Distribution of the ironstone within the quarry is interpretative and indicates the probable original extent of the ironstone at the modern floor level. A shallow sill, through which there was a tramway tunnel, separates the main quarry from the eastern extension, which was connected by a second tunnel running under the road, from the north-east corner of the quarry, to the main tramway of the St Tudwall's Ironstone Company. This tramway ran east to the quay at Penrhyn Du. The structure of the quarry is a faulted south-east-verging, north-east-plunging anticline.

More significant attempts at manganese exploitation have occurred in the Trwyn-y-Fulfran Formation of the Middle Cambrian of the St Tudwal's Peninsula. Trial workings and adits mark the entire length of the outcrop of the base of the formation [2894 2476 to 2880 2383]. The age of these trials is unknown, as is their degree of success. An inclined adit has been exposed by recent quarrying of the Trwyn-y-Fulfran Formation for aggregate [2890 2430]. Old workings still exist at several points, notably a series of adits probably serving a drift working [2878 2426 to 2886 2419] and a cluster of trial adits around a shaft [2878 2391].

A major manganese mining belt lies a little to the west of Rhiw, around the Nant and Benallt Mines, within the adjacent Bardsey Island district (Gibbons and McCarroll, 1993), and a small area of unmineralised rocks attributable to the horizons associated with this mineralisation is present within the Pwllheli district. These crop

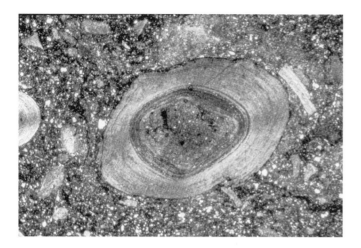

Plate 25   Partially phosphatised chamosite pisoid and ooids in Hen-dy-capel Ironstone (GS674).

The nucleus of pisoid is ferruginous peloid with relict clastic texture. The cortex of pisoid shows abrasion and fracturing produced by reworking and transport. Pen-y-Gaer Quarry B (Young, 1991b) [2984 2829]. Field of view: 7 mm. Crossed polarised light.

out in an area south of Treheli [237 279] where sandstones of the Trygarn Formation rest on highly sheared mudstones similar to those of the Wig Member at Benallt Mines. The mineralisation occurs at the base of the Trygarn Formation and is associated with a zone of enhanced deformation, coarser sedimentation, and localised igneous activity (synsedimentary basic sills and the Mynydd Rhiw Rhyolitic Tuff Member), all suggesting that this belt represents a zone of late Arenig to early Llanvirn faulting, probably along the margin of a basin centred to the south-east.

Vein mineralisation

A small orefield of former economic importance is located in the northern part of the St Tudwal's Peninsula (Figure 56). Mining of lead and copper occurred from at least the early part of the 17th century (Foster-Smith, 1977). The heyday of mining was probably the third quarter of the 19th century. There has been no exploitation of these ores since 1892, and detailed information on the workings of the mines is now sparse. The principal orebody was the 'Main Vein'. This vein, or vein system, runs from Penrhyn Mine in the east [3228 2625] to Porth Neigwl Mine, near Llanengan, in the west [2948 2678]. Where the 'Main Vein' would be expected to reach the east coast of the St Tudwal's Peninsula three faults are exposed in the cliffs which exhibit mineralisation. These faults [at 3269 2603, 3266 2609, 3262 2618] strike at N085° dipping 85°S, N298° dip 73°N and N082° dip 84°S. All three faults, however, show an apparent downthrow to the north of approximately 20 m. Some mineralisation also occurs in the same area on the south-south-east-trending reverse faults, and some trial workings were attempted [e.g. at 3275 2575] but these trials do not appear to have proved economic deposits.

In the main mining area, there is some suggestion, from the alignment of Pant-gwyn Mine and the alignment of the two West Assheton Mine adits with the four shafts near Bwlchtocyn Hotel, that veins trending at approximately N170° were also exploited.

The mineral veins contain quartz, baryte, galena, sphalerite and chalcopyrite, but there is no information on the distribution of the minerals within the veins. Depths of working have been recorded for Penrhyn Mine (15, 26 and 35 fathoms), Assheton (165 m/540 feet, vein stoped to 110 m/360 feet) and Porth Neigwl (165 m/540 feet, vein stoped to 146 m/480 feet). The depths suggest that workings in the Penrhyn Mine and Assheton Mine were within the Llanengan and St Tudwal's Formations, whereas the Porth Neigwl Mine extended well down into the Cambrian Hell's Mouth Formation. Although the depth of working for the Bwlchtocyn Mine is not recorded, the mine dumps [313 267] contain large amounts of mudstone derived from the Ceiriad and/or Nant-y-big formations, suggesting the mining reached depths of at least 100 m. The Deucoch Mine appears to have worked veins hosted by the Nant Ffrancon Subgroup.

Consideration of structural data for the area (Figures 56, 57) suggests that the vein system overlies a major flexure of the cover strata, probably draping over a basement fault. The height of the top of the Cambrian succession decreases rapidly north of the mining belt, with the overlying Ordovician succession overridden by the Ordovician rocks in the hanging wall of the Sarn–Abersoch Thrust only a short distance to the north.

The limited production figures available (Forster-Smith, 1977) suggest that the eastern mines (Penrhyn and Assheton) produced a larger proportion of zinc than those to the west. Only the westerly mines of the Bwlchtocyn area produced significant quantities of copper. This apparent variation in the mineralogy of the vein minerals may be related to variations in host rocks, with lower stratigraphical formations exploited by the western mines.

In the southern part of the St Tudwal's Peninsula, several mineralised faults are exposed in Porth Ceiriad. The fault cutting the Maentwrog Formation [at 3101 2483] strikes at N117° and dips at 80°S and has indications of a complex history of movement, in which the baryte mineralisation appears to be a late phase. At the west end of the same bay, mineralisation is associated with faulting [around 3045 2465], where veins occur near the intersection of a fault striking at N266° and dipping 73°N with a major north-north-west-trending reverse fault. Small trial adits have been dug in the cliff and are almost certainly those trials for copper and lead at Pared Mawr discussed by Forster-Smith (1977), probably dating to around 1851.

A reconnaissance geochemical drainage survey undertaken by BGS has identified a grouping of base metal anomalies within the dark grey mudstones of the Nant Ffrancon Subgroup. The anomalies occur to the south-west of Llanbedrog and between Nanhoron and Llaniestyn where they occupy a north-west-trending belt extending for a distance of about 4 km. An adit leading

Figure 56 Map of the
St Tudwal's orefield, with
estimated depths to the top of
the Cambrian.

A — A indicates the line of
section of Figure 57.

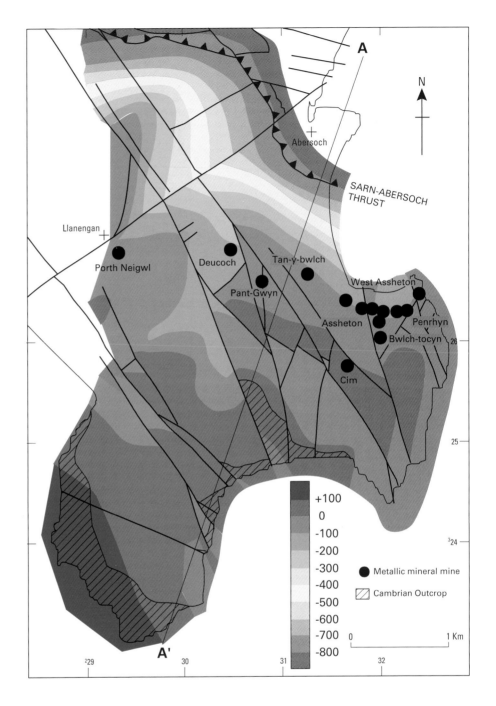

to a small flooded stope near Bodlondeb [287 315] may
represent an early attempt to exploit this mineralisation.
There are no obvious signs of mineral veining either
within or around the adit, but enhanced levels of copper,
lead and zinc were identified in panned concentrates
taken from the stream which passes over the mouth of
the adit (Leake and Marshall, 1994).

DETAILS OF MINES

Penrhyn [3228 2625]

This is probably the oldest mine in the region. There are
records of mining here in the mid-18th century. The

'old' mine was reopened in 1751 following the discovery
of copper. After a prolonged early history, it was
reopened in 1851, but only sporadic production figures
are available. In 1851, 17 tonnes lead ore concentrate are
recorded, with 20 tonnes in 1855, 10 tonnes in 1856 and
17 tonnes in 1871. The mine was operated in the 19th
century by Cornish miners; a Cornish engine house, the
miners cottages ('Cornish Row') and the remains of the
Cornish-language school are still to be seen. At least five
shafts existed, of which two still remain, together with an
adit in Porth Bach [3241 2648], which may have served
for both drainage and transport of ore to the cove for
shipping. A probable drainage adit also exists beside the
track from the mine down to Borth Fawr [3219 2633].

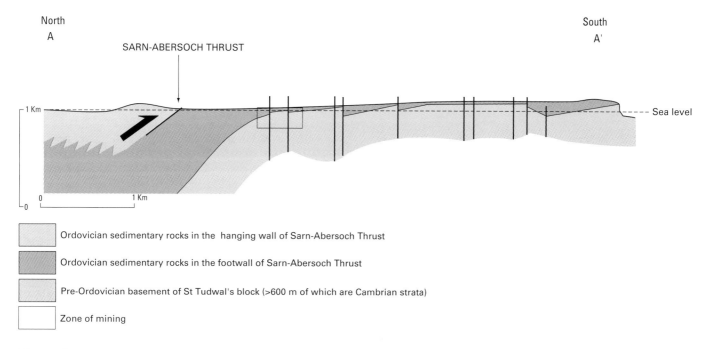

North
A

SARN-ABERSOCH THRUST

South
A'

Sea level

1 Km

0

1 Km

0

Ordovician sedimentary rocks in the hanging wall of Sarn-Abersoch Thrust

Ordovician sedimentary rocks in the footwall of Sarn-Abersoch Thrust

Pre-Ordovician basement of St Tudwal's block (>600 m of which are Cambrian strata)

Zone of mining

Figure 57   Cross-section through the St Tudwal's orefield along line A–A of Figure 56.

Assheton [3198 2624]

Production for 1870 to 1889 indicates 3120 tonnes of lead ore concentrates and 1020 tonnes of zinc ore concentrates. Several shafts exist around the site of the mine [3196 2601, 3194 2616, 3199 2623]. Drainage of the mine was apparently via the West Assheton Mine adits. In the later period of operation at least, the two mines were probably operated together.

West Assheton [3178 2633]

Production for 1876 to 1881 gives a total of 1895 tonnes of lead ore concentrates and 864 tonnes of zinc ore concentrates. A drainage adit opens onto the shore [3184 2649], with another a little higher on the hillside. Shafts associated with this occur on the hilltop at Machroes [3190 2627, 3192 2631, 3178 2633] and there were probably major workings a little farther west [3178 2635].

Cim [3168 2569]

The only written records for Cim are for a trial in 1854, stated to be in search of copper (Foster-Smith, 1977), but clearly full-scale extraction took place here too. There are three shafts close to the house, one dated 1854.

Bwlchtocyn [3128 2657]

No production figures for this mine exist prior to 1888 when output was combined with that from Pant-gwyn and Tan-y-bwlch mines. Together they produced 2991 tonnes of lead ore concentrates and 255 tonnes of zinc ore concentrates between 1888 and 1892. This mine,

together with Tan-y-bwlch and Pant-gwyn, was served from 1846 to 1885 by the tramway built by the St Tudwalls Iron Ore Company to bring iron-ore from the Hen-dy-capel mine to the quay at Penrhyn Du.

Tan-y-bwlch (Tan-yr-allt)

The mine is known to have been in existence in 1851, and was at work again between 1873 and 1886 when 8722 tonnes of lead ore concentrates and 447 tonnes of zinc ore concentrates were produced. From 1870 to 1892, the orefield produced 8123 tonnes of copper ore concentrate, largely from Tan-y-bwlch and Pant-Gwyn mines.

Pant-Gwyn [3080 2660]

The earlier period of this mine (1882 to 1887) saw production of 2333 tonnes of lead ore concentrate. Later production figures are included with those of Tan-y-bwlch and Bwlchtocyn. Some of the copper production mentioned above under Tan-y-bwlch Mine probably came from Pant-gwyn.

Deucoch [3057 2699]

This mine was worked in conjunction with Tan-y-bwlch Mine between 1873 and 1892. It appears to have worked in the stratigraphically highest levels of the mining area.

Porth Neigwl [2948 2678]

Production figures exist only for the period 1874 to 1883 with 879 tonnes of lead ore concentrate. The filled main shaft still exists, as does a further shaft on the hill above and the mine flue and chimney.

Building stone and aggregate

Little building stone is now produced in the district. In the past the Nanhoron Granophyric Microgranite [287 329] and the Carreg-yr-Imbill Dolerite [386 343] have been extensively quarried. Exploitation of the Mynydd Tir-y-cwmwd Microgranite was undertaken in several large quarries along its south-east margin [328 304 to 337 308], partly for setts and partly for aggregate. On a more local basis, stone for building and walling has been quarried in the past from the exposures of almost all the more resistant lithologies in the district. In the St Tudwal's Peninsula, the Trwyn-yr-Wylfa Member of the St Tudwal's Formation has been extensively quarried as building stone. Dolerites have been worked in the past at various small quarries (Pen-y-gaer [2975 2832], Nant y Carw [236 323], Dinas [273 359]), as has the Sarn Complex granite (Pen-yr-Orsedd [242 353]), the Wyddgrug Microgranite (Wyddgrug [286 366]), the Foel Gron Microgranite (Mynytho [303 311]) and the Carneddol Rhyolitic Tuff Formation (Carreg y Defaid [341 326], Bodgadle [311 352]). Currently, production from the Nanhoron Microgranite [287 329] is largely for aggregate, although quarrying of large blocks for sea-defences is also important.

One interesting early use of stone in the district was the exploitation of cherty hornfelsed volcaniclastic sediments from the Trygarn Formation of Mynydd Rhiw [234 299] for the manufacture of polished axes in the Neolithic period (Houlder, 1961).

Sand and gravel

The constructional drift topography of the north of the district, the terraces surrounding the Cors Geirch, those north of Abersoch and the sandur spread west of Efail-newydd represent a significant sand and gravel resource. Small disused pits in the terraces surrounding the Cors Geirch occur near Traian [3301 3621], south-west of Pont Rhyd Beirion [3222 3423] and near Bodvel Hall [3437 3673]. Small pits in isolated ridges and mounds occur north of Sarn Bach [3048 2697], at Bryn Bugail [3071 3123], and near Cefn Madryn [2770 3652]. There are disused pits in blown sand south of Cim [3193 2512] and sand and gravel is still extracted for local use from terraces at The Warren [3194 2997].

A reconnaissance assessment of sand and gravel resources in eastern Llŷn carried out by the University of Liverpool (Crimes et al., 1988) includes the eastern half of the Pwllheli district. The study identified a sandur deposit sloping at a low angle to the south, in the area to the north-west of Pwllheli. This deposit was considered to warrant further investigation, although its resource potential may be limited by the existence of rock at shallow depths.

INFORMATION SOURCES

Further geological information held by the British Geological Survey relevant to the Pwllheli district is listed below. It includes published maps, memoirs and borehole logs. Enquiries concerning geological data for the district should be addressed to the Manager, National Geological Records Centre, BGS, Keyworth.

Searches of indexes to some of the BGS collections can be made on the Geoscience Data Index system in British Geological Survey libraries and at the web site http://www.bgs.ac.uk. This is a developing computer-based system that carries out searches of indexes to collections and digital databases for specified geographical areas. The indexes include:

- boreholes
- topographical backdrop based on 1:250 000 scale maps
- outlines of BGS maps at 1:50 000, 1:10 000, 1:10 560 and County Series maps
- chronostratigraphical boundaries and areas from British Geological Survey 1:250 000 maps
- geochemical sample locations on land
- aeromagnetic and gravity data recording stations
- land survey records

Material collected during the course of this survey are archived at Department of Earth Sciences, University of Wales, Cardiff.

MAPS

Geology

1:1 500 000
Tectonic map of Britain, Ireland and adjacent areas, 1996

1:1 000 000
Pre-Permian geology of the United Kingdom, 1985

1:625 000
Solid geology map UK (south), 2001

1:250 000
52N 06W Cardigan Bay Solid geology, 1982
52N 06W Cardigan Bay Quaternary geology, 1990
52N 06W Cardigan Bay Sea-bed sediments, 1982

1:50 000 and *1:63 360*
Sheet 119 Snowdon (S), 1996
Sheet 133 Aberdaron (S) (D), 1994
Sheet 135 Harlech (S) (S&D), 1982
Sheet 163 Cadair Idris (S&D), 1995

1:10 000
The following list shows the 1: 10 000 Series maps included partly or wholly within the 1:50 000 Series Sheet 134 Pwllheli. All the maps are on National Grid lines, lying within the 100 kilometre square SH. Uncoloured dye-line copies of all the maps are available from BGS, Keyworth. Surveyors of the 1:10 000 maps were W Gibbons and T P Young (solid) and D McCarroll (drift).

SH 22SE	Trwyn Cilan	D McC, TPY	1988–91
SH 22NE	Llanengan	D McC, TPY	1988–91
SH 22NW	Rhiw	D McC, TPY	1988–91
SH 23SE	Botwnnog	D McC, TPY	1988–91
SH 23SW	Sarn	D McC, TPY	1988–91
SH 23NE	Edern	D McC, TPY	1988–91
SH 23NW	Tudweiliog	WG, D McC, TPY	1988–91
SH 32SW	Porth Ceiriad	D McC, TPY	1988–91
SH 32NW	Abersoch	D McC, TPY	1988–91
SH 33SE	Pwllheli Harbour	WG, D McC	1988–91
SH 33SW	Llanbedrog	D McC, TPY	1988–91
SH 33NE	Pwllheli	WG, D McC	1988–91
SH 33NW	Boduan	D McC, TPY	1988–91
SH 43NE	Llanystumdwy	WG, D McC, TPY	1988–91
SH 43NW	Chwilog	WG, D McC	1988–91

Hydrogeological map

1:625 000
Sheet 18 England and Wales, 1977

Geochemistry maps

1:625 000
Methane, carbon dioxide and oil susceptibility, Great Britain–north and south, 1995.
Radon potential based on solid geology, Great Britain–north and south (in Appleton and Ball, 1995)
Distribution of areas with above national average background concentrations of potentially harmful elements (As, Cd, Cu, Pb & Zn), Great Britain–north and south, 1995

Geophysical maps

1:1 500 000
Colour shaded relief gravity anomaly map of Britain, Ireland and adjacent areas, 1996

Colour shaded relief magnetic anomaly map of Britain, Ireland and adjacent areas, 1996

1:250 000
Cardigan Bay (52N 06W) Aeromagnetic anomaly, 1980
Bouguer gravity anomaly, 1980

1:50 000
Geophysical information maps; plot-on-demand maps are available which summarise graphically the publicly available geophysical information held for the sheet in the BGS databases.

Features include:

- Regional gravity data: Bouguer anomaly contours and location of observations.
- Regional aeromagnetic data: total field anomaly contours and location of digitised data points along flight lines.
- Gravity and magnetic fields plotted on the same base map at 1:50 000 scale to show correlation between anomalies.
- Separate colour contour plots of gravity and magnetic fields at 1:125 000 scale for easy visualisation of important anomalies.
- Location of local geophysical surveys.
- Location of public domain seismic reflection and refraction surveys.
- Location of deep boreholes and those with geophysical logs.

Minerals

1:1 000 000
Industrial minerals resources map of Britain, 1996

BOOKS AND REPORTS

Memoirs, books, reports and papers relevant to the district arranged by topic. These may be consulted at BGS and other libraries.

Books

British regional geology, North Wales, 3rd edition, 1961.
United Kingdom Offshore Regional Report

The geology of the Irish Sea, 1995.

Memoirs
Geology of the country around Aberdaron, Sheet 133, 1993
Geology of the country around Snowdon, Sheet 119, 1997
Geology of the country around Harlech, Sheet 135, 1985
Geology of the country around Cadair Idris, Sheet 163, 1995

MATERIAL COLLECTIONS

Geological Survey photographs

Copies of the photographs that appear in this memoir are deposited for reference in the British Geological Survey library, Keyworth. Colour or black and white prints and transparencies can be supplied at a fixed tariff.

Petrological and palaeontological collections

Samples collected during the course of this geological survey are held in the Department of Earth Sciences, Cardiff University.

Borehole sample collection

At present (2002) there are samples from 17 boreholes in the district which are registered in the BGS borehole collection; two of these are over 30 m depth.

BGS Lexicon of named rock unit definitions

Definitions of the named rock units shown on BGS maps, including those shown on the 1: 50 000 Series Sheet 134 Pwllheli are held in the Lexicon database. This is available on Web site http://www.bgs.ac.uk. Further information on the database can be obtained from the Lexicon Manager at BGS Keyworth.

Geochemical data

Regional multi-element geochemical data are available for stream-sediment, stream-water and soil samples from the area. Enquiries should be directed to the Data Manager, G–BASE, BGS, Keyworth.

Minerals

Directory of Mines and Quarries
United Kingdom Minerals Yearbook

MINGOL is a GIS based minerals information system, from which hard-copy and digital products tailored to individual clients' requirements can be obtained.

ADDRESSES FOR DATA SOURCES

Department of Earth Sciences,
Cardiff University
PO Box 914
Park Place
Cardiff   CF1 3YE

Telephone   029 20874830
Fax   029 20874326
Web site   http://www.cf.ac.uk

British Geological Survey
Hydrogeology Group
Maclean Building
Crowmarsh Gifford
Wallingford
Oxfordshire   OX0 8BB

Telephone   01491 838800
Fax   01491 692345

London Information Office at the Natural History Museum
Earth Galleries
Exhibition Road
South Kensington
London   SW7 2DE

Telephone   0171 589 4090
Fax   0171 584 8270

British Geological Survey (Headquarters)
Keyworth
Nottingham   NG12 5GG

Telephone   0115 936 3100
Fax   0115 936 3200
Web site   http://www.bgs.ac.uk.

REFERENCES

Most of the references listed below are held in the Library of the British Geological Survey at Keyworth, Nottingham. Copies of the references can be purchased subject to the current copyright legislation.

ALLEN, P M, and JACKSON, A A. 1985.   Geology of the country around Harlech.   *Memoir of the British Geological Survey*, Sheet 135 with part of 149, (England and Wales).

ALLEN, P M, JACKSON, A A, and RUSHTON, A W A. 1981.   The stratigraphy of the Mawddach Group in the Cambrian succession of North Wales.   *Proceedings of the Yorkshire Geological Society*, Vol. 43, 295–329.

AUSTIN, W E N, and McCARROLL, D. 1992.   Foraminifera from the Irish Sea glacigenic deposits at Aberdaron, western Lleyn, North Wales: palaeoenvironmental implications.   *Journal of Quaternary Science*, Vol. 7, 311–317.

BASSETT, D A, and WALTON, E K. 1960.   The Hell's Mouth Grits: Cambrian greywackes in the St Tudwal's Peninsula, North Wales.   *Quarterly Journal of the Geological Society of London*, Vol. 116, 85–110.

BASSETT, M G, OWENS, R M, and RUSHTON, A W A. 1976.   Lower Cambrian fossils from the Hell's Mouth Grits, St Tudwal's Peninsula, North Wales.   *Journal of the Geological Society of London*, Vol. 132, 623–644.

BATE, D G, and RUSHTON, A W A. 1991.   Preliminary report on fossils from a locality near Garn Bach, Llŷn.   *Technical Report, Stratigraphy Series*, No. WH 91/175R, *Biostratigraphy and Sedimentology Group Report*, No. PD 91/165, British Geological Survey.

BATTIAU–QUENNEY, Y. 1984.   The pre-glacial evolution of Wales. *Earth Surface Processes and Landforms*, Vol. 9, 229–252.

BECKINSALE, R D, EVANS, J A, THORPE, R S, GIBBONS, W, and HARMON, R S. 1984.   Rb-Sr whole-rock isochron ages, $\delta^{18}O$ values and geochemical data for the Sarn Igneous Complex and the Parwyd gneisses of the Mona Complex of Llŷn, N. Wales. *Journal of the Geological Society of London*, Vol. 141, 701–709.

BECKLY, A J. 1985.   *The Arenig Series in North Wales.* Unpublished PhD thesis, University of London.

BECKLY, A J. 1987.   Basin development in North Wales during the Arenig.   *Geological Journal*, Vol. 22, 19–30.

BECKLY, A J. 1988.   The stratigraphy of the Arenig Series in the Aberdaron to Sarn area, western Llŷn, North Wales.   *Geological Journal*, Vol. 23, 321–337.

BECKLY, A J, and MATLETZ, J. 1991.   The Ordovician graptolites *Azygograptus* and *Jishougraptus* in Scandinavia and Britain. *Palaeontology*, Vol. 34, 887–925.

BENNETT, M A. 1989.   Quartz-spessartine metasediments (coticules) and their protoliths in North Wales.   *Geological Magazine*, Vol. 126, 435–442.

BEVINS, R E, BLUCK, B J, BRENCHLEY, P J, FORTEY, R A, HUGHES, C P, INGRAM, J K, and RUSHTON, A W A. 1992.   Ordovician. 19–36 in Atlas of Palaeogeography and Lithofacies. COPE, J C W, INGRAM, J K, and RAWSON, P E (editors).   *Special Publication of the Geological Society of London*, Memoir No. 13.

BEVINS, R E, LEES, G J, and ROACH, R A. 1991.   Ordovician bimodal volcanism in SW Wales: geochemical evidence for petrogenesis of the silicic rocks.   *Journal of the Geological Society, London*, Vol. 148, 719–729.

BEVINS, R E, and ROWBOTHAM, G. 1983.   Low-grade metamorphism within the Welsh sector of the paratectonic Caledonides.   *Geological Journal*, Vol. 18, 141–167.

BOULTON, G S. 1977.   A multiple till sequence formed by a late Devensian Welsh ice cap: Glanllynnau, Gwynedd.   *Cambria*, Vol. 1, 10–31.

BOWEN, D Q. 1969.   A new interpretation of the Pleistocene succession in the Bristol Channel area.   *Proceedings of the Ussher Society*, Vol. 2, 86.

BOWEN, D Q. 1973.   The Pleistocene succession in the Irish Sea.   *Proceedings of the Geologists' Association*, Vol. 84, 249–272.

BOWEN, D Q. 1974.   The Quaternary of Wales.   373–426 in *The Upper Palaeozoic and post-Palaeozoic rocks of Wales*. OWEN, T R (editor). (Cardiff University of Wales Press).

BOWEN, D Q. 1977.   The coast of Wales.   223–256 in The Quaternary history of the Irish Sea. KIDSON, C, and TOOLEY, M J, (editors). *Geological Journal Special Issue*, No. 7. (Liverpool: Seel House Press.)

BOWEN, D Q. 1991.   Time and space in the glacial sediment systems of the British Isles.   In *Glacial Deposits of Great Britain and Ireland*. EHLERS, J, GIBBARD, P L, and ROSE, J (editors). (Rotterdam: Balkema.)

BOWEN, D Q, ROSE, J, McCABE, A B, and SUTHERLAND, D G. 1986. Correlation of Quaternary glaciations in England, Ireland, Scotland and Wales.   *Quaternary Science Reviews*, Vol. 5, 299–340.

BOWEN, D Q, and SYKES, G A. 1988.   Correlation of marine events and glaciations on the northeast Atlantic margin. *Philosophical Transactions of the Royal Society*, B318, 619–635.

BOWEN, D Q, SYKES, G A, REEVES, A, MILLER, G H, ANDREWS, J T, BREW, J S, and HARE, P E. 1985.   Amino acid geochronology of raised beaches in south–west Britain.   *Quaternary Science Reviews*, Vol. 4, 279–318.

BREMER, H. 1980.   Landform development in the humid Tropics, German Geomorphological research.   *Zeitschrift für Geomorphologie*, Vol. 36, 162–175.

BROWN, E H. 1960.   *The relief and drainage of Wales*.   Cardiff University of Wales Press.

BROWN, M J, and EVANS, A D. 1989.   Geophysical and geochemical investigations of the manganese deposits of Rhiw, western Llŷn, North Wales.   *British Geological Survey Technical Report*, WF/89/14 (BGS Mineral Reconnaissance Programme Report 102)

BRUNSDEN, D. 1980.   Applicable models of longterm landform evolution.   *Zeitschrift für geomorphologie*, supplement band, Vol. 36, 16–26.

BÜDEL, J. 1957.   Die 'Doppelten Einebnungsflachen' in den feuchten Tropen.   *Zeitschrift für Geomorphologie* N.F. Vol. 1, 201–288.

BÜDEL, J. 1979.   Reliefgenerationem und klimageschichte in Mitteleuropa.

BUTTLER, C J. 1991. Bryozoans from the Llanbedrog Mudstones (Caradoc), north Wales. *Bulletin of the British Museum, Natural History* (Geology Series), Vol. 47, 153–168.

CAMPBELL, S, and BOWEN, D Q. 1989. *Geological Conservation Review: the Quaternary of Wales.* Nature Conservancy Council.

CAMPBELL, S D G, REEDMAN, A J, HOWELLS, M F, and MANN, A C. 1987. The emplacement of geochemically distinct groups of rhyolites during the evolution of the Lower Rhyolitic Tuff caldera (Ordovician), North Wales, U.K. *Geological Magazine*, Vol. 124, 501–511.

CANTRILL, T C, and SHERLOCK, R L. 1920. Chapter 2: Pre-Carboniferous bedded ores. 4–29 in Bedded Iron Ores; Pre-Carboniferous and Carboniferous. STRAHAN, A, GIBSON, W, CANTRILL, T C, SHERLOCK, R L, and DEWEY, H. *Memoir of the Geological Survey–Special Report on the Mineral Resources of Great Britain*, Volume 13.

CASTRO, A, MORENO-VENTAS, I, and DE LA ROSA, J D. 1990. Microgranular enclaves as indicators of hybridisation processes in granitoid rocks, Hercynian Belt, Spain. *Geological Journal*, Vol. 25, 391–404.

CATTERMOLE, P J. 1969. A preliminary geochemical study of the Mynydd Penarfynydd intrusion, Rhiw Igneous Complex, south-west Lleyn. 435–446 in *Precambrian and Lower Palaeozoic rocks of Wales*. WOOD, A (editor). (Cardiff: University Press.)

CATTERMOLE, P J. 1976. The crystallization and differentiation of a layered intrusion of hydrated alkali olivine-basalt parentage at Rhiw, North Wales. *Geological Journal*, Vol. 11, 45–70.

CATTERMOLE, P J, and ROMANO, M. 1981. Lleyn Peninsula. *Geologists' Association Guide*, No. 39, 39pp.

COCKS, L R M, and RONG, J Y. 1988. A review of the late Ordovician *Foliomena* brachiopod fauna with new data from China, Wales and Poland. *Palaeontology*, Vol. 31, 53–67.

COLHOUN, E A, and MCCABE, A M. 1973. Pleistocene glacial, glaciomarine and associated deposits of Mell and Tullyallen townlands, near Drogheda, eastern Ireland. *Proceedings of the Royal Irish Academy*, Vol. 73B, 165–206.

CONNEL, E R, and HALL, A M. 1984. Kirkhill Quarry: correlation. 80 in *Buchan Field Guide*. Hall, E M (editor). (Quaternary Research Association Cambridge.)

COOPE, G R, and BROPHY, J A. 1972. Late-glacial environmental changes indicated by a coleopteran succession from North Wales. *Boreas*, Vol. 1, 97–142.

COOPE, G R, and JOACHIM, M J. 1980. Lateglacial environment changes interpreted from fossil coleoptera from St Bees, Cumbria, northwest England. 55–68 in *Studies in the Lateglacial of Northwest Europe*. LOWE, J J, GRAY, J M, and ROBINSON, J E. (Oxford: Pergamon.)

COOPE, G R, and PENNINGTON, W. 1977. The Windermere Interstadial of the Late Devensian. *Philosophical Transactions of the Royal Society, Series B*, Vol. 208.

COWIE, J W. 1974. The Cambrian of Spitsbergen and Scotland. 123–155 in *Lower Palaeozoic rocks of the World, Vol. 2, Cambrian of the British Isles, Norden and Spitsbergen*. HOLLAND, C H (editor). (London: John Wiley and Sons.)

COWIE, J W, RUSHTON, A W A, and STUBBLEFIELD, C J. 1972. A correlation of the Cambrian rocks in the British Isles. *Special Report of the Geological Society of London*, No. 2, 40 p.

CRIMES, T P. 1966. The relative age of some concretions in Cambrian sediments of St Tudwal's Peninsula, North Wales. *Geological Journal*, Vol. 5, 33–42.

CRIMES, T P. 1969a. *The stratigraphy, structure and sedimentology of some of the Pre-Cambrian and Cambro-Ordovician rocks bordering the Southern Irish Sea.* Unpublished PhD thesis, University of Liverpool.

CRIMES, T P. 1969b. Trace fossils from the Cambro-Ordovician rocks of North Wales, UK, and their stratigraphical significance. *Geological Journal*, Vol. 6, 333–338.

CRIMES, T P. 1970a. A facies analysis of the Cambrian of Wales. *Palaeogeography, Palaeoclimatology, Palaeoecology*, Vol. 7, 113–170.

CRIMES, T P. 1970b. A facies analysis of the Arenig of Western Llŷn, North Wales. *Proceedings of the Geologists' Association*, Vol. 81, 221–240.

CRIMES, T P, CHESTER, D K, DAVIES, H, HUNT, C, MCCALL, G J, MUSSET, A E, PIPER, J D A, and THOMAS, G S P. 1988. *Assessment of sand and gravel resources in the eastern Llŷn Peninsula, north Gwynedd, North Wales.* Open File Report, Department of Environment, London, 122p.

CRIMES, T P, CHESTER, D K, and THOMAS, G S P. 1992. Exploration of sand and gravel resources by geomorphological analysis in the glacial sediments of the eastern Lleyn Peninsula, Gwynedd, North Wales. *Engineering Geology*, Vol. 32, 137–156.

CRIMES, T P, and OLDERSHAW, M A. 1967. Palaeocurrent determinations by magnetic fabric measurements on the Cambrian rocks of St Tudwal's Peninsula, North Wales. *Geological Journal*, Vol. 5, 217–232.

CRIMES, T P, and SLY, P G. 1964. Implication of certain sedimentary structures within the Cambrian succession of the St Tudwal's Peninsula, southwest Caernarvonshire. *Nature*, Vol. 204, 174.

CROUDACE, I W. 1980. *The geochemistry and petrogenesis of the Lower Paleozoic granitoids of North Wales.* Unpublished PhD thesis, University of Birmingham.

CROUDACE, I W. 1982. The geochemistry and petrogenesis of the Lower Paleozoic granitoids of the Lleyn Peninsula, North Wales. *Geochimica et Cosmochimica Acta*, Vol. 46, 609–622.

DAVIES, G, GLEDHILL, A, and HAWKESWORTH, C. 1985. Upper crustal recycling in southern Britain: evidence from Nd and Sr isotopes. *Earth and Planetary Science Letters*, Vol. 75, 1–12.

DOWDESWELL, J A, and SHARP, M J. 1986. Characterization of pebble fabrics in modern glacigenic sediments. *Sedimentology*, Vol. 33, 699–710.

DOWNIE, C. 1982. Lower Cambrian acritarchs from Scotland, Norway, Greenland and Canada. *Transactions of the Royal Society of Edinburgh, Earth Sciences*, Vol. 72, 275–285.

EBY, G N. 1992. Chemical subdivisions of the A-type granitoids: Petrogenesis and tectonic implications. *Geology*, Vol. 20, 641–644.

EDGE, M. 1990. Cors Geirch-Maesoglan. 48 in *The Quaternary of North Wales Field Guide*: ADDISON, K., EDGE, M J, and WATKINS, R (editors). (Quaternary Research Association Coventry.)

ELLES, G L. 1909. The relationship of the Ordovician and Silurian rocks of Conwy (North Wales). *Quarterly Journal of the Geological Society of London*, Vol. 129, 621–641.

ELLES, G L. 1922. A new *Azygograptus* from North Wales. *Geological Magazine*, Vol. 59, 299–301.

EMBLETON, C. 1964. The planation surfaces of Arvon and adjacent parts of Anglesey: a re-examination of their age and origin. *Transactions of the Institute of British Geographers*, Vol. 35, 17–26.

EVANS, J A. 1990. *Resetting of Rb/Sr whole-rock isotope systems during low-grade metamorphism, North Wales.* Unpublished PhD Thesis, University of London.

EYLES, C H, and EYLES, N. 1984. Glaciomarine sediments of the Isle of Man as a key to late Pleistocene stratigraphic investigations in the Irish Sea Basin. *Geology*, Vol. 12, 359–364.

EYLES, C H, EYLES, N, and MCCABE, A M. 1985. Glaciomarine sediments of the Isle of Man as a key to late Pleistocene stratigraphic investigations in the Irish Sea Basin: a reply. *Geology*, Vol. 13, 446–447.

EYLES, N, and MCCABE, A M. 1989a. Glaciomarine facies within subglacial tunnel valleys: the sedimentary record of glacio-isostatic downwarping in the Irish Sea Basin. *Sedimentology*, Vol. 36, 431–448.

EYLES, N, and MCCABE, A M. 1989b. The Late Devensian (< 22 000 YBP) Irish Sea Basin: the sedimentary record of a collapsed ice sheet margin. *Quaternary Science Reviews*, Vol. 8, 305–351.

EYLES, N, and MCCABE, A M. 1991. Glaciomarine deposits of the Irish Sea Basin: the role of glacioisostatic disequilibrium. 311–331 in *Glacial Deposits of Great Britain and Ireland*. EHLERS, J, GIBBARD, P, and ROSE, J (editors). (Rotterdam: Balkema)

FEARNSIDES, W G. 1905. On the geology of Arenig Fawr and Moel Llyfnant. *Quarterly Journal of the Geological Society of London*, Vol. 61, 608–640.

FEARNSIDES, W G. 1910a. The Tremadog Slates and associated rocks of south-east Carnarvonshire. *Quarterly Journal of the Geological Society of London*, Vol. 66, 142–188.

FEARNSIDES, W G. 1910b. Geology of North and Central Wales. In: *Geology in the field*, Jubilee Volume, Geologists' Association.

FITCH, F J. 1967. Ignimbrite volcanism in North Wales. *Bulletin Volcanologique*, Vol. 30, 199–219.

FORSTER-SMITH, J R. 1977. The mines of Anglesey and Caernarvonshire. *British Mining*, No. 4. (Skipton: Northern Mines Research Society.)

FORTEY, R A, BECKLY, A J, and RUSHTON, A W A. 1990. International correlation of the base of the Llanvirn Series, Ordovician System. *Newsletters in Stratigraphy*, Vol. 23, 119–142.

GIBBONS, W. 1980. *The geology of the Mona Complex of the Lleyn Peninsula and Bardsey Island, North Wales.* Unpublished PhD thesis, CNAA (Portsmouth).

GIBBONS, W. 1983. The Monian Penmynydd Zone of metamorphism in Llŷn, North Wales. *Geological Journal*, Vol. 18, 1–21.

GIBBONS, W. 1987. The Menai Strait Fault system: an early Caledonian terrane boundary in North Wales. *Geology*, Vol. 15, 744–747.

GIBBONS, W. 1989. Basement-cover relationships around Aberdaron, Wales, U.K.: the fault-reactivated northwestern margin of the Welsh Basin. *Geological Magazine*, Vol. 126, 363–372.

GIBBONS, W. 1990. Pre-Arenig terranes of northwest Wales. 28–43 in *Avalonian and Cadomian Geology of the North Atlantic*. STRACHAN, R, and TAYLOR G K (editors). (Glasgow and London: Blackie.)

GIBBONS, W, and BALL, M J. 1991. Discussion on Monian Supergroup stratigraphy in northwest Wales. *Journal of the Geological Society of London*, Vol. 148, 5–8.

GIBBONS, W, and HARRIS, A L. 1994. A revised correlation of Precambrian rocks in the British Isles. *Special Report of the Geological Society of London*, Special Report No. 22, 1–110.

GIBBONS, W, and HORAK, J M. 1996. The evolution of the Neoproterozoic Avalonian subduction system: Evidence from the British Isles. 269–280 in Avalonian and Related Peri-Gondwanan Terranes of the Circum-Atlantic. NANCE, R D, and THOMPSON, M D (editors). Boulder, Colorado. *Geological Society of America Special Paper*, No. 304

GIBBONS, W, and MCCARROLL, D. 1993. Geology of the country around Aberdaron, including Bardsey Island. *Memoir of the British Geological Survey*, sheet 133 (England and Wales).

GIBBONS, W, and YOUNG, T P. 1999. Mid-Caradoc magmatism in central Llŷn, rhyolite petrogenesis, and the evolution of the Snowdonia Volcanic corridor in NW Wales. *Journal of the Geological Society of London*, Vol. 156, 301–316.

GOLDRING, R. 1985. The formation of the trace fossil *Cruziana*. *Geological Magazine*, Vol. 122, 65–72.

GRAY, J M. 1991. Glaciofluvial landforms. 443–454, in *Glacial deposits in Great Britain and Ireland*. EHLERS, J, GIBBARD, P L, and ROSE, J (editors). (Rotterdam: Balkema.)

GREENLY, E. 1919. The geology of Anglesey. *Memoir of the Geological Survey of the United Kingdom* (2 vols.). (London: HMSO.)

GREENLY, E. 1938. The age of the mountains of Snowdonia. *Quarterly Journal of the Geological Society of London*, Vol. 94, 117–122.

GROVES, A W. 1952. Wartime investigations into the hematite and manganese resources of Great Britain and Northern Ireland. *Permanent Records of Research and Development, Ministry of Supply, London*, No. 20, 703.

HALL, A M. 1985. Cenozoic weathering covers in Buchan, Scotland, and their significance. *Nature*, Vol. 315, 392–395.

HALL, A M. 1986. Deep weathering patterns in northeast Scotland and their geomorphological significance. *Zeitschrift für geomorphologie*, Vol. 30, 407–422.

HARKER, A. 1889. *The Bala Volcanic Series of Carnarvonshire and associated rocks.* Cambridge.

HARLAND, W B, ARMSTRONG, R L, COX, A V, CRAIG, L E, SMITH, A G, and SMITH, D G. 1990. *A geologic time scale 1989.* (Cambridge: Cambridge University Press.)

HARPER, J C. 1956. The Ordovician succession near Llanystumdwy, Caernarvonshire. *Liverpool and Manchester Geological Journal*, Vol. 1, 385–393.

HARRIS, C, and MCCARROLL, D. 1990. Glanllynnau. 38–47 in *The Quaternary of North Wales: Field Guide*. ADDISON, K, EDGE, E J, and WATKINS, R (editors). (Coventry: Quaternary Research Association.)

HARRISON, R K. 1971. The petrology of the Upper Triassic rocks in the Llanbedr (Mochras Farm) borehole. *Institute of Geological Sciences Report*, No. 71/18, 37–72.

HAWKINS, T R W. 1970. Hornblende gabbros and picrites at Rhiw, Caernarvonshire. *Geological Journal*, Vol. 7, 1–24.

HICKS, H. 1878. On some new Pre-Cambrian areas in Wales. *Geological Magazine*, Vol. 5, No. 10, 460–461.

HICKS, H. 1879. On the Pre-Cambrian (Dimetian, Arvonian and Pebidian) rocks in Carnarvonshire and Anglesey. *Quarterly Journal of the Geological Society of London*, Vol. 35, 295.

HOARE, P G. 1991. Late Midlandian glacial deposits and glaciation in Ireland and the adjacent offshore regions. In *Glacial Deposits of Great Britain and Ireland*. EHLERS, J, GIBBARD, P L, and ROSE, J (editors). (Rotterdam: Balkema.)

HOFMANN, H J. 1975. *Bolopora* not a bryozoan, but an Ordovician phosphatic oncolitic accretion. *Geological Magazine*, Vol. 112, 523–526.

HORAK, J. 1993. *The Late Precambrian Coedana and Sarn Complexes, northwest Wales — a geochemical and petrological study.* Unpublished PhD thesis, University of Wales, 415 pp.

HORAK, J M, DOIG, R, EVANS, J A, and GIBBONS, W. 1996. Avalonian magmatism and terrane linkage : new isotopic data from the Precambrian of North Wales. *Journal of the Geological Society of London*, Vol. 153, 91–99.

HOULDER, C H. 1961.   The excavation of a neolithic stone implement factory on Mynydd Rhiw in Caernarvonshire. *Proceedings of the Historic Society*, New Series, 27, (5), 108–143.

HOWELLS, M F, LEVERIDGE, B E, ADDISON, R, and REEDMAN, A J. 1983. The lithostratigraphic subdivision of the Ordovician underlying the Snowdon and Crafnant Volcanic Groups, North Wales. *Report of the Institute of Geological Sciences*, No. 83/1, 11–15.

HOWELLS, M F, LEVERIDGE, B E, and EVANS, C D R. 1973. Ordovician ashflow tuffs in eastern Snowdonia.   *Report of the Institute of Geological Sciences*, No. 73/3.

HOWELLS, M F, LEVERIDGE, B E, and EVANS, C D R. 1978. *Classical areas of British Geology: Capel Curig and Betws y Coed: Description of 1:25 000 sheet SH75.*   (London: HMSO for Institute of Geological Sciences.)

HOWELLS, M F, LEVERIDGE, B E, EVANS, C D R, and NUTT, M J C. 1981.   *Classical areas of British Geology: Dolgarrog: Description of 1:25 000 sheet SH76.*   (London: HMSO for Institute of Geological Sciences.)

HOWELLS, M F, REEDMAN, A J, and CAMPBELL, S D G. 1991. *Ordovician (Caradoc) marginal basin volcanism in Snowdonia (north-west Wales).*   (London: HMSO for British Geological Survey.)

HOWELLS, M F, REEDMAN, A J, and LEVERIDGE, B E. 1985.   *Geology of the country around Bangor. Explanation for 1:50 000 sheet 106 (England and Wales).*   (London: HMSO for British Geological Survey.)

HOWELLS, M F, and SMITH, M. 1997.   Geology of the country around Snowdon.   *Memoir of the British Geological Survey*, Sheet 19 (England and Wales).

HUTCHINSON, R D. 1962.   Cambrian stratigraphy and trilobite faunas of southeastern Newfoundland.   *Geological Survey of Canada, Bulletin*, Vol. 88, 156 p.

INSTITUTE OF GEOLOGICAL SCIENCES. 1979.   *Geological Map of the United Kingdom, South*, 3rd Edition (1:625 000 Scale).   Institute of Geological Sciences.

JEHU, T J. 1909.   The glacial deposits of west Caernarvonshire. *Transactions of the Royal Society of Edinburgh*, Vol. 47, 17–56.

JOHN, B A. 1970.   Pembrokeshire.   229–265 in *The glaciations of Wales and adjoining regions*. LEWIS, A (editor).   (London: Longman.)

JONES, R L. 1977.   Late Devensian deposits from Kildale, northeast Yorkshire.   *Proceedings of the Yorkshire Geological Society*, Vol. 41, 185–188.

KEAREY, P, and BROOKS, M. 1991.   *An introduction to geophysical exploration.* 2nd Edition.   (Oxford: Blackwell Scientific Publications.)

KEEN, D H, JONES, R L, and ROBINSON, J E. 1984.   A Late Devensian fauna and flora from Kildale, northeast Yorkshire. *Proceedings of the Yorkshire Geological Society*, Vol. 441, 385–397.

KING, C A M. 1963.   Some problems concerning marine planation and the formation of erosion surfaces.   *Transactions of the Institute of British Geographers*, Vol. 33, 29–43.

KOKELAAR, P. 1988.   Tectonic controls of Ordovician arc and marginal basin volcanism in Wales.   *Journal of the Geological Society of London*, Vol. 145, 759–775.

LAKE, P. 1906–1946.   A monograph of the British Cambrian trilobites.   *Palaeontographical Society Monograph*, 350pp.

LEAKE, R C, and MARSHALL, T R. 1994.   Reconnaissance drainage survey for base-metal mineralisation in the Lleyn peninsula, North Wales.   *British Geological Survey Technical Report*, WF/94/3, 31p (Mineral Reconnaissance Programme Report 132).

LEAT, P T, and THORPE, R S. 1986.   Geochemistry of an Ordovician basalt-trachybasalt-subalkaline/peralkaline rhyolite association from the Lleyn Peninsula, North Wales, U.K. *Geological Journal*, Vol. 21, 29–43.

LEWIS, C. 1894.   *The glacial geology of Britain and Ireland.*

LINDMAR-BERGSTRÖM, K. 1982.   Pre-Quaternary geomorphological evolution in southern Fennoscandia. *Sveriges Geologiska Undersokning*, C, Vol. 785, 1–202.

LOWE, J J, and WALKER, M J C. 1984.   *Reconstructing Quaternary Environments.*   (London: Longman) 389pp.

MANNERFELT, C M. 1945.   Nöagra glacialmorfologiska formelement.   *Geografiska Annaler*, Vol. 27, 1–239.

MARTIN, F, and DEAN, W T. 1981.   Middle and Upper Cambrian and Lower Ordovician acritarchs from Random Island, eastern Newfoundland.   *Geological Society of Canada, Bulletin*, Vol. 343, 43 pp.

MARTIN, F, and DEAN, W T. 1983.   Late early Cambrian and early Middle Cambrian acritarchs from Manuels river, eastern Newfoundland.   *Current research, Part B, Geological Survey of Canada*, Paper 83–1B, 353–363.

MARTIN, F, and DEAN, W T. 1988.   Middle and upper Cambrian acritarch and trilobite zonation at Manuels river and Random Island, eastern Newfoundland.   *Geological Survey of Canada, Bulletin*, Vol. 381, 91pp.

MATLEY, C A. 1928.   The Pre-Cambrian and associated rocks of south-western Lleyn (Caerns).   *Quarterly Journal of the Geological Society of London*, Vol. 84, 440–504.

MATLEY, C A. 1932.   The geology of the country around Mynydd Rhiw and Sarn, South-western Lleyn, Caerns.   *Quarterly Journal of the Geological Society of London*, Vol. 88, 238–273.

MATLEY, C A. 1936.   A 50-foot coastal terrace and other late-glacial phenomena in the Lleyn Peninsula.   *Proceedings of the Geologists' Association*, Vol. 47, 221–233.

MATLEY, C A. 1938.   The geology of the country around Pwllheli, Llanbedrog and Madryn, southwest Carnarvonshire. *Quarterly Journal of the Geological Society of London*, Vol. 94, 555–606.

MATLEY, C A, and HEARD, A. 1930.   The geology of the country around Bodfean (South-western Carnarvonshire).   *Quarterly Journal of the Geological Society of London*, Vol. 86, 130–168.

MATLEY, C A, NICHOLAS, T C, and HEARD, A. 1939.   Summer field meeting to the western part of the Lleyn Peninsula. *Proceedings of the Geologists' Association*, Vol. 50, 83–100.

MATLEY, C A, and SMITH, B. 1936.   The age of the Sarn Granite. *Quarterly Journal of the Geological Society of London*, Vol. 92. 188–200.

McCABE, A M. 1986a.   Late Pleistocene tidewater glaciers and glacial marine sequences from north County Mayo, Republic of Ireland.   *Journal of Quaternary Science*, Vol. 1, 73–84.

McCABE, A M. 1986b.   Glaciomarine facies deposited by retreating tidewater glaciers. An example from the Late Pleistocene of Northern Ireland.   *Journal of Sedimentary Petrology*, Vol. 56, 886–894.

McCABE, A M. 1987.   Quaternary deposits and glacial stratigraphy in Ireland: a review.   *Quaternary Science Reviews*, Vol. 6, 259–300.

McCABE, A M, DARDIS, G F, and HANVEY, P M. 1984. Sedimentology of a Late Pleistocene submarine-moraine complex, County Down, Northern Ireland. *Journal of Sedimentary Petrology*, Vol. 54, 716–730.

McCabe, A M, Dardis, G F, and Hanvey, P M. 1987. Sedimentation at the margins of a Late Pleistocene ice-lobe terminating in shallow marine environments, Dundalk Bay, eastern Ireland. *Sedimentology*, Vol. 34, 473–493.

McCabe, A M, and Eyles, N. 1988. Sedimentology of an ice-contact delta, Carey Valley, Northern Ireland. *Sedimentary Geology*, Vol. 39, 1–14.

McCabe, A M, Haynes, J R, and Macmillan, N F. 1986. Late Pleistocene tidewater glaciers and glaciomarine sequences from north County Mayo, Republic of Ireland. *Journal of Quaternary Science*, Vol. 1, 73–84.

McCabe, A M, and Hirons, K R (editors). 1986. *Field Guide to the Quaternary deposits in southeast Ulster.* (Cambridge: Quaternary Research Association).

McCarroll, D. 1990. The ice ages in the Isle of Man; an historical perspective. In: *The Isle of Man: celebrating a sense of place.* Robinson, V, and McCarroll, D (editors). (Liverpool University Press.)

McCarroll, D. 1991. Ice directions in western Lleyn and the status of the Gwynedd readvance of the last Irish Sea glacier. *Geological Journal*, Vol. 26, 137–143.

McCarroll, D. 1995. Geomorphological evidence from the Lleyn Peninsula constraining models of the magnitude and rate of isostatic rebound following deglaciation of the Irish Sea Basin. *Geological Journal*, Vol. 30, 157–163.

McCarroll, D, and Harris, C. 1990. Aberdaron. 52–56 in *The Quaternary of North Wales: Field Guide.* Addison, K, Edge, J M, and Watkins, R (editors). (Coventry: Quaternary Research Association.)

McCarroll, D, and Harris, D. 1992. The glacigenic deposits of western Lleyn, north Wales: terrestrial or marine? *Journal of Quaternary Science*, Vol. 7, 19–29.

McDonald, A J W, Fletcher, C J N, Carruthers, R M, Wilson, D, and Evans, R B. 1992. Interpretation of the regional gravity and magnetic surveys of Wales, using shaded relief and Euler deconvolution techniques. *Geological Magazine*, Vol. 129, 523–531.

Merriman, R J, Bevins, R E, and Ball, T K. 1986. Geochemical variations within the Tal y Fan intrusion: implications for element mobility during low-grade metamorphism. *Journal of Petrology*, Vol. 27, 1409–1436.

Merriman, R J, and Roberts, B. 1985. A survey of white mica crystallinity and polytypes in pelitic rocks of Snowdonia and Llŷn, North Wales. *Mineralogical Magazine*, Vol. 49, 305–319.

Merriman, R J, Roberts, B, and Hirons, S R. 1992. Regional low grade metamorphism in the central part of the Lower Palaeozoic Welsh Basin: an account of the Llanilar and Rhayader Districts, BGS 1:50K sheets 178 & 179. *British Geological Survey Technical Report*, WG/92/16.

Mitchell, G F. 1960. The Pleistocene history of the Irish Sea. *Advancement of Science*, Vol. 17, 313–325.

Mitchell, G F. 1972. The Pleistocene history of the Irish Sea: second approximation. *Scientific Proceedings of the Royal Dublin Society*, Section A, Vol. 4, 181–199.

Molyneux, S G. 1988. A re-assessment of the evidence for the ages of ironstones at Pen-y-gaer and Hen-dy-Capel. *British Geological Survey Technical Report, Stratigraphy Series*, WH/88/340R, Unpublished.

Nakamura, N. 1974. Determination of REE, Ba, Fe, Mg, Na and K in carbonaceous and ordinary chondrites. *Geochimica Cosmochimica Acta*, Vol. 38, 757–776.

Nicholas, T C. 1915. Geology of the St Tudwal's Peninsula. *Quarterly Journal of the Geological Society of London*, Vol. 71, 83–143.

Nicholas, T C. 1916. Notes on the trilobite faunas of the Middle Cambrian of the St Tudwal's Peninsula (Caernarvonshire). *Quarterly Journal of the Geological Society of London*, Vol. 71, 451–472.

Niedermeyer, R O, and Langbein, R. 1989. Probable microbial origin of Ordovician (Arenig) phosphatic pebble coats (*'Bolopora'*) from North Wales, U.K. *Geological Magazine*, Vol. 126, 691–698.

Ollier, C. 1981. *Tectonics and landforms.* (London: Longman.)

Orton, G. 1992. Geochemical correlation of Ordovician ash flow tuffs in North Wales. *Geological Journal*, Vol. 27, 317–338.

Palmer, D. 1980. *The generalised reciprocal method of seismic refraction interpretation.* Society of Exploration Geophysics, Tulsa, USA.

Paul, M A, and Eyles, N. 1990. Constraints on the preservation of diamict facies (melt-out tills) at the margins of stagnant glaciers. *Quaternary Science Reviews*, Vol. 9, 51–69.

Pearce, J A. 1983. The role of sub-continental lithosphere in magma genesis at destructive plate margins. 2230–2249 in *Continental basalts and mantle xenoliths*, Hawkesworth, C J, and Norry, M J (editors). (Nantwich: Shiva Geology Series.)

Pearce, J A, Harris, N B W, and Tindle, A G. 1984. Trace element discrimination diagrams for the tectonic interpretation of granitic rocks. *Journal of Petrology*, Vol. 25, 956–983.

Penny, L F, Coope, G R, and Catt, J A. 1969. Age and insect fauna of the Dimlington silts, east Yorkshire. *Nature*, Vol. 224, 65–67.

Pratt, W T. 1995. Discussion on Cambrian stratigraphy of St Tudwal's Peninsula, Gwynedd, northwest Wales. *Geological Magazine*, Vol. 132, 616–622.

Pratt, W T, Woodhall, D G, and Howells, M F. 1995. Geology of the country around Cadair Idris. *Memoir of the British Geological Survey*, Sheet 149 (England and Wales).

Price, D. 1981. Ashgill trilobite faunas from the Llŷn Peninsula, North Wales, U.K. *Geological Journal*, Vol. 16, 201–216.

Raisin, R A. 1889. On some nodular felstones of the Lleyn. *Quarterly Journal of the Geological Society of London*, Vol. 45, 247–269.

Ramsey, A C. 1866. The geology of North Wales. *Memoir of the Geological Survey*, 3 (2nd Edition 1881).

Reedman, A J, Howells, M F, Orton, G, and Campbell, S D G. 1987. The Pitts Head Tuff Formation: a subaerial to submarine welded ashflow tuff of Ordovician age, North Wales. *Geological Journal*, Vol. 124, 427–439.

Rice, R J, and Douglas, T. 1991. Wolstonian glacial deposits and glaciations in Britain. In *Glacial Deposits of Great Britain and Ireland.* Ehlers, J, Gibbard, P L, and Rose, J (editors). (Rotterdam: Balkema.)

Roberts, B. 1967. Succession and structure in the Llwyd Mawr Syncline, Caernarvonshire, North Wales. *Geological Journal*, Vol. 5, 369–390.

Roberts, B. 1979. *The geology of Snowdonia and Llŷn: an outline and fieldguide.* (Bristol: Adam Hilger.) 183 pp.

Roberts, B. 1981. Low grade and very low grade regional metabasic Ordovician rocks of Llŷn and Snowdonia, Gwynedd, North Wales. *Geological Magazine*, Vol. 118, 189–200.

Roberts, B, and Merriman, R J. 1985. The distinction between Caledonian burial and regional metamorphism in metapelites from North Wales: an analysis of isocryst patterns.   *Journal of the Geological Society of London*, Vol. 142, 615–624.

ROBERTS, B, and MERRIMAN, R J. 1990.   Cambrian and Ordovician metabentonites and their relevance to the origins of associated mudrocks in the northern sector of the Lower Palaeozoic Welsh marginal basin.   *Geological Magazine*, Vol. 127, 3–43.

ROBERTS, B, MERRIMAN, R J, and PRATT, W. 1991.   The influence of strain, lithology and stratigraphical depth on white mica (illite) crystallinity in mudrocks from the vicinity of the Corris Slate Belt, Wales: implications for the age of metamorphism in the Welsh Basin.   *Geological Magazine*, Vol. 128, 633–645.

ROBINSON, D. 1987.   The transition from diagenesis to metamorphism in extensional and collisional settings.   *Geology*, Vol. 15, 866–869.

ROBINSON, D, WARR, L N, and BEVINS, R E. 1990.   The illite 'crystallinity' technique: a critical appraisal of its precision.   *Journal of Metamorphic Geology*, Vol. 8, 333–344.

ROBINSON, J E (editor).   *Studies in the Lateglacial of Northwest Europe.*   (Oxford: Pergamon Press.)

ROSE, J. 1985.   The Dimlington stadial/Dimlington chronozone: a proposal for naming the main glacial episode in the Late Devensian in Britain.   *Boreas*, Vol. 14, 225–230.

ROSE, J. 1987.   The status of the Wolstonian glaciation in the British Quaternary.   *Quaternary Newsletter*, Vol. 53, 1–9.

ROWLANDS, P H. 1971.   Radiocarbon evidence of the age of an Irish Sea glaciation in Vale of Clwyd.   *Nature*, Vol. 230, 9–11.

RUDDIMAN, W F, SANCETTA, C D, and McINTYRE, A. 1977.   Glacial/interglacial response rate of subpolar North Atlantic water to climatic change: the record in ocean sediments.   *Philosophical Transactions of the Royal Society of London*, Series B, Vol. 280, 119–142.

RUSHTON, A W A. 1974.   The Cambrian of Wales and England. 43–121 in *Cambrian of the British Isles, Norden and Spitsbergen.* HOLLAND C H (editor). (London: J Wiley and Son.)

RUSHTON, A W A, and HOWELLS, M F. 1998.   *British Geological Survey Report*, 98/01.

RUSHTON, A W A, and ZALASIEWICZ, J. 1991.   Report on mid-Ordovician graptolites from the Pwllheli area, Llŷn. Report WH91/239 R.   *Biostratigraphy Research Group Report* PD 91.221, Unpublished Technical Report British Geological Survey.

SAUNDERS, G E. 1968a.   Fabric analysis of the ground moraine deposits of the Lleyn Peninsula of southwest Caernarvonshire. *Geological Journal*, Vol. 6, 105–118.

SAUNDERS, G E. 1968b.   Reappraisal of glacial drainage phenomena in the Lleyn Peninsula.   *Proceedings of the Geologists' Association*, Vol. 79, 305–324.

SAUNDERS, G E. 1968c.   Glaciation of possible Scottish readvance age in northwest Wales.   *Nature*, Vol. 218, 76–78.

SAUNDERS, G E. 1968d.   *The glacial and postglacial evolution of landforms in the Lleyn Peninsula.*   Unpublished PhD Thesis, University of London.

SAUNDERS, G E. 1973.   Vistulian periglacial environments in the Lleyn Peninsula.   *Biuletyn Periglacalny*, Vol. 22, 257–269.

SEDGWICK, A. 1843.   Outline of the geological structure of North Wales.   *Proceedings of the Geological Society*, Vol. 4, 212–224.

SEDGWICK, A. 1844.   On the older Palaeozoic (Protozoic) rocks of North Wales.   *Quarterly Journal of the Geological Society of London*, Vol. 1, 5–22.

SEDGWICK, A. 1847.   On the classification of the fossiliferous slates of North Wales, Cumberland, Westmoreland, and

Lancashire (being a supplement to a paper read to the society, March 12, 1845).   *Quarterly Journal of the Geological Society of London*, Vol. 3, 133.

SHACKLETON, N J, and OPDYKE, N D. 1973.   Oxygen isotopes temperatures and ice volumes on a 10^5 and 10^6 year scale. *Quaternary Research*, Vol. 3, 39–55.

SHACKLETON, N J, and OPDYKE, N D. 1976.   Oxygen isotope stratigraphy of core V28–239, Late Pliocene to Late Holocene. *Geological Society of America Memoirs*, No. 145, 449–464.

SHACKLETON, R M. 1956.   Notes on the structure and relation of the Pre-Cambrian and Ordovician rocks of South Western Lleyn (Caernarvonshire).   *Liverpool and Manchester Geological Journal*, Vol. 1, 400–409.

SHACKLETON, R M. 1959.   The stratigraphy of the Moel Hebog district between Snowdonia and Tremadog.   *Liverpool and Manchester Geological Journal*, Vol. 2, 216–251.

SHARPE, D. 1846.   Contributions to the geology of North Wales. *Quarterly Journal of the Geological Society of London*, Vol. 2, 283.

SHEEHAN, P M. 1973.   Brachiopods from the Jerrestad Mudstone (early Ashgill, Ordovician) from a boring in Southern Sweden.   *Geologia et Palaeontologia*, Vol. 7, 59–76.

SIMPKINS, K. 1968.   *Aspects of the Quaternary history of central Caernarvonshire, Wales.*   Unpublished PhD Thesis, University of Reading.

SIMPKINS, K. 1974.   The late-glacial deposits of Glanllynnau, Caernarvonshire.   *New Phytologist*, Vol. 73, 605–618.

SISSONS, J B. 1979.   Palaeoclimatic inferences from former glaciers in Scotland and the Lake District.   *Nature*, Vol. 278, 518–521.

STRAHAN, A, and CANTRILL, T C. 1904.   The geology of the South Wales Coalfield. Part 6: the country around Bridgend. *Memoir of the Geological Survey*, Sheets 261, 262 (England and Wales).

STRECKHEISEN, A. 1976.   To each plutonic rock its proper name. *Earth Science Review*, Vol. 12, 1–33.

SYNGE, F M. 1964.   The glacial succession in west Caernarvonshire.   *Proceedings of the Geologists' Association*, Vol. 75, 431–444.

SYNGE, F M. 1970.   The Pleistocene Period in Wales. LEWIS, C A. (editor).   315–350 in *The glaciations of Wales and adjoining regions.* (London: Longman.)

TAWNEY, E B. 1883.   Woodwardian laboratory notes: North Wales rocks.   *Geological Magazine*, Vol. 5, 65.

THOMAS, G S P. 1976.   The Quaternary stratigraphy of the Isle of Man.   *Proceedings of the Geologists' Association*, Vol. 87, 307–323.

THOMAS, G S P. 1977.   The Quaternary of the Isle of Man. Quaternary History of the Irish Sea. KIDSON, C, and TOOLEY, M J (editors).   *Geological Journal Special Issue*, No. 7.

THOMAS, G S P, CHESTER, D K, and CRIMES, T P. 1990.   Eastern Llŷn.   30–35 in *The Quaternary of North Wales field guide.* ADDISON, K, EDGE, M J, and WATKINS, R (editors). (Coventry: Quaternary Research Association.)

THOMAS, M F. 1974.   *Tropical geomorphology: a study of weathering and landform development in warm climates.*   (London: Macmillan.)

TRAYNOR, J-J. 1990.   Arenig sedimentation and basin tectonics in the Harlech Dome area (Dolgellau Basin), North Wales. *Geological Magazine*, Vol. 127, 13–30.

TREMLETT, W E. 1962.   The geology of the Nefyn-Llanaelhaearn area of North Wales.   *Liverpool and Manchester Geological Journal*, Vol. 3, 157–176.

TREMLETT, W E. 1964. The geology of the Clynnog-Fawr district and Gurn Ddu Hills of northwest Lleyn. *Geological Journal,* Vol. 4, 207–223.

TREMLETT, W E. 1965. The geology of the Chwilog area of southeastern Lleyn (Caernarvonshire). *Geological Journal,* Vol. 4, 435–448.

TREMLETT, W E. 1969. Caradocian volcanicity. 357–385 in *The Precambrian and Lower Palaeozoic Rocks of Wales.* WOOD, A (editor). (Cardiff: University of Wales Press.)

TREMLETT, W E. 1972. Some geochemical characteristics of Ordovician and Caledonian acid intrusions of Lleyn, North Wales. *Proceedings of the Yorkshire Geological Society,* Vol. 39, 33–57.

TRYTHALL, R J B. 1989a. The mid-Ordovician oolitic ironstones of North Wales: a field guide. 213–220 in Phanerozoic Ironstones. YOUNG, T P, and TAYLOR, W E G (editors). *Geological Society Special Publication,* No. 46.

TRYTHALL, R J B. 1989b. *The Mid-Ordovician oolitic ironstones of North Wales.* Unpublished PhD thesis, CNAA, Luton CHE.

TRYTHALL, R J B. 1993. Discussion of: 'A revision of the age of the Hen-dy-capel ooidal ironstone (Ordovician), Llanengan, North Wales' by T P Young. *Geological Journal,* Vol. 28, 205–207.

TRYTHALL, R J B, ECCLES, C, MOLYNEUX, S G, and TAYLOR, W E G. 1987. Age and controls of ironstone deposition (Ordovician) North Wales. *Geological Journal,* Vol. 22, 31–43.

TWIDALE, C R. 1976. On the survival of palaeoforms. *American Journal of Science,* Vol. 276, 77–95.

VERNON, R H. 1983. Restite, xenoliths and microgranitoid enclaves in granites. *Journal and Proceedings, Royal Society of New South Wales,* Vol. 116, 77–103.

VOLKOVA, N A. 1990. Middle and Upper Cambrian acritarchs in the East-European Platform. *Academy of Sciences of the USSR, Transactions,* 454, 116 pp.

WALSH, P T, ATKINSON, K, BOULTER, M C, and SHAKESBY, R A. 1987. The Oligocene and Miocene outliers of west Cornwall and their bearing on the geomorphological evolution of Oldland Britain. *Philosophical transactions of the Royal Society of London,* Series A, Vol. 323, 211–245.

WARREN, W P. 1991. Fenitian (Midlandian) glacial deposits and glaciation in Ireland and the adjacent offshore regions. *Glacial Deposits of Great Britain and Ireland.* EHLERS, J, GIBBARD, P L, and ROSE, J (editors). (Rotterdam: Balkema.)

WATSON, E. 1981. Characteristics of ice-wedge casts in west central Wales. *Buletyn Periglacjalny,* Vol. 28, 163–177.

WESTERGARD, A H. 1946. Agnostidea of the Middle Cambrian of Sweden. *Sveriges Geologiska Undersokning,* C477, 141pp.

WILKINSON, I, and SMITH, M. 1988. Basement fractures in North Wales: their recognition and control on Caledonian deformation. *Geological Magazine,* Vol. 125, 301–306.

WILLIAMS, H. 1927. The geology of Snowdon, North Wales. *Quarterly Journal of the Geological Society of London,* Vol. 83, 346–431.

WINCHESTER, J A, and FLOYD, P A. 1977. Geochemical discrimination of different magma series and their differentiation products using immobile elements. *Chemical Geology,* Vol. 20, 325–343.

WHITTOW, J B. 1957. *The Lleyn Peninsula, North Wales. A geomorphological study.* Unpublished PhD thesis, University of Reading.

WHITTOW, J B. 1965. The interglacial and postglacial strandlines of North Wales. 94–117 in *Essays in geography for Austin Miller (Reading)* WHITTOW, J B, and WOOD, P D (editors).

WHITTOW, J B, and BALL, D F. 1970. North-west Wales. LEWIS, C A (editor). 21–58 in *The Glaciations of Wales and Adjoining Areas* (London: Longman.)

WINTLE, G A, and CATT, J A. 1985. Thermoluminescence dating of the Dimlington Stadial deposits in eastern England. *Boreas,* Vol. 14, 231–234.

WOOD, D S, and HARPER, J C. 1962. Notes on a temporary section in the Ordovician at Conway, North Wales. *Liverpool and Manchester Geological Journal,* Vol. 3, 177–185.

WOODCOCK, N H. 1990. Sequence stratigraphy of the Palaeozoic Welsh Basin. *Journal of the Geological Society of London,* Vol. 147, 537–547.

YOUNG, T P. 1991a. The Ordovician ironstones of North Wales. *Jurassic and Ordovician ooidal ironstones,* YOUNG, T P (editor). 13th International Sedimentological Congress Fieldguides.

YOUNG, T P. 1991b. A revision of the age of the Hen-dy-capel ooidal ironstone (Ordovician), Llanengan, N. Wales. *Geological Journal,* Vol. 26, 317–327.

YOUNG, T P. 1992. Ooidal ironstones from Ordovician Gondwana: a review. *Palaeogeography, Palaeoecology, Palaeoclimatology,* Vol. 99, 321–347.

YOUNG, T P. 1993. A revision of the age of the Hen-dy-capel ooidal ironstone (Ordovician), Llanengan, N. Wales–Reply. *Geological Journal,* Vol. 28, 207–210.

YOUNG, T P, and DEAN, W T. 1995. Cambrian stratigraphy of St Tudwal's Peninsula, northwest Wales. Reply to discussion by W T Pratt. *Geological Magazine,* Vol. 132, 619–624.

YOUNG, T P, MARTIN, F, DEAN, W T, and RUSHTON, A W A. 1994. Cambrian stratigraphy of St Tudwal's Peninsula, Gwynedd, north-west Wales. *Geological Magazine,* Vol. 131, 335–360.

ZALASIEWICZ, J. 1984. A re-examination of the type Arenig Series. *Geological Journal,* Vol. 19, 105–124.

AUTHOR CITATIONS FOR FOSSIL SPECIES

To satisfy the rules and recommendations of the international codes of botanical and zoological nomenclature, authors of cited species are listed below.

Adara alae Martin in Martin & Dean, 1981
Agnostus exaratus Gronwall, 1902
Agnostus pisiformis var obesus Belt
Agraulos longicephalus Hicks
Amphitryron radians (Barrande)
Amplexograptus arctus Elles and Wood
Amplexograptus confertus (Lapworth)
Annulum squamaceum (Volkova) Martin in Martin & Dean, 1983
Arbusculidium filamentosum (Vavrdová) Vavrdová, 1972
Arbusculidium gratiosum Cramer and Diez
Arthrorachis tarda (Barrande)
Azygograptus eivionicus Elles
Azygograptus lapworthi Nicholson
Azygograptus suecicus Moberg, 1892

Bailiaspis glabrata (Angelin)
Barakella fortunata Cramer and Diez
Broeggerolithus nicholsoni (Reed)
Broeggerolithus soudleyensis (Bancroft)
Brongniartella minor (Salter)

Centropleura pugnax Illing
Ceraurinella intermedia (Kielan)
Christiania nilssoni Sheehan
Climacograptus antiquus Lapworth
Climacograptus scharenbergi Lapworth
Climacograptus (Normalograptus) miserabilis Elles and Wood
Climacograptus (Normalograptus) mohawkensis Ruedemann
Conolichas melmerbiensis (Reed)
Corynexochus cambrensis Nicholas
Corynoides cf. *curtus* Lapworth
Cristallinium cambriense (Slavíková) Vanguestaine, 1978
Cristallinium cf. *C. randomense* Martin in Martin & Dean, 1981 emend. Martin in Martin & Dean, 1988
Cybeloides (Paracybeloides) girvanensis (Reed)
Cymatogalea aspergillum
Cymatiogalea cf. *C. cristata*, (Downie) Rauscher, 1974

Deacybele pauca Whittington
Decoroproetus calvus (Whittard)
Desmochtina minor cf. *typica* Eisenach, 1931
Dicranograptus clingani Carruthers resicis Williams
Didymograptus cf. *deflexus* Elles and Wood

Didymograptus extensus Hall
Didymograptus hirundo Salter
Didymograptus superstes Lapworth
Didymograptus (D.) spinulosus Perner
Dindymene longicaudata Kielan
Dionide richardsoni Reed
Diplograptus compactus Elles and Wood
Diplograptus ellesi Bulman
Diplograptus foliaceus (Murchison)
Dolichometopus suecicus Angelin
Duftonia geniculata Ingham

Eliasum llaniscum Fombella, 1977
Encrinuroides sexcostatus (Salter)
Eodiscus punctatus (Salter)
Estoniops alifrons (McCoy)

Flexicalymene planimarginata (Reed)
Foliomena folium (Barrande)
Frankea hamata Burmann, 1970
Frankea hamulata Burmann, 1970
Frankea longiusucula Burmann, 1970

Glyptograptus dentatus Brongniart
Glyptograptus teretiusculus Hisinger
Gravicalymene pontilis Price

Hallograptus bimucronatus (Hall)
Hamatolenus (Myopsolenus) douglasi Bassett, Owens & Rushton
Harperopsis scripta (Harper)
Heliosphaeridium llynense Martin *in* Young et al., 1994
Homagnostus obesus (Belt)

Kerberodiscus succinctus Bassett, Owens & Rushton
Kloucekia apiculata (McCoy)

Leiofusa stoumonensis Vanguestaine, 1973
Leiofusa simplex (Combaz) Martin, 1975
Leiofusa cf. *L. gravida* Pittau, 1985
Leptestiina prantli (Havlicek)
Liocnemis recurvus (Linnarasson)
Linguagnostus aristatus Fedjanina
Lonchodomas drummockensis (Reed)

Maneviella venulosa (Salter)
Michrystridium acum brevispinosum? Turner, 1984

Nankinolithus granulatus (Wahlenberg)

Opsimasaphus radiatus (Salter)
Orthisphaeridium quadrinatum (Burmann, 1970) Eisenack et al., 1976
Orthograptus amplexicaulis (Hall)
Orthograptus calcaratus (Lapworth)
Orthograptus calcaratus var. acutus Elles and Wood

Panderia megalophthalma Linnarsson
Paradoxides davidis Salter
Paradoxides hicksii Salter

Parasolenopleura applanata (Salter)
Peramorpha manuelsensis Martin in Martin & Dean, 1983
Peronopsis scutalis (Hicks)
Phillipsinella parabola (Barrande) aquilona Ingham
Pirea lagenaria (Burmann) Eisenack, Cramer and Diez, 1976
Placoparia cambriensis Hicks
Platylichas nodulosus McCoy
Playlichas glenos Whittington
Plutonides hicksii (Salter)
Poikilofusa cf. *P. squama* (Deunff) Martin, 1973
Poikilofusa cf. *P. chalaza* Rasul, 1979
Primaspis semievoluta (Reed)
Pseudoclimacograptus scharenbergi? (Lapworth)
Pseudophyllograptus angustifolius (Hall)
Pseudosphaerexochus seabornei Price
Ptychagnostus longifrons (Nicholas)
Ptychagnostus punctuosus (Angelin)

Raphiophorus tenellus (Barrande)
Retisphaeridium dichamerum Staplin, Jansonius and Pocock 1975
Retisphaeridium howellii Martin in Martin & Dean, 1983

Salix herbacea (Musøyre)
Scopelochasmops cambrensis (Whittington)
Sericoidea abdita complicata Williams
Skiagia scottica Downie, 1982
Solenopleura variolaris (Salter)
Solenopleuropsis variolaris (Salter)
Stellechinatum celestum (Martin) Turner
Stelliferidium pingiculum Martin in Martin & Dean, 1988
Striatotheca frequens Burmann, 1970
Striatotheca quieta (Martin, 1969) Rauscher, 1974

Tetragraptus amii Elles and Wood
Tetragraptus serra Brongniart
Timofeevia lancarae (Cramer and Diez, 1972) Vanguestaine, 1978
Timofeevia microretis Martin in Martin & Dean, 1981
Timofeevia pentagonalis (Vanguestaine, 1974) Vanguestaine, 1978
Timofeevia phosphoritica Vanguestaine, 1978
Tomagnostus fissus (Linnarsson)
Tretaspis caritus Price
Tretaspis hadelandica Størmer brachysticus Ingham

Veryhachium dumontii Vanguestaine, 1973
Veryachium trispinosum (Eisenack, 1938) Deunff, 1959
Vulcanisphaera turbata Martin in Martin & Dean, 1981

INDEX

See also Contents (p.v) for principal headings and lithological units.

BRITISH GEOLOGICAL SURVEY

Keyworth, Nottingham NG12 5GG
0115 936 3100

Murchison House, West Mains Road, Edinburgh EH9 3LA
0131 667 1000

London Information Office, Natural History Museum
Earth Galleries, Exhibition Road, London SW7 2DE
020 7589 4090

Exeter Business Centre, Forde House, Park Five Business
Centre, Harrier Way, Sowton, Exeter, Devon EX2 7HU
01392 445271

The full range of Survey publications is available from the BGS
Sales Desks at Nottingham and Edinburgh; see contact details
below or shop online at www.bgs.co.uk

The London Information Office maintains a reference
collection of BGS publications including maps for
consultation.

The Survey publishes an annual catalogue of its maps and
other publications; this catalogue is available from any of the
BGS Sales Desks.

*The British Geological Survey carries out the geological survey of Great
Britain and Northern Ireland (the latter as an agency service for the
government of Northern Ireland), and of the surrounding continental
shelf, as well as its basic research projects. It also undertakes
programmes of British technical aid in geology in developing countries
as arranged by the Department for International Development and
other agencies.*

*The British Geological Survey is a component body of the Natural
Environment Research Council.*

the StationeryOffice

Published by The Stationery Office and available from:

The Stationery Office
(mail, telephone and fax orders only)
PO Box 29, Norwich, NR3 1GN
Telephone orders/General enquiries 0870 600 5522
Fax orders 0870 600 5533

www.the-stationery-office.com

The Stationery Office Bookshops
123 Kingsway, London WC2B 6PQ
020 7242 6393 Fax 020 7242 6394
68–69 Bull Street, Birmingham B4 6AD
0121 236 9696 Fax 0121 236 9699
33 Wine Street, Bristol BS1 2BQ
0117 926 4306 Fax 0117 929 4515
9–21 Princess Street, Manchester M60 8AS
0161 834 7201 Fax 0161 833 0634
16 Arthur Street, Belfast BT1 4GD
028 9023 8451 Fax 028 9023 5401
The Stationery Office Oriel Bookshop
18–19 High Street, Cardiff CF1 2BZ
029 2039 5548 Fax 029 2038 4347
71 Lothian Road, Edinburgh EH3 9AZ
0870 606 5566 Fax 0870 606 5588

The Stationery Office's Accredited Agents
(see Yellow Pages)

and through good booksellers